About Island Press

Island Press is the only nonprofit organization in the United States whose principal purpose is the publication of books on environmental issues and natural resource management. We provide solutions-oriented information to professionals, public officials, business and community leaders, and concerned citizens who are shaping responses to environmental problems.

In 2005, Island Press celebrates its twenty-first anniversary as the leading provider of timely and practical books that take a multidisciplinary approach to critical environmental concerns. Our growing list of titles reflects our commitment to bringing the best of an expanding body of literature to the environmental community throughout North America and the world.

Support for Island Press is provided by the Agua Fund, Brainerd Foundation, Geraldine R. Dodge Foundation, Doris Duke Charitable Foundation, Educational Foundation of America, The Ford Foundation, The George Gund Foundation, The William and Flora Hewlett Foundation, Henry Luce Foundation, The John D. and Catherine T. MacArthur Foundation, The Andrew W. Mellon Foundation, The Curtis and Edith Munson Foundation, National Environmental Trust, The New-Land Foundation, Oak Foundation, The Overbrook Foundation, The David and Lucile Packard Foundation, The Pew Charitable Trusts, The Rockefeller Foundation, The Winslow Foundation, and other generous donors.

The opinions expressed in this book are those of the author(s) and do not necessarily reflect the views of these foundations.

THE
ENDANGERED
SPECIES ACT
AT
THIRTY

Volume 2

Volume 1
Renewing the Conservation Promise

Volume 2
Conserving Biodiversity in Human-Dominated Landscapes

THE ENDANGERED SPECIES ACT AT THIRTY

Conserving Biodiversity in Human-Dominated Landscapes

Edited by
J. Michael Scott, Dale D. Goble,
and Frank W. Davis

ISLANDPRESS

Washington · Covelo · London

Figure 7.1 on page 87 of *The Endangered Species Act at Thirty: Renewing the Conservation Promise* is patterned after a Figure in Taylor, N. T., K. F. Suckling, and J. R. Rachlinskí 2005. The effectiveness of the Endangered Species Act: A Quantitative Review. *Bioscience* 55: 360–367.

Library of Congress Cataloging-in-Publication Data

Library of Congress Cataloging-in-Publication Data
The Endangered Species Act at thirty / edited by J. Michael Scott, Dale D. Goble, and Frank W. Davis.
    p. cm.
  Includes bibliographical references and index.
  ISBN 1-59726-054-1 (cloth : alk. paper) — ISBN 1-59726-055-X (pbk. : alk. paper)
  1. Endangered species—Law and legislation—United States. 2. Endangered species—United States. 3. Wildlife conservation—United States. I. Scott, J. Michael. II. Goble, Dale. III. Davis, F. W. (Frank W.), 1953–
  KF5640.E482 2005
  346.7304'69522—dc22
                                                            2005026419
British Cataloguing-in-Publication Data available

Book design by Brighid Wilson
Composition by Karen Wenk

Printed on recycled, acid-free paper

Manufactured in the United States of America
09 08 07 06 05 04 03   10 9 8 7 6 5 4 3 2 1

Contents

Preface   x

PART I   CONSERVATION GOALS

Chapter 1   Introduction   3
Frank W. Davis, J. Michael Scott, and Dale D. Goble

Chapter 2   Evolution of At-Risk Species Protection   6
Dale D. Goble

Chapter 3   Endangered Species Time Line   24
Leona K. Svancara, J. Michael Scott, Dale D. Goble, Frank W. Davis,
and Donna Brewer

Chapter 4   Explicit and Implicit Values   36
J. Baird Callicott

Chapter 5   Toward a Policy-Relevant Definition
of Biodiversity   49
Bryan Norton

PART II   CONSERVATION SCIENCE

Chapter 6   Space, Time, and Conservation Biogeography   61
Mark V. Lomolino

Chapter 7   Preserving Nature   70
Shahid Naeem, Robin S. Waples, and Craig Moritz

Chapter 8   Preserving Ecosystem Services   80
               Shahid Naeem and Claire Jouseau

Chapter 9   Science and Controversy   97
               Holly Doremus

Chapter 10   Science and Implementation   104
               Mary Ruckelshaus and Donna Darm

Chapter 11   Distinct Population Segments   127
               Robin S. Waples

Chapter 12   Hybrids and Policy   150
               Susan M. Haig and Fred W. Allendorf

Chapter 13   Critical Habitat   164
               J. Michael Reed, H. Resit Akcakaya, Mark Burgman, Darren Bender,
               Steven R. Beissinger, and J. Michael Scott

PART III   CONSERVATION POLICY AND MANAGEMENT

Chapter 14   Benefits and Costs   181
               Jason F. Shogren

Chapter 15   Economic Impacts   190
               David L. Sunding

Chapter 16   Land Use Planning   206
               Thomas A. Scott, Linda Fernandez, and Michael F. Allen

Chapter 17   Arbitrage and Options   218
               Geoffrey Heal

Chapter 18   Conservation Banking   228
               Jessica Fox, Gretchen C. Daily, Barton H. Thompson Jr., Kai M. A. Chan,
               Adam Davis, and Anamaria Nino-Murcia

Chapter 19   Working Seascapes   244
               Paul R. Armsworth, Carrie V. Kappel, Fiorenza Micheli,
               and Eric P. Bjorkstedt

Chapter 20   Agricultural and Urban Landscapes   256
               Berry J. Brosi, Gretchen C. Daily, and Frank W. Davis

Chapter 21   Cities and Biodiversity   275
               Timothy Beatley

Chapter 22   Conserving Biodiversity in Human-Dominated
Landscapes   288
Dale D. Goble, J. Michael Scott, and Frank W. Davis

Contributors   291

Notes   299

References   301

Index   349

Preface

This book grew out of a multidisciplinary, multi-interest evaluation of the Endangered Species Act that coincided with the act's thirtieth anniversary. The project—known informally as the Endangered Species Act at Thirty project—began in the winter of 2001 when Dale Goble (University of Idaho College of Law) and J. Michael Scott (U.S. Geological Survey and University of Idaho College of Natural Resources) began an in-depth evaluation of the act. Frank Davis (University of California, Santa Barbara, Donald Bren School of Environmental Science and Management) and Geoffrey Heal (Columbia University, Graduate School of Business) joined as organizers the following spring and fall. With the generous support of Dennis J. Aigner, dean of the Bren School, the project was housed there.

Two principles guide the project. First, all analyses of the act should be scientifically rigorous. Thus, papers that form the basis for subsequent discussion have been through multiple peer reviews. Second, discussion should engage the full spectrum of perspectives on the act. To that end, the project has involved groups as diverse as the American Farm Bureau Federation, the National Cattlemen's Beef Association, Plum Creek Timber Company, Environmental Defense, the National Wildlife Federation, and the Center for Biological Diversity.[1] The organizers also have benefited from the ongoing involvement of four individuals who have played significant roles in the evolution of the Endangered Species Act: Michael J. Bean (director of wildlife program, Environmental Defense), James L. Caswell (administrator, Office of Species Conservation, State of Idaho), William J. Snape III (Defenders of Wildlife), and Steven P. Quarles (attorney, Crowell & Mooring, LLP). Others who have been generous with their time are Holly Doremus (University of California, Davis), Peter Kareiva (The Nature Conservancy), and Buzz Thompson (Stanford University); they have led author groups and chaired topic sessions for the November

2003 conference, solicited additional contributed papers, and prepared substantial papers of their own.

The Endangered Species Act at Thirty project began in mid-November 2002 with a gathering of a select group of nearly thirty scholars and practitioners—biologists, economists, geographers, land use planners, natural resource lawyers, philosophers, and policy analysts[2] —for a two-day discussion of the Endangered Species Act. Following this initial meeting, the attendees drafted some forty papers that examined the act from multidisciplinary perspectives. After an initial round of peer review, these papers served as the analytical basis for a two-day conference held in Santa Barbara in mid-November 2003. A group of nearly a hundred individuals representing a diverse cross section of the interests affected by the act—nongovernmental organizations from both the conservation and development communities as well as federal, state, and local government representatives—met to discuss the papers and share ideas. The group was addressed by Bruce Babbitt (secretary of the interior in the Clinton administration), Dirk Kempthorne (governor of Idaho and then-chair of the National Governors Association), and Craig Manson (assistant secretary for fish and wildlife and parks, Department of the Interior).

The discussions produced a remarkable degree of consensus on potential avenues for increasing the act's effectiveness. These ideas have been further refined at a series of workshops convened by Goble and Scott with the guidance of an ad hoc steering committee composed of Michael Bean, Sharon Oxley (National Center for Housing and the Environment), and Bill Snape. Participants were again chosen to provide a multi-interest perspective. In addition to agency personnel with managerial responsibility for workshop topics, representatives from a full range of the impacted community were involved. In the workshops, participants developed detailed proposals for implementing the points of consensus. To date, workshops have been held on diverse topics such as identifying species that could be delisted quickly (hosted by Environmental Defense, in Washington, D.C.), conservation-reliant species (hosted by the U.S. Fish and Wildlife Service, in Arlington, Va.), recovery management agreements (hosted by the National Cattlemen's Beef Association, in Washington, D.C.), streamlining habitat conservation plans (hosted by the National Center for Housing and the Environment, in Washington, D.C.), state-based programs (hosted by the National Center for Housing and the Environment, in Atlantic City, N.J.), creating a single source of permitting information (cohosted by the University of Idaho and the Center for Research on Invasive Species and Small Populations [CRISSP], in Moscow, Idaho), and landowner incentives (hosted by Defenders of Wildlife, in Washington, D.C.). An additional workshop is planned on large-area, multiparty conservation agreements (hosted by Soulen Livestock Company and CRISSP, in Boise, Idaho).

The organizers have also presented preliminary findings to a variety of involved groups, including several groups of U.S. Fish and Wildlife Service directors and staff; the staff of Senate Committee on Environment and Public Works; the Western Association of Fish and Game Agencies; and the Nature Conservancy–Smith Fellows. The results of the workshops and consultations were presented at a senate policy briefing in the Dirksen Senate Office Building in Washington, D.C.; the assistant secretary of the interior and his staff were briefed the following day. We have benefited from the discussions that these presentations stimulated.

The Endangered Species Act at Thirty project has produced two books. The first, *The Endangered Species Act at 30: Renewing the Conservation Promise,* emphasized policy issues; it was published by Island Press in 2005. The book you hold in your hands, *The Endangered Species Act at 30: Conserving Biodiversity in Human-Dominated Landscapes,* examines several issues in detail: the use of science in implementing the Endangered Species Act, the appropriate conservation units, and the challenges and consequences of maintaining endangered species in human-dominated landscapes.

The project has been assisted at every stage by many people and institutions. The sponsors of the preconference authors meeting, the conference, and the postconference workshops were very generous in their support; they include the National Center for Housing and the Environment, Defenders of Wildlife, Donald Bren Foundation, Idaho Office of Species Conservation, National Wildlife Federation, Turner Endangered Species Fund, Donald Bren School of Environmental Science and Management, University of California, Los Angeles, Evan Frankel Environmental Law and Policy Program, and the colleges of law and natural resources at the University of Idaho.

Our host institutions, the University of California, Santa Barbara; University of Idaho; and U.S. Geological Survey, have provided both financial and in-kind support. They have also fostered the project by providing supportive working environments. We would like particularly to thank our deans, Dennis Aigner, Donald L. Burnett (University of Idaho College of Law), and Steven Daley Laursen (University of Idaho College of Natural Resources).

To Jennifer L. Purcell, fund-raiser extraordinaire, a special thanks for her enthusiasm for our effort. We could not have completed the project without B. J. Danetra, a one-woman tactical team. And we are in debt to Gina Wilson, computer whiz extraordinaire, for fine-tuning the figures. Students, as always, played indispensable roles in handling the myriad details—none more than Leona Svancara, Durward Bagley, Aarika Dobbins, and Katherine Strickler.

This project has worked only because of the willing participation of individuals who have played major roles in the implementation of the act. Our thanks to the Honorable Dirk Kempthorne, the Honorable Craig Manson, and the

Honorable Bruce Babbitt. These individuals provided a policy context for our endeavor that was essential to its success. Employees of the U.S. Fish and Wildlife Service were generous with their time and information. Michael Franz was particularly helpful in tracking down information in the Fish and Wildlife Service endangered species database and explaining the vagaries of its Web site. Others were incredibly helpful in explaining subtle issues of policy and law: thanks to John Fay, Claire Cassell, Gary Frazer, Michelle Morgan, Donna Brewer, Elizabeth H. Stevens, Debby Crouse, Wendi Weber, and Laverne Smith. Jim Tate (senior science advisor to Secretary of the Interior Gale Norton) was helpful in many ways.

Our steering committee has provided wise counsel on a number of issues. We owe its members, Michael Bean, James Caswell, Steve Quarles, and Bill Snape, a particular debt of gratitude for helping to ensure the participation of well-informed individuals from all points of view on the Endangered Species Act and helping us to identify the issues and frame the questions for participants.

The publication of a book with as many authors as this one has presents special challenges. We had a great editorial team from Island Press. Barbara Dean, a professional's professional and a truly nice person to boot, has guided us through the complexities of publication starting with writing the prospectus; from the project's beginning, she has been unfailingly encouraging. Our thanks as well to Barbara Youngblood for guiding us through the production process and Erin Johnson for her vigilant eyes and insightful questions.

Finally, to all of the participants, a special thanks for your participation and your candor.

J.M.S.
D.D.G.
F.W.D.

Part 1 Conservation Goals

Americans value species for a variety of intrinsic and extrinsic reasons. It shows in the language of the Endangered Species Act, which declares that "fish, wildlife and plants are of esthetic, ecological, educational, recreational, and scientific value to the nation and its people." In principle, the Endangered Species Act does not confer higher value on some species than others. For example, threatened and endangered species are listed alphabetically within a taxonomic group, suggesting that all species are equally deserving. In reality, a small subset of species receive a disproportionate share of funding and conservation attention, usually because of their symbolic value, as in the case of the bald eagle (*Haliaeetus leucocephalus*), their aesthetic value, as in the case of the California condor (*Gymnogyps californianus*), or simply because they are more familiar to us: vertebrates are disproportionately represented over invertebrates.

Confronted with scarce fiscal resources and growing need, public agencies, nongovernmental organizations, and the scientific community continue to debate conservation priorities and the appropriateness of a species-level national biodiversity conservation policy. Scientific dimensions of this issue are explored in part 2. Economic and management dimensions are considered in part 3. The chapters in this part probe the philosophical and legal historical roots of American nature conservation and of species conservation in particular, and provide a conceptual and legal foundation for the chapters that follow.

In chapter 2, Dale Goble tracks the legal record from the colonial laws of the late seventeenth century through the passage of the act in 1973 to the administrative reforms of the 1990s. In chapter 3, to help us navigate the complex history of U.S. conservation policy, Leona Svancara and colleagues provide a time line of significant twentieth-century legal actions, ending with the thirtieth anniversary of the act in 2003. In chapters 4 and 5, Baird Callicott and Bryan Norton offer contrasting philosophical perspectives on how we define and value biodiversity. Callicott examines how we assign instrumental and intrinsic value to species in the context of the Endangered Species Act and considers the role of the marketplace versus the legislature in establishing those values. Norton focuses instead on how we define and measure biodiversity and on the relationship between its biological meaning and public policy.

I   Introduction

Frank W. Davis, J. Michael Scott, and Dale D. Goble

More than thirty years after its passage, the Endangered Species Act (ESA) of 1973 continues to be a cornerstone of U.S. biodiversity policy and among our most powerful environmental laws. The ESA set the nation's biodiversity conservation policy on a path that emphasized species-based conservation and triggered action only when a species faced imminent extinction. However, promoting recovery has proven more challenging than the original designers of the law anticipated. The number of listed species has mushroomed from 78 in 1973 to 1,267 in 2005, while in that time only 13 species have recovered sufficiently to be removed from the list (Scott et al. 2006).

As described in *The Endangered Species Act at 30: Renewing the Conservation Promise*, the act has proven remarkably durable in spite of nearly continuous political assaults and legal and scientific challenges (Goble et al. 2006). The contributing authors to that volume describe a variety of factors responsible for the act's endurance. Public support for species conservation has remained strong, especially for high-visibility species such as the bald eagle (*Haliaeetus leucocephalus*) and grizzly bear (*Ursus arctos horribilis*) but also for less-charismatic taxa. The act has been championed by environmental groups in part for its power to control development, a role supported by a majority of the American public (Czech and Krausman 1997). Reforms have also been important to the act's continuance. In particular, implementation has evolved over the years from an absolute prohibition on take of endangered species to a more flexible permitting system, thereby defusing potentially explosive conservation conflicts on private lands. The act has also catalyzed administrative and legal reforms at all levels of government that have led to positive changes in natural resource management in rural areas and in urban open space planning.

The future viability of the Endangered Species Act, however, is uncertain. Over the next few decades the sheer magnitude of the conservation challenge will almost certainly defy species-by-species conservation (Woodwell 2002). We now live in a human-dominated world of a rapidly changing climate and increasingly biologically impoverished ecosystems (Millennium Ecosystem

Assessment 2005a). As the conservation need grows, scientists have recommended putting more effort and resources toward protecting ecosystem services rather than simply preserving biodiversity for its own sake (Folke et al. 1996; Balvanera et al. 2001). This tension between investing in species for their intrinsic value versus their utility is likely to increase. The number of at-risk species in the United States is already five to ten times greater than the number of species currently protected under the ESA (Scott et al. 2006) and the gap will almost certainly continue to widen.

The cost of saving species must also be reevaluated. As our understanding of ecosystem dynamics and species requirements has improved, we see more clearly that our nature reserves are neither large enough nor represent environmental variation well enough to buffer species against continued habitat loss, degradation, or geographic displacement under climate change (Scott et al. 2001; Rosenzweig 2003a). Perhaps more to the point, many of the species at greatest risk are on private lands where political and economic costs of reserve-based species conservation are highest.

In other words, broad socioeconomic and environmental trends, combined with advances in conservation science, predict a rapidly widening gap between the goal of the Endangered Species Act, "to provide a means whereby the ecosystems upon which endangered species and threatened species depend, [and] to provide a program for the conservation of such endangered species and threatened species" (sec. 2(b)), versus what the law can actually deliver or what conservation scientists would argue is needed. For this reason, we believe an examination of the Endangered Species Act at thirty is not complete without revisiting some of the basic questions that pertain to U.S. policy for biodiversity conservation:

• What are we trying to protect and why?
• What are the limits of local species-based conservation for protecting biodiversity at multiple spatial scales and levels of organization?
• How can we conserve the biodiversity of the United States in increasingly human-dominated landscapes?
• Can we move beyond the tradition of biological reserves for rare and endangered species toward a conservation strategy that is more ecologically and economically viable?

The first volume, *The Endangered Species Act at 30: Renewing the Conservation Promise*, examined the implementation record, key actors and institutions, successes and failures, and opportunities to increase the act's effectiveness. This companion volume examines the four questions posed above in more detail, offering perspectives from environmental philosophers, conservation biologists, ecologists, and economists. Together the two books present a thorough examination of America's most powerful environmental law at a critical juncture in its history.

Chapters are organized into three parts: "Conservation Goals," "Conservation Science," and "Conservation Policy and Management." Chapters in the first part examine the historical and philosophical underpinnings of nature conservation in general and species conservation in particular. In the second part, biogeographers, geneticists, ecologists, and conservation biologists consider biodiversity conservation at multiple scales and levels of organization, the effectiveness of the Endangered Species Act in protecting different kinds of biodiversity, and ways of improving the role of science in its implementation. Chapters in the third part examine prospects for conserving biodiversity in human-dominated ecosystems from economic, ecological, and social perspectives. The emphasis is on conserving biodiversity on private lands outside of nature reserves in urban and agricultural landscapes. Several chapters explore new approaches such as conservation banks and markets for species and ecosystem services.

The chapters in this volume are more technical than those in the first volume and readers may find the juxtaposition of so many disciplines thought provoking. Their scope varies widely. Some chapters are broad and conceptual while others more narrowly focus on specific aspects of conservation science or policy. The underlying theme throughout, however, is that biodiversity conservation in human-dominated landscapes requires a different mindset than the view prevailing in 1973. At the time, it was thought that single-species conservation could be achieved by "cease-and-desist" orders and nature set-asides; instead, we find ourselves in an increasingly complicated world of multispecies- and ecosystem-based conservation over large landscapes, active adaptive management of nature, and dynamic biodiversity markets.

Despite the extraordinary challenge of biodiversity conservation in the twenty-first century, however, the authors are decidedly positive and pragmatic in their outlooks. We hope that the reader will find, as we have, that the forward-looking ideas and approaches presented here create a sense of excitement and renewed hope for restoring and maintaining the diversity of nature in America.

2   Evolution of At-Risk Species Protection

Dale D. Goble

Wildlife conservation has historically employed two sets of tools. The first, "hook-and-bullet" game management, relies on take restrictions such as closed seasons and bag limits to maintain huntable populations; its use can be traced back nearly a millennium (Goble and Freyfogle 2002; Bean and Rowland 1997). The second, habitat protection, is equally ancient. Both the king in Parliament and colonial American legislatures routinely restricted land uses to conserve habitat (Goble and Freyfogle 2002; Hart 1996). The tools—take prohibitions and habitat protection—authorized by the Endangered Species Act (ESA) thus are familiar, but the act's objectives are not. Indeed, the notion that "saving all the pieces" is important is a change in perspective that remains intensely contested.

This chapter examines the evolution of wildlife conservation in the United States from game law to endangered species preservation, roughly divided into four overlapping periods. The first period lasted from the arrival of Europeans in North America to the rise of industrialism. The second was defined by the transformations produced by industrialization and the triumph of an unrestrained market. The third, from the end of the nineteenth century to the 1960s, was a reaction to the excesses of the market: conservationists sought reform by mandating scientific management of natural resources. The final period is the still-uncertain present. It began with the dramatic burst of federal legislation that transformed wildlife law—legislation that produced a corporate-fueled reaction.

The Myth of Abundance

The first stories from America were tales of exuberant bounty: Thomas Morton described a Massachusetts with "Fowles in abundance, Fish in multitude, and . . . Millions of Turtledoves one the greene boughes: which sate pecking, of the full ripe pleasant grapes, that were supported by the lusty trees" (Morton 1637; Cronon 1983). Richard Whitbourne's description of the now-extinct great auk

(*Alca impennis*), of its ability to "multiply so infinitly," and of God's gift of "the innocency of so poore a creature, to become such an admirable instrument for the sustenation of man" (Whitbourne 1620), captures two of the central precepts of the period: nature was both inexhaustibly fecund and created for the use of our species, and it was a continuously replenished storehouse. The innumerable flocks of passenger pigeons (*Ectopistes migratorius*) and the horizon-darkening herds of buffalo (*Bison bison*) made a mockery of restraint, and a policy of free access was simply assumed.

Experience soon demonstrated, however, that although wildlife might be abundant, it was not infinite. Massachusetts Bay adopted a closed season on deer in 1693; by the Revolution, every colony except Georgia had similar laws (Hynning 1939; Lund 1976). Colonial and state governments also regulated land uses to protect wildlife habitat (Goble and Freyfogle 2002; Hart 1996). The most common examples involve anadromous fish because of their importance to local communities. John Hart (2004), for example, has found that "[b]y 1800, thirteen states had laws prohibiting mill dams on some or all of their rivers from obstructing the passage of fish" (292). As the Massachusetts Supreme Judicial Court noted in one early decision contesting a requirement that the dam owner install fish passage facilities, "every owner of a water-mill or dam holds it . . . under the limitation, that a sufficient and reasonable passageway shall be allowed for the fish" (*Inhabitants of the Towns of Stoughton, Sharon, Canton v. Baker* 1808, 528).

Industrialization brought dramatic change: the relatively static society of the early Republic with its emphasis on community (Novak 1996) was fundamentally transformed.

The Triumph of the Market

The common law allocated resources through property rules. One result was the protection of settled expectations; stability and continuity were dominant values. In colonial America, for example, access to fish was determined by long usage of fishing places (*Carson v. Blazer* 1810; *Freary v. Cooke* 1779; *Pitkin v. Olmstead* 1790). This understanding of "property" was swept away during the industrial transition between 1750 and 1850 (Horwitz 1977; Nelson 1975). Older communitarian restraints—the web of kin, community, and reciprocity—that supported an economic order based on a combination of subsistence, barter, communal labor, and limited markets, gave way to economic individualism, wage labor, and market dominance (Kulik 1985; Thompson 1985). Wildlife was often a victim of this transformation.

In the United States, industrialization began on the small rivers of New England, which were easily tapped for their waterpower. The owners of grist- and

sawmills—the previous users of the waterpower—traditionally had been required to open their dams to permit passage of anadromous shad, salmon, and
alewives to their upstream spawning grounds. Owners of the new blast furnaces
opposed such requirements because the furnaces required a continuous supply
of waterpower; they also opposed mandatory fishways because such facilities required spilling water and thus reduced production. Also, unlike mills, the furnaces (and the cotton mills that succeeded them) were market concerns that
employed wage workers, produced commodities for regional, national, or international markets, and were owned by capitalists living outside the community.
The result was conflict between competing visions of the public good, between
the agrarian, communitarian economic order and the industrial, individualistic
market-based relations (Hartley 1957; Steinberg 1991). Although the issue was
not settled nationally until after the Civil War, the mill owners in New England
set the precedent when they succeeded in changing both the pattern of river use
and the laws protecting fish (e.g., *McFarlin v. Essex Company* 1852). In exempting dams from the requirement of fishways, legislators chose economic development and private gain; both farmers and fish lost.

This pattern repeated itself on increasingly larger scales in the post–Civil
War period. Nature was simply a "resource" that existed to be exploited as rapidly as possible; judges and legislators reconstructed the law on the assumption
that the land and its wealth were infinite and available for capture (Goble 1999;
Hurst 1956). As Supreme Court Justice Stephen J. Field wrote, "[t]he wild bird
in the air belongs to no one, but when the fowler brings it to earth and takes it
into his possession it is his property. . . . So the trapper of the plains and the
hunter of the north have a property in the furs they have gathered, though the
animals from which they were taken roamed at large and belonged to no one"
(*Spring Valley Water Works v. Schottler* 1884).

If this scramble to convert natural capital into private wealth led to the extirpation of the resource, it was accepted fatalistically (Martin 1879). Fatalism
also describes the resignation greeting the destruction of wildlife habitat as a
by-product of economic activities. In 1878, for example, the California Commissioners of Fisheries noted that "one-half of the streams in this State to
which salmon formerly resorted for spawning, have, for this purpose been destroyed by mining. As mining is the more important industry, of course, for
this evil there is no remedy" (Commissioners of Fisheries of the State of California 1878, 5).

By the last decade of the nineteenth century, the white pine forests of the
upper Midwest had been turned into board feet; the herds of bison had been replaced with cattle (Flores 1980; Isenberg 2000); the once-uncountable flocks of
passenger pigeons were gone (Halliday 1980; Schorger 1955). The 1890 census
noted that the "unsettled" area had been broken into isolated fragments. Fred-

erick Jackson Turner pondered the significance of the closing of the frontier in American history (Turner 1894) and Theodore Roosevelt nostalgically asserted that the destruction of the buffalo demonstrated that "the frontier had come to an end; it had vanished" (Roosevelt 1893, 12–13).

Progress had its costs.

Progressives and the Belief in Scientific Management

Destruction of the passenger pigeon and American bison—species that had once seemed impossibly innumerable—demonstrated the myth of abundance. As the costs of unbridled exploitation became increasingly apparent, concern coalesced into the Progressive movement (Hays 1957; Link and McCormick 1983; McGerr 2003). In natural resources, the Progressives urged conservation as an alternative to the market-driven waste. Emphasizing the role of government in protecting the public welfare, they sought to harness the new forces in American life—science, technology, and industrial management—to achieve efficiency in resource use. It was an optimistic and mechanistic view: science could transform nature into a multiple-use, sustained-yield machine (Goble 1999). As preached by Theodore Roosevelt and Gifford Pinchot, management by apolitical, scientific professionals would ensure that natural resources were used to provide the greatest good for the greatest number (Hays 1959; Pisani 1996). In his 1905 instructions as chief of the newly created U.S. Forest Service, Pinchot was explicit on the goals of progressive conservation: "In the administration of the forest reserves . . . all land is to be devoted to its most productive use for the permanent good of the whole people, and not for the temporary benefit of individuals or companies. All resources of forest reserves are for *use*, . . . under such restrictions only as will insure the permanence of these resources" (Pinchot 1947, 261).

The Progressives' focus was utilitarian; wildlife was to be managed to be used. As with the industrialism Progressives sought to reform, nature was a collection of resources. The movement's wildlife conservation program proved remarkably durable, lasting through the 1960s. It included take restrictions and habitat protection administered by a professional cadre of managers.

Curbing the Slaughter: Regulating the Direct Killing of Wildlife

The massive, often-wasteful slaughter of wildlife that characterized the end of the nineteenth century produced a coalition that sought to conserve wildlife by closing down game markets (Barrow 1998; Doughty 1975). Given the post–Civil War period's understanding of constitutional limits, this was a state-by-state process. Although most states had established fish and game agencies by the end of the nineteenth century (Hynning 1939), these agencies "were often ineffective, and enforcement of regulations was uneven at best" (Meine 1995, 17). Furthermore, many of the states crucial to the protection of migratory waterfowl were slow to act: in the South, not a single state had a wildlife agency in 1900. The inability of conservationists to secure enactment of effective statutes in every state dramatized the federal problem: as one "ardent sportsman" from Louisiana said, "The birds [snipe] were such migrants, and only in the country for a short time, I had no mercy on them, and killed all I could, for a snipe once missed might never be seen again" (Phillips 1934, 7). This problem is inherent in the federal system itself: in the politic—and bloodless—language of a contemporaneous senate report, the "strong temptation pressing upon every state to secure its full share of edible game birds during the spring and fall migrations . . . rendered harmonious and effective State supervision impossible" (U.S. Congress 1912, 1; Coggins 1983). The inability of conservationists to achieve unanimity led them to seek federal protection.

Among the first fruits of the new approach was the enactment by Congress of the Lacey Act (Act of May 25, 1900; Cart 1973; Dorsey 1998). Although national in scope, the act nonetheless remained faithful to the then-restrictive understanding of the federal government's power: Congress did not seek to supplant state law but rather to reinforce it by criminalizing the interstate shipment of animals when possession or shipment of the wildlife was illegal under the laws of either the sending or the receiving state.

The Lacey Act, however, failed to prevent the continuing decline of migratory birds, and conservationists pressed Congress to regulate their killing (Fox 1981; Hornaday 1931). The first bill to do so was introduced in Congress in 1903, but it took Congress another ten years to enact the Weeks-McLean Migratory Bird Act (Act of March 3, 1913), which asserted federal authority over migratory birds. The act was immediately challenged by hunters and quickly declared unconstitutional (*United States v. Shauver* 1914; *United States v. McCullagh* 1915).

Conservationists shifted tactics again, internationalizing the issue by pressing the federal government to negotiate a treaty with Great Britain (acting for Canada) to protect migratory birds. Congress ratified the treaty in 1916 (Convention with Great Britain for the Protection of Migratory Birds 1916) and enacted the Migratory Bird Treaty Act to implement it in 1918 (Act of July 3, 1918). This act too was challenged as unconstitutional. In *Missouri v. Holland*, however, the U.S. Supreme Court bluntly rejected the attack, observing that "it is not sufficient to rely upon the States. The reliance is vain" (*Missouri v. Holland* 1920, 435).

For the next fifty years, Congress acted sporadically, and generally in an ancillary role, to restrict the take of wildlife. Not until 1940 did Congress again preempt state law by restricting take. Concluding that the bald eagle (*Haliaeetus leucocephalus*)—"no longer a mere bird of biological interest but a symbol of American ideals of freedom"—was threatened with extinction, Congress enacted the Bald Eagle Protection Act (Act of June 8, 1940). In 1940, the United States also signed the first wildlife protection treaty since the Migratory Bird Treaty. The Convention on Nature Protection and Wild Life Preservation in the Western Hemisphere committed the United States and the hemisphere's other nations "to protect and preserve *in their natural habitat* representatives of all species and genera . . . in sufficient numbers and over areas extensive enough to assure them from becoming extinct through any agency within man's control" (Convention on Nature Protection and Wild Life Preservation in the Western Hemisphere 1940, preamble; italics mine).

Apart from migratory birds and a symbolic species, the shifting understanding of federalism ushered in by the New Deal had little effect on wildlife conservation. In part, this reflected the fact that until the mid-1930s "wildlife" was little more than a synonym for "game" and there was no political pressure on Congress to federalize the regulation of hunting. It was not until the mid-1960s that Congress again became actively involved in regulating the killing of wildlife.

Preserving Habitat: Preventing the Indirect Killing of Wildlife

Progressive conservationists also took steps to protect wildlife habitat. In 1903, President Theodore Roosevelt created the first federal wildlife refuge when he issued an executive order reserving the federally owned "Pelican Island . . . as a preserve and breeding ground for native birds" (Fischman 2003, 34–35).

The process remained ad hoc. In part, this reflected the focus of the conservation movement on game *protection*: hunting restrictions, predator control, and artificial propagation were viewed as solutions to declines in game populations. A variety of studies in the 1920s, however, demonstrated a strong correlation between wildlife populations and land use (Leopold 1933; Meine 1995). Congress, again relying on the Migratory Bird Treaty, responded by enacting the Migratory Bird Conservation Act (Act of February 18, 1929), authorizing the secretary of the interior to acquire lands "suitable for use as an inviolate sanctuary . . . for migratory birds." Five years later, Congress created a permanent funding source for refuge acquisition when it enacted the Migratory Bird Hunting Stamp Act of 1934 ("Duck Stamp Act"; Act of March 16, 1934). The act mandated a federal hunting license the fees from which were used for "acquisition of suitable areas for migratory bird refuges."

During the 1930s, the emerging science of ecology revolutionized understanding of the interrelationships between land, plants, and wildlife (Dunlap 1988). As habitat became increasingly central to theories on wildlife conservation, conservationists stepped up efforts to create a truly national wildlife refuge system. The Depression led to New Deal programs with the dual purpose of rebuilding wildlife populations and providing unemployment relief. In 1933, for example, President Franklin D. Roosevelt appointed a committee that included Aldo Leopold and J. N. "Ding" Darling to prepare a plan for land acquisition that sought both to remove "submarginal" land from agricultural production (and hence to increase commodity prices) and to acquire refuges. The committee targeted some 17 million acres and Congress quickly responded by appropriating funds. Conservation was again a politically powerful idea (Cart 1972).

Professionalizing Wildlife Management

The third innovation that transformed wildlife conservation was professionalization. Gifford Pinchot provided the model when he created a cadre of professionally trained forest managers by encouraging the establishment of forestry schools and by helping to found a professional forestry organization (Hein 1995; Meine 1995). Forestry captured the emphasis on science and professionalism central to Progressive ideology. It was not until the 1930s, however, that professionalization reached wildlife management—and then it was largely the result of the work of Aldo Leopold, who began his career as a forest ranger in Pinchot's Forest Service (Meine 1988).

The sharp decline in game following World War I prompted a series of studies that led to a shift from game protection (i.e., hunting restrictions) and game supplementation (i.e., artificial propagation and the introduction of exotic species) to game management. The culmination of this transition can be seen in two documents: a report of a committee chaired by Leopold—the American Game Policy of 1930 (Leopold 1930)—and the first textbook in the emerging field, Leopold's *Game Management* (1933). Both documents focused on the importance of habitat. In *Game Management*, Leopold restated a central thesis of the Progressives that active management could produce sustained yield: "game can be restored by the *creative use* of the same tools which have heretofore destroyed it—axe, plow, cow, fire, and gun" (Leopold 1933, xxxi). Leopold's ideas gave shape to an emerging consensus.

The transition occurred rapidly: "wildlife" replaced "game" as the defining term; "management" shifted from captive breeding and predator-control programs to preservation and restoration of habitat. By 1940, wildlife management was a recognized discipline with a text (Leopold's *Game Management*), a journal (*Journal of Wildlife Management*), and a professional society (the Wildlife Society) (Meine 1995).

Professionalization quickly produced reform in the federal government. Congress had long shown interest in applying science to the management of fish and wildlife. In the nineteenth century it established the Bureau of Sports Fisheries (1871) and the Division of Economic Ornithology and Mammalogy (1886) (Cameron 1929). These agencies were moved to the Department of the Interior in 1939; in 1940, they were combined and renamed the Fish and Wildlife Service.

Congress also provided the impetus that brought scientific management to many states when it enacted the Federal Aid in Wildlife Restoration Act (Act of September 2, 1937). The statute reflected the evolving understanding of wildlife management: by providing federal funds to states for "wildlife-restoration projects," Congress defined the objectives in terms of habitat. And funding was conditioned on the requirement that a state's proposed projects satisfy federal standards—a provision that gave the federal agency power to require that states employ trained wildlife scientists. Furthermore, the act mandated that a state's fish and wildlife agency would be eligible for funding only if the state had "a prohibition against the diversion of license fees paid by hunters for any other purpose than the administration" of the state fish and game department. The objective was apparent: to free agencies from dependence on state legislatures, increasing the role of science while decreasing the role of politics.

The Progressive Era Wildlife-Management System

The Progressive era created a wildlife management system that survived without significant change until the 1960s. A central element of this system was the allocation of responsibility between federal and state governments. The federal government managed migratory birds with an emphasis on maintaining huntable populations of migratory waterfowl; the states managed all other wildlife. The primary regulatory instruments employed by both were closed seasons and bag limits.

A second component of the management system was the creation of wildlife refuges. At the federal level, funds generated by the Duck Stamp Act were used to establish refuges. Although the refuge system focused on migratory waterfowl, it also included lands intended to protect some nongame species. In the states, on the other hand, the focus was almost exclusively on game species, in part because the state fish and game agencies were dependent upon hunters and fishers for their funding.

Finally, the system was utilitarian. The initial push to save migratory birds at the turn of the nineteenth century focused on economic arguments—nongame birds, for example, were described as eating insects and rodents (e.g., Palmer 1899).

Although the system was concerned primarily with game species, there was some recognition that species threatened with extinction required special management. For example, in 1936, Aldo Leopold published an article entitled

"Threatened Species" in which he argued that preservation of species such as the grizzly bear (*Ursus arctos horribilis*) and the ivory-billed woodpecker (*Campephilus principalis*) was "a prime duty of the conservation movement" (Leopold 1991). The following year, the U.S. Biological Survey acquired land in Texas to protect the wintering grounds of the critically imperiled whooping crane (*Grus americana*) (Allen 1952; McNulty 1966). And in 1942, a joint committee from the U.S. Fish and Wildlife Service and National Park Service produced a book entitled *Fading Trails: The Story of Endangered American Wildlife*. The book was written

> to show how certain forms of wildlife have approached the brink of extinction. . . . It attempts to explain the poor economy of allowing any wildlife species to pass completely from being, if it is possible for such disaster to be averted. All forms of animal life, whether they be game species, fur bearers, predators, or what, are valuable in nature's enduring battle for perfection. Each form of life does its bit to help maintain the elusive "balance" between all living things. (Beard et al. 1942, ix)

The blending of economic, ecological, and ethical arguments pointed to the future.

The Sixties and Beyond: The Environmental Movement and Its Enemies

As species continued to decline, it became increasingly clear that existing safeguards for wildlife were insufficient and that fundamental changes were needed. In the early 1950s, the plight of a gangly looking bird caught the attention of the nation and the whooping crane became the poster child of wildlife conservation. The crane had been in trouble since the end of the nineteenth century as a result of habitat loss and hunting: by 1938, when the Aransas National Wildlife Refuge was established in Texas, the population had declined to a mere eighteen birds (Allen 1952). The public began to follow the species' plight, and by the middle of the 1950s, newspapers were reporting the annual count of whooping cranes (McNulty 1966). Thus the cranes contributed to a broadly based environmental consciousness beginning to stir in America (Dunlap 1988; Worster 1977; Yaffee 1982). In response to a growing consensus that the "environment" needed protection, the federal government took a series of steps beginning in the mid-1960s that fundamentally transformed environmental law by shifting the locus of legislation from the states to the national government.

The paradigmatic statute of the period was the Wilderness Act of 1964 (Act of September 3, 1964; Wilkinson 1992). It opens with language that differs dramatically from the usual lawyerly "whereases" and "heretofores":

A wilderness, in contrast to those areas where man and his own works dominate the landscape, is hereby recognized as an area where the earth and its community of life are untrammeled by man, where man himself is a visitor who does not remain. (Act of September 3, 1964, sec. 2)

Wilderness is not Pinchot's forest; it is not land for the production of commodities. The drafters of the Wilderness Act sought instead to preserve the land for the aesthetic experiences it offers. In 1965, President Lyndon Johnson wrote of the need for a "new conservation": "Our conservation must be not just the classic conservation of protection and development, but a creative conservation of restoration and innovation. Its concern is not with nature alone, but with the total relation between man and the world around him. Its object is not just man's welfare but the dignity of man's spirit" (Johnson 1965, 2087).

The new conservation extended to wildlife. Beginning in the 1960s, Congress enacted a series of statutes restricting the taking of protected species. In 1971, it passed the Wild Free-Roaming Horses and Burros Act (Act of December 15, 1971) to protect feral horses and burros as the "living symbols of the historic and pioneer spirit of the West." The following year Congress federalized the conservation of marine mammals in the Marine Mammal Protection Act (Act of October 21, 1972). And in 1976, the United States enacted the Magnuson Fisheries Conservation and Management Act (Act of April 13, 1976), creating a complex structure of regional management councils to manage the marine fisheries.

Federal habitat conservation statutes also became markedly more expansive. The National Environmental Policy Act (NEPA) (Act of January 1, 1970) and the wildlife-consideration mandates applicable to the federal land-managing agencies—the National Park Service (Act of August 25, 1916), the Forest Service (Act of June 4, 1897; Act of June 12, 1960; Act of October 22, 1976), and the Bureau of Land Management (Act of October 21, 1976; Act of Oct. 25, 1978)—were broadly restructured to redefine decision making on wildlife. Finally, fitfully, Congress moved to create the National Wildlife Refuge System (Act of October 15, 1966a, 1966b; Act of October 9, 1997).

Still, the paradigmatic wildlife statute of the period—the Wilderness Act of wildlife conservation—was the Endangered Species Act of 1973.

Endangerment as a National Concern: Endangered Species Protection before 1973

Two decades after the publication of *Fading Trails*, the Department of the Interior created the Committee on Rare and Endangered Wildlife Species (Yaffee 1982). In 1966, the committee published a preliminary list of 331 species divided into three categories of concern (Committee on Rare and Endangered

Wildlife Species 1966). The "Redbook," as the list was known, lacked legal force; indeed, it contained one species, the Utah prairie dog (*Cynomys parvidens*), that another federal agency was trying to eradicate. The Redbook did, however, increase awareness of the risk of extinction.

The first legislative response to increasing public concern for endangered wildlife came in 1964. Acknowledging that habitat loss was a significant cause of extinction, Congress included a provision in the Land and Water Conservation Fund Act (Act of May 28, 1963) allowing monies to be used for the acquisition of land "for the preservation of species of fish or wildlife that are threatened with extinction" (Act of May 28, 1963, sec. 460l-9(a)(1)). This language embodied two fundamental changes: it provided for the preservation of wildlife rather than the management of game species, and it specified that protection was to be accomplished through habitat preservation rather than take regulation. Zoos—like the Victorian curio cabinet—were no longer sufficient: wildlife must be preserved in the wild.

ENDANGERED SPECIES PRESERVATION ACT OF 1966

The first federal endangered species act was the Endangered Species Preservation Act of 1966 (ESPA). As with the Land and Water Conservation Fund, the ESPA's focus was habitat protection. Acknowledging that "one of the unfortunate consequences of growth and development" is the extermination of wildlife, Congress announced a national policy for the "conservation, protection, restoration, and propagation" of native fish and wildlife "that are threatened with extinction" (ESPA sec. 1(a)).

As is often the case, the grand scope of the act's policy statement gave way to a more modest implementation scheme: Congress authorized the secretary to spend up to $15 million from funds already available under the Land and Water Conservation Fund (ESPA sec. 2(c)). The ESPA did, however, direct the secretary of the interior to publish a formal list of endangered species of "native fish and wildlife" (sec. 1(c)). In 1967, the secretary officially listed seventy-eight species as endangered (U.S. Department of the Interior 1967; Wilcove and McMillan 2006).

ENDANGERED SPECIES CONSERVATION ACT OF 1969

The Endangered Species Preservation Act's focus on habitat ignored the impact of taking and commercial activities on wildlife populations. It also ignored the international aspect of extinction: the American market often caused problems elsewhere. The failure to regulate these activities was partially remedied in 1969 when Congress extensively supplemented the ESPA and renamed it the Endangered Species Conservation Act (ESCA). The ESCA provided a more comprehensive but still limited program that emphasized the regulation of interstate and foreign commerce in species listed as endangered.

Although the ESCA's domestic provisions were only a modest modification of existing law, its provisions on international commerce marked a fundamental change. The earlier Endangered Species Preservation Act had authorized a largely hortatory list of endangered "native fish and wildlife" (sec. 1(c)); the Endangered Species Conservation Act focused instead on international commerce in wildlife by prohibiting the importation of species listed by the secretary of the interior as "threatened with worldwide extinction" (sec. 3(a)). The prohibition was backed by stiff civil and criminal sanctions (sec. 4).

CONVENTION ON INTERNATIONAL TRADE IN ENDANGERED SPECIES OF
WILD FAUNA AND FLORA
In the Endangered Species Conservation Act, Congress also instructed the secretaries of the interior and state to call an international conference on protecting endangered species. The conference that finally convened in Washington, D.C., in February 1973 reflected a convergence of interests between wildlife-exporting and -importing nations. Exporting states had increasingly recognized that conservation measures were necessary to prevent the extermination of economically valuable resources; importing nations, on the other hand, were responding to public opinion that increasingly favored wildlife preservation (Schonfeld 1985). The result was the Convention on International Trade in Endangered Species of Wild Fauna and Flora (CITES), a multilateral treaty that established an international system of import and export permits to regulate international commerce in species designated for protection.

The Evolution of the Endangered Species Act of 1973

Although it is common to speak of "the Endangered Species Act of 1973," there have in fact been several Endangered Species Acts of 1973. Not only has the act been amended by Congress, it has also been modified by the agencies responsible for its implementation. And although the act has been both praised and condemned as "the pit bull of environmental laws," the reality has become something more ambiguous. In *Tennessee Valley Authority v. Hill* (1978), the U.S. Supreme Court noted that the prohibitions on jeopardizing a listed species "admit to no exception"; the Court could have written the same phrase about the prohibition against "take" (ESA secs. 9(a)(1)(B), 3(18)). A combination of legislative and administrative amendments has, however, transformed the act from a prohibitive law into a flexible, permitting statute (Houck 1993).

THE FIRST ENDANGERED SPECIES ACT OF 1973
Substantive and procedural requirements of the Endangered Species Act are covered in five sections:

- *Section 4* establishes procedures for listing species as either threatened or endangered, for designating critical habitat, and for preparing recovery plans for listed species.
- *Section 7* requires federal agencies that authorize, fund, or carry out an action—"federal action agencies"—to consult with the U.S. Fish and Wildlife Service in the Department of the Interior or the National Marine Fisheries Service in the Department of Commerce—the "federal fish and wildlife agencies"—to "insure" that their actions are not likely "to jeopardize the continued existence" of listed species.
- *Section 9* prohibits any person from taking or engaging in commerce in endangered species.
- *Section 10* provides exemptions, permits, and exceptions to section 9 prohibitions.
- *Section 11* specifies the civil and criminal penalties applicable to the violations enumerated in section 9.

Although the act has been amended several times, these five sections remain the core mechanism for protecting species faced with extinction.

As this outline suggests, the ESA sets in motion a linear process: when a species is at risk of extinction, it is listed as either endangered or threatened and its critical habitat is designated. The wildlife agency prepares a recovery plan for the species that specifies how threats to its continued existence will be ameliorated so that the species no longer requires protection under the act. In the interim, the species is protected under sections 7, 9, and 11 from all activities not permitted pursuant to section 10.

THE SECOND ENDANGERED SPECIES ACT OF 1973:
THE 1978 AND 1979 AMENDMENTS
In *Tennessee Valley Authority v. Hill* (1978), the U.S. Supreme Court held that Tellico Dam could not be completed to avoid extirpating the snail darter, a small species of perch. The Court's decision made the darter a national symbol assigned diametrically different meanings by different groups. The problem was that *Tennessee Valley Authority v. Hill* pitted two popular species against one another: an endangered species and pork (Coggins and Russell 1982). The Supreme Court's resolution of the conflict presented Congress with a dilemma: how to protect both at-risk species and pork-barrel spending. Congress responded with "flexibility." In the Endangered Species Act Amendments of 1978 (Act of November 10, 1978; Act of December 28, 1979), Congress crafted language that offered something for both "species." While leaving the act's substantive standards generally intact, Congress significantly modified its procedures.

Listing: The transformation from prohibitive to permissive can be clearly seen in the 1978 amendments to the listing process. Congress amended—or, perhaps more accurately, burdened—the listing process by substantially expanding the procedural requirements to list a species. It imposed additional notice provisions, required local hearings, and mandated the designation of critical habitat as part of the listing determination. While increasing the complexity of the procedures, the amendments also imposed a time limit; listings that had not been completed within two years must be withdrawn.

When James Watt became secretary of the interior in 1981, listing stopped as the Reagan administration added a requirement that listings be economically justified (Office of the President 1981). The combined effect of the legislative and administrative changes was dramatic: less than 5 percent of the more than two thousand species formally proposed for listing in November 1978 were listed; in mid-December 1979, the USFWS withdrew proposals to list 1,876 species (USFWS 1979; Greenwald et al. 2006).

Critical habitat: Congress also revised critical habitat provisions in the 1978 amendments to the ESA. First, it required critical habitat to be designated at the time a listing determination is made. Second, Congress defined "critical habitat" to emphasize "conserving" listed species, which in turn is defined as recovery (ESA sec. 3(5)).

Consultation and jeopardy: In the 1973 act, section 7 required action agencies to "insure that actions authorized, funded, or carried out by them do not jeopardize the continued existence" of a listed species. As the Supreme Court noted in *Tennessee Valley Authority v. Hill,* "This language admits of no exceptions" (Tennessee Valley Authority v. Hill 1978, 173). In the 1978 amendments, Congress softened the "do not" to "not likely to" and substantially expanded (and complicated) the consultation procedures: the slightly more than one hundred words in the original section became the first subsection of a section that now filled nearly eight pages in the *Statutes at Large.* Finally, Congress created a new entity, the Endangered Species Committee (nicknamed the "God Squad") and empowered it to grant exemptions from the act's prohibitions.

In the 1978 amendments, Congress transformed what had been a relatively simple statute into something procedurally complex. Because an agency is more likely to be reversed for procedural rather than substantive errors, procedural complexity empowers those opposed to an agency's decisions. By modifying the procedures, Congress was able to restructure the act without changing its substantive standards and in the process the statute's original prohibitive severity was substantially softened.

THE THIRD ENDANGERED SPECIES ACT OF 1973: THE 1982 AMENDMENTS
If the theme of the 1978 amendments was "flexibility," the dominant concern in 1982 was "discretion." On the one hand, the detailed, time-consuming procedures added in 1978, particularly when coupled with the Reagan

administration's emphasis on economics, had stalled listings. On the other, Congress was concerned with James Watt, a secretary of the interior openly hostile to endangered species preservation. Watt—like President Ronald Reagan— had declared himself a "sagebrush rebel" (Cawley 1993), aligning himself with a coalition of Western ranchers and legislators who opposed environmental protection when it limited the traditional commodity uses of the public lands (Snow 1996). The 1982 amendments, in other words, moved in more than one direction (Act of October 13, 1982).

Listing: The amendments restricted the secretary's discretion by specifying that the listing determination be made "*solely* on the basis of the best scientific and commercial data available"; economics were not to be considered in determining whether a species was threatened or endangered. Section 4 was also amended to restructure the listing procedure into a three-step process with specific deadlines for each step. In addition, the linkage between listing a species and designating its critical habitat was relaxed. The intent of these changes was to put the secretary back in the business of listing species.

At the same time, Congress added new procedures that effectively reduced the stringency of the substantive requirements. The most significant was the creation of a new status, "warranted but precluded," that allowed wildlife agencies to determine that listing a species while warranted was precluded by other pending actions—a category that has become a black hole.[1]

Consultation and jeopardy: The consultation and exemption procedures were also substantially rewritten: steps were deleted and deadlines tightened, but the substantive standards were again left untouched.

Incidental take: The most significant amendments were to section 10. The ESA's take prohibition in section 9 applies to all "persons"—a term defined broadly to include not only individuals but also business organizations and federal and state government agencies (sec. 3(8)). As a result, prohibited takes of listed species can occur both within the context of an agency action subject to consultation under section 7 and on private lands owned by a developer who has no need for a federal permit and is therefore not required to consult with the wildlife agency. In 1982, Congress created "incidental take" provisions for both situations. For actions requiring consultation under section 7—events that require some federal action such as the issuance of a permit—Congress added a provision that authorized the wildlife agency to include an "incidental take statement" to permit take as long as it does not jeopardize the continued existence of the species (ESA sec. 7(b)(4)). And, to "addres[s] the concerns of private landowners who are faced with having otherwise lawful actions not requiring Federal permits prevented by section 9 prohibitions against taking," Congress added an "incidental take permit" to section 10 (Act of October 13, 1982). The amendment authorized the issuance of incidental take permits in conjunction with the development of a habitat conservation plan (HCP) prepared by the applicant; the secretary was required to determine that the take incidental to the HCP would not "appreciably reduce the likelihood of the survival and recovery of the species in the wild" (ESA sec. 10(a)(2)(B)). Thus, an incidental take permit effectively authorizes the developer—in J. B. Ruhl's phrase—to kill endangered species, legally (Ruhl 1999).

Although the incidental take provisions were significant steps in transforming the act from prohibitive to permitting, the amendments also restricted the secretary's discretion by imposing additional requirements on the permitting authority. Prior to the amendments, the secretary had proposed to authorize take of listed species in conjunction with HCPs that did not include the congressionally mandated findings.

THE FOURTH ENDANGERED SPECIES ACT OF 1973: THE ADMINISTRATIVE
AMENDMENTS OF THE NINETIES

Much of the transformation of the Endangered Species Act from prohibitive to permitting is a result of administrative rather than legislative actions. As with habitat conservation plans (Thompson 2005; Tarlock 2005), Congress has often acted to ratify and restrain agency initiatives. The wildlife agencies have repeatedly pushed the statute's boundaries. For example, in 1986 they finalized regulations to implement the 1982 amendments to the consultation requirements of section 7. The regulations redefined several crucial terms, including the phrase "destruction or adverse modification [of critical habitat]" (ESA sec. 7(a)(2)). The new definition was effectively identical to the definition of "jeopardize the continued existence of [a listed species]" (Code of Federal Regulations 2004) and thus collapsed the two standards into one. As a result, the wildlife agencies have subsequently argued that critical habitat adds nothing to the jeopardy prohibition and the designation of critical habitat is therefore an expensive, time-consuming process that does nothing to conserve listed species.

Similarly, the 1978 amendments to section 4 added a requirement that listing determinations be made "after taking into account those efforts, if any, being made by any State or foreign nation" (sec. 4(b)(1)(A)). The first Bush and Clinton administrations relied upon this language in a series of decisions concluding that it was not necessary to list a species because some state or federal entity would independently take steps to protect the species (Goble and Freyfogle 2002).

Following Republican congressional victories in 1994, the ideologically divisive politics—characterized by House Speaker Newt Gingrich and the Contract with America—increased debate on the ESA. In response to the hostility toward endangered species openly expressed by some members of Congress, Secretary of the Interior Bruce Babbitt "resolve[d] to save the Endangered

Species Act by implementing a series of reforms on the implementation of the act from top to bottom, particularly as it applied to private lands". The secretary advocated "incentive-based strategies to try and reconcile endangered species conservation with economic development" (Barry 1998, 131).

The centerpiece of this initiative was a series of agreements that could be offered to private landowners which included assurances from the U.S. Fish and Wildlife Service that the agency would not impose additional restrictions—the "No Surprises" policy (USFWS and NMFS 1998). Although the details of the agreements— habitat conservation plans (USFWS and NMFS 1996a), candidate conservation agreements (USFWS 1999f), and safe harbor agreements (USFWS 1999f)—varied, they were intended to make the ESA more developer friendly by balancing two competing goals: flexibility (to adapt to changing biological circumstances and new information) and certainty (to allow the permittee to make economic decisions).

Under the second Bush administration, administrative modifications of the act slowed, and the emphasis shifted to reevaluating previous listing decisions (Milstein 2004). Congress, however, is again showing interest in legislation; in October 2005 the House passed a bill that made fundamental changes to the act.

Conclusion

Early America was about abundance—and wildlife was a dramatic example. Flocks of passenger pigeons that darkened the skies (Audubon n.d.) produced a profligate perspective. There were voices in opposition: James Fenimore Cooper has Leather-stocking issue a biblical denunciation on the wasteful slaughter of pigeons (Cooper 1823) and Henry David Thoreau considered using a crowbar against the Billerica dam to open a passage for the shad (Thoreau 1849). But such concerns were lost in the westward sweep of Manifest Destiny: we were taming the wilderness, building a nation, celebrating material progress, and the loss of species was simply an unfortunate cost of progress. The shift in scale that followed the Civil War gave Leather-stocking's perspective broader appeal: the Progressive conservationists urged that waste be replaced with scientific management; the increasing understanding of ecology made Thoreau seem prescient. In response to these shifting perceptions, the law has moved from the free-wheeling rule-of-capture, to game protection, to wildlife management, and finally to species preservation.

The reality behind these terms—the law on the ground—is often very different than the law in the statute books. Game protection, for example, requires law enforcement and the anecdotal evidence suggests that closed seasons and bag limits were often only paper restrictions. Similarly, the U.S. Supreme Court's description of the ESA as "language [that] admits of no exception" (*Tennessee Val-*

ley Authority v. Hill 1978) is no longer accurate. The combined effect of the legislative and administrative amendments to the act has been to transform the prohibitive statute into a more flexible permitting system. This is not, however, the public perception. The act at thirty remains a lightning rod—a fact that itself may impede the recovery of at-risk species.

3 Endangered Species Time Line

Leona K. Svancara, J. Michael Scott, Dale D. Goble, Frank W. Davis, and Donna Brewer

The Endangered Species Act (ESA) is embedded in a web of statutes designed to regulate relationships between humans and other species that stretch back nearly a millennium (Goble, this volume; Goble and Freyfogle 2002). This chapter presents a time line of federal actions taken to protect wildlife beginning with passage of the Land and Water Conservation Fund Act in 1963 (Act of May 28, 1963). Earlier laws to protect wildlife are discussed elsewhere (Goble, this volume). The time line emphasizes federal actions that conserve species at risk of extinction and significant events in the course of implementing the Endangered Species Act.

The story is one of expanding protection, moving from the Land and Water Conservation Fund Act's recognition of species threatened with extinction, through the protection of migratory birds, to the first federal statutes to protect endangered species—the Endangered Species Preservation Act (Act of October 15, 1966a), the Endangered Species Conservation Act (Act of December 5, 1969), and the Endangered Species Act itself in 1973. In this progression, federal law has moved from protection of only fish and game to include nearly all at-risk plants and animals.

The enactment of the ESA in 1973 was not the end of the story, however. The act has been amended several times over the past thirty years and administrative actions have also modified its on-the-ground application. The original ESA embodied a top-down regulatory approach but the subsequent amendments have increased incentives that would encourage private landowners, government agencies, and other organizations to collaborate in recovery efforts for endangered species.

1963

- Land and Water Conservation Fund Act (Act of May 28, 1963)

- Seeks to ensure "adequate outdoor recreation resources" by providing funds to the Department of the Interior and to states for land acquisition
- Provides the first formal recognition of endangered species by Congress through authorization to purchase land "for the preservation of species of fish or wildlife that are threatened with extinction"

1964

- Department of the Interior appoints the Committee on Rare and Endangered Wildlife Species

1966

- Committee on Rare and Endangered Wildlife Species publishes *Rare and Endangered Fish and Wildlife of the United States* (Committee on Rare and Endangered Wildlife Species 1966). The book

  - Is known as the "Redbook" because of its red cover
  - Is the first official listing of species considered in danger of extinction
  - Contains 331 species in three categories of concern: 130 rare and endangered species, 74 peripheral species, and 127 species of undetermined status

- Endangered Species Preservation Act (Act of October 15, 1966a)

  - Is the first federal endangered species legislation
  - Authorizes the secretary of the interior to list native species of fish and wildlife as endangered
  - Authorizes acquisition of endangered species habitat for inclusion in the newly established National Wildlife Refuge System
  - Encourages cooperation with states to conserve endangered species

1967

- The first formal listing of endangered species is made: fourteen mammals, thirty-six birds, three reptiles, three amphibians, and twenty-two fish (see Wilcove and McMillan 2006)

1968

- U.S. Fish and Wildlife Service buys the first habitat to protect an endangered species: 2,300 acres in Florida for the Key deer (*Odocoileus virginianus clavium*)

1969

- Endangered Species Conservation Act (Act of December 5, 1969), amends and renames the Endangered Species Preservation Act of 1966 to extend protection to species in danger of "worldwide extinction" by

  - Increasing the procedural formality for listing species as endangered
  - Extending protection to some invertebrates
  - Requiring a five-year review of the endangered species list
  - Directing the secretaries of state and the interior to convene a meeting to develop international conventions on the conservation of endangered species (which eventually led to the enactment of the Convention on International Trade in Endangered Species of Wild Fauna and Flora [CITES])

- Nevada enacts the first state endangered species act, which

  - Provides limited protection for species and explicit exceptions to protect agricultural interests

1973

- Convention on International Trade in Endangered Species of Wild Fauna and Flora (CITES 1973) (entered into force July 1, 1975)

  - Restricts international trade in plant and animal species at risk of extinction

- Endangered Species Act (Act of December 28, 1973)

  - Is signed by President Richard M. Nixon on December 28
  - Authorizes the listing of species as endangered and threatened
  - Requires federal agencies to ensure that actions they authorize, fund, or carry out do not jeopardize the existence of listed species or modify critical habitat
  - Prohibits unauthorized taking, possession, sale, and transport of endangered wildlife species; the secretary of the interior is authorized to extend the prohibitions to threatened species by regulation
  - Provides authority to acquire land for the conservation of listed wildlife species
  - Authorizes cooperative agreements and grants-in-aid to states that establish adequate programs for conservation of endangered and threatened wildlife species
  - Imposes civil and criminal penalties for violating the act or regulations

- Implements CITES and the Convention on Nature Protection and Wild Life Preservation in the Western Hemisphere

1976

- Endangered Species Act Amendments of 1976 (Act of July 12, 1976)

  - Simplifies administrative processes in emergency situations, clarifies enforcement procedures, provides for disposal of forfeited and abandoned property, and clarifies the definition of "commercial activity"
  - Exempts from ESA prohibitions whale parts and products (scrimshaw) held lawfully before the date of enactment

1977

- First plant species are listed as endangered: San Clemente Island Indian paintbrush (*Castilleja grisea*), San Clemente Island larkspur (*Delphinium variegatum* ssp. *kinkiense*), San Clemente Island broom (*Lotus dendroideus* ssp. *traskiae*), and San Clemente Island bush-mallow (*Malacothamnus clementinus*)

1978

- First recovery plan is published for Kirtland's warbler (*Dendroica kirtlandii*)
- *Tennessee Valley Authority v. Hill* (1978)

  - U.S. Supreme Court holds that Tellico Dam cannot be completed because it would extirpate the snail darter

- Section 7 regulations are promulgated
- Endangered Species Act Amendments of 1978 (Act of November 10, 1978)

  - Reauthorizes the Endangered Species Act
  - Expands listing procedures by adding additional requirements, including the opportunity for public hearings
  - Directs the secretary of the interior to review the list of endangered and threatened species every five years
  - Adds a requirement that critical habitat generally be designated at the time of species listing
  - Requires consideration of economics in designating critical habitat
  - Directs secretaries of the interior and agriculture to develop a program for conserving listed species

- Amplifies and formalizes consultation provisions, including a requirement that federal agencies prepare biological assessments in cases where the secretary of the interior has advised that a listed species may be present
- Establishes a cabinet-level Endangered Species Committee with authority to exempt federal actions from compliance with the jeopardy prohibition of section 7
- Obligates the Endangered Species Committee to grant an exemption when the secretary of defense requests it based on national security
- Authorizes cooperative agreements with states for the conservation of endangered and threatened plants
- Restricts the definition of "species" by excluding "populations" of invertebrates

1979

- Energy and Water Development Appropriations Act (Act of September 25, 1979)

  - Authorizes the completion of Tellico Dam by exempting it from all federal statutes, including the Endangered Species Act

- Endangered Species Act Amendments (Act of December 28, 1979)

  - Extends and increases the authorization of appropriations
  - Directs the secretary of the interior to designate the Endangered Scientific Authority for the implementation of CITES
  - Creates the International Convention Advisory Commission
  - Directs the U.S. Fish and Wildlife Service to establish a prioritization system for listing
  - Extends scrimshaw exemptions for an additional three years

1981

- Secretary of the Interior James Watt seeks to redefine the regulatory definition of "harm"; when the proposal produces a storm of negative comments, the term is only cosmetically modified (USFWS 1981a, 1981b)
- Lacey Act Amendments (Act of November 16, 1981); prohibits interstate and foreign shipment of wildlife and plants illegally taken, possessed, transported, or sold under federal, tribal, state, or foreign law
- Listing priority guidelines are promulgated

1982

- Endangered Species Act Amendments of 1982 (Act of October 13, 1982)
  - Reauthorizes the Endangered Species Act
  - Significantly restructures listing procedures, including a requirement that determination of a species' status generally be made within one year of the listing proposal
  - Specifies that listing is to be made "solely on the basis of the best scientific and commercial data available" and hence that economics are not to be considered
  - Authorizes the development of habitat conservation plans (HCPs) as a condition for issuing permits to private parties to take a listed species when incidental to otherwise lawful activities
  - Adds "warranted but precluded" category to listing provisions
  - Establishes procedures for reintroducing experimental populations of listed species
  - Prohibits removing listed plants from land under federal jurisdiction
  - Extends annual authorizations under the act through fiscal year 1985

1983

- First habitat conservation plan is approved for the San Bruno elfin butterfly (*Callophrys mossii bayensis*) in San Bruno Mountain, California
- Listing and recovery priority guidelines are promulgated (USFWS 1983a, 1983b)

1985

- Exemptions regulations are promulgated (Endangered Species Committee 1985)
  - Establishes procedures for applying for an exemption to allow a federal action that jeopardizes the continued existence of a listed species
  - Provides procedures and standards for evaluating such applications by the secretary of the interior and the Endangered Species Committee
- First delisting due to recovery occurs (brown pelican [*Pelecanus occidentalis*])

1986

- Interagency cooperation section 7 consultation regulations are promulgated (USFWS and NMFS 1986)

1987

- Last dusky seaside sparrow (*Ammodramus maritimus nigrescens*) dies in captivity (Walters 1992)

1988

- Endangered Species Act Amendments of 1988 (Act of October 7, 1988)
  - Reauthorizes the Endangered Species Act
  - Redefines "person" to clarify the inclusion of municipalities
  - Provides equal authority to the departments of the interior and agriculture for enforcing restrictions on import and export of listed plants
  - Requires the secretary of the interior to monitor all petitioned species that are candidates for listing
  - Emphasizes that the act's emergency listing procedures are available for delisted species that again became threatened
  - Directs the secretary of the interior to develop and review recovery plans for listed species without showing preference for any taxonomic group
  - Specifies minimum content requirements for recovery plans
  - Requires reports on recovery plans and on the status of listed species to Congress every two years
  - Provides for public review of new or revised recovery plans prior to final approval
  - Requires monitoring of recovered species that have been delisted
  - Clarifies permissible uses of funds allocated to states and establishes criteria for these allocations
  - Prohibits damaging or destroying endangered plants on federal lands and on private lands when it is a violation of state law
  - Increases civil and criminal penalties provided under section 11
  - Requires the secretary of commerce to contract for a National Academy of Sciences study for conservation status of sea turtles and provides for establishment of a sea turtle coordinator
  - Requires the administrator of the Environmental Protection Agency in cooperation with the secretaries of the interior and agriculture to conduct a study identifying reasonable and prudent means to implement an endangered species pesticide labeling program and to report to Congress within one year
  - Extends the exemption from criminal sanctions for sales of pre-act scrimshaw
  - Authorizes the U.S. Fish and Wildlife Service to monitor the import and export of protected plants

1990

- Guidelines on the recovery planning for listed species are issued (USFWS 1990b)
- First salmonid (Sacramento River evolutionarily significant unit of chinook salmon [*Oncorhynchus tshawytscha*]) is listed as endangered

1991

- National Marine Fisheries Service issues its definition of evolutionarily significant unit (see Waples, this volume)

  - A distinctive group of Pacific salmon (*Oncorhynchus* spp.), steelhead (*Oncorhynchus mykiss*), or sea-run cutthroat trout (*Oncorhynchus clarki*) that are uniquely adapted to a particular area or environment and cannot be replaced
  - A population that is reproductively isolated from other population units of the same species and represents an important component of the evolutionary legacy of the biological species

- An injunction is issued by U.S. District Court Judge William Dwyer prohibiting timber harvesting of federal old-growth forests in the Pacific Northwest to protect the northern spotted owl (*Strix occidentalis caurina*); the decision is based on the National Forest Management Act rather than on the Endangered Species Act

1992

- Endangered Species Act authorization expires; the act remains in force through annual appropriations for the departments of commerce and the interior

1994

- Section 7 draft guidelines are issued
- "No Surprises" policy is announced; the policy guarantees that participants in a habitat conservation plan would suffer no further restrictions without compensation, even if the species continues to decline

  - Intended to minimize social and economic impacts consistent with timely recovery of a species listed as threatened or endangered
  - Provides a participation plan process involving all appropriate agencies in a strategy to implement one or more recovery actions

- Six joint ESA policies are issued by the U.S. Fish and Wildlife Service and the National Marine Fisheries Service regarding
  - Peer review in ESA activities and associated regulations (USFWS and NMFS 1994a)
  - An ecosystem approach under the ESA (USFWS and NMFS 1994b)
  - Information standards to provide criteria, establish procedures, and provide guidance to ensure decisions made by the agencies under the ESA represent the best commercial and scientific data available (USFWS and NMFS 1994c)
  - Section 9 prohibitions to establish a procedure at the time a species is listed as threatened or endangered in order to identify the maximum extent of activities that may violate section 9 of ESA and to increase understanding of the prohibitions by the public (USFWS and NMFS 1994d)
  - The role of state agencies in ESA activities (USFWS and NMFS 1994e)
  - Recovery plan participation and implementation (USFWS and NMFS 1994f)

1995

- First safe harbor agreement approved
- *Babbitt v. Sweet Home* (1995)
  - U.S. Supreme Court upholds the U.S. Fish and Wildlife Service definition of "harm" to include destroying or modifying habitat for an endangered or threatened species if the action results in the taking of the species
- Budget rider prohibits the listing of additional species and further designation of critical habitat until end of fiscal year 1995, effectively eliminating all funding for listing and prelisting activities under the ESA
- Gray wolf (*Canis lupus*) is reintroduced into Yellowstone National Park and central Idaho

1996

- Petition management guidelines are issued (USFWS and NMFS 1996d)
- Listing priority guidelines are issued for all emergency listings, for review status of all other proposed and candidate species, and for delisting actions (USFWS 1996c)
- Final guidelines for habitat conservation plans are issued (USFWS and NMFS 1996a)
- Policy is issued entitled "Policy Regarding the Recognition of Distinct Vertebrate Population Segments (Vertebrate Population Policy)" (USFWS and NMFS 1996b; see Waples, this volume)

- Clarifies interpretation by the U.S. Fish and Wildlife Service and National Marine Fisheries Service of the phrase "distinct population segment of any species of vertebrate fish or wildlife"
- Policy for Conserving Species Listed or Proposed for Listing under the ESA While Providing and Enhancing Recreational Opportunities (USFWS and NMFS 1996c)

1997

- Secretarial order on native Americans and the Endangered Species Act is issued (U.S. Department of the Interior and U.S. Department of Commerce 1997)
- Safe harbor agreements draft policy is issued
- Candidate conservation agreements draft policy is issued

1998

- "No Surprises" rule is revised (USFWS and NMFS 1998)
  - Provides regulatory assurances to the holder of a habitat conservation plan that no additional land use restrictions or financial compensation will be required for species covered by the permit
  - Precludes the federal government from requiring certain conservation measures from the permit holder
- First marine plant (Johnson's seagrass [*Halophila johnsonii*]) is listed as threatened

1999

- Section 7 handbook final guidelines are issued (USFWS and NMFS 1999a)
- Safe harbor agreements final policy is issued (USFWS and NMFS 1999b)
  - Provides incentives for private and other nonfederal property owners to restore, enhance, or maintain habitats for listed species
  - Specifies that future safe harbor agreements will be formalized by issuance of a permit to "enhance the propagation or survival" of an endangered or threatened species
  - Requires that actions undertaken by the landowner produce a "net conservation benefit" to the species
  - Specifies how baseline conditions are to be determined
  - Provides participating landowners with technical assistance to develop safe harbor agreements

- Candidate conservation agreements with assurances final policy is issued (USFWS and NMFS 1999c)

  - Provides for issuing assurances as an incentive for nonfederal landowners to implement conservation measures for species that are candidates for listing or are likely to become candidates in the near future

- Regulations are issued for safe harbor and candidate conservation agreements (USFWS 1999f)

  - Codifies minimum permit requirements and conditions that must be met for nonfederal landowners to receive the assurances

- Listing priority guidelines are issued for fiscal year 2000 (USFWS 1999j)

2000

- Final addendum to the Handbook for Habitat Conservation Planning and Incidental Take Permitting Process (USFWS and NMFS 2000a)

  - Provides guidance for conducting the incidental take permitting program by ensuring that biological goals are identified
  - Expands the public comment process

- *Wyoming Farm Bureau Federation v. Babbitt* (2000)

  - U.S. Court of Appeals for the Tenth Circuit upholds reintroduction of wolves in Yellowstone National Park as an experimental population

- Controlled Propagation of Listed Species Policy (USFWS and NMFS 2000c)

  - Provides guidance and consistency for use of controlled propagation as a component of a species recovery strategy
  - Ensures smooth transitions between various phases of conservation efforts such as propagation, reintroduction, and monitoring
  - Authorizes the controlled propagation of listed species when recommended in an approved recovery plan or when necessary to prevent extinction of a species

2001

- *Sierra Club v. U.S. Fish and Wildlife Service* (2001)

  - U.S. Court of Appeals for the Fifth Circuit holds that the U.S. Fish and Wildlife Service has acted arbitrarily and capriciously in failing to designate critical habitat for the Gulf sturgeon (*Acipenser oxyrinchus desotoi*)

- Fifth Circuit's interpretation of the scope of habitat protection may prove significant

2003

- Conservation Banking Guidance (USFWS 2003g)

    - Addresses the establishment, use, and operation of conservation banks to offset adverse impacts to listed species

- Draft candidate conservation agreements handbook is issued (USFWS 2003j)
- Policy is issued for evaluating conservation efforts when making listing decisions (USFWS and NMFS 2003a)

    - Identifies criteria to be used in determining whether conservation efforts yet to be implemented can be relied upon to avoid listing a species as threatened or endangered
    - Provides guidance to U.S. Fish and Wildlife Service personnel to determine whether a recently adopted or implemented conservation effort contributes to unnecessarily listing a species or to listing a species as threatened rather than endangered
    - Provides information to groups interested in developing agreements or plans that would make it unnecessary for agencies to list a species under the Endangered Species Act

- *Spirit of the Sage Council v. Norton* (2003)

    - U.S. District Court for the District of Columbia invalidates the permit revocation rule and remands the "No Surprises" rule to the agency, holding that it is procedurally invalid
    - Revises safe harbor agreements and candidate conservation agreements with assurances (USFWS 2003h)

4   Explicit and Implicit Values

J. Baird Callicott

All environmental policy is grounded, ultimately, on values. In some instances, values are explicitly stated; in others, they remain implicit, either because they seem so universally shared as to make expressing them unnecessary or because they are so inchoate as to make expressing them difficult. Some of the values served by the Endangered Species Act (ESA) are explicitly stated; the most important value, however, is unstated. This chapter explores the ESA's explicit, instrumental values and its implicit, intrinsic value and explains how instrumental values are objectified and quantified for purposes of comparison and choice. It also explains the domain in which intrinsic value is objectified and suggests a metric for its quantification. Finally, it discusses how these two incommensurable kinds of value interact in the real world.

Instrumental and Intrinsic Values

In the literature of environmental philosophy—which emerged at about the same time the Endangered Species Act became law—values are classified dichotomously as either *instrumental* or *intrinsic*. A value is instrumental when it is a means to some other end. A value is intrinsic when it is an end in itself. Some things may be both instrumentally and intrinsically valuable—an employee, for example. Other things may be valued in only one way. A shovel is valued only instrumentally; an infant child is valued by its parents only intrinsically. Intrinsic value is also deontological—or duty generating.

In the Western tradition, human beings are usually assumed to be the only intrinsically valuable ends. All other things are instrumentally valuable in relation to humans. In the jargon of contemporary environmental ethics, the Western tradition of thought has been anthropocentric. Moreover, Western moral philosophy has been militantly anthropocentric, vigorously justifying the exclusive claim of humans to intrinsic value. Contemporary environmental ethics challenges the assumption of anthropocentrism and its defense in Western moral philosophy.

Anthropocentrism and instrumentalism are closely linked because anthropocentrism assigns only instrumental value to all nonhuman natural entities. If we acknowledge, however, that other-than-human beings can also be valuers, then we must also acknowledge that they value things instrumentally. Squirrels, for example, value acorns instrumentally. Holmes Rolston argues that if other-than-human beings can also be valuers, then we must also acknowledge that they, no less than we, value themselves intrinsically—even if they do not do so self-consciously (Rolston 1994).

The Instrumental Values of the ESA and Their Quantification

The Endangered Species Act specifies that nonhuman species "are of aesthetic, ecological, educational, historical, recreational, and scientific value to the Nation and its people" (sec. 2(a)(3)). These values are listed alphabetically.

These explicit values appear to be purely instrumental. Indeed, delivering the majority opinion in *Tennessee Valley Authority v. Hill* (1978, 178–79), Chief Justice Warren Burger summarizes the legislative history of the ESA as emphasizing the utility of species: "Congress was concerned about the *unknown* uses that endangered species might . . . have." He quotes expert testimony declaring that "it is in the best interests of mankind to minimize the losses of genetic variations. The reason is simple: they are potential resources."

To the extent that the values are exclusively instrumental, they may be quantified in a monetary metric in order to compare them with other things that have instrumental value—such as pasture for livestock, farmland, and shopping malls—for purposes of making rational choices between competing uses (Freeman 1993).

Some environmental philosophers object to valuing nonhuman species (and other aspects of the natural environment) in a monetary metric because to do so "reduces" aesthetic, ecological, educational, historical, recreational, and scientific values to "economic" value (Hargrove 2000). From the perspective of contemporary economics, such objections are unfounded. Humans instrumentally value things in many ways. A car may be instrumentally valued as a means of transportation, as an object of aesthetic delight, and as a symbol of status. To aggregate the diverse values comprising a car, we need a common metric. Money is a convenient metric because it is quantitative and fungible. A car's market price is the sum of its diverse values expressed in a monetary metric. Its price is not an additional "economic" value of the car; rather it is the quantification of its transportation, aesthetic, and status-symbol values. Thus, from the point of view of environmental economics, to quantify the total instrumental values of endangered species in monetary terms is not to reduce these values to some other value but rather to express them in the same metric in which other competing instrumental values are expressed (Freeman 1993). Discomfort with quantifying the values of endangered species in a monetary metric may suggest, instead, a feeling that the values of endangered species are not solely instrumental—that such species are also intrinsically valuable.

Commodities derived from natural capital (such as lumber) are traded in markets and thus have a price. Outdoor recreation may also be a bundle of commodities and services for sale at a price. For example, in a "canned hunt" on private land a paying customer is guided to a confined game animal for the ego-affirming experience of killing it and acquiring a mounted trophy (Norris et al. 2001). The value of a wooded property clearcut for lumber can thus be compared with its value preserved for canned hunts—because both can be measured in a monetary metric. Nonconsumptive recreation involving endangered species, such as searching the piney woods of East Texas for red-cockaded woodpeckers (*Picoides borealis*), also can be measured in the same metric, even though they may not have a price tag. Using a "travel-cost method," environmental economists calculate the amount of money people spend on transportation, food, and lodging plus the opportunity costs of foregoing alternative money-making activities. In addition to such "implicit pricing methods," the aesthetic, ecological, educational, historical, and scientific values of the red-cockaded woodpecker—for which there is no market to determine their price—are expressible in the monetary metric by other, indirect, methods, such as "contingent valuation" (Freeman 1993).

Some endangered species are keystone species—"a species whose ecological impact is . . . disproportionately large relative to its abundance" (Power et al. 1996). For example, the southern sea otter (*Enhydra lutris nereis*) was nearly extirpated through overexploitation for its valuable fur. As a result, the underwater kelp "forests" on the continental shelf off the west coast of the United States began to disappear—because of the grazing by irrupting populations of sea urchins—with cascading ecological effects. Sea otters prey on sea urchins and as otter populations rebounded, urchin populations were reduced allowing the kelp forests to return and again provide habitat for many other species (Van-Blaricom and Estes 1998). Because sea otters are vital to the persistence of kelp-dominated aquatic communities that are important to other, commercially valuable species, the instrumental ecological value of otters, expressed in the monetary metric, probably exceeds their value as a commodity resource, expressed in the same metric.

Unlike the southern sea otter, few endangered species are likely to be essential to the provision of ecosystem services. As David Ehrenfeld notes, "the species whose members are the fewest in number, the rarest, the most narrowly distributed—in short, the ones most likely to become extinct—are obviously the ones least likely to be missed by the biosphere. Many of these species were never common or ecologically influential; by no stretch of the imagination can we make them out to be vital cogs in the ecological machine" (Ehrenfeld 1988, 215). The red-cockaded woodpecker, for example, is not a keystone species nor does it appear to play any other vital role in its ecosystem. Similarly, its recreational value, calculated by the travel-cost method, does not appear to be large. Indeed, the fact that it is endangered by lumbering suggests that the woodpecker's total value—understood to be instrumental and thus quantifiable in the monetary metric—competes poorly with the instrumental value of lumber, quantified in the same metric.

According Intrinsic Value to Listed Species Through the ESA

The goal of the Endangered Species Act is clearly to temper "economic growth and development" by "adequate concern" for species "in danger of or threatened with extinction" leading to "conservation" of them (ESA sec. 2(a)(1)). But, as noted, the values identified in section 2(a)(3) when quantified in the monetary metric do not appear adequate to achieve conservation of such species by purely market forces. This suggests that the act implicitly recognizes the intrinsic value of listed species, effectively exempting their conservation from purely instrumental—and thus purely economic—considerations.

The locus classicus of the concept of intrinsic value and its antithetical relationship to the monetary metric is found in the influential moral philosophy of Immanuel Kant, who wrote,

> [E]verything has either a *price* or a *dignity*. Whatever has a price can be replaced by something else as its equivalent; on the other hand, whatever is above all price, and therefore admits of no equivalent, has a dignity.
>
> That which is related to general human inclinations and needs has a *market price*. That which, without supposing any need, accords with a certain taste, i.e., with pleasure in the mere purposeless play of our faculties, has an *affective price*. But that which constitutes the condition under which alone something can be an end in itself does not have a mere relative worth, i.e., a price, but an intrinsic worth, a *dignity*. (Kant 1785, 53)

The distinction that Kant draws between a market price and an affective price is roughly the distinction that economists make between a market price and a shadow price. Things that people want (the objects of "human inclinations") are traded in markets and thus have a market price. Some objects of aesthetic experience—things that involve "pleasure in the mere purposeless play of our faculties," such as works of art—have a market price; those that do not—for example, many environmental amenities, such as wild and scenic rivers and clear viewsheds—have an affective price. That is, they have a value that can be expressed in the monetary metric. But it is, Kant thinks, inappropriate to price things that have intrinsic value. In a spirit of Kantian deontology and in the name of judicial restraint, the U.S. Supreme Court decided in *Tennessee Valley Authority v. Hill* that the Endangered Species Act exempted listed species from valuation (by the federal courts, at least) on the monetary metric in 1978—despite the emphasis on their instrumental value in the majority opinion. When completion of the Tellico Dam was stopped—to protect the snail darter (*Percina tanasi*)—the Court was "urged to view the Endangered Species Act 'reasonably' and to provide an interpretation 'that accords with some modicum of common sense and the public weal'" (*Tennessee Valley Authority v. Hill* 1978, 194). Burger rejected the invitation, holding that the language of the ESA "admits of no exception" when it "affirmatively command[s] all federal agencies 'to *insure* that actions authorized, funded, or carried out by them do not jeopardize the continued existence' of [a listed] species or 'result in the destruction or modification of habitat of such species.'" In *Tennessee Valley Authority v. Hill* (1978, 173), Burger alludes more than once to the economic impact of the Endangered Species Act—its effect in the domain of the market. Perhaps most unequivocally, he writes, "The plain intent of Congress in enacting this statue was to halt and reverse the trend toward species extinction, whatever the cost" (*Tennessee Valley Authority v. Hill* 1978, 184). Strictly interpreted, the ESA "will produce results requiring the sacrifice of the anticipated benefits of the project and of many millions of dollars in public funds" (*Tennessee Valley Authority v. Hill* 1978, 174). And although

> the burden on the public through the loss of millions of unrecoverable dollars would [seem to] greatly outweigh the loss of the snail darter . . . neither the Endangered Species Act nor Article III of the Constitution provides federal courts with authority to make such fine utilitarian calculations. On the contrary, the plain language of the Act, buttressed by its legislative history, shows clearly that Congress viewed the value of endangered species as "incalculable." Quite obviously, it would be difficult for a court to balance the loss of a sum certain—even $100 million— against a congressionally declared "incalculable" value, even assuming we had the power to engage in such a weighing process, which we emphatically do not. (*Tennessee Valley Authority v. Hill* 1978, 187–88)

The Court's refusal to value the snail darter economically—that is, to express its value in the monetary metric—and weigh that value against the price of the Tellico Dam affirms the intrinsic value of the species; the snail darter has value that cannot be expressed in terms of a price. But all instrumental values are expressible in terms of a price, either a market price or an affective (or shadow) price. Thus the value of the snail darter is noninstrumental; that is, intrinsic. It has a dignity, not a price.

Further, while the explicit language of the act and of *Tennessee Valley Authority v. Hill* is free of references to "intrinsic value," deontological rhetoric occasionally bubbles to the surface in the latter. For example, "It is conceivable that the welfare of an endangered species may weigh more heavily upon the public conscience, as expressed by the final will of Congress, than the write-off of those millions of dollars already expended . . . for Tellico in excess of its present salvageable value" (*Tennessee Valley Authority v. Hill* 1978, 169–70). The loss of something of mere instrumental value might be regrettable but hardly a matter of conscience. And while the expert testimony before Congress quoted in *Tennessee Valley Authority v. Hill* focuses on the "incalculable" (187–88) utility of species, such rationales are characterized as "the most narrow possible point of view"—the noninstrumental point of view, presumably, being the more expansive one.

Finally, although *Tennessee Valley Authority v. Hill* concludes that "Congress was concerned about the unknown uses that endangered species might . . . have" (178–), the Court concludes that Congress was also concerned "about the unforeseeable place such creatures may have in the chain of life on this planet." That may simply express a risk-averse instrumental concern for potential ecological services (although the concept was not current in 1978) parallel to a risk-averse instrumental concern for potential ecological goods—that is, natural resources. But it may, on the other hand, express a noninstrumental, deontological concern for biodiversity and ecological integrity.

Dispute rages about the ontological status of intrinsic value in the large literature of environmental philosophy (Symposium 1992). Is intrinsic value—as its name would suggest—an objective property of something that has intrinsic value, like its length or weight? Or is intrinsic value subjectively conferred, like something being loved or hated? In 1973, did Congress implicitly ratify a new moral *discovery* that endangered species have intrinsic value—analogous to a new scientific discovery such as the new forms of life near volcanic vents on the ocean's floor? Or did Congress implicitly *grant* endangered species intrinsic value—as it might grant a disenfranchised group of citizens the right to vote? There is an even larger literature in legal philosophy on the ontological status of rights (Wellman 1985). Are rights natural and real or are they artificial and conventional? While these questions are philosophically interesting and important, their answers make no practical difference. Whether endangered species literally *have* intrinsic value (like birds have feathers) or *are valued* intrinsically (like X is a target only when Y aims at it), the practical consequences are the same.

Tempering the Excesses of Utilitarian Welfare Calculus

Two schools of thought have dominated Western moral culture since the late eighteenth century—utilitarianism and Kantianism.

In the former, the aim of both private persons and public policy should be to achieve "the greatest happiness of the greatest number" (of human beings)— "happiness" then being understood to consist in a greater balance of pleasure over pain (Bentham 1789; Mill 1863). Later, utilitarians substituted "welfare" for happiness and defined welfare in terms of "preference satisfaction" (Baumol 1952). In themselves, preferences are regarded as neither good nor bad and they are aggregated among preference-satisfying individuals, who are regarded as counting equally. Thus, a preference for the music of Beethoven is not deemed to be better than a preference for that of LL Cool J. Nor are those who prefer Beethoven's music given more weight in welfare calculations than those who prefer that of LL Cool J. The "rational" aim of each private person is to maximize his or her own welfare and the aim of public policy is to maximize aggregate welfare.

Aggregate preference satisfaction may, however, be maximized in some circumstances at an extreme cost to a few individuals. For example, the aggregate welfare of a preindustrial slave-owning society may be greater than that of a preindustrial egalitarian society (Rawls 1971). Ancient Athenian society might be a case in point. Without slaves to do the physical work, the Athenian intelligentsia would have lacked the leisure to create the science, philosophy, literature, and art that we still enjoy two and a half millennia later. Thus, no self-consistent utilitarian argument can be deployed against the institution of slavery. The most graphic example is gladiator shows: thousands of Romans took pleasure in watching a few people fight to the death in the Coliseum (Kyle 1998). The modest welfare gain of a gladiatorial spectator multiplied by fifty thousand might well outweigh the extreme welfare loss of a few vanquished gladiatorial contestants.

The Kantian conceptual constellation of intrinsic value, dignity, and rights counters the potentially repugnant outcome of the unbridled utilitarian welfare calculus. According to Kant, rationality is the sole intrinsic-value-conferring property (Kant 1785). And, although he held open the possibility that other rational beings may inhabit the universe, humans were the only rational beings of which Kant was aware and thus the only entities to which he accorded intrinsic value. The clearest effect of recognizing the intrinsic value of human beings has been to make a market in human beings illegal and to prohibit such things as gladiator shows (Sawyer 1986). Similarly, some aspects of humanity such as sexuality and chemically unaltered states of human consciousness are also accorded a dignity and intrinsic value (Decker 1979; Inciardi 1986). With the advent of organ-transplant techniques, a market in human organs is now prohibited in the United States and many other Western countries (Rothman et al. 1997).

Proposals to accord intrinsic value to nonhuman beings dominate the animal-rights and environmental-ethics literatures. To argue that some nonhuman animals (such as primates and cetaceans) are rational and thus should be accorded intrinsic value departs least from the Kantian paradigm (Savage-Rumbaugh and Lewin 1994). To argue that other intrinsic-value-conferring properties should be substituted for rationality preserves the structure of Kant's ethic but alters, to some extent, its content. Substitutes proposed include being a "subject of a life," being a "teleological center of life," having a good of one's own, and having interests (Regan 1983; Goodpaster 1978; Taylor 1986; Varner 1998). Some proposals have been successfully incorporated into public policy. Although robust markets in animals still exist—everything from livestock markets to puppy mills to the zoo trade—the increasing body of law governing the humane treatment and care of animals in agriculture, biomedical research, and rodeos suggest that pleas for animal rights have had some measurable effect on public policy (Cohen 2000). The ESA is outstanding in this regard for two reasons. First, it accords listed species intrinsic value, albeit only implicitly. Second, the theoretical justification of intrinsic value for species is less well developed than the theoretical justification of animals' rights (Callicott 1986). There has been no success in translating into law the claim that *individual* plants and other subsentient organisms—except for specimens of listed endangered species—have intrinsic value.

It should now be clear why the ethical concept of intrinsic value should not be conflated with the economic concept of existence value, as some economists propose (Aldred 1994). Existence value is a personal preference. Some would, for example, prefer that black-footed ferrets (*Mustela nigripes*) remain in existence rather than suffer extinction (Vargas et al. 1966). This kind of preference may be expressed in the monetary metric, either by contingent valuation (asking respondents how much they would be willing to pay to keep black-footed ferrets in existence) or by estimating what fraction of the total monetary support donated to such organizations as the Nature Conservancy and Defenders of Wildlife might be fairly allocated to the conservation of black-footed ferrets (Aldred 1994). To accord something intrinsic value, on the other hand, is to declare that it has a dignity and that it should not be subject to pricing of any kind.

There is another, more intuitive way of highlighting the difference between intrinsic and existence value. In modern Western moral culture, human beings are recognized to have intrinsic value. But for each of us, only our respective family members, friends, neighbors, colleagues, and acquaintances have measurable existence value. I would be willing to pay all the money I could get my hands on to preserve my son (my only child) if his existence were threatened. Understandably, most readers would be willing to pay a great deal less to assure the existence of *my* son. When one factors in consideration of every other mother's son, the existence value of individual human beings to whom one is unrelated and with whom one is unacquainted shrinks to infinitesimal amounts. (I can get my hands on only so much money and there are more than six billion human beings in existence. So what honest answer could I give if asked how much I would be willing to pay to preserve the existence of say an individual Swede whom I've never met?) Although all human beings have intrinsic value and all have it equally in modern Western moral culture—as reflected in concepts such as universal human rights and the U.S. Constitution's Fourteenth Amendment ideal of equal protection under the law (United Nations 1996; Nowak and Rotunda 2000)—the existence value of any given human being varies wildly with circumstance. For example, the existence value of the scion of a very wealthy family may approach a billion dollars; that of a street urchin in Rio de Janeiro may approach zero. To conflate existence and intrinsic value is to think like a kidnapper rather than like a member of Kant's idyllic Kingdom of Ends (Kant 1785).

Dual Democracy of Value Objectification: The Market and the Legislature

The domain in which our utilitarian values are appropriately expressed is the market. As noted, the market is not perfectly efficient in part because not all of the things we value instrumentally are routinely bought and sold and thus do not have actual prices. Nonetheless, the market is, on the whole, democratic. People "vote" with their dollars for such things as McDonald's food and Coca Cola. Things for which people do not "vote" in the market soon disappear. Infamous examples are Edsel automobiles and Beta videotape cassette players. Looking around we can literally see the democratic common denominator of aggregated individual preferences—massaged, of course, by advertising—in contemporary society: fast-food chain restaurants, cell phones, lite beer, Wal-Mart superstores, and the like.

According to Mark Sagoff, the appropriate democratic domain for the expression of our nonutilitarian values is the legislature (Sagoff 1988). Arguably, both our utilitarian and nonutilitarian values are subjective. Preferences—such as for Coca Cola over RC Cola—are incontestably subjective. The market and its surrogates, however, serve in a way to objectify such preferences. The belief that some things have intrinsic value while others do not also appears to be subjective. Some people—members of People for the Ethical Treatment of Animals, for example—believe that individual animals have intrinsic value (and ought to have rights to life, liberty, and the pursuit of happiness), while others (still in the majority) do not. Analogous to the way the market objectifies preferences, legislatures objectify noninstrumental values. Thus, in contemporary Western democratic societies the intrinsic value accorded human beings is legislatively objectified by laws prohibiting murder, slavery, other forms of human trafficking, prostitution, the sale of human organs, and the sale or possession of mind-altering drugs. Other values objectified by legislation (or so fundamental as to be institutionalized in the U.S. Constitution) orbit the intrinsic value of human beings—for example, freedom of speech and religion, property rights, and the right to privacy.

That preferences are not the same as intrinsic value and the values that orbit it is indicated by the different way each is objectified. Preferences are objectified through aggregate choice. Intrinsic values are objectified through public debate. The wider extension of intrinsic value by legislation—to human fetuses, for example—is the subject of intense and often acrimonious public debate. Remarkably, the Endangered Species Act implicitly objectifies the intrinsic value of listed species—a decision that was indirectly affirmed by the U.S. Supreme Court in its refusal to express the value of a listed species in the metric appropriate for comparing things of instrumental value. In this sense, the intrinsic value of listed endangered species has become objective.

A Suggested Metric for Quantifying Intrinsic Value

Recognition of parallel domains—the market and the legislature—for the objectification of instrumental values on the one hand and intrinsic values on the other, suggests that there might be parallel metrics for the quantification of these different kinds of value. As noted, a common monetary metric enables us to compare the relative value of different kinds of instrumentally valuable things of unequal utility—the value of a car, for example, versus the value of a house. But, again, the monetary metric is inappropriate for quantifying intrinsic value—things, as Kant put it, that should have a dignity, not a price.

So what is an appropriate common metric for quantifying dignity? The question itself may seem impious until we reflect that, when objectified by legislative fiat, intrinsic value (like utility) is not distributed equally. A human being has greater dignity (greater intrinsic value) than most aspects of humanity—chemically unaltered states of human consciousness, for example, or sex. How do we know? Because the relative quantitative difference in the distribution of intrinsic value—as objectified democratically by legislative action—is reflected in the penalties for violating the legislation. The penalties for murder and kidnapping are severe; penalties for prostitution or soliciting a prostitute are relatively modest. Penalties for possessing prohibited mind-altering drugs are usually less severe than for trafficking in such drugs but more severe than for trafficking in sex (except when sex traffic involves minors). Thus, it appears that chemically unaltered states of human consciousness have a greater degree of democratically objectified dignity than does sex among adults (table 4.1). Sec-

TABLE 4.1 Sample federal crimes and associated penalties as an approximate metric for quantifying intrinsic value

Federal crimes	Associated penalties
First-degree murder	Death, or life prison term
Second-degree murder	10-year-to-life prison term
Voluntary manslaughter	10-year maximum prison term and unspecific fine
Kidnapping	20-year maximum prison term
Wholesale distribution of controlled substance	10-year-to-life prison term and $4 million maximum fine
Retail distribution of controlled substance	4-year maximum prison term and $30,000 maximum fine
Simple possession of controlled substance	1-year maximum prison term and $1,000 fine
Trafficking in human organs	5-year maximum prison term and $50,000 maximum fine
Prostitution (not a federal crime)	6-month jail term and/or $500 fine (California)
Taking listed endangered species	1-year maximum prison term, and/or $50,000 maximum fine

Source: Legal Information Institute 2005.

tion 11(b)(1) of the Endangered Species Act specifies a fine of up to $50,000 and a prison term of up to one year for "any person who knowingly violates any provision of this Act." Although the penalty metric for quantifying intrinsic value is far less sensitive than the monetary metric for quantifying instrumental value, it does seem to reflect the inequality in the distribution of intrinsic value as it is recognized through legislative action.

Penalty and Monetary Metrics: Their Interactions in the Real World

While Sagoff and others draw a sharp boundary between the market and legislative domains for the democratic objectification of utilitarian and deontological values, such values necessarily interact in a single arena—the real world (Sagoff 1988). Money influences legislation/regulation and legislation/regulation has an economic impact.

Legislative action is notoriously subject to monetary manipulation. In the United States, this commonly occurs through the system of legal bribery called campaign contributions (Corrado 2000). Thus, the democratic objectification of what should or should not be accorded intrinsic value may be thwarted by wealthy individuals and corporations. For example, David Bengston and his associates found that popular values regarding the national forests are shifting away from instrumental toward intrinsic (Bengston et al. 1999; Xu and Bengston 1997). Members of Congress and politically appointed heads of federal agencies, however, seem more responsive to the (financial) interests of the timber, oil and gas, and grazing industries than to this shift in popular values (Sierra Club 2003).

If a thing's intrinsic value is democratically objectified by legislative action, then it has an impact on the market (and its monetary metric) that sometimes varies proportionately to the strength of the signal it registers on the penalty metric. Often the intent of such legislation is to place its subject beyond the pale of the free market and thus ensure that it has no price, for example prohibiting the sale of controlled substances, sex, and human organs. One consequence of such legislation is to create a black market in which prices are generally higher than in a free market. For example, the relatively severe penalties for the sale of marijuana and cocaine have wildly inflated their prices on the black market (Desimone and Farrelly 2001). The relatively inconsequential penalties for the sale of sex (among adults) have not created much difference in its illegal and legal market price (Morris 1997). In the absence of uniform legislation banning such sales, an international gray market in very pricey human organs has emerged (Rothman et al. 1997). Similarly, the ESA and the Convention on International Trade in Endangered Species of Wild Flora and Fauna (CITES) have created a black market in endangered species such as Bengal tiger bones and African elephant tusks (Woods 1997; Stuart and Stuart 1996).

Because instrumental and intrinsic values must interact in the real world, Congress responded to the *Tennessee Valley Authority v. Hill* decision by amending the Endangered Species Act to create a cabinet-level committee (the Endangered Species Committee) invested with the power to override the protective provisions of the act when the costs of species conservation rise beyond a prohibitive threshold.

The procedures the committee uses to review applications for exemptions to the act illustrate another fundamental, easily overlooked way in which legislatively objectified intrinsic value affects instrumental values objectified by the market: the burden of proof is shifted to competing utilitarian values (Fox 1993). For example, the burden of proof rests on the state or federal government when it is threatening the liberty or life of an intrinsically valuable human being by prosecuting him for a crime that is punishable by imprisonment or execution. Similarly, because the intrinsic value of listed species has been implicitly objectified, an application for an exemption to the act's provisions can be granted only when it will not jeopardize the species. The ESA shifts the burden to the applicant to meet stringent, multiple criteria. Among these are the necessity to show that "the benefits of any such action [that would violate the act] clearly outweigh the benefits of alternative courses of action consistent with conserving the species or its critical habitat" (ESA sec. 7(h)(2)). Moreover, the benefits must not be solely private profit; the applicant must demonstrate that the action is "in the public interest." Given the burdens placed on the exemption applicant, it is not surprising that the committee has only been convened three times and has approved only one exemption (Buck et al. 2001).

Finally, the intrinsic value implicitly accorded listed species by Endangered Species Act has created an emerging legal market in conservation credits. For example, International Paper's habitat conservation plan for the red-cockaded woodpecker includes provisions for the sale of conservation credits to other owners of woodpecker habitat. Under the terms of the agreement, the company will dedicate 1,300 acres (eventually expanding to 5,000 acres) to intensive management of woodpecker habitat (Environmental Defense 2003). On this land, the company will consolidate eighteen nesting "clusters" of woodpeckers. As the number of nesting clusters rises above eighteen, International Paper may sell woodpecker conservation credits to other private landowners who may then log their woodpecker habitat without violating the ESA. The U.S. Fish and Wildlife Service has stated, "This plan also marks the establishment of the first mitigation bank for endangered species created in the Southeast on private land. This concept enables International Paper to increase its red-cockaded woodpecker population by assuming red-cockaded woodpecker mitigation responsibilities of other landowners who desire timely land management flexibility at market-driven rates" (USFWS 1999i).

The ESA's treatment of listed species demonstrates the difference between utilitarian and intrinsic values. Criminal penalties attached to conduct that violates the act objectifies the relative intrinsic value of listed species. And the continuing controversy swirling around the act also exemplifies the controversy that accompanies extension of intrinsic values to things through legislative fiat.

5 Toward a Policy-Relevant Definition of Biodiversity

Bryan Norton

The Endangered Species Act of 1973 (ESA) was a bold departure in environmental legislation; it has become perhaps the most powerful environmental statute in the United States, and it has been employed both as a weapon—to stop threatening projects—and as a tool—to bring opposed interests to a bargaining table. Commentators have noted that species endangerment is only one aspect of the biological impoverishment of the world's ecosystems; some have suggested that references to "species" in the legislation (which includes species, subspecies, and distinct population segments of vertebrates) should be viewed as a surrogate for protecting living things and the natural systems in which they are embedded.

This chapter examines these broader concerns. To do so, we focus on the term "biological diversity," or "biodiversity," which has come to function as a label for the broad concerns for nature, its life forms, and its processes. We address two questions:

1. How should we *define* the term "biodiversity?"
2. How should we *characterize* and *measure* the *value* of biodiversity?

These questions are important because they acknowledge that saving species serves as a proxy for a broader social goal—the interruption of a seemingly inexorable trend toward the impoverishment of the biological world.

Defining biodiversity is no simple act of lexicography; biologists, for example, offer varied definitions of the term. Similarly, because this book addresses policy, we cannot avoid addressing social goals and values as well as science. Choosing a definition in a context in which concepts and arguments of science and public policy interact forces us to face a strategic dilemma: should we start with a scientifically accurate definition before identifying values that would accrue from systems that are diverse in the biologists' sense of the term, or should we ask what we value about biological diversity and then seek a definition that captures those values?

Because the act explicitly refers to the objects of study of biological science, it is tempting to think that biology should determine the meaning of the term. But it should not be forgotten that the context of the act is a list of social values identified in its preamble—"esthetic, ecological, educational, historical, recreational, and scientific"—so that understanding these values is essential to identifying what should be saved. Furthermore, the context set by this book's topic dictates a definition of biodiversity that fulfills the purposes of *policy discourse*, even as we recognize that any definition must achieve *biological respectability*. When we think about apparently scientific concepts like biodiversity in a conservation context, we are forced to conclude that we cannot know what we mean until we know what we care about. By judging our definition by a dual criterion, we may ignore some things important to biologists because we seek a definition that can improve communication regarding policy goals. A definition that can fulfill these twin purposes is a *bridge term*, a term that links discourse about policy goals to scientific data and theory, all within a discourse about policy choices that will determine the future of life on earth. In this chapter, I explore how to articulate a policy based on reasonable conservation targets, focusing on the Endangered Species Act as a starting point.

First, we must carefully define key terms such as "biodiversity." In 1909, John Dewey delivered a lecture, "The Influence of Darwinism on Philosophy" (1910), in which he argued that the publication of Darwin's *Origin of Species* (1859) undermined a foundational idea in Western thought: the assumption that our categories "correspond" to an existing, "deeper" reality. Whether referring to Platonic "forms," Aristotelian "essences," or Kantian "categories," Western philosophy had argued that the world is intelligible to the human mind on the assumption that the world has a prelinguistic structure and that language functions by labeling prepackaged objects. Words, according to this traditional view, get their meaning from their connections to objective reality; sentences correspond to preexistent facts.

Darwin's discovery (implicitly) required the conclusion that the definition of a species is not an act of labeling, but a *decision* to draw a line across a continuum of change. This holds true for all linguistic stipulations: words do not correspond to preexisting objects or categories. Through an act (usually implicit) of choice, the development of a vocabulary to discuss observable phenomena "constitutes" the objects and categories we recognize and manipulate linguistically. This position, sometimes referred to as "conventionalism," emphasizes the social uses of language and the role that language plays in interpreting our shared realities.

Dewey recognized that the categories of biology (and of language more broadly) are tools that gain reality by functioning within communicative contexts, not by correspondence to prior realities. Communicative usefulness, not truth-by-correspondence, should determine our definitions. But usefulness implies we must carefully examine the shared purposes of the communication—and that leads back to the subject of social values and commitments.

Dewey's argument—and the Darwinian basis for it—are especially relevant here because they remind us that there is no "correct" biological definition to be "found," as one might discover a gem under a rock. We are looking for a definition that is *useful* in deliberative discourse on how to preserve biological diversity, however defined. Dewey recognized that all of our categories, including biological categories, develop from the need to communicate and to act together.

Social Goals and Policy Objectives in Protecting Biodiversity

The strategy of beginning with a biological definition before addressing the values question, although attractive, cannot do justice to the role Congress gave values in the preamble to the Endangered Species Act. An alternative starting point is the current discourse regarding the values of biodiversity and the ideas that shape discussion of endangered species. This discourse, however, is in poor shape, suffering from an excess of ideology and an associated polarization of the debate. Accordingly, debaters speak past each other. By *ideology*, I mean beliefs and conceptualizations based on preexperiential commitments. For example, a theory exists that environmental values are, or can be measured as, economic values. This view privileges the market, shifting the burden to those who would interfere with markets; growth is implicitly accepted as a dominating good. On the other hand, advocates for a theory that nature has "intrinsic" value call for deeply revising growth plans, citing obligations to the natural world as overriding human-oriented values. Proponents on both sides of this debate base their arguments on a *theory* of value rather than on attempts to use ideologically neutral language to describe and to test hypotheses about values.

Commitment to a *theory* of value shapes the values noticed by advocates of that theory, identifies the noticed values with a *type* of value, and creates the categories cited in arguments to protect species and biodiversity. If we choose our biological categories because of a priori, preexperiential theory, it will be difficult to link science and values together, because the terminology, observations, and data sought will differ according to a nonempirical theory. I have argued elsewhere that this polarization results from the misleading opposition between anthropocentric economists and advocates of intrinsic value in nature (Norton 1991, 2005). Because advocates of these two theories/paradigms for expressing environmental values characterize values in incommensurable ways, discourse is characterized by disagreements about the nature of the problem, the goals to be pursued, and the nature of the social values considered worth protecting. These very different perspectives for valuing nature set the tone for a noisy, but unproductive, debate about goals for protecting species and biological diversity.

I disagree with those who argue that the Endangered Species Act should be interpreted as attributing intrinsic value to species. The admission that intrinsic value claims are largely unresolvable by experience or empirical evidence makes them ideological—and positively unhelpful in the policy debates. It polarizes discussion by highlighting differences about *why* we should save species, when the real problem is the need to *do* something, cooperatively, to protect biodiversity, since it is widely valued for many reasons.

It can be argued that the most divisive aspect of this polarization is that both sides insist they have *the* correct theory of value, and that all values that count must count in *their* accounting framework. This insistence locks both sides into a framework of analysis that expresses their ideological commitment to a theory about the "nature" of environmental value; communication and compromise become unlikely. Such theories have been characterized by Christopher Stone as "monistic"—defined as the belief that there is a "single coherent and complete set of principles capable of governing all moral quandaries" (Stone 1987, 199). We can bypass this turf war by adopting a pluralistic stance based on the observable fact that people express their valuing of nature in many ways, all of which can legitimately be called "human values."

In fact, the original authors of the Endangered Species Act listed the social values they thought would be served by protecting species without *interpreting* these values as fitting either of the competing, single-valued theories of value. Once we adopt this reasonable, if unranked, list of values—aesthetic, ecological, educational, historical, recreational, and scientific—discussion will shift from a tug-of-war over values to a more focused discussion of goals.

However that debate comes out, the point is that saving biodiversity supports a range of values. The list is not competitive from a policy standpoint; stronger biodiversity legislation would protect all of these values. In many cases, we know what should be done, even if supporters of pro-environmental policies offer different justifications based in different worldviews, and using very different language. On the nonideological, pluralistic view, values associated with protection are additive, not competitive. What is important is to motivate governments and communities to address the biodiversity crisis; we do not have to agree on an abstract characterization of "the value of biodiversity" to agree that actions to protect biodiversity are justified. The same policies—those that successfully protect the most important kinds of biodiversity—are likely to protect all or most of these values. Saving biodiversity is good policy, however it is justified.

Value pluralism can be wedded to an experimental spirit ("adaptive management") in which discussion participants are encouraged to express values in their own terms but to then explain and discuss these values with others; this process encourages creation of common concepts for expressing values (Norton and Steinemann 2003). Over time, we can assess whether the terms and definitions of value categories serve the purpose of communication. This process, in other words, opens the possibility of consciously developing more effective linguistic tools for characterizing environmental values and threats to them. Defining biodiversity thus becomes part of this ongoing quest for a definition that captures both the values of a diverse biota and the best science of the day while also encouraging an open discussion of the importance of protecting biodiversity.

Since it seems impossible to save all of life's diversity, we are faced with choices. The mandate to conserve biodiversity must be accompanied by an understanding of which aspects of diversity should be saved if we are to preserve the values that justify conservation policies. The dilemma: which comes first, the egg of social values or the chicken of good biological science? By using the list in the Endangered Species Act as a tentative list of social values associated with biodiversity protection, we can state a clear definition for policy contexts: *biodiversity* should refer to those aspects of natural variety that are socially important enough to obligate protection of those aspects for future generations.

We must examine the best thinking of biologists on defining the term "biodiversity" before returning to the policy implications of our argument.

Biological Definitions of Biodiversity

Diversity has long been an important term in the literature of both biology and ecology, so, from the perspective of biologists, biodiversity is simply the diversity that exists in the biological world. However, diversity has been given several meanings. For example, there is a longstanding debate about whether diversity is better captured by total species counts or whether some degree of evenness in the comparative size of populations should also be taken into account. More profoundly, biodiversity is *multifaceted*—it encompasses diversity at multiple, nested scales of complex systems. R. H. Whittaker referred to three types: Alpha, Beta, and Gamma diversity, which today are usually referred to as "within-habitat," "cross-habitat," and "total diversity" (Whittaker 1960; Norton 1987).

Inventory Definitions and Difference Definitions

David Takacs asked twenty-one leading biologists to define biodiversity (Takacs 1996). The answers range widely, and few stress the same aspects of biologically diverse systems. One important difference is the extent to which they emphasize the dynamic aspects of biodiversity. There is a common-sense distinction, of course, between products and processes, between stocks of diverse entities and the ongoing flow of evolutionary processes. These processes generate and sustain biodiversity, so it is important to include them in a definition.

The definitions can usefully be divided into two types: *inventory definitions* and *difference definitions*. E. O. Wilson, for example, provides an inventory when he defines biodiversity as "the variety of life across all levels of organization from genic diversity within populations, to species, which have to be regarded as the pivotal unit of classification, to ecosystems. Each level can be treated either independently or together to give a total picture. And each can be treated either locally or globally" (Takacs 1996, 50). Similarly, Daniel Janzen defines biodiversity as "the whole package of genes, populations, species, and the cluster of interactions that they manifest" (Takacs 1996, 48). Peter Brussard recognizes the prominence of inventory-type definitions, asserting that the "standard definition" of biodiversity is species diversity, diversity of communities or habitats that species combine into, and the genetic diversity within species (Takacs 1996, 46).

Difference definitions, on the other hand, emphasize the complexities and interrelations among biological entities. Several of Takacs's scientists reflect this emphasis: "I think of it as fundamentally a measure of difference," says Donald Falk (Takacs 1996, 47); Paul Wood says simply that biodiversity is "the sum total of differences among biological entities" (Wood 1997, 2000, 41).

Difference definitions link biodiversity to a "difference" function. They emphasize differences among entities rather than inventorying entities that exemplify differences. Wood captures this variation in types of definitions by noting that we can characterize diversity in terms either of "biological entities that are different from one another," or as "differences among biological entities" (Wood 2000, 41). The former approach emphasizes the entities involved, while the latter focuses on "an environmental *condition or state of affairs* relative to the entities" (Wood 2000, 41). At the species level, for example, a difference definition would emphasize species that are the only one in their genus and would favor genera with no close relatives. Inventory definitions, which identify biodiversity with the sum total of entities that differ from each other, aspire to being additive—one increases biodiversity of a collection by adding elements different from that collection; the relative novelty of a species is not important to an inventory definition.

Both inventory definitions and difference definitions can capture the dynamic aspects of diversity. An "inventory" of diverse entities can, in principle, include dynamic aspects. Janzen, for example, says that biodiversity is "[the] whole package of genes, populations, species, and the cluster of interactions that they manifest" (Takacs 1996, 48) thus including interactive processes as part of his inventory. Another definition simply refers to biodiversity as the sum total of the processes creating biodiversity. For example, Terry Erwin defines biodiversity as "the product of organic evolution, that is, the diversity of life in all its manifestations," which emphasizes processes even when the focus is on the products of processes. While both inventory definitions and difference definitions *can* include the dynamic aspects of biodiversity, the latter focus on this aspect and thus more accurately portray the function of process in maintaining biodiversity (Takacs 1996, 47).

Difference definitions help us to see what is most valuable in diversity at all levels because they reveal the role of diversity in biological creativity. R. H. Whittaker hypothesized that "diversity begets diversity," that diverse elements undergoing diverse processes will generate more diversity (Whittaker 1960). This hypothesis also suggests that losses of diversity can create further losses: species become threatened as their mutualists become endangered or extinct. Diversity provides options for further creativity—and diversity is important as a contributor to that dynamic. Consider agricultural crops: most production comes from domesticated and even genetically modified seed stock, while wild varieties produce only a tiny portion of the world's food crops. If, however, a major disease breaks out in domestic lines, the existence of wild varieties—with their greater genetic and morphological diversity—might contain the genetic resistance needed to reestablish domestic productivity.

Biological diversity is thus not a resource among other resources. That is, differences in biological entities contribute only indirectly to agricultural production. Differences among biological entities are the *source* of substitutions, of improved seeds, and of new adaptations (Wood 2000). This has strong implications for the ways we assign values to diverse ecosystems. For example, it calls into question the goal of equating the values found in nature to the concept of "ecosystem services" and to the monetary values derived from these services because, if biodiversity cannot be represented as an additive quantity, it seems unlikely that it can be represented as a quantity of dollar values. (Daily [1997, 366] acknowledges this point. See also Paul Wood's [1997] argument that biodiversity cannot be considered a "resource" among other resources because it is in fact the "source" of biological resources.)

Employing the distinction between inventory and difference definitions, I argue for two theses. First, neither type of definition can provide a comprehensive accounting of what we mean by biodiversity. Second, there are nevertheless good *biological* reasons to favor difference definitions over inventory definitions. However, inventory definitions may nonetheless prove important in public discourse.

The Impossibility of Addition

Biodiversity cannot be defined in such a way as to make it a measurable quantity. That is, we cannot provide an *index* allowing us to rate ecosystems or collections of entities according to their degree of diversity. Wood explains this point by noting that because diversity is multidimensional and because its dimensions are not commensurable, it is difficult to define. Diversity cannot therefore be reduced to one commensurable statistic (2000, 49).

To illustrate Wood's concern, consider the following case: assume a functioning ecological system made up of n species; if one more species invades the system and establishes itself, without losing any species, there is an increment in diversity to the level $n + 1$. Suppose instead we expand the system by adding another *system*—another habitat that shares some species with the original—for example, a storm opens a large clearing in a once-dense forest—but the new system has additional species and a range of relationships and functions that were not present in the original system (this would be an increase in "cross-habitat diversity" rather than "within-habitat diversity"). We might avoid double-counting in an inventory-style definition by not counting the duplicative species in the added system, but the resulting list of species would not capture the real impact on biodiversity represented by additions of cross-habitat diversity. Adding cross-habitat diversity also introduces a range of genetic and behavioral functions and relationships that are important to biodiversity but not captured in the new species list. Thus, as a technical matter, inventory definitions imply a form of commensurability and ability to aggregate across collections that is impossible and thus misleading.

A similar argument applies also to difference definitions. Philosopher of biology Sahotra Sarkar (2005), citing similar reasons, suggests that no satisfactory definition of biodiversity is possible. He argues that biodiversity is usually understood to include two hierarchies—a spatial hierarchy from biological molecules to communities and ecosystems, and a taxonomic hierarchy based in genetic lineages—but that the differences mapped by these hierarchies are not additive. Each hierarchy represents a significant and different form of diversity, a form that must be included in any comprehensive accounting of differences among biological entities (Sarkar 2005, 178). Again, we are forced to conclude that biodiversity—whether conceived as an inventory of differing objects or as a difference function applicable to groups of entities—cannot be defined as an additive index capable of ranking systems or collections of entities as more or less diverse.

The conclusion that biodiversity cannot be defined as an additive quantity may initially seem disastrous. If biologists cannot provide a quantitative index of biodiversity, does it follow that their recommendation that we preserve biodiversity is meaningless? Does it mean that biologists do not have a common understanding of what we should be trying to save? Perhaps not. Biologists can often decide how to save biodiversity even when they cannot define it. For many purposes, the term "works" to guide action because we can act cooperatively on the assumption that "we know it when we see it." To *define* a term, on the other hand, is to connect it to other words—not actions—that are theoretically, and often ideologically, loaded. It may be that the variation in definitions has more to do with biologists' linguistic habits and their theoretical commitments than with their conservation activities.

Furthermore, we need not be dismayed by the lack of a quantifiable definition of biodiversity, given what we learned from Dewey. We should not expect that biodiversity will denote some preexistent, biological parameter; nor should we expect biodiversity to be precisely measurable. What we are looking for is a term and attendant definition that fulfills two conditions. It must be "clear enough" to enable communication about what to do. That is, can practitioners use the term to agree upon policies that will protect biodiversity, as understood in that community? Second, it must be rich enough to capture all that we mean by, and value in, nature. These features are so diverse that they cannot be made precise and measurable. The question is not, can we precisely define it? Rather, the question is, are members of the community able to act in concert? The answer is that major conservation groups in the United States agree about many of the steps required to protect biodiversity. Although disagreements exist regarding priorities and tactics, conservation groups generally agree about the need for policies that create open space, protect riparian corridors, and so forth. The term is clear enough to usefully guide policy within the community of practitioners and advocates.

The remaining question is whether the term will be politically successful in communicating the importance of biodiversity to policy makers and the public. Ideally, public discourse about biodiversity protection would suggest better ways to articulate the needs of biological conservation.

Biodiversity in Public Policy Discourse

A major task of environmentalists and conservation biologists should be to develop better means of communicating biological and ecological information to policy makers and the public.

When Thomas Lovejoy, a respected scientist and a policy leader, was asked by Takacs about the meaning of biodiversity, he said "The term is really supposed to mean diversity at all levels of organization. But the way it's most often used is basically relating to species diversity. I think for short operational purposes, that *species diversity* is good shorthand. . . . It's the most easily measured, and it's the one at which the measures are the least controversial. But you're really talking about more than that. You're talking about the way species are put together into larger entities and you're talking about genetic diversity within a species" (Takacs 1996, 48). Here, then, we have a leading biologist and conservationist advocating a more complex definition for scientific accuracy but a simpler definition for shorthand in policy contexts.

The arguments suggest that difference definitions are superior for capturing the biological understanding of biodiversity, while the interests of communication with policy makers and the public are better served by inventory definitions. It is perhaps ironic that a key biological weakness of inventory definitions—their tendency to encourage false hope of a quantified measure of biodiversity—also makes them popular with policy makers intent on tallying wins and losses in the effort to save biodiversity. Difference definitions, on the other hand, show the value of biodiversity as a source of options and opportunities—but these fare poorly in policy debates.

Perhaps this highlights the importance for scientists and policy makers of talking openly about ways to improve communication. Rather than clinging to definitions that don't work, we can investigate which terms and linguistic forms are conducive to communication and cooperative behavior within the community seeking to protect the wonders of the biologically diverse world. As noted earlier, we can use bridge terms, such as "ecological integrity," that have both empirical and evaluative content. An alternative strategy is to pair terms; for example, "biodiversity" would be paired with another, less technical, term that would be used in discourse with the public and policy makers. Recent opinion research shows that less than 60 percent of Americans are familiar with the term "biodiversity" and some are actively hostile toward it. On the other hand, the phrase "web of life" seems to resonate better with many Americans. This empirical information suggests that "web of life" be used in place of "biodiversity" when addressing policy makers and the public. "Biodiversity" could then maintain its scientific rigor while linked to a more intuitive idea with broader public appeal.

Part II   Conservation Science

The practice of science is fundamental to conducting the business of the Endangered Species Act (ESA) and achieving its goals of preventing extinction and promoting recovery. Recently, there has been much discussion in the public arena about the quality of science, and Congress has introduced several bills addressing the issue. However, there is little evidence to support contentions that science has failed us (National Research Council 1995). Tools for identifying species and mapping their distributions and habitat needs are greater now than when the act was passed, but inadequate information on the taxonomy (Raven and Wilson 1992), geography (Lomolino, this volume), and natural history of species still presents a major hurdle to effective listing and recovery.

The chapters in this part provide ideas about how, despite shortfalls in knowledge, to make better use of available information, ask more policy- and recovery-relevant questions, and more effectively communicate the findings in science to policy makers. They also describe how species concepts have been used in the implementation of the act. In chapter 6, Mark Lomolino frames the spatial and temporal context in which we conserve endangered species and explains the relevance of the Wallacean shortfall to effective implementation of the act. In chapter 7, Shahid Naeem and his colleagues examine how well the Endangered Species Act has protected ecological and evolutionary processes upon which, as stated in the act, "endangered species and threatened species depend." In a similar vein, Shahid Naeem and Claire Jouseau explore in chapter 8 how endangered species protection relates to the protection of ecosystem services such as net primary production and nutrient retention.

Much of the controversy surrounding the use of science in implementing the Endangered Species Act comes from lack of knowledge of or misunderstanding about its limits and confusion about the role of scientists in informing policy and decision makers. In chapter 9, Holly Doremus provides a historical overview and in-depth discussion of the legislative mandates for science, the legal impact of the "best available science" mandate, political controversies surrounding the use of science in implementation of the act, and competing models of scientific decision making. Mary Ruckelshaus and Donna Darm address these issues in chapter 10 and provide a general review of how science is used to implement the ESA in the areas of listing decisions, designation of critical habitat, actions under sections 7 and 10 of the ESA, and recovery planning.

Biological systematics is basic to implementing the Endangered Species Act, not only in defining species but also in establishing significant variation within species. In chapter 11, Robin Waples presents a case study of Pacific salmon (*Oncorhynchus* spp.) that illustrates the power of modern genetic tools for achieving particularly descriptions of species. In chapter 12, Susan Haig and Fred Allendorf review the definition and place of hybrids in the implementation of the Endangered Species Act and how "hybrid policy" has changed since the first consideration of hybrids in the late 1970s. And in chapter 13, Mike Reed and his colleagues discuss the use of science to define what has become one of the most hotly contested concepts in the Endangered Species Act: critical habitat (Suckling and Taylor 2006).

Overall, these chapters underscore the need for improved use of science in protecting imperiled taxa, as well as evolutionary and ecosystem processes.

6 Space, Time, and Conservation Biogeography

Mark V. Lomolino

One assumption of this volume is that thirty years is a sufficient period to evaluate the strategies, successes, and shortcomings of the Endangered Species Act (ESA). While three decades may exceed the generation time of our own species and greatly exceeds the administrative cycles and presidential tenures in the United States, it falls far short of the time likely required to recover most imperiled species. Moreover, these species and their associated communities and ecosystems diverged and developed over millennia and many generations and have been influenced by processes operating at landscape to regional scales. These elements of biological diversity developed from populations that slowly spread from their origins to distant areas, expanding their geographic ranges and interacting with many other species, extant and now extinct. They diverged and diversified in isolation, again over many millennia and across what came to be broad and sometimes disjunct ranges, ultimately either surviving or succumbing to a combination of extinction forces. While endangerment and extinction may appear to occur rapidly, they are simply the last stages in the long evolutionary and ecological history of imperiled species.

The long-term and broad-scale historical development and decline of biological diversity may be far more relevant to conservation biology than is currently appreciated. As the insightful paleontologist and biogeographer George Gaylord Simpson (1966) observed, "The extent to which we can hope to understand ourselves and to plan our future depends in some measure on our ability to read the riddles of the past." Some conservation biologists appreciate the applied as well as heuristic values of the long-term and large-scale history of biological diversity. Recently, Gunderson and Folke (2003) called upon conservation biologists to look toward the "science of the long view"—to expand our studies to integrate disciplines over decades and centuries, and to develop new models and approaches to understand how ecosystems operate over broad temporal and spatial scales.

A growing number of today's conservation biologists are calling for strategies to preserve the ecological, biogeographic, and evolutionary context of endangered species, allowing them to persist in their natural form and not merely as curios in captivity or museums (Goble, this volume). Perhaps it is best not to stipulate a time frame, such as populations persisting for at least the next five years or into the "foreseeable future." Although most of what we study has a limited temporal scale, extinction and, therefore, the challenge for conservation biologists is a long-term process. As Michael Soulé (1983) put it, "The extinction problem has little to do with the death rattle of its final actor. The curtain in the last act is but a punctuation mark—it is not interesting in itself. What biologists want to know about is the process of decline in range and numbers." The process of range decline is indeed a very long-term and large-scale process.

By increasing the temporal and spatial extent of the Endangered Species Act and of conservation biology in general, we can work toward two additional, insightful goals:

• Inclusion of historical factors (in the broad evolutionary and biogeographic sense) that contribute to a better understanding of the causes of extinction and better assessments of endangerment
• Reestablishment of the geographic and evolutionary context of endangered life forms (see Peery et al. 2003; Lomolino 2004)

In this chapter I suggest a strategy for conserving endangered species at scales that are ecologically, biologically, and evolutionarily significant.

An Introduction to Conservation Biogeography

Consideration of the geographical and evolutionary history of species, and using them to establish recovery goals, are central to an emerging discipline and new synthesis in science—conservation biogeography. In a nutshell, conservation biogeography is an applied science based on geographically explicit insights from many fields, all of which can be distilled to a relatively simple, two-part paradigm:

• Success in conserving biological diversity depends heavily on our understanding of the geography of nature (a geography that has both temporal and spatial dimensions)
• Conservation of the natural character (morphological, physiological, behavioral, ecological, and evolutionary) of native biotas can best be achieved by conserving their geographic context

Ecological interactions, dispersal, extinction, speciation, and evolutionary divergence occur in particular places and times, each result serving as a precursor to the next; together these events comprise a distinct series and, ultimately, a set of unique species that cannot be replicated. Change any stage or major event—for example, as in the extreme case of the collision of an asteroid some 66 million years ago or the emergence of a superspecies such as *Homo sapiens*—and the very face of nature itself will be forever altered. Dinosaurs have yet to reevolve and longhorn cattle can never replace North America's Pleistocene megafauna.

The lesson is not just that the natural world has changed in dramatic and irreversible ways, or that our own species may fundamentally change the geography and evolutionary trajectories of Earth's life forms. Claims that in recent decades were dismissed as alarmist hyperbole (e.g., that most historic and many prehistoric extinctions are/were anthropogenic) have now become consensus opinions among respected scientists. Yet we often fail to appreciate the linkage between temporal and spatial time scales. Processes that play out over large spatial scales also require long time periods to take fruition. If we are to be truly successful at conserving the natural character of native species and the ecosystems they inhabit, we should realize that ecological and evolutionary processes—those fundamental to conserving biological diversity—typically involve substantial time lags. David Tilman and his colleagues (1994) call attention to "extinction debts"—essentially time delays between various disturbances and their ultimate effects on biological diversity. The longer the generation time or the larger and more broadly distributed the species, the longer the time lag between cause and effect—extinction debts sometimes measure decades to centuries. Given this, a thorough understanding of the threats and declines of endangered species (seemingly precursory to listing decisions and conservation plans) may well require that we dig deep into the historic and prehistoric record.

It follows that the sciences of prehistoric life forms—paleobiogeography, historical biogeography, evolutionary biology, and related disciplines—may provide invaluable insights for conserving today's life forms. George Gaylord Simpson's call to learn from "the riddles of the past" continues to grow in its relevance to today's dilemmas.

John Byers (1997) describes one of these "riddles of the past" in his account of pronghorn antelopes. One of the most singular curiosities of this species is its ability to avoid predators by virtue of group vigilance combined with amazing speed and endurance. Across the relatively planar landscapes of interior North America, pronghorn sentinels can detect approaching predators from great distances and quickly issue warning calls. If signaled to flee, pronghorns can slice across the prairie and savanna at 100 kilometers per hour and continue their flight for many minutes. But the singular question is not why can pronghorns run the way they do, but what are they running from? There are no lions, cheetahs, or other large cursorial predators in North America; but there once were.

As Byers observes, pronghorns and the complement of North America's diverse, former collection of large grazing herbivores were plagued by a battalion of large predators, including hyenas, cheetahs, lions, saber-toothed cats, four species of wolves, plundering dogs, and dire wolves. This continent's Pleistocene herbivores coevolved with this nightmare assemblage of large, cursorial predators. Those that persisted did so by either outgrowing their predators or, as in the case of pronghorns, outrunning them.

The lesson from biotas past is far from an isolated and banal, academic exercise. In this particular case, if we are to preserve the natural character of North America's sole surviving antelope—its size, great speed and endurance, and complex social system—we may need to maintain a diversity of its populations across its historic range and within ecosystems that continue to challenge it to survive by vigilance and speed (see Dudley 1999 for a similar case study for rare plants and now-vanished herbivores; see also Burney et al. 2001).

Significance of Conservation Biogeography

Preservation of native biotas in their natural state as integral components of functioning ecosystems and as significant and adaptable evolutionary units means that we should strive to preserve the geographic context of endangered biotas. This is not just a purist's vision. Conservation of imperiled species requires that they maintain the speed, size, reproductive, predatory and avoidance behaviors, immune responses, and the many other survival strategies that in the past were maintained as responses to natural selection regimes across the species' historic range. This, of course, requires a better understanding of the geographic structure of native species and their communities. The task, however, is plagued by an insidious catch-22 of conservation biology: we need to know the most about the rarest species—those that are likely atypical and difficult to study. We can develop sound inferences not just from the few snapshots and glimpses we have in recent time and limited locations but also from the wealth of studies on the history and prehistory of these and related species. How were they distributed in the past? How did their distributions change with climatic conditions, habitat shifts, or invasions by other species, including humans? Based on phylogenetic and phylogeographic reconstructions, we can determine the distinctiveness of focal species along with when, where, and in what forms their relatives persisted and perished (Avise 2000; Lockwood et al. 2002).

David Steadman, Timothy Flannery, Paul Martin, and other distinguished scientists have chronicled the ecological history and biotic upheavals of the late Pleistocene and early Holocene (e.g., see Martin 1984; Flannery 1995, 2001; Steadman 1995; Steadman and Martin 1984). Their work has convinced many that few regions exist where ecological and evolutionary conditions are similar to those that produced any extant species. We do not have to dig too deeply into the fossil record to reconstruct these ghosts of communities and ecosystems past. The remains of native rodents of the Galapagos Islands, hundreds of species of Pacific island birds, and many thousands of other species of animals and plants from around the world have been collected just a few centimeters below the surface. These have provided us with a more complete picture of the natural, intact ecosystems as well as clues to the origins, persistence, and extinction of native biotas.

Some two decades ago, bones were discovered, not beneath the soil but along the windswept ice sheets of Wrangel Island off the northern coast of Siberia (Vartanyan et al. 1993). The bones were those of mammoths with a fascinating story to tell: Over time, these "mammoths" had declined in size to one-third the mass of their mainland ancestors. This is an intriguing but common trend in insular mammals—the "island rule." Otherwise large mammals such as mammoths, elephants, and deer, if they persist, tend to become dwarfed on islands, while species of small mammals such as mice and voles tend toward gigantism. On Wrangel Island, woolly mammoths persisted in a fundamentally altered ecological and evolutionary arena—one limited in space and resources and devoid of large predators. While ancestral pronghorns evolved to outrun their predators, Pleistocene elephants, mastodons, and mammoths on the continents simply outgrew them. Now, in Wrangel's ecologically simple and predator-free system, selective pressures shifted to favor smaller size.

Again, this lesson of species past has valuable applications to conservation of modern-day "mammoths." If we continue to maintain individuals in small, ecologically simple enclosures and reserves—systems that fail to simulate natural selective pressures—then future generations of elephants may become tame, tuskless, and anthropogenically dwarfed. Perhaps many will dismiss this as futuristic science fiction, but there is mounting evidence that many native biotas are being downsized (Lomolino et al. 2001; Dudley 1999; Whitehouse 2002; Raubenheimer 2000). Some populations of elephants are already genetically fixed on tusklessness, and body size changes have been reported across a diversity of species, including mammals and birds inhabiting fragmented landscapes of northwestern Europe (Schmidt and Jensen 2003) and key subspecies such as Mexican wolves (*Canis lupus baileyi*) that appear to be undergoing genetic dwarfing (Fredrickson and Hedrick 2002).

There also is a second and equally compelling lesson from the "parable of the woolly mammoth," one with especially important insights for conserving biological diversity. The mammoth bones discovered on Wrangel Island were not just small, they were also fresh—at least in a relative sense. Prior to this discovery, the woolly mammoth was thought to have perished (on the Eurasian mainland) approximately eleven thousand years ago. But these bones were just thirty-six hundred years old. Mammoths survived well into the Holocene (a prolonged extinction debt, indeed) and, more important, they survived in isolation along the extreme periphery of their range. This is fundamentally counter to what we thought we knew about the geography of extinction—that peripheral populations should be the first to go and that central populations should persist in the latter stages of geographic range collapse and extinction (Channell and Lomolino 2000a, 2000b; Lomolino and Channell 1995, 1998; Abbitt et al. 2000; Nielsen et al. 2001). Conservation biologists generally relegated peripheral regions of a species' historic range to the land of the walking dead, the domain of zombies with little value for conserving biological diversity. We were told to devalue such areas and peripheral populations to low status and to avoid the range periphery when locating nature reserves or selecting sites for biological surveys, reintroductions, and translocations.

It turns out, however, that the "exceptional" case of the woolly mammoth, persisting in isolation, was actually the rule. Even for contemporary patterns of extinction and endangerment, the general pattern is that of persistence of peripheral, rather than central, populations. Viewed over the entire temporal extent of range collapse from a once broadly distributed species, the process typically begins with collapse of one of its many peripheral populations (typically that first encountered by the spreading extinction factor), then the extinction front spreads to overwhelm the central populations; the final, persistent populations are found along the most remote reaches (extreme periphery, islands, or highest elevations) of the historic range (Lomolino and Channell 1995, 1998; Channell and Lomolino 2000a, 2000b). Conservation guidelines need to expand to include the periphery of historic and prehistoric ranges, again emphasizing a need to increase the spatial and temporal extent of our mandates to better assess the historic geographic range (Foin et al. 1998).

We are still left with a significant, but surmountable, challenge—one I have referred to as the *Wallacean Shortfall* in honor of Alfred Russel Wallace and his contributions to the field of biogeography. In addition to providing us with fundamental insights into the geography of nature, on evolutionary spread, and the ultimate decline and extinction of species, Wallace made prescient observations for conserving biological diversity:

> So we find, both in Australia and South America, that in a quite recent period many of the largest and most specialized forms have become extinct, while only the smaller types have survived to our day—a group progressing and reaching a maximum size or complexity and then dying out, or leaving at most but a few pygmy representatives. (Wallace 1901, 394)
>
> It is clear, therefore, that we are now in an altogether exceptional period of earth's history. We live in a zoologically impoverished world, from which all the hugest, and fiercest, and strangest forms have recently disappeared; and it is, no doubt, a much better world for us now they have gone. (Wallace 1876, 150)

No doubt many twenty-first-century conservation biologists question whether it is a "better world" without these great beasts, but few can question his prescience in one of the earliest statements on the very problem the Endangered Species Act seeks to solve. Perhaps the greatest challenge to achieving the goals of the act and conserving biological diversity is our very limited understanding of biological diversity itself. During the early 1990s, Peter Raven and Edward O. Wilson (1992) called on conservation biologists to address the *Linnaean Shortfall* (i.e., the discrepancy between the list of described species and the total number species believed to inhabit this planet). Conservation biologists, however, are faced with a more challenging shortfall. The lists of described species are just that—lists of Latin binomials with descriptions of identifying characteristics. For an overwhelming majority of them, however, we know precious little of their distributions (either past or present). This is the *Wallacean Shortfall,* the paucity of information on the geographic distributions of species. How can we understand patterns in endangerment, hot spots of diversity and endemicity, and optimal sites and scales for conservation actions (e.g., translocations, introductions, and configuration of reserve networks) without understanding the distributions of the species we are trying to conserve?

The success in identifying (through listing processes) and conserving native species (through recovery plans, habitat conservation plans, and related activities) will depend to a significant degree on our knowledge of current and past distributions of species, on geographic variation of their populations, and on the geographic dynamics of extinction forces. Few would argue for mixing locally adapted populations from different regions. It is now equally evident that searches for undiscovered populations of imperiled species or for sites for introductions should include the periphery of historic and possibly prehistoric ranges. But, for how many species can we accurately estimate the current range let alone historic and prehistoric ranges?

Perhaps the most famous case is that of the California condor (*Gymnogyps californianus*). Although limited to the state of California in recent times, its populations occupied a broad expanse of the North American continent during the Holocene, stretching from the Northeast down to Florida and across the Southeast to the Southwest, to Baja California, and up to British Columbia (Channell and Lomolino 2000b). Reintroductions of condors to central areas of its most recent range (i.e., in California) were unsuccessful, largely because factors causing its decline still persisted in those areas. However, reintroductions of condors to Vermillion Cliffs in northern Arizona, a region not occupied by the species for some two millennia, is now celebrated as an encouraging success.

Unfortunately, similar efforts to recover endangered species, even those as critically threatened as condors and black-footed ferrets (*Mustella nigripes*), are challenged by the gap in our knowledge of the geography of native biotas, past and present. There is, however, cause for optimism. Information on the geography of endangered species and ecosystems, and our abilities to record and analyze such information, has increased at an impressive rate, especially during the past two decades. The list of initiatives by dedicated agencies including programs such as GAP (Scott et al. 1993), RAP, WorldMap (Williams and Humphries 1996), the Human Footprint and the Last of the Wild (Sanderson et al. 2000), and the Alliance for Zero Extinctions (Ricketts et al. 2005) continues to grow. Scientific societies such as the Society for Conservation Biology, the Ecological Society of America, and the International Biogeography Society continue to increase their involvement in these and other conservation initiatives. While much work remains, the gap is closing.

Conclusion and Recommendations

The Endangered Species Act and the recovery process should be periodically revised and updated as we increase our understanding of the natural world and, in particular, of the geography of extinction, endangerment, and conservation. In closing, I offer the following recommendations:

- Whenever possible, phylogenetic and phylogeographic analyses and reconstructions should be conducted to assist listing decisions and recovery planning
- Recovery strategies should include increased emphasis on peripheral populations, and the option to list geographically distinct populations (now only permitted for vertebrates) should be extended to other taxa
- Information on historic and prehistoric populations, along with cost-effective biological surveys of extant populations, should be used to (1) determine habitat affinities, ecological associations and geographic distributions, and variation among populations, both past and present, and to (2) structure recovery goals by biogeographic and evolutionary distinct subregions of a species' historical range
- These and related lines of information should be incorporated into the recovery planning process to develop geographically explicit models to predict and project the spatial dynamics of extinction forces; in other words, how, when, and where they will impact focal populations in the future

These recommendations constitute a challenging research agenda. However, we have the technology and expertise to expand the temporal and spatial scales of conservation initiatives and to develop more effective strategies for conserving native species. We will need to muster the political will, and we should enlist what Daniel Simberloff (1988) once referred to as the army of unemployed and underemployed scientists to collect relevant data on distributions and geographic variation. We need to heed the esteemed late Senator Paul Tsongas's call to think across generations. We will conduct the essential biological surveys, analyze the spatially explicit information, close the gap on the Wallacean Shortfall, and meet the challenge of conserving the geographic and evolutionary context, and the natural character of imperiled biotas.

7   Preserving Nature

Shahid Naeem, Robin S. Waples, and Craig Moritz

To consider the broader environmental significance of protecting species at risk of extinction, we must first consider the roles or functions that species fulfill in nature. Although "nature" has many definitions, here we define it to mean the end product of ecological and evolutionary processes. That is, within a habitat, region, or biosphere, the condition of the soil, water, air, and biota reflects the outcome of physical, chemical, ecological, and evolutionary processes. We refer to this combination of abiotic and biotic conditions as "nature" and to the ecological and evolutionary processes that create it as "natural processes."

Using these definitions, we propose three approaches in which environmental actions can protect or conserve nature. The first approach is to preserve natural processes by directly managing them or providing suitable substitutions. For example, we can directly manage a polluted watershed to restore its water quality, or we can build expensive water treatment facilities to treat the water (Chichilnisky and Heal 1998). The second approach is to protect nature itself, assuming that with adequate protection nature and its natural processes will persist. For example, we can designate marine protected areas that exclude human activities. The third approach is to protect the biotic components of nature that govern the environment. This approach encompasses the intent of the Endangered Species Act (ESA): to protect nature by protecting species.

In this chapter, we examine the broader environmental significance of the Endangered Species Act by reviewing the roles species play in natural processes and by examining how natural processes govern our environment, how human activities modify nature, and how the Endangered Species Act can ameliorate the impacts of human activities.

Ecological and Evolutionary Processes

At any scale, from microsite to the biosphere, natural environments consist of matter cycling between organic and inorganic material. These cycles are driven by a diversity of organisms that consume energy. The simplest is the "green-slime perspective" in which photosynthetic biomass consumes solar energy and inorganic nutrients and produces biomass. This autotrophic biomass is consumed by heterotrophic organisms that convert the organic biomass they consume back to inorganic matter through mineralization and respiration. Many computer-based ecosystem and climate models use this approach.

In fact, at the level of the biosphere, biomass consists of tens to hundreds of millions of species each composed of highly dynamic populations constantly evolving and adapting to ever-changing environmental conditions. The role a species plays in ecological and evolutionary processes is determined by where it resides in the complex structure of earth's biota. Important features of this structure concern what species eat (trophic structure, or linkages), how species interact with it in other ways (community structure, or biotic linkages), where species are found (distribution and abundance), how matter is cycled between inorganic and organic forms by the biota (biogeochemistry, or ecosystem processes), and the evolutionary relationships among species and populations (evolutionary processes). If natural processes were largely random and nature merely the epiphenomenon of such randomness, we could do little to understand or manage it, and there would be little motivation to study it. Nature, however, is not the random end-product of biomass (e.g., green slime) exhibiting metabolic processes. Rather, it is a patterned distribution of interacting species whose dynamics cycle matter between organic and inorganic forms. Through competitive, facilitative, and trophic interactions a web of interconnectedness regulates the dynamics and stability of natural processes. This diversity is generated by evolutionary and coevolutionary processes in which the origin and extinction of species constantly yields a biota that adapts to Earth's changing conditions. The evolutionary trajectories species take are governed by the number of populations, their connectivity, and the impacts of ecosystem change on all populations, both central and peripheral.

A Summary of Human Impacts on Nature

In the previous section, we described a world in which species play key roles in structuring and regulating the magnitudes and dynamics of the ecological and evolutionary processes that govern our environment. The modern world, however, is increasingly one in which humans are the dominant species, governing the environment. In this section we examine major human impacts that have altered nature.

Most prominent among these impacts are human influences on rates of biological invasion, extinction, biogeochemical processes, climate change, and habitat modification. These changes also occur naturally, but humans have invariably increased their rate and frequency.

Biological invasions The distribution of a species is often constrained by physiological barriers (e.g., tropical plants lacking frost tolerance) or physical barriers (e.g., inability of most species to cross oceans). Deliberate or inadvertent human transport of biota has removed many of these limits to movement, leading to a vast degree of biotic homogenization (Drake et al. 1989; Lodge 1993; Mack et al. 2000). In addition, invaders also intensify local rates of extinction of native species (Wilcove et al. 1998).

Extinction Although difficult to quantify precisely, there is little question that extinction rates due to human activities are orders of magnitude higher than rates of extinction due to natural processes (Wilson 1988a; Soulé 1991; Jenkins 1992; Lawton and May 1994; Heywood 1995; May et al. 1995). The most dramatic declines are due to local extinctions—the loss of diversity on a per-unit area basis—rather than to global extinctions. Such declines in local diversity occur through habitat modification or habitat degradation in which managed or degraded systems steadily replace natural or wild systems (Wilcove et al. 1998; Balmford et al. 2002). Harvest can also be a significant factor, especially in marine systems (Myers and Worm 2003).

Biogeochemical processes Humans dominate a number of biogeochemical processes. For example, humans have doubled atmospheric carbon dioxide (CO_2), consume nearly 50 percent of net primary productivity, and have doubled nitrogen (N) deposition in terrestrial ecosystems (Vitousek et al. 1997b).

Climate change Earth's biota and ecosystems are experiencing unprecedented levels of climate change. Climate change has been and continues to be a common feature of nature, but anthropogenic acceleration of the process has raised a number of concerns about the ability of populations and natural systems to adapt to such change (Peters and Lovejoy 1994; Huntley 1995; Parmesan and Yohe 2003). Recently, increasing attention has focused on abrupt climate changes—such as the melting of polar ice caps or reorganization of the oceans' circulation patterns—and how anthropogenic climate change may trigger such events (Broecker 1997; Alley et al. 2003). Thus, not only are the rates of climate change likely to be higher than experienced in the past, but the frequency of abrupt changes may be on the rise as well.

Habitat modification Balmford et al. (2002) noted that the majority of Earth's wildlands have continued to decline in spite of the Earth Summit in 1992 in Rio de Janeiro and 2002 in Johannesburg, suggesting that the summit has had little effect in halting the continued transformation of natural or wild habitat to managed or degraded habitats. According to one estimate, twenty-seven ecosystems have declined in area by 98 percent, and what is protected is often dominated by poor-quality habitat not suitable for cultivation (Shaffer et al. 2002). On top of such change, habitat fragmentation, also an increasingly common feature of landscapes, alters food webs (Terborgh et al. 2001), biomass (Laurance et al. 1997), species interactions (Fagan et al. 1999), and the survivorship and persistence of populations and species (Bascompte and Solé 1996; Lens et al. 2002).

Summary The distribution and abundance of species is determined by many factors, some of the most important being invasion, extinction, biogeochemistry, climate change, and habitat loss. Although natural processes affect all of these factors, today they are dominated by human activities. Collectively, these activities are resulting in ecosystems that are more homogeneous in their species composition, increasingly species poor, and changing chemically and physically at untypically high rates—with the possible exception of such extreme events as asteroid impacts.

The Role of Species in the Modern World

Human influences have altered the world to a degree that ecological and evolutionary processes are increasingly less relevant to environmental processes. Earlier, we described how species collectively regulate the environment and also how biodiversity is declining rapidly, both taxonomically and ecologically. In this section we consider the significance of this decline.

Biodiversity and ecosystem functioning Ecosystem processes are regulated by their biota, and changes in local biodiversity can affect the magnitude and stability of such processes, although there is debate over the specific mechanisms and magnitudes involved (Loreau et al. 2001). This ecological perspective is a novel way to consider the importance of biodiversity since it ascribes an active role for diversity in regulating the environment rather than assuming that biodiversity is a passive epiphenomenon of abiotic processes such as climate (Schulze and Mooney 1993; Loreau et al. 2002; Naeem 2002b).

For our purposes, the most important idea from this work is its suggestion that loss of biodiversity will decrease the magnitude of (Naeem et al. 1994; Naeem et al. 2000a; Tilman et al. 2001a) and stability (Tilman and Downing 1994; Naeem and Li 1997; Pfisterer and Schmid 2002) of ecosystem functioning.

Biodiversity and invasion Although Charles Elton proposed that biodiversity was an important element in determining the susceptibility of an ecosystem to biological invasion (Elton 1958; Levine and D'Antonio 1999), only recently has empirical investigation of this possibility intensified (Palmer and Maurer 1997; Tilman 1997; Naeem et al. 2000b; Kennedy et al. 2002; Levine et al. 2002). As in the case of ecosystem functioning, it is difficult to tease apart extrinsic factors that regulate invasion from that of biodiversity since the two are correlated (Stohlgren et al. 1999; Levine 2000; Rejmánek 2003; Stohlgren et al. 2003).

Biodiversity and phylogenetic information   A region's biota is its repository of phylogenetic information. Anthropogenically enhanced rates of extinction are producing extinction rates higher than origination rates thereby driving down biodiversity not only in regions but also across landscapes and in the biosphere itself. Such change threatens phylogenetic information—a primary motivation for identifying and concentrating efforts on biodiversity hotspots that contain particularly high levels of phylogenetic information (Myers et al. 2000; Sechrest et al. 2002).

Some analyses suggest that considerable levels of extinction are required before phylogenetic information is lost (Nee and May 1997) but this applies only if extinction is random. Extinction, however, is seldom random, more often exhibiting a pattern in which related species share similar fates. For example, with respect to carnivores and primates, 50 percent of the variance in the World Conservation Union's threat status is explained by high trophic level, low population density, slow life history, and small geographic range; the rest is attributed to anthropogenic factors such as hunting or habitat modification (Purvis et al. 2000b). Under such circumstances, the loss of phylogenetic information is more severe than one might expect from random extinction (Purvis et al. 2000a).

There are ecological consequences of such nonrandom extinction. For example, carnivores and top predators often face higher extinction rates for a variety of reasons (Purvis et al. 2000b; Gittleman and Gompper 2001), which means that changes in community structure or possibly predator regulation of lower trophic-level densities are likely to occur in the face of higher extinction rates. These could lead to cascades of extinction if such top predator species are keystone species.

Finally, loss of biodiversity through its impacts on biocomplexity can affect the sustainability and resilience of communities and ecosystems. For example, Hilborn et al. (2003) demonstrate that stock and life history differences among Alaskan sockeye salmon (*Oncorhynchus nerka*) stocks contributed to high levels of productivity over a fifty-year period.

Summary   The modern world is increasingly depauperate, with habitats that are increasingly species poor and increasingly homogeneous. Contemporary studies suggest that biodiversity loss is changing the way ecosystems function and the way our biota serves as repositories of phylogenetic content necessary for its evolution in the face of changing environments. This depauperate world may be less stable, lower in its rates of ecosystem functioning, and less capable of adapting to environmental change.

Species Preservation

The significance of the Endangered Species Act in slowing biodiversity loss is demonstrated by an imaginary game based on contemporary patterns of extinction. Imagine a grid in which each square carries a multitude of colored pieces. Each square is different. Some, like the tropical regions, carry many differently colored pieces (species) but few of each color; others, like the tundra, carry many pieces but only a few colors. We now set a game in motion in which we throw a die once for each square. This is the extinction die. It has as many faces as there are colors of pieces, and when the die is thrown, each square loses whatever piece shows on the top of the die. If the die comes up a color that is not on the square, then no species pieces are removed from the square. The other rule specifies that if the colored piece is the last of that color on the board, the Endangered Species Act is invoked and the persistence of that color (i.e., species) is guaranteed somewhere on the board. The end result would be a board with one piece of each color someplace on the board. This game demonstrates how, under these rules, a species is listed only when on the brink of extinction. By manipulating species independent of their population, community, and ecosystem roles, we ensure the preservation of phylogenetic information. But in the absence of multiple populations, community structure, and ecosystem function, ecological or evolutionary processes are generally lost.

Reality adds some subtle complexities to the game. Because the ESA allows for subspecies and races to be preserved (closely colored pieces treated as different), some retention of population structure and of heritable variability may occur. Also, because some states list species endangered in their state, we may have more individuals of a color if a square actually represents two or more states that both list the same species. Further, most species management plans do not save just one individual but aim to maintain a population of individuals that would ensure persistence of the species. So a colored piece actually represents a minimally viable population.

In an alternative game, the rules might require that each square must retain at least one piece of each color (species) it originally had—it does not matter if the color is on the board elsewhere—it is not allowed to go extinct on its square. Thus, each square (e.g., county) must conserve whatever species is endangered in its habitat, even if it is not endangered elsewhere on the board (the United States). In this variation of the game, our board shows the same color patterns observed at the outset, but by the end of the game the pattern is thinner, because only one individual of each color is present in a square where previously many were found. Biologically, the result is a landscape more likely to ensure phylogenetic content, some degree of population structure, and some ecosystem functioning, but it would consist of species-rich squares each low in density and thereby consisting of readily invaded habitats, expressing low levels of functioning, and exhibiting little resilience. This landscape would lack biological complexity.

The point that emerges from our game playing is that divesting a species of (or disassociating it from) its function or role in evolutionary or ecological processes is the environmental equivalent of extinction. Yet the language of the Endangered Species Act suggests that it recognizes that species must be preserved in the wild, for it is in the context of natural environments their true value emerges. The ESA does not espouse housing remaining individuals of a threatened species in zoos or pickling them for museums; but ranching or relocating threatened species to a protected park is little different from placing them in a zoo or pickling them. Such actions divest species of their roles in ecological and evolutionary processes. The role of a nitrogen fixer is retained only if it continues to fix nitrogen in that ecosystem at the same rate. If the species is a pollinator, its community role is only retained if it continues to pollinate its native plants. If a species is to persist through the vagaries of environmental change, effective protection needs to ensure genetic robustness such that the species contains sufficient genetic variability to accommodate local or even global environmental change. If a species is to be the source of newly adapted subpopulations, subspecies, or even new species, effective protection needs to ensure its ability to serve in those roles.

Shoring Up the Disentangled Bank

Our consideration of the role of species in natural processes fits the entangled bank metaphor of Darwin's famous closing passage in *The Origin of Species by Means of Natural Selection, or the Preservation of Favoured Races in the Struggle for Life* (Darwin 1859, chap. 14). Darwin envisioned nature as an entangled bank, "clothed with many plants of many kinds, with birds singing on the bushes, with various insects flitting about, and with worms crawling through the damp earth" (459). Clearly, nature is diverse and interconnected, and, most important, these elaborately constructed forms, so different from each other, and dependent on each other in so complex a manner, have all been produced by laws acting around us. In this chapter we have rephrased this entangled-bank description of nature, describing it instead as the collection of interacting species whose diversity is governed by evolutionary processes and whose distribution and abundance is governed by ecological processes. We have further shown that the environment is derived from the biogeochemical processes governed by these species.

The metaphor for the modern world is that of a *disentangled* bank. Habitat modification and degradation and biological invasion yield simpler, species-poor, ordered communities. Prairie grasslands, for example, that once contained hundreds of species have been replaced by managed grasslands such as corn, wheat, soybean crops, and rangelands. Complex forests have been replaced by monoculture plantations. Natural stocks of Pacific salmon in northwestern North America have declined while sea-ranching hatcheries and salmon farming of large pens of Atlantic salmon have grown to take their place. As discussed above, such depauperate systems provide needed ecosystem goods and services but with lower levels of ecosystem functioning, less resiliency, and lower adaptability to changing conditions. While the methods used to assess the costs of the loss of natural ecosystem services are controversial, preliminary estimates suggest that these costs are likely to be enormous (Costanza et al. 1997; Balmford et al. 2002).

The scientific basis for biodiversity as a critical factor in governing Earth's environment is not without controversy, but its central premise has been recognized by the majority of the world's countries. In 1992, the Earth Summit in Rio de Janeiro established a strategy for sustainable development, allowing extraction of natural resources necessary for sustaining human populations while ensuring the same privileges for future generations. The Convention on Biological Diversity arose from this meeting and was signed by the majority of the world's governments. Its premise: maintaining biodiversity is the equivalent of maintaining the world's ecological underpinnings; but it also allows participants to continue economic development.

The Convention on Biological Diversity and the Endangered Species Act are similar in structure. The convention's emphasis on conservation and sustainability does not preserve interconnectivity among species and ecosystem resilience necessary for biodiversity to persist in the face of environmental change and variability (Knapp 2003). Likewise, the ESA aims to conserve species by rescuing them from extinction, but it has little investment in notions of ecosystem resilience (though delisting requires demonstration of long-term persistence of a population) and no investment in interconnectivity among species.

For thirty years, the Endangered Species Act has been shoring up the entangled bank by preserving its components. The act's emphasis on species independent of their roles in ecological and evolutionary processes is the best strategy available in the absence of knowledge about the specific roles a species may play; it allows at least core species richness to be maintained.

The wording of the act clearly recognizes the importance of species as agents of natural processes. Its execution, however, has focused on the preservation of the species to the exclusion of their ecological and evolutionary role. When a species has declined to the point that it is considered threatened under the ESA, its role in ecological or evolutionary processes is usually severely diminished; but it can return to this role with sufficient shepherding. Over the long term, continued rescuing of our nation's species can provide not only natural services but also the stability that comes with diverse habitats.

Conclusion

The Endangered Species Act, like many environmental statutes, follows a command-control format. Standards, such as allowable concentrations of sulfur in smokestack emissions, permissible arsenic concentrations in drinking water, or minimal viable population sizes, are key elements of such statutes. They are the bases for regulations (commands) that control activities to ensure standards are met. By themselves, command-control approaches lead to complex rules and regulations; the federal Environmental Protection Agency has become an organization that manages and enforces an enormous array of regulations of almost incomprehensible complexity (Dietz and Stern 2002).

Command-control works best for point-source problems, but when the problem is diffuse, other approaches are necessary (Dietz and Stern 2002). Over the past thirty years, the ESA has treated the problem of biodiversity loss as a point-source problem. For example, establishing minimal viable populations is an attempt to establish the equivalent standards, but such activities have never had the same degree of precision or ready application as other environmental standards—a standard of 10 parts per million of arsenic, no matter how contentious, is easy to understand and implement. Protecting fifty individuals within a species, however, is not easily applied to all species. The command-control approach has been a good start, but it requires modification when applied to natural processes and nature.

The suggestion that emerges is to reconfigure the game rules governing allowable changes in our biota. Under such a scenario, the landscape would consist of ecoregions based on the ecological and evolutionary roles species play within these regions. That way, when the roll of the die names a species, the rules for removing or conserving a piece would be based not only on the presence or absence of that species, but also on the extent to which the loss of that species in that habitat affects the ecological and evolutionary role the species plays in the landscape. Proposing changes to the Endangered Species Act requires a more rigorous, quantitative approach—assessing its existing ability to ensure species' roles and determining how it could better safeguard not only the persistence of species but also their ecological and evolutionary roles.

This proposition—to modify the Endangered Species Act to allow it to regulate the ecological and evolutionary roles species play—has complex implications for policy, property rights, jobs, and management. On the surface, it could be misconstrued as a vehicle by which we replace our increasingly anthropic environment with wild nature. Presented in this light, such a proposition would not sit well with Americans who support the ESA's role in preventing extinction but are generally in favor of regulating nature through fire suppression, flood regulation, pest control, and genetic engineering. Currently, the ESA confronts property rights, jobs, and management issues when a species is directly threatened by such activities, and such confrontations will likely escalate. It is one thing to challenge property rights when an owner's land use jeopardizes the persistence of a species; it is quite another to challenge them because an owner's land use jeopardizes a species' role in an ecological or evolutionary process.

For now, the Endangered Species Act at least preserves the many colored pieces on the board so that if we decide to change the rules and look more to nature and natural services, our game board will contain more than just a handful of playing pieces.

8   Preserving Ecosystem Services

Shahid Naeem and Claire Jouseau

Increasing conversions of natural ecosystems to managed ecosystems (such as grasslands to farms, or forests to plantations), climate change (such as elevated atmospheric carbon dioxide and global warming), and pollution, the spread of invasive species, and other anthropogenic environmental changes invariably lead to dramatic reductions in native species in virtually all ecosystems of the world. When such reductions are so extreme that one or more native species may suffer global extinction and disappear, we stand to lose the values ascribed to such species, whether cultural or economic. The Endangered Species Act (ESA), *regardless of its original intent*, has the potential to preserve all these values (Callicott, this volume; Norton, this volume). That is, the act, though it was never intended to be, is a value-neutral statute in the sense that threat of extinction is the only criterion by which a species is listed.

This is a little-appreciated virtue that may help to preserve biodiversity in the long run. Consider, for example, jaguars and burying beetles: Listing the jaguar (*Panthera onca*) preserves not only its cultural value to humans but also its ecological value as a carnivore able to regulate populations of wild mammalian herbivores that harbor infectious diseases and destroy vegetation. The American burying beetle (*Nicrophorus americanus*), also listed and therefore also protected under the Endangered Species Act, has arguably less inspirational value than a jaguar, but the ecological value of its role in decomposition (the recycling of organic matter back into inorganic matter), an important ecosystem function, is likewise preserved. These examples clearly illustrate that although the act is not "value-neutral," and we do not label it so, it has value-neutral features in the sense that if it saves species, for whatever values motivate saving species, other values are unintentionally saved. The ESA was not designed to be value-neutral—it simply functions that way.

Section 2 of the Endangered Species Act stipulates that "species of fish, wildlife, and plants are of esthetic, ecological, educational, historical, recreational, and scientific value to the Nation and its people." Of the many values one can ascribe to biodiversity (Humphries et al. 1995; Perlman and Adelson

1997), the category of ecological value is probably the most widely recognized and least appreciated. *Ecological value* is an imprecise term, and many have adopted the term *ecosystem services* instead. Ecosystems provide a wealth of services, such as greenhouse gas regulation, soil production, biocontrol, and reduction of infectious diseases (De Groot 1992; Baskin 1997; Costanza et al. 1997; Daily et al. 1997; Naeem 2001). Ecosystem services are distinct from *ecosystem functions*, the latter being any activity (e.g., production, decomposition, and other biogeochemical activities) of an ecosystem independent of its significance to human well-being. Ecologists study and measure ecosystem functions while social scientists and natural scientists translate how such activities affect human well-being. For example, ecologists often measure *net primary production* (NPP), or how much plants photosynthesize minus what they respire, to gauge the potential biogeochemical activity of an ecosystem, but NPP must be translated into actual lumber, food, and biofuels before it can be understood as an ecosystem service.

In this chapter we examine biotically driven geochemical processes or biogeochemical functions and, by extension, the ecosystem services derived from them. These processes, functions, and services were chosen in part because of the wealth of theoretical and empirical ecological research conducted in these areas over the last decade (Loreau et al. 2001, 2002) and because of the significant role species play in governing such processes. Net primary production, for example, is controlled largely by plants and the organisms they interact with and is a biogeochemical function from which well-known ecosystem services are derived. Human well-being benefits from NPP through climate modulation, agricultural production, and the resource base (e.g., food) for the rest of the biota that provide other services within ecosystems (see reviews in Roy et al. 2001). Similarly, *nitrogen fixation* by microbes that draw nitrogen (N) from the atmosphere and make it available to plants is a biogeochemical function that affects primary production, soil fertility, and, as a consequence, human well-being (Vitousek et al. 1997a). The complement to nitrogen fixation is *nitrogen mobilization*, which liberates nitrogen from its organic forms and completes the cycle.

Such biogeochemical functions involve networks of interacting organisms that, through production, predation, competition, facilitation, disease, and other interactions, determine the magnitude, rates, and stability of these functions (May 1974; DeAngelis 1992; McCann et al. 1998). In particular, the trophic structure of a community—the pattern of feeding among species in an ecosystem—is critical to ecosystem functioning (Schindler et al. 1997; Naeem 2002a; Paine 2002; Raffaelli et al. 2002). Net primary production, for example, may seem to be associated exclusively with plants, but all organisms interacting with plants play equally important roles and are connected through the carbon cycle and the flow of energy through the ecosystem. NPP represents a movement of carbon out of the atmosphere by plants via photosynthesis and into the biosphere in the form of autotrophic (e.g., producers such as plants or algae) biomass. This producer biomass is eventually consumed by other organisms (e.g., herbivores), and these consumers are then in turn consumed by others (e.g., carnivores), and so on, until finally all matter enters the pool of dead organic matter. Decomposers then return the organic matter back to its inorganic form (e.g., carbon dioxide [CO_2] and dinitrogen [N_2], the atmospheric form of nitrogen) thus completing the cycle. NPP and related ecosystem services are thus intimately linked to the trophic structure of the community within the ecosystem.

Given the importance of biogeochemical functions like net primary production and nitrogen mobilization, it is essential to understand how the Endangered Species Act may maintain these services by protecting both species and the ecosystem's inherent trophic structure. Do ecosystems with the highest level of function receive the same level of protection as ecosystems with lower levels? Does the ESA preserve trophic structure within an ecosystem? If so, is trophic structure maintained equally well across all levels of function?

Because data to establish species richness baselines were unavailable, we focused instead on determining how an ecosystem-function perspective can inform the listing of species under the Endangered Species Act. To do so, we used broad-based estimates of ecosystem functioning, broadly defined ecoregions that we treated as ecosystems, and rough estimates of the basic components of trophic structure in those ecosystems. We explored these data for significant patterns of association between currently listed endangered species and our estimates of ecosystem functioning and trophic structure. Although our findings are necessarily general, they provide interesting insights into the act's potential role as our national safeguard of biodiversity and ecosystem functioning.

Biodiversity and Ecosystem Functioning

The relationship between biodiversity and ecosystem functioning has drawn considerable attention over the last decade as another way of assessing the relevance of biodiversity (Naeem 2002b). The issues associated with this new perspective have been reviewed recently (Loreau et al. 2001, 2002), and so we provide only a brief overview as it relates to the Endangered Species Act. Our approach is to treat biodiversity as the independent variable and ecosystem processes and properties as the dependent variable. This sharply contrasts with decades of ecological research that has taken the opposite approach—treating ecosystem functions as extrinsic factors that regulate the distribution and abundance of species (Gaston 2000).

The concern is how biodiversity loss (or gain) impacts ecosystem functions and ecosystem properties, such as resiliency (the ability to bounce back after a perturbation), resistance to invasion, and other aspects of ecosystem stability. One of the critical elements of the ecosystem-function perspective is the value of an individual species. Understanding whether species are redundant or play unique roles in an ecosystem is critical to understanding how their loss or gain affects ecosystem functioning (Walker 1992; Lawton and Brown 1993; Ehrlich and Walker 1998; Naeem 1998). Evaluating ecological redundancy requires understanding the functional roles species play in ecosystem processes and how they may be grouped into functional groups, the assumption being that species within functional groups are likely to be redundant (Díaz and Cabido 2001; Hooper et al. 2002; Lavorel and Garnier 2002; Naeem and Wright 2003). Although the concept of ecological redundancy would seem anathema to the business of species preservation, there is a sense that redundant species have value as entities that can ensure ecosystem function by compensating for the loss of functionally equivalent species from the ecosystem (i.e., the insurance hypothesis) (Perrings 1995; McCann 2000). Thus, to be ecologically redundant is not to be without value, but to have a different sort of value, one to be appreciated over the longer term. By analogy, a spare tire may seem insignificant in the short term (e.g., during a short trip to the local market) since it is redundant with the other four tires on one's automobile, but over the long term the value of the redundant tire becomes clear when a blowout occurs.

There has been considerable debate surrounding biodiversity ecosystem-functioning research (Guterman 2000; Naeem 2000; Wardle et al. 2000), but consensus and synthesis are emerging (Loreau et al. 2001, 2002).

Listed Species In Relation to Ecosystem Functioning

If the listing process of species is biased toward certain groups of species rather than providing protection across a spectrum of species and ecosystems, then the Endangered Species Act may not be preserving ecosystem functions. To examine the issue of bias, we take a statistical approach, analyzing patterns of association among listed species, the ecosystems within which they are found, the ecosystem functions of those ecosystems, and what kinds of species (in this case, whether species are producers, carnivores, omnivores, or herbivores) are listed.

Interpreting the Relationship Between Listed Species and Ecosystem Functions

We classified species by their respective ecoregions based on their known geographic range and a modified version of the World Conservation Union

(IUCN) three-tiered habitat classification system (Olson et al. 2001). We also classified species trophically based on derived life history data. Finally, we selected two ecosystem functions for analysis that are known to be key functions and provide important services to society.

ENDANGERED SPECIES DATA

The list of endangered species was culled from the January 2003 federal list of threatened and endangered native species made available through the Endangered Species Program of the U.S. Fish and Wildlife Service (USFWS). Information on the ecology, geographic distribution, and life history of each species was primarily obtained from NatureServe (see http://www.natureserve.org/). Once species had been assigned to specific ecoregions and trophic levels based on ecology and life history data, the number of ecoregions was reduced to better match the habitat designations of the available measures of ecosystem functions—estimates for net primary production and nitrogen mobilization.

ECOREGIONS

Based on the collected ecological and geographical data, species were assigned to one or several of the 173 specific habitat subclasses (e.g., shrub-scrub-dominated wetland) derived from the IUCN habitat classification system. Following the specific habitat assignments, subclasses were combined to form approximately thirty more general classes (e.g., wetland). Finally, these general categories were merged into major habitat designations (e.g., transitional region) to facilitate the alignment of species habitats with the broader categories used in ecosystem biogeochemical assessment and to obtain suitable sample sizes for analysis. Consequently, we can examine the Endangered Species Act with respect to ecosystem function at the national scale.

ECOSYSTEM FUNCTIONS

Estimates for yearly average NPP in terrestrial ecosystems were determined by McGuire and others (1992) from models of potential vegetation across ecosystems in the United States. Aquatic ecosystem estimates of NPP were obtained from Barnes and Mann (1991) and Wetzel (2001). Estimates of nitrogen mobilization were obtained primarily from the NASA Earth Observing System Terrestrial Ecosystem Model (Schlesinger 1997; Roy et al. 2001; McGuire et al. 1992).

STATISTICS

In our analyses we used standard parametric statistical methods. These methods included analysis of variance (ANOVA), analysis of covariance (ANCOVA), and linear regressions. In our ANCOVAs we used two steps, the first testing for homogeneity of slopes of the relationship between the dependent variable and the covariate by testing for interactions between the covariate and main effect or categorical variables. If this interaction was significant, then the test for homogeneity of slopes failed, and we ended the analysis. If the slopes were homogeneous, then we removed the nonsignificant main effect-covariate interaction term and reanalyzed the data to test for significant differences among intercepts. We also used chi-square tests to examine possible differences between expected and observed frequencies where appropriate. All calculations were made using SYSTAT statistical analysis software (version 10.2).

Interpreting Analyses of the Relationship Between Listed Species and Ecosystem Functions

Our statistical analyses provide quantitative assessments of the relationship between listed species and ecosystem function.

PROTECTED DIVERSITY BY MAJOR ECOREGION

The number of endangered species listed under the Endangered Species Act appears unbiased within major categories of ecoregions (ANOVA; df = 3, 19; $F = 0.417$, $P = 0.743$; fig. 8.1). There is a trend in which terrestrial ecoregions appear to have on average more species listed, while transition areas have fewer

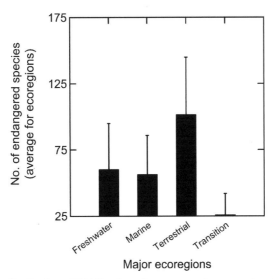

Figure 8.1. The distribution of ESA listed species among major categories of ecoregions. Bars equal means for ecoregions within category. Error bars equal the standard error of the mean (SE). (Data from U.S. Fish and Wildlife; ecoregions categorization based on IUCN classification system.)

(fig. 8.1), but the variance among ecoregions is quite high so we could not reject the hypothesis of no difference among major categories of ecoregions by ANOVA.

PROTECTED DIVERSITY AND ECOSYSTEM FUNCTION

Not surprisingly, major ecoregions show considerable differences in NPP for the compiled data (fig. 8.2). Endangered species listed under the Endangered Species Act are biased toward ecosystems of low productivity. There is a clear but nonsignificant (linear regression; df = 1, 21; F = 3.45, R^2 = 0.10, P = 0.07), negative (constant = 0.112, slope = −0.36) trend for ecoregions exhibiting higher NPP to have fewer numbers of endangered species (fig. 8.3). Analysis of covariance (ANCOVA), in which NPP is treated as a covariate, indicates that the slopes of the relationship between endangered species and NPP among major regions (marine, terrestrial, freshwater, and transition) are not different, but, again, a trend is apparent (interaction between NPP and major region nonsignificant; P = 0.09; table 8.1, *top*). Using the more conservative critical value of 0.05, we assumed the slopes were homogeneous and thus continued the ANCOVA and tested for significant differences among intercepts (homogene-

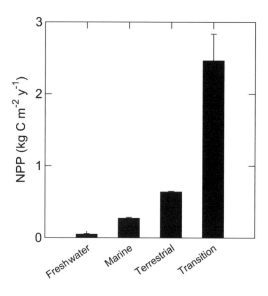

Major ecoregions

Figure 8.2. Net primary production (NPP) and major categories of ecoregions. Bars equal means for ecoregions within category. Error bars equal the SE. (NPP data from McGuire et al. 1992; ecoregions categorization based on IUCN classification system.)

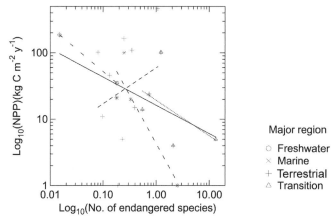

Figure 8.3. The relationship between NPP and species currently listed under the Endangered Species Act. Dashed lines represent linear relationships by major regions whereas the single continuous line indicates the linear relationship across all regions. The solid line represents the linear approximation of the overall relationship across all regions while the wide-spaced, intermediate-spaced, closely-spaced, and dotted lines represent fresh water, marine, terrestrial, and transition regions, respectively. Note that the test for homogeneity of slopes was not rejected, thus differences among major regions are not considered to be different, in spite of the seemingly strong difference between terrestrial ecoregions and the other ecoregions. (NPP data from McGuire et al. 1992.)

ity of intercepts, or magnitudes of the relationship between NPP and endangered species). The magnitudes were significantly different, though the covariate was not (table 8.1, *bottom*).

Nitrogen mobilization data for the thirteen terrestrial ecoregions with available data showed a significant inverse relationship with listed endangered species (linear regression; constant = 0.286; slope = −0.189; df 1, 45; R^2 = 0.144, $P < 0.01$; fig. 8.4). Because this ecosystem function concerned only terrestrial ecoregions, we did not conduct an ANCOVA by major region as with NPP.

ENDANGERED SPECIES AND THE PRESERVATION OF TROPHIC STRUCTURE
Endangered species are not uniformly distributed among trophic groups with respect to ecoregion categories. The frequency of listed endangered species occurring in each major ecoregion category with respect to trophic class is not uniform (Pearson chi-square = 261.264, df = 9, $P < 0.001$; table 8.2). There is distinct bias toward listing carnivores, although producers are heavily represented in terrestrial ecoregions (fig. 8.5). Likewise, the frequency of occurrence of each trophic group by major ecoregion category is not uniform and shows a bias toward carnivores (Pearson chi-square; df = 3, $P < 0.001$; fig. 8.6).

TABLE 8.1 Analysis of covariance results for the relationship between endangered species and ecoregion net primary production

Source	Sums of squares	Degrees of freedom	Mean square	Ratio of two squares	Probability
	Test for homogeneity of slopes				
Major region (main effects)	1.906	3	0.635	3.725	**0.039**
Number of endangered species (S_E) (covariate)	1.070	1	1.070	6.274	**0.026**
(S_E) x major region	1.380	3	0.460	2.698	0.089
Error	2.217	13	0.171		
	Test for homogeneity of intercepts				
Major region (main effects)	3.042	3	1.014	4.511	**0.018**
Number of endangered species (S_E) (covariate)	0.203	1	0.203	0.903	0.356
Error	3.597	16	0.225		

Note: If a critical value of 0.10 is used rather than 0.05, then the interaction between main effect (ecoregion) and covariate (number of endangered species) rejects the test for homogeneity of slopes. At the critical value of 0.05, the test for homogeneity of slopes fails and the test for homogeneity of intercepts is considered (bottom half of table). SS = sums of squares; DF = degrees of freedom; MS = mean square. Boldface indicates statistical significance ($P < 0.05$).

ECOSYSTEM FUNCTION, TROPHIC STRUCTURE, AND ENDANGERED SPECIES
Among trophic classes of species, there is a tendency for ecosystems with lower productivity to have higher numbers of listed species, even though trophic categories differ in total numbers of species listed. That is, fewer numbers of carnivore, herbivore, omnivore, and producer species tend to be listed at higher NPP even though there are more carnivore species listed overall. This interpretation is based on ANCOVA results that show the relationship between number of endangered species and NPP is not significantly different among trophic classes (slopes are homogeneous or no significant interaction between model terms and trophic class; table 8.3).

The negative relationship between nitrogen mobilization and endangered species is indistinguishable among different trophic classes of species. This interpretation is based on ANCOVA results that show the relationship between number of endangered species and nitrogen mobilization is not significantly different among trophic classes (slopes are homogeneous; fig. 8.4, table 8.4).

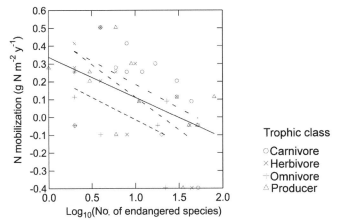

Figure 8.4. The relationship between nitrogen mobilization and trophic categories of endangered species listed by the Endangered Species Act. Each point represents an ecoregion within the broad biome class indicated in the legend. The solid line, wide-spaced, intermediate-spaced, and closely-spaced dashed lines represent carnivores, herbivores, omnivores, and producers, respectively. Note that test for homogeneity of slopes was not rejected and there was no significant differences among intercepts (see table 8.4 for ANCOVA results). (Data derived from Schlesinger 1997; Roy et al. 2001; McGuire et al. 1992.)

TABLE 8.2 Frequency of species occurring in each major ecoregion category with respect to trophic class

Trophic class	Freshwater	Marine	Terrestrial	Transition	Total
Carnivore	66	158	412	44	680
Herbivore	13	20	226	14	273
Omnivore	28	24	96	28	176
Producer	13	21	578	15	627
Total	120	223	1,312	101	1,756

Note: Entries are numbers of endangered species or subspecies.

Benefits of an Unbiased Endangered Species Act

The current endangered species listed under the ESA reflects several trends with respect to the three aspects of ecosystem functioning we have examined—NPP, nitrogen mobilization, and trophic components. Terrestrial ecoregions appear to have the largest number of listed species (fig. 8.1), while transition ecoregions have the fewest and are also the most productive (fig. 8.2). There is a trend for ecoregions with higher ecosystem functioning (for both NPP and nitrogen mo-

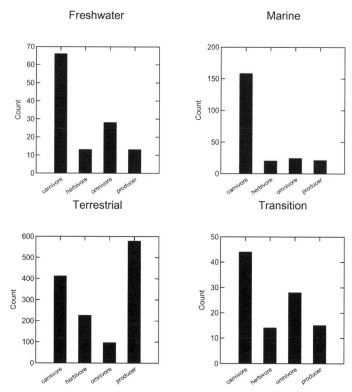

Figure 8.5. Frequency of species among trophic classes with respect to different categories of ecoregions.

bilization) to have fewer species listed (figs. 8.3 and 8.4; table 8.1). Finally, carnivores are listed more frequently than any other trophic class (table 8.2) with the exception of terrestrial ecoregions where producers also exhibit a high number of listed species (figs. 8.5 and 8.6). These negative patterns of association between ecosystem function and endangered species appear to be the same regardless of the trophic class of endangered species examined (tables 8.3 and 8.4).

The observed patterns of association between listed species and NPP or nitrogen mobilization are likely to be similar to those found in nature. There is evidence, for example, that NPP and species richness are inversely related or exhibit a hump-shaped relationship, both of which suggest that ecoregions of the highest NPP may have low levels of diversity. Transition zones, such as wetlands, frequently have fewer species, and thus it is logical that fewer listed species are found in transition ecosystems and more in terrestrial ecosystems. Likewise, carnivores are often the most susceptible to the negative effects of human activities, and thus it is logical that more carnivores are listed than other

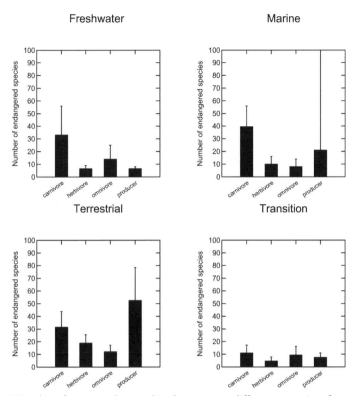

Figure 8.6. Number of species within trophic classes among different categories of ecoregions. Bars equal mean number of endangered species within trophic class while error bar equals the standard error (SE).

species in most ecoregions. In terrestrial ecosystems, producers (plants) are well represented in the listing compared to marine, freshwater, and transition areas since these ecosystems tend to have fewer plant species.

Our findings illustrate that patterns in currently listed endangered species in relation to ecosystem services are consistent with what might be expected for a value-neutral policy. We conclude that the ESA has protected the role of species in ecosystem processes and trophic structure in ways that appear to be consistent with the patterns observed in nature.

Can the Endangered Species Act Preserve Ecosystem Services and Functions?

Because the Endangered Species Act protects threatened and endangered species in an unbiased fashion, as we have established above, it likely also preserves

TABLE 8.3 ANCOVA results, test for homogeneity of slopes, for $\log_{10}$(net primary production) as a function of major ecoregion category, trophic class, and $\log_{10}$(number of endangered species) as a covariate

Source	Sum of squares	Degrees of freedom	Mean square	Ratio of two squares	Probability
Major ecoregion category (MEC)	6.549	3	2.183	13.308	**<0.001**
Trophic class (T)	0.447	3	0.149	0.909	0.443
Log10(number of en-dangered species) (S)	2.024	1	2.024	12.337	**0.001**
MEC*S	2.979	3	0.993	6.053	**0.001**
T x S	0.475	3	0.158	0.965	0.416
T x MEC x S	0.764	9	0.085	0.518	0.855
Error	8.366	51	0.164		

TABLE 8.4 ANCOVA results for nitrogen mobilization in terrestrial ecoregions

Source	Sum of squares	Degrees of freedom	Mean square	Ratio of two squares	Probability
Test for homogeneity of slopes					
Trophic class	0.082	3	0.027	0.599	0.620
Log$_{10}$(number of endangered species) (S) (covariate)	0.743	1	0.743	16.379	**<0.001**
Trophic class x S	0.033	3	0.011	0.242	0.826
Error	1.634	36	0.045		
Test for homogeneity of intercepts					
Trophic class	0.198	3	0.066	1.546	0.218
Log$_{10}$(number of endangered species) (S) (covariate)	0.797	1	0.797	18.648	**<0.001**
Error	1.667	39	0.043		

Note: Trophic class represents the main effect and $\log_{10}$(number of endangered species) represents the covariate. Boldface highlights statistically significant results.

ecosystem function—a welcome but unintended consequence. We would surmise that by the time a species is listed, population density is so low that its effect on ecosystem functioning is minimal; but protections under the ESA designed to prevent further population decline will almost certainly prevent further decline in the species' role in ecosystem functioning. Likewise, microbial communities, which are key to ecosystem functions and services, are not protected under the Endangered Species Act, but they too may benefit from protections specifically bestowed on birds, mammals, lizards, fish, butterflies, and flowers. However, quantitative data are lacking to conclusively prove these assertions.

Can the Endangered Species Act Conserve Ecosystem Services?

As discussed earlier, the neutrality of the Endangered Species Act in preserving ecosystem functioning is by chance rather than by design. However, if ecosystem services were considered in listing decisions, critical habitat designation, or recovery efforts, the act could serve as an active and deliberate safeguard of ecosystem services.

The listing process is haphazard at best (Gordon et al. 1997) and blind to the ecosystem values of the species in question. Candidate species are recommended through petitions or lawsuits and evaluated first on the magnitude and then on the immediacy of the threat, and finally on taxonomic distinctiveness—all criteria unrelated to ecosystem services. From a scientific perspective, priorities for determining species listings would, ideally, include the following: (1) total number of species benefiting from the listing, (2) a candidate's ecological role, (3) a candidate's recovery potential, and (4) a candidate's taxonomic distinctiveness (Carroll et al. 1996). Unfortunately, neither evaluation method addresses the scientifically recognized link between biodiversity and ecosystem services, and thus overlooks a critical link between human well-being and species preservation.

Although bias was not intentionally written into the Endangered Species Act, concern exists that the act is used to list and manage more popular, "charismatic," megafauna species, such as the jaguar. If this were true, the value-neutral nature of the act and its role in preserving diversity important to ecosystem functioning and services would be compromised. However, the ESA listings show considerably less bias than other published reviews of species threats and global lists of endangered species compiled by organizations such as the World Conservation Union (table 8.5). If we better understood ecological functions such as production, nutrient retention, and, especially, decomposition (where many seemingly minor species play important roles), the listing process would better serve all species, including humans. Additionally, such an ecosystem function or ecosystem services-based approach might reduce species management costs involved in listing species that are directly critical to or represent a particular service, indirectly supporting other species through habitat protection.

In single-species recovery plans, the concept of ecosystem services may support designation of *umbrella species,* species whose preservation also protects habitats of secondary species. For example, the bay checkerspot butterfly (*Euphydryas editha bayensis*) of central California is currently protected under the Endangered Species Act. In the umbrella-species approach, if the act mandates a threat-based conservation effort, then measures would be adopted that protect only the largest remnant butterfly populations. On the other hand, by focusing efforts on ecosystem function or service, all habitats where the butterfly occurs could be preserved, including some marginal habitat patches. The indirect benefit of this second approach would be the additional protection of 98 percent of spring-flowering plant species also found in the serpentine grassland (Launer and Murphy 1994). Ecosystem services that might be used in such efforts include recreation, aesthetic beauty, and the maintenance of biodiversity through which agricultural, medicinal, and industrial

TABLE 8.5 Endangered species listed under the Endangered Species Act by taxonomic group, comparing treatment by other organizations

Taxonomic group	% listed under the ESA	% targeted by conservation research	% listed by IUCN as threatened worldwide	Species extinction risk (%)
Plants	**60.4**	20	**18**	**33**
Vertebrates (total)	**24.4**	69	**3**	—
Birds	31.7	39	19	14
Mammals	26.9	40	9	16
Fish	29.3	8	48	37
Reptiles	6.8	8	15	—
Amphibians	5.2	6	9	—
Invertebrates (total)	**15.2**	**11**	**79**	—
Molluscs	40.6	19	6	69
Crustaceans	12.9	8	3	59
Insect	23.9	68	80	—
Other	22.6	6	11	43

Sources: Data for percentage targeted by conservation research and percentage listed by IUCN as threatened worldwide from Clark and May 2002; data for species extinction risk from Stein et al. 2002.

Note: Extinction risk represents the percentage of U.S. species as a whole (*n* = 20,897) within each taxonomic group that have been classified as extinct, imperiled, or vulnerable.

advances are made. Such a hybrid approach may prove more successful than either a species-focused ESA approach or a broader ecosystem management approach.

The U.S. Fish and Wildlife Service has been under increasing pressure to move from single-species recovery plans to multispecies plans as a means of more effectively protecting and improving the standing of listed species. But studies have demonstrated that multispecies plans are less effective than the single-species models at maintaining and increasing populations of listed species, suggesting that this approach should be reevaluated (Clark and Harvey 2002). This somewhat counterintuitive finding may in part result from a poorer understanding of the ecology of species listed in the multispecies plans, a lack of adaptive management provisions, infrequent revisions, and a grouping based on "threat similarity" alone. The ecosystem service concept may effectively address several of these issues, and the service-based approach may yield more coherence in management and be a superior alternative to the "threat similarity" criteria binding multispecies recovery plans. In addition, lack of species-specific ecological knowledge may be mitigated by an improved grouping of a common service-based method as opposed to just threat. Adaptive management may also benefit from a function-based focus in which monitoring of ecosystem service recovery may be more effective than measuring population numbers directly.

Finally, assigning critical habitat may be facilitated by incorporating the value of ecosystem service preservation. In some cases it may be easier to identify habitat types that provide key services than to assess whether or not a habitat is "critical" to a listed species.

What Is the Right Path?

We believe that value-neutral protection under the Endangered Species Act for species facing extinction, regardless of their perceived value, is currently the most effective means of protecting ecosystem services. But is it the right path to take? On the surface, value-neutrality seems uninformed by *the best available science* and thus the less-desirable choice. But in the absence of the data needed to properly investigate the role species play in ecosystem functioning, a value-neutral approach continues to be our best option.

Still, we do not want to blindly wander the same path for the next thirty years; we would like to see listing and delisting decisions eventually made based on the importance of species to ecosystem functioning within ecoregions, which would better protect ecosystem services. The latter approach reflects two reasons for protecting species: if a species faces extinction, not only is the species threatened but also the functioning of its ecosystem; if the functioning of an ecosystem is threatened, so are we.

We thank the University of Washington and Columbia University for support to C. Jouseau and the National Science Foundation (NSF DEB 9996117) to Shahid Naeem. We thank S. F. Tjossem, E. Sterling, R. Gnam, and two anonymous reviewers for critically reading the manuscript.

9   Science and Controversy

Holly Doremus

When the Endangered Species Act (ESA) was enacted in 1973, no one worried much about the role of science in its implementation. To the extent that there was any disagreement as the act made its way through a nearly unanimous Congress, it was about the respective roles of state and federal governments,[1] not about the use of science (Goble, this volume; U.S. Congress 1972). Legislators, building on a tradition of science-based conservation policy, confidently directed the administrative agencies charged with implementing the new law to use the best available scientific data. Legislators offered little indication of why they felt that consideration of the best available scientific data was important, or what agencies should do if the available scientific data proved incomplete or equivocal.

Today, more than thirty years later, those questions can no longer be ignored. The scientific underpinnings of ESA implementation are bitterly contested in court, in the halls of Congress, in outside scientific reviews, and in the battle for public opinion. This chapter provides a historical overview of the legislative mandates for science, together with a discussion of the legal impact of "best available science," and the controversies surrounding the use of science in the implementation of the Endangered Species Act.

Legislative Mandates for Use of Best Available Science

The first federal endangered species legislation, the Endangered Species Preservation Act of 1966, charged the secretary of the interior with identifying species threatened with extinction. As part of the listing process, the secretary was directed to seek the advice and recommendations of experts "including, but not limited to, ornithologists, ichthyologists, ecologists, herpetologists, and mammologists" (Act of October 15, 1966a, sec. 1(c)). The next version, the Endangered Species Conservation Act of 1969, explicitly required that the secretary base listing decisions on the best scientific data available (sec. 4(b)(1)). The accompanying reports called for consultation with appropriate scientific organizations and individual specialists (Act of December 5, 1969, sec. 1(c)), suggesting that the wording had changed but the intention had not. The mandate that listing decisions be made on the basis of the best scientific data available was carried over unchanged into the 1973 Endangered Species Act (sec. 3(a)).

Little thought seems to have been given to these provisions. Like similar requirements in other conservation laws of the era, they seem to have been intended to encourage objective, apolitical, value-neutral decision making (Doremus 1997). No one raised the question of how to address uncertain scientific data or suggested that science might not be capable of answering all questions relevant to identifying groups for protection.

Since 1973, requirements for use of the best available scientific data have been extended to provisions of the ESA addressing biological assessments (sec. 7(c)), the impact of proposed federal action on listed species and designated critical habitat (sec. 7(a)(2)), and the definition of critical habitat (sec. 4(b)(2)). Perhaps surprisingly, several important sections of the Endangered Species Act are not explicitly subject to the best available science mandate. The recovery planning provision (sec. 4(f)), for example, does not mention scientific information. Neither does the section allowing relaxation of the prohibition on taking for threatened species (sec. 4(d)), or the section allowing issuance of incidental take permits (sec. 10(a)(2)). Those omissions highlight the curious nature of the best available science mandate. Science would seem to be as important for recovery plans or incidental take permit decisions as for listing or jeopardy determinations. That Congress did not expressly address the use of science in developing recovery plans or making permit decisions suggests an unquestioned assumption that regulatory agencies must use the best available scientific data when making decisions with a high scientific content. It is curious, then, that in so many of the ESA's provisions Congress felt the need to make that obligation explicit.

There has been only one substantive modification of a best available science mandate. In 1982, Congress amended the Endangered Species Act to require that listing decisions be based "solely" on the best available scientific data (Act of October 13, 1982). That change responded to the Reagan administration's imposition of an economic impact analysis requirement on listing proposals and to suspicion that the White House's Office of Management and Budget was pressuring the Department of the Interior to avoid listing species whose protection might carry high economic costs. A legislative report explained that "nonbiological considerations," particularly economics, could no longer play a role in listing decisions (U.S. Congress 1982, 20). At the same time, Congress imposed strict new deadlines on finalizing proposed listings, subject to brief extension if the secretary found "substantial disagreement regarding the sufficiency or accuracy" of the relevant scientific data (ESA sec. 4(b)(6)(B)(i)).

Legal Impact of the Mandates

In some respects, the ESA's repeated and explicit directive to the implementing agencies to use the best available scientific evidence in making decisions simply makes explicit a background principle of rationality that already applies to all federal agency decision making. Under the Administrative Procedure Act (Act of June 11, 1946), federal courts will set aside any federal agency decision that is "arbitrary, capricious, an abuse of discretion, or otherwise not in accordance with law" (5 U.S.C. sec. 706(2)(A)). Modern judicial interpretations of the Administrative Procedure Act require agencies to support their factual findings with some evidence and to provide a plausible explanation for their decisions. Even without an explicit mandate to consider the best available scientific evidence, therefore, a decision that ignored relevant scientific evidence brought to the agency's attention probably would not survive judicial review.

The best available science mandates do make it clear that ESA decisions need not be supported by conclusive evidence. The agencies must act on the basis of the evidence available, even if it is limited. They cannot delay listing, for example, until it is clear that the species is disappearing (*Defenders of Wildlife v. Babbitt* 1997). They must, instead, use their best professional judgment to interpret the evidence available and act on the basis of that interpretation.

The best available science mandate should protect agencies against unrealistic demands from courts for scientific certainty. Some courts, however, have demanded levels of specificity in the designation of critical habitat that would be difficult for science to provide. Critical habitat is defined as areas requiring special management where physical or biological features essential to the conservation of the species are found (ESA sec. 3(5)(A)(i)). The U.S. Fish and Wildlife Service has resisted critical habitat designation for years, seeing it as a difficult task with limited conservation benefits (USFWS 1999e). The statute, however, requires that critical habitat designation accompany listing in most cases, and a rash of lawsuits has forced the listing agencies to comply. They typically do so by identifying a geographic area they believe is essential to the species, perhaps simply because it is where the species is most commonly seen. In two recent cases, courts have complicated the already difficult task of critical habitat designation by insisting on specific identification of essential features of that habitat, such as water quality and quantity levels required by the listed species (*Middle Rio Grande Conservancy District v. Babbitt* 2000; *Home Builders Association of Northern California v. U.S. Fish and Wildlife Service* 2003). Particularly because critical habitat designation, like listing and consultation decisions, must be accomplished on tight statutory deadlines, courts should be careful not to impose unrealistic demands on the science.

Taking a broad view of the word "available," the best available science mandate could be construed to impose on the agencies implementing the Endangered Species Act an affirmative obligation to develop or analyze relevant data to the extent feasible. A few early cases did read it that way (*Roosevelt Campobello International Park Commission v. U.S. Environmental Protection Agency* 1982; *Connor v. Burford* 1988). More recently, though, courts have tended to take a narrow view of what it means for information to be available, ruling that the agency has no obligation to conduct even relatively simple studies (*Southwest Center for Biological Diversity v. Babbitt* 2000).

Science at the Center of Controversy

Although it was not an issue in the 1973 enactment of the Endangered Species Act, the role of science in implementation of the new law quickly became a focus of controversy and dispute. That should not be surprising. The act is, at least on paper, the strongest of the U.S. federal environmental laws, requiring protection of almost any dwindling species[2] and imposing nearly insurmountable barriers to almost any type of action that threatens the survival of a listed species.[3] Although it has never been implemented as aggressively as its language seems to authorize, the ESA does potentially stand in the way of many kinds of economic activity. People who stand to profit from those activities have strong incentives to fight its application. From the other side, environmentalists often see the Endangered Species Act as their best hope for blocking development.

The scientific underpinnings of ESA implementation invite challenges from both sides because the available scientific data is so often incomplete and uncertain. Given the almost unavoidable human tendency to interpret equivocal evidence as supporting one's preferred outcome, incomplete data tend to polarize debate as each side finds confirmation of its views (Sarewitz 2004).

This dynamic has played out since the Endangered Species Act was first passed, becoming more intense as its power became apparent. Shortly after the U.S. Supreme Court decided *Tennessee Valley Authority v. Hill* (1978), legislators worried about the potential reach of the ESA began introducing amendments demanding that regulatory decisions meet higher scientific standards (Doremus 1997). Recent proposals would have required that the regulatory agencies give greater weight to field work and peer-reviewed data, that data used by the agency meet standards set by the Office of Management and Budget under the Data Quality Act (Act of December 21, 2000), and that critical habitat be limited to areas shown by field surveys to be occupied by the species (U.S. Congress 2005).

Battles over the role of science are not new and have not been limited to the legislature. Dozens of lawsuits have challenged the scientific underpinnings of particular ESA decisions. Environmentalists were the first to head to the courtroom, but development interests have caught the litigation fever as well.

The scientific community is the latest front line. Two early reviews of the general scientific foundations of the Endangered Species Act, one requested from the National Research Council (NRC) and the other volunteered by the Ecological Society of America, were positive (National Research Council 1995; Carroll et al. 1996) The general principles of the ESA—that careless human activity threatens other species, that species need habitat protection to survive, and that species are a sensible focus for conservation efforts—are widely accepted.

Specific decisions are more of a challenge. As the NRC committee that reviewed the scientific basis for the Endangered Species Act in 1995 noted, "critical data to make informed decisions on proposals for listing, to designate critical habitat, and to develop recovery and management plans are usually lacking" (National Research Council 1995, 182). Recently, as the limits of the data supporting those decisions have become more widely understood, both the regulated community and the action agencies that serve them have begun to question wildlife agencies more aggressively. That dynamic has led to lawsuits, but also to a series of solicited NRC reviews of specific ESA decisions. Over the last ten years, the National Research Council has been asked to review decisions regarding listing of Pacific and Atlantic salmon; management decisions concerning the Colorado, Missouri, Platte, Klamath, and Columbia river systems; and the decline of the Steller sea-lion (*Eumetopias jubatus*), among others (National Research Council 1996a, 1999a, 2002a, 2003a, 2004a, 2004b, 2004c, 2004d, 2005). Those reviews, with the conspicuous exception of the Klamath study, have generally endorsed wildlife agency decisions, but all have noted the thin information base on which those decisions must be made.

Competing Models of Scientific Decision Making

One reason the science of ESA implementation has been so controversial is that legislators, and much of the public, seem to expect certainty from science-based regulatory decisions. That expectation dovetails with a widespread public belief that science provides reliable yes-or-no answers to questions asked of it. The hard reality is that the scientific information available to support ESA decisions is frequently incomplete, ambiguous, and contested. An array of critical interpretive judgments are needed to translate that kind of science into policy decisions. Most ESA decisions do not, and never will, fit the simpleminded public vision of science as objective decision maker.

The key question, which has not been explicitly addressed by the legislature, the regulatory agencies, or the law's critics, is which principles should guide the inevitable judgments that ultimately determine regulatory choices. Instead of directly addressing the question, public debate has centered around differing characterizations of what it means for policy decisions to be "scientific." Antiregulatory interests, including some lawmakers, promote a model that would require what they call "sound science" to justify regulatory intervention. Proregulatory environmental interests, on the other hand, call for a model that would give great deference to the views of conservation scientists.

The "sound science" model seeks to import what its proponents claim are norms of research science. Research scientists know that their measurements are never perfect, that many features of the natural world can be highly variable, and that factors outside their control may confound their results. Professional incentives favor early claims of proof, but if those claims are incorrect, they can set the field back rather than advance it. To deal with the complications and incentives of research science, scientists have developed general norms for what the authors of a study can claim to have shown. Those norms vary somewhat among fields, but often they require that statistical tests demonstrate a high probability (typically 95 percent) that a claimed effect did not arise by chance. "Sound science" proponents argue that similar standards of proof should apply before economic activity is restricted.

They also draw parallels with the use of science in the courtroom, arguing that data not meeting specific standards should play no role in regulatory decisions. The U.S. Supreme Court ruled in *Daubert v. Merrell Dow Pharmaceuticals* (1993) that expert scientific testimony is not admissible in federal court unless the judge finds that it is both reliable and relevant to the decision. Reliability is evaluated on the basis of several factors, including testability, peer review, potential error rate, and acceptance of the technique within the relevant scientific community. Antiregulatory interests argue that it is just as important to keep unreliable scientific data (a category they see encompassing all but the most conclusive studies) out of regulatory decisions. The Data Quality Act is a general attempt to limit the use of such data. Legislative proposals to require specific kinds of data and mandate peer review before ESA decisions are finalized are intended to serve similar functions.

Environmentalists, on the other hand, have sought to strengthen the role of scientists in regulatory decisions. Conservation scientists, not surprisingly, tend to favor protective regulatory outcomes more strongly than the general public does. Environmentalists, therefore, would specifically delegate regulatory decisions to the career scientific staff of the wildlife agencies and would encourage those scientists to consider any and all data available, no matter how inconclusive.

They too are able to claim that the norms of science support their preferred model for decision making. Scientific claims are properly evaluated by the relevant scientific community, not by the general public. In scientific practice, support of the most distinguished members of the field plays a key role in acceptance of a claim or theory. Environmental groups regularly submit letters signed by large numbers of practicing scientists in support of their arguments for stronger regulation and accuse the decision makers of misusing science if the decision does not go their way.[4]

A More Productive Vision of Scientific Decision Making

Moving beyond current disputes about the use of science in ESA implementation will require a new vision of scientifically credible regulation. That vision must acknowledge uncertainties in the data, and directly address decision making in light of those uncertainties. The appropriate burden of proof will depend on the probabilities and relative costs of errors of over- and underregulation, as well as incentives (or lack of incentives) to produce or disclose information. A precautionary approach would allow the regulatory agencies to mandate conservation action on the basis of thin but suggestive information.

Such a precautionary approach would be more palatable, and easier to justify, if it were accompanied by a clear commitment to improving the information base over time and updating regulatory decisions accordingly. Regulatory agencies should be required to explicitly acknowledge at the outset any gaps in the data; explain how filling those gaps might change the regulatory decision; and address whether the needed data can be generated, at what cost, and on what timeline. Some of the burden of filling crucial data gaps can fairly be placed on those who would profit from development, but Congress should also provide targeted funding for data gathering and analysis, with the highest priority given to filling information needs relevant to the most immediate and sharpest conflicts between conservation and development. Finally, the agencies should regularly update their regulatory decisions, conducting status reviews as required of listed and "warranted but precluded" species and reinitiating consultation for ongoing activities. Agency budgets do not currently include sufficient funding for this kind of updating; they should be increased as needed to allow regular review and updating of all key ESA decisions.

I O Science and Implementation

Mary Ruckelshaus and Donna Darm

The U.S. Endangered Species Act (ESA) relies heavily on science, and not surprisingly science has become a major battleground in the controversy surrounding its implementation (Doremus, this volume). Apparently, Congress hoped that ESA decisions could be made based on science alone and thereby insulated from politics (U.S. Congress 1982, 19). This hope was unrealistic for at least two reasons. First, science cannot answer with certainty many of the questions that must be answered in ESA decision making, especially in the time frames demanded by the statute. Second, while science has a central role in informing natural resource decisions, scientific information alone cannot "make decisions." Criticizing the science seems to be one outcome of hard policy choices (Mapes 2001; Boyle 2002; Dalton 2002; *Seattle Times* 2002; Stokstad 2002; Strassel 2002; Pianin 2003; *Sacramento Bee* 2003a and 2003b; Cart and Weiss 2004).

The ESA requires agency reliance on science in several areas: The secretaries of commerce and the interior must designate critical habitat based on the best available scientific data (ESA sec. 4(b)(2)); federal agencies must rely on the best available scientific and commercial data but ensure that their actions will not jeopardize the continued existence of listed species or adversely modify their critical habitat (ESA sec. 7(a)(2)); and recovery plans must adopt objective criteria for delisting (ESA sec. 4(f)(1)(B)(ii)). In requiring that decisions affecting endangered species be made primarily on the basis of science, Congress sought to insulate agencies from political pressure. Instead, perversely, intense political pressure has forced underground the agency policy choices inherent in science-based decisions (Doremus 1997).

Some scholars have argued that "better science" will not reduce the controversy surrounding the act. Instead, they call for more openness about the policy choices embedded in ESA decisions (Doremus 1997; Myer 2001; Yaffee 2006). The authors wholeheartedly agree, but we also believe that better scientific information and processes of eliciting and translating science can improve decision making under the act.

The ESA has been the subject of intense debate in the scientific literature in terms of its effectiveness in protecting species (Schwartz 1999; Boersma et al. 2001; Crouse et al. 2002; Scott et al. 2006, chap. 2). Federal agency use of scientific information in implementing the act was evaluated by the National Research Council (1995). In this chapter, we focus on the role of science in the act and how the agencies use science in practice. We address the following questions for each stage of the ESA process from listing through recovery planning: (1) What is the role of science, and what has agency practice revealed to be the difficulties of incorporating science? (2) How have the public and courts responded? (3) How could either the science or the process of providing science be improved? We also consider whether decision makers are prepared to make and explain decisions based on incomplete science. We close with suggestions for how scientists can better serve decision making under the act.

The Science Underlying Listing Determinations

Two biological questions are central to the listing process: What is the species (or biological unit) to be listed? And what is the species' likely risk of extinction? The U.S. Fish and Wildlife Service (USFWS) and National Marine Fisheries Service (NMFS) have developed interagency guidance on how to manage listing petitions (USFWS and NMFS 1996d, 1999d) but that guidance does not offer biological criteria to address the issues below.

What is a Listable Unit?

The Endangered Species Act protects "subspecies and any distinct population segment of any species of vertebrate fish or wildlife which interbreeds when mature" (sec. 3(15)). Four difficult science issues have emerged in practice: Do all subspecies have equivalent "significance" taxonomically? What is a distinct population segment (Waples, this volume)? How does hybridization between taxa affect species identification (Haig and Allendorf, this volume)? How should artificially propagated individuals be considered?

SPECIES AND SUBSPECIES

The accuracy and degree of revisions of taxonomic classifications at the subspecies level vary greatly among species. The U.S. Fish and Wildlife Service has frequently encountered situations in which it was uncertain whether a group of individuals should be classified as a distinct population segment, a subspecies, or even a separate species (e.g., interior least tern [USFWS 1985], lower Keys rice rat [USFWS 1991a], Mississippi gopher frog [*Rana capito sevosa*], California red-legged frog [*Rana aurora draytonii*] [USFWS 1996a], and California

tiger salamander [*Ambystoma californiense*] [USFWS 2003c]). The listing determinations for the coastal California gnatcatcher (*Polioptila californica californica*) (USFWS 1993), dusky seaside sparrow (*Ammodramus maritimus nigrescens*) (Avise and Nelson 1989), and Florida panther (*Puma concolor coryi*)
(Culver et al. 2000) aroused enormous controversy over the issue of whether the
groups were significantly divergent from more common sister taxa to be considered subspecies and therefore listable units. The social and political fallout from
these listing decisions continues today (e.g., Carlson 2003; *Miami Herald* 2003;
Pfeifer 2003; Wilson 2003a). In some respects the controversy is misplaced because even if not considered subspecies, many of these population groups can be
listed as distinct population segments (Stanford Environmental Law Society
2001). In other cases, new information about the lack of reproductive isolation
may lead USFWS and NMFS biologists to conclude that a group of populations is neither a subspecies (contrary to a published classification) nor a distinct
population segment, as in the case of the western sage grouse (USFWS 2004a).

DISTINCT POPULATION SEGMENT
The U.S. Fish and Wildlife Service and National Marine Fisheries Service have
a joint distinct population segment (DPS) policy (USFWS and NMFS 1996e)
that provides two tests of distinctness: (1) Is the population or group of populations markedly separate from other populations of the same species? (2) Is it significant? NMFS adopted a policy for designating distinct population segments
of Pacific salmon and steelhead (NMFS 1991; Waples 1991, 1995), which relies on identification of *evolutionarily significant units* (ESUs) before the joint
DPS policy was implemented (Waples, this volume). In delineating a DPS,
agencies must establish the significance of intraspecific variation in life history,
genetic, or morphological traits. It is important to determine the relationship of
life history variants (e.g., races) to one another in order to decide into how
many pieces a species could or should be divided for listing determinations
(Waples, this volume).

The coastal California gnatcatcher illustrates the difficulty in determining
the significance of within-species variation. The birds were originally identified
as a subspecies based on bill size and shape, tail length, and overall coloration—
all characteristics used by ornithologists to establish taxonomic classifications
(USFWS 1993). These characteristics evolved since the last ice age, when the
birds expanded northward from a refuge in Mexico—evolutionarily a very short
time frame. Skeptical of the listing, private-sector interests sponsored research
suggesting morphological variations may not be genetically based. In response,
the USFWS proposed listing the coastal California gnatcatcher as a distinct
population segment (USFWS 2003a). As a practical matter, in spite of a rash of
new scientific information gathering and analyses, the listing of the gnatcatcher

as a DPS rather than a subspecies has had little, if any, effect on the degree of protection it is afforded under the Endangered Species Act.

How important is intraspecific variation to long-term persistence of the subspecies or species? Should relatively recently evolved forms be protected? Some observers (and plaintiffs) argue that the act is meant to protect morphologically unique forms as "distinct" population segments (Doremus 1997). Others suggest that the relevant inquiry should be whether, if lost, the variation could evolve again in a time span meaningful to humans (such as a few generations) (Ruckelshaus et al. 2002b; Waples et al. 2004).

Once a distinct population segment is delineated, scientists must assess the importance of different morphological or life history forms to the continued existence of the DPS (or species or subspecies) as a whole.

HYBRIDS

Hybridization between closely related taxa can create listing challenges, especially when one of the hybridizing species is common and the other rare (Haig and Allendorf, this volume). For example, the red wolf (*Canis lupus rufus*), which is listed as endangered under the ESA, may interbreed with the unlisted eastern gray wolf (*Canis lupus lycaon*) (Wayne and Jenks 1991; Dowling et al. 1992; Nowak 1992; Brownlow 1996). An equally vexing example is the westslope cutthroat trout (*Oncorhynchus clarki lewisi*), which hybridizes with introduced rainbow trout (*O. mykiss*) in the western United States (Allendorf and Leary 1988; Behnke 1992; Rubidge et al. 2001; Rubidge 2003; Taylor et al. 2003). In that case, after legal challenge and extensive discussion, the U.S. Fish and Wildlife Service decided not to list the trout despite a proposed policy on considering hybrids (or intercrosses) under the act (USFWS and NMFS 1996f; USFWS 2003f).

ARTIFICIAL PROPAGATION

Both the U.S. Fish and Wildlife Service and the National Marine Fisheries Service have had to consider artificially propagated individuals occurring in natural habitats (e.g., fish produced in a hatchery, captively bred birds). Until recently, both agencies judged the danger of extinction and the state of recovery based on naturally reproducing populations. NMFS has proposed a policy that considers the risk of extinction of species based on the combined artificially propagated and naturally produced components of populations (NMFS 2004a, 2005a). The proposal raises interesting policy and science questions. The policy side must address the acceptable degree of risk, both with respect to biological issues (such as likelihood of persistence) and management issues (such as the likelihood of continued funding for artificial propagation programs). On the science side, biologists must incorporate artificial propagation into extinction risk models despite poor data on breeding patterns, reproductive success, and movement of hatchery and wild fish. At the interface between science and policy, there is the question of the importance of a species' "evolutionary trajectory." Is a distinct population segment in danger of diverging from a natural evolutionary trajectory because of artificial selection also "in danger of extinction? Presumably it could be if the artificial selection makes it likely the distinct population segment will no longer be significant to the taxon (or evolutionarily significant, in the case of an evolutionarily significant unit; Myers et al. 2004).

PUBLIC AND COURT REACTION

Courts are generally unwilling to second-guess agency biologists when it comes to taxonomic classification or evaluation of extinction risk. The General Accounting Office reviewed sixty-four listing decisions by the U.S. Fish and Wildlife Service between 1999 and 2002 and found that peer reviewers "overwhelmingly supported" the science behind the decisions. Courts overturned only two listing decisions because of improper use of scientific data (GAO 2003). However, courts will intervene when judges believe the National Marine Fisheries Service or U.S. Fish and Wildlife Service have failed to follow the statute, regulations, or policies, or when the judge believes the agencies have failed to adequately explain the connection between the data and the conclusion. For example, a district court invalidated NMFS's decision to list naturally spawned but not hatchery-spawned Oregon coast coho salmon, even though the agency found them to comprise a single evolutionarily significant unit (*Alsea Valley Alliance v. Evans* 2001). A court of appeals threw out the USFWS's decision to list a population of the cactus ferruginous pygmy-owl (*Glaucidium brasilianum cactorum*) because the agency failed to explain how the population was "significant" and therefore a distinct population segment under the joint DPS policy (*National Association of Home Builders v. Norton* 2003). And a district court concluded that NMFS did not use the best available science when it relied on an outdated taxonomic classification for the killer whale (*Orcinus orca*) (*Center for Biological Diversity v. Lohn 2003*).

ADVANCING THE ROLE OF SCIENCE

The NRC review of use of science in the Endangered Species Act was supportive of the "evolutionary unit" concept (National Research Council 1995). Much of the ongoing scientific debate over DPS/ESU identification involves technical points, such as how best to describe evolutionarily significant variation for protection (summarized in Ruckelshaus et al. 2002b; Waples, this volume). Some observers feel the U.S. Fish and Wildlife Service and National Marine Fisheries Service have defined distinct population segments too narrowly (Doremus 1997), arguing that the Endangered Species Act was intended to protect populations that have aesthetic value, are keystone species within their ecosystems, or are in some other sense unique. The concern is that the rigid "scientific" approach embodied in ESU and DPS policies ignores other equally valid values that Congress intended to protect. The policies in most cases provide workable guidance in determining whether a species exists for purposes of the act.

Extinction Risk

Once the listable unit (i.e., species, subspecies, or distinct population segment) is identified, its risk of extinction must be estimated under section 4(a) of the Endangered Species Act (table 10.1). The act defines an "endangered species" to be "in danger of extinction throughout all or a signficant portion of its range" (sec. 3(6)) and a "threatened species" to be "likely to become an endangered species within the foreseeable future" (sec. 3(19)).

THE ROLE OF SCIENCE IN AGENCY PRACTICE

Risk evaluations are necessarily a combination of scientific analyses and policy judgments about the degree of "acceptable" risk and the time frames over which risk should be evaluated (Burgman 2005). Decision makers must then interject a judgment about whether a species' risk of extinction triggers the statutory definitions of "endangered" or "threatened."

Qualitative approaches to estimating species risk, if transparent and systematic, can be as reliable as quantitative approaches (e.g., Keith et al. 2004; McCarthy et al. 2004). Neither the U.S. Fish and Wildlife Service nor the National Marine Fisheries Service regularly use widely accepted qualitative approaches to estimating extinction risk (IUCN 1994; NatureServe 2003). NMFS implemented its own risk evaluation matrix to assess the status of over fifty ESUs of Pacific salmonids (Wainwright and Kope 1999). This matrix accounted for diversity and spatial distribution in addition to conventional population status analysis (e.g., Allendorf et al. 1997; Shelden et al. 2001).

Quantitative extinction risk models (known collectively as *population viability analyses*, or PVAs) require information on population size, population growth rate, and variability in population growth rate over time (Dennis et al. 1991; Boyce 1992; Morris et al. 1999). The critical first step of identifying demographically independent populations is almost never done in PVAs despite evidence that ignoring population structure can cause grave errors in estimates of extinction risk (Morris et al. 1999). In a recent counterexample, NMFS identified independent populations before conducting viability modeling for Pacific salmonids (McElhany et al. 2000; Ruckelshaus et al. 2002a).

The data needed to parameterize even the simplest PVA models are almost always incomplete (Reed et al., this volume). Additional uncertainties arise with

TABLE 10.1 Key science-related provisions within the Endangered Species Act

ESA provision	Science-related question addressed by provision	Further work needed on analyses pertaining to provision	Further work needed on application of provision
4(a) Listing	Is there a "species"?	Improved definition of the "distinct population segment/evolutionarily significant unit" concept	Agency guidance on how to address hybridization, definition of taxonomic "significance," and artificially propagated individuals
4(a) Listing	What is the species' risk of extinction?	Improved definition of time scales, attention to multiple indicators of risk, methods of estimating rates of reproduction of at-risk species	Agency guidance on consideration of extinction risk and "significant portion" of range
4(b) Critical habitat designation	What habitat features are essential to species' conservation and how much habitat is needed for conservation?	Relationship between habitat quality/quantity and species extinction risk	Agency guidance on designating critical habitat, how to weigh benefits/costs; consider sequence of application
7(a)(2) Federal consultation 10(a)(1)(B) Habitat conservation plans	What effect will a particular action have on species' survival or recovery? Does an action result in take, and if so, how much?*	Relative importance of different limiting factors in extinction risk; how effects of individual actions relate to whole population/species impacts	More-open science process in section 7 consultations; guidance on considering piecemeal vs. whole life-cycle approach
4(f) Recovery planning	What are the characteristics of a recovered species? What factors are limiting recovery? What habitat is essential to recovery?	All of the above	More public participation in policy oversight of the planning process

* This question also arises in section 9 enforcement actions, which are not addressed in this chapter.

model structure—for example, how to depict population responses at small sizes, the effects of density-dependent population regulation, and choice of a quasi-extinction threshold (Morris et al. 1999). For these reasons it is important to explore the sensitivity of PVA results to alternative assumptions (e.g., Dennis et al. 1991; Holmes 2001; Holmes and Fagan 2002), as NMFS has done for estimating the status of Pacific salmon and Steller sea-lions (*Eumetopias jubatus*) in listing and recovery decisions (Gerber and VanBlaricom 2001; NMFS 2003a; Puget Sound Technical Recovery Team 2002; Willamette–Lower Columbia Technical Recovery Team 2003).

Applications of PVA generally assume that past trends and variability in input parameters can be used to project future population dynamics. This is almost certainly an incorrect assumption given climate change, changes in human management of the landscape, introduction and spread of nonindigenous species, and changing rates and intensity of human-influenced catastrophes (e.g., fire, toxic, or oil spills). A promising approach is to use scenario planning whereby scientists ask whether an estimated risk of extinction (or any population outcome) changes under alternative views of future conditions (see "The Science Underlying Recovery Planning" in this chapter; Clark et al. 2001; Carpenter 2002; Peterson et al. 2003).

An emerging issue for the U.S. Fish and Wildlife Service and National Marine Fisheries Service is interpretation of the statutory definition of an endangered species as one that is in danger of extinction "throughout all *or a significant portion* of its range" (emphasis added). Recent practice has been to rely on the identification of a distinct population segment. Dissatisfied with some determinations not to list, plaintiffs have begun to challenge the agencies for failure to separately examine whether a species, subspecies, or DPS is in danger of extinction in at least a portion of its range (*Defenders of Wildlife v. Norton* 2001, 2002; *Environmental Protection Information Center [EPIC] v. National Marine Fisheries Service [NMFS]* 2004.) While the two agencies have not yet explicitly interpreted this statutory phrase, recent USFWS decisions have applied a biological test, similar to the significance test of the DPS policy, examining whether a population group is biologically significant even though it is not discrete (e.g., USFWS 1998, 2000). It is unclear whether the two agencies believe that a species in danger of extinction in only a portion of its range must be listed throughout its entire range (see *Marbled Murrelet v. Lujan* 1992).

PUBLIC AND COURT REACTION

Doremus (1997) suggested that the public reacts negatively to unbridled agency discretion in identifying species and determining risk of extinction. However, it seems this reaction is less about whether the U.S. Fish and Wildlife Service and National Marine Fisheries Service have misapplied science than it is an objection to protecting such creatures as rats and bugs, often against private interests. Courts tend to defer to agency listing determinations (GAO 2003), except when they conclude that the agencies failed to follow the statute or agency regulations. Although public comment on listing proposals often contests the agencies' analysis of extinction risk, the authors are unaware of any successful court challenges in that area.

ADVANCING THE ROLE OF SCIENCE

The U.S. Fish and Wildlife Service and National Marine Fisheries Service recently outlined criteria by which they will evaluate the effects of federal, state, and local conservation efforts when making listing decisions (USFWS and NMFS 2003b). These so-called "conservation measures" have been or soon will be implemented, although it is still too soon to evaluate their effects on extinction risk. The question is a scientific one that can be exceedingly challenging to address (see discussion in "The Science Underlying Recovery Planning" below).

The two agencies would be well served by adopting recommendations acknowledging that making listing determinations is not just a science exercise but has three important policy components: (1) the time period over which persistence should be measured, (2) the level of risk that results in a threatened or endangered finding, and (3) the burden of proof for demonstrating the effects of conservation measures. Such recommendations must be flexible enough to account for the inaccuracy of extinction risk estimates and for biological differences among species. For example, the time period over which extinction is considered may depend upon the inherent variability in demographic characteristics of a species or the ability of scientists to forecast long-term trends. Recommendations would need to leave room for decision makers and scientists to work together to understand the biological implications of alternative risk levels (e.g., modelers can illuminate for decision makers what a 0.99, 0.95, or 0.80 probability of extinction looks like) (Doremus, this volume).

Research is needed on how best to make population or species demographic parameter estimates from spotty census information (Reed et al., this volume). Abundance information for many species of conservation concern consists of presence/absence data, index counts, or censuses during a specific life stage that are easy to count, such as breeding aggregations. Making a determination about the viability status of a species requires that these sample data be translated into whole population or species counts. What are the best methods for making that translation? What are the advantages and pitfalls associated with different approaches to estimating species numbers from population subsamples?

Finally, accounting for environmental factors and species interactions that accelerate or mitigate downward population trends could significantly improve quantitative models of extinction risk (see also "The Science Underlying Recovery Planning" below; National Research Council 1995).

The Science Underlying Critical Habitat Designations

Within one year of listing, the U.S. Fish and Wildlife Service and National Marine Fisheries Service must designate critical habitat to the maximum extent prudent and determinable (table 10.1). The Endangered Species Act defines critical habitat as "the specific areas within the geographical area occupied by the species . . . on which are found those physical or biological features . . . essential to the conservation of the species," and "specific areas outside the geographical area occupied by the species . . . upon a determination by the Secretary that such areas are essential for the conservation of the species" (USFWS and NMFS 1999e, 31872). From this construction, the statute seems to contemplate an approach to critical habitat designation that favors occupied areas: the agencies first identify habitat elements essential to species conservation (for example, a particular type of tree for nesting, vegetation for forage or cover, gravel streambeds for spawning, etc.) and then designate areas within the species' present range where those elements are present. Only for areas outside the species' present range must there be a determination that the area itself is "essential for conservation." In practice, the agencies, plaintiffs, and some courts have blurred the two standards and require that all areas, occupied or unoccupied, meet the test for unoccupied habitat: the area itself must be essential for conservation. For example, in a case involving the Rio Grande silvery minnow (*Hybognathus amarus*), the court stated that critical habitat "must be limited geographically to what is essential to the conservation of the threatened or endangered species" (*Middle Rio Grande Conservancy District v. Babbitt* 2000). And in a case involving the Alameda whipsnake (*Masticophis lateralis euryxanthus*) the court observed that "critical habitat for occupied land is defined in part . . . as specific areas 'essential to the conservation of the species' " (*Home Builders Association of Northern California v. U.S. Fish and Wildlife Service* 2003).

The USFWS and NMFS have long maintained that critical habitat designation adds little to species protection (Clark 1999). Section 7 of the ESA requires federal agencies to ensure that their actions do not jeopardize species' continued existence and do not destroy or adversely modify their critical habitat. The two agencies have usually treated an action that adversely modifies critical habitat as also jeopardizing the species' continued existence, making the prohibition against adverse modification redundant. Agency regulations defining both jeopardy and adverse modification in similar terms (actions affecting "both the survival and recovery" of the species) have reinforced this approach. Critics point out that critical habitat designation is especially important for species protection in unoccupied habitat, where the USFWS and NMFS may be less likely to reach a jeopardy finding (Taylor et al. 2003, 2005). Two separate reviews examined effects of critical habitat designations on reported trends in species abundance and content of recovery plans, and the results were mixed (Clark et al. 2002; Hoekstra et al. 2002b; Taylor et al. 2003, 2005). Recent court decisions have invalidated the agencies' regulatory definition of adverse modification as not being sufficiently tied to conservation (*Gifford Pinchot Task Force v. U.S. Fish and Wildlife Service* 2004; *Sierra Club v. U.S. Fish and Wildlife Service* 2001). As future section 7 practice adjusts to the new legal rulings, the two tests may prove not to be redundant and the designation of critical habitat may indeed provide increased protection for listed species. The authors believe the current landscape is too unsettled to draw a reliable conclusion from past practice.

Critical habitat designations, where they have been made, have lacked meaningful analysis of the economic impact (see *New Mexico Cattle Growers Association v. U.S. Fish and Wildlife Service* 2001). Successful court challenges to designations (or lack of designations) have led to multiple requirements for the USFWS to designate habitat in very short time frames. Moreover, courts have ordered the agencies to consider economic impacts of designation, even if they are "coextensive" with the impacts of applying the section 7 jeopardy requirement (*New Mexico Cattle Growers Association v. U.S. Fish and Wildlife Service* 2001). This requirement is contrary to the best available science regarding economic analysis, which would require an estimate of the costs of designation based on a comparison of the world with and without the designation (Office of Management and Budget 2003).

In response, the U.S. Fish and Wildlife Service has vigorously objected to the requirement (e.g., testimony of Assistant Secretary of the Interior Craig Manson, [Manson 2003]). Past congressional efforts have failed to amend the ESA to change the timing of critical habitat designation to coincide with recovery planning instead of listing, but it remains a topic of congressional interest.

The Role of Science in Agency Practice

Section 4(b)(2) of the Endangered Species Act requires critical habitat designation to be based on the best scientific data available, although the U.S. Fish and Wildlife Service and National Marine Fisheries Service may exclude areas from designation if economic or other relevant impacts outweigh the benefits of designation. However, often agencies know little about species' habitat needs at the time of listing and thus identification of critical habitat is highly uncertain.

The agencies' joint designation of critical habitat for the Gulf sturgeon (*Acipenser oxyrinchus desotoi*) illustrates this. The two agencies examined the population structure and concluded that the seven extant populations were largely reproductively isolated. They reasoned that the populations at the extremes of the range are important for conserving genetic diversity and that the intermediate populations are important for connectivity, and concluded that all habitat currently occupied by the seven populations is essential for conservation (USFWS 2003i). Like the judgments made in analyzing extinction risk, these were clearly not made in a policy vacuum. The question of how many populations are needed for conservation and how much habitat each needs for conservation are not just scientific questions. The answers depend upon tolerance to risk and time scales over which the risk is considered.

One of the more contentious debates surrounding critical habitat designation concerns the consideration of economic costs of designation by the U.S. Fish and Wildlife Service and National Marine Fisheries Service and their discretion under section 4(b)(2) of the ESA to exclude areas from designation if the benefit of exclusion outweighs the benefit of designation. The two agencies have only recently begun to apply economic analysis in their designations, and their use of the science of economics is not well developed. Their past practice of collapsing the jeopardy and adverse modification requirements into a single test has complicated the economic analysis. Furthermore, at the time of listing, information is lacking on land use patterns and how economic activities would be modified as a result of section 7 consultations.

Public and Court Reaction

Provisions in the Endangered Species Act for critical habitat designations have proven a major flash point for both advocates and critics of species protection (e.g., *Sacramento Bee* 2003b; Wilson 2003b; Cart and Weiss 2004). For advocates, the provisions give them their strongest tool for protecting habitat. For critics, the provisions are among the few places in the statute where economics comes into play, making them a rallying point for the development-regulated community. Further, many landowners assume that when private land is designated as critical habitat the federal government is in effect "taking" their property and will restrict its use. And, finally, the U.S. Fish and Wildlife Service and the National Marine Fisheries Service, arguing that critical habitat designation adds nothing to species protection, have resisted designating habitat altogether or have simply designated habitat without sufficient analysis (Patlis 2001). It is not surprising, therefore, that the agencies often fail to make critical habitat designations and when they do, the designations frequently end up in court (GAO 2003).

The courts have responded to such treatment with impatience, chastising agency reluctance to designate critical habitat and ordering that designations be completed expeditiously. Further complicating the situation are court decisions finding the agencies' regulatory definition of adverse modification invalid. The lack of guidance by the two agencies and a growing number of court opinions make the situation still more uncertain.

Advancing the Role of Science

There are promising biological approaches that could be used to at least partially address the question of how much occupied and unoccupied habitat is needed for species persistence (Hanski 1999), but the data requirements are daunting. For instance, population matrix models can be used to address the question of how changes in survival at particular life stages affect overall population dynamics or persistence (Caswell 2001). One example of such an application with a listed species is the endangered Kemp's ridley sea turtle (*Lepidochelys kempii*), in which matrix models suggest that the survival of subadults and adults in the ocean was most critical to overall population status (Heppell et al. 1996; Heppell and Crowder 1998). Another approach is to predict how changes in habitat will impact species status based on empirical habitat suitability models (e.g., Jenkins et al. 2003). Unfortunately, we have limited ability to directly address the question of critical habitat—what habitat conditions or amounts significantly affect life-stage-specific survivals?

The science of economics also could contribute to improving the designation process. Section 4(b)(2) of the Endangered Species Act requires the U.S. Fish and Wildlife Service and National Marine Fisheries Service to consider the impacts of designation and balance the benefits of exclusion against the benefits of designation. Federal guidelines recommend putting the two types of benefits into the same metric in a cost-benefit framework (Office of Management and Budget 2003). Although information may be readily available that allows economic impacts to be quantified and monetized, quantifying the benefits to species from critical habitat designation is more difficult.

Thus, best economics practice would have the agencies measure the incremental impact and benefit of designation; the courts, however, have ruled otherwise (*New Mexico Cattle Growers Association v. U.S. Fish and Wildlife Service* 2001). How should the agencies proceed in this situation? Best economic practice would have them conduct a formal cost-benefit analysis, yet the short statutory time frames, limited information and resources, and considerable latitude for discretion suggest formal cost-benefit analysis may be neither possible nor necessary. One observer has suggested that approaches other than cost-benefit analysis, such as a cost-effectiveness framework, may be more appropriate (Sinden 2004). This recommendation is consistent with Office of Budget and Management guidance in cases where benefits are difficult to monetize (such as benefits to health or the environment).

The National Research Council recommended identification of habitat critical to survival at time of listing and designating the rest of critical habitat at the time of recovery planning (National Research Council 1995). These changes would require legislative reform of the act, but tying critical habitat designation to recovery planning has many proponents. The Department of the Interior has gone on record supporting such a connection (Manson 2004). The General Accounting Office recommends that the USFWS and NMFS adopt guidance on critical habitat designation (GAO 2003).

Until the agencies amend the regulatory definition of adverse modification, it will be unclear what standard they are applying in their section 7 consultations and whether they continue to view the prohibitions against jeopardy and adverse modification of critical habitat as providing redundant protection. Guidance on the economic analysis called for in the act would also help the USFWS and NMFS expedite designations. In particular, criteria for determining whether consideration of economic or other relevant impacts outweigh the benefits of designation would be helpful.

The Science Underlying Limitations on Federal Actions

When a federal agency intends an action that may affect a listed species, it must consult with the listing agency (table 10.1). For actions that adversely affect the species, the agency provides its biological opinion as to whether the action as proposed is likely to jeopardize the continued existence of a listed species or adversely modify its critical habitat. If the agency's opinion is that the action is likely to cause jeopardy or adverse modification, it must offer a reasonable and prudent alternative. The statute requires that all agencies "shall use the best scientific and commercial data available" in fulfilling the consultation requirement.

Analysis of jeopardy and adverse modification is one of the most common tasks required of the U.S. Fish and Wildlife Service and National Marine Fisheries Service yet one in which the standards are most obscure (Rohlf 1989, 2001). The statute does not define jeopardy or adverse modification. The two agencies have adopted regulatory definitions of these terms (USFWS and NMFS 1999e), but their consultation handbook lays out an analytical approach that does not track the regulatory definitions. The regulations define "jeopardize the continued existence of" to mean "to engage in an action that reasonably would be expected, directly or indirectly, to reduce appreciably the likelihood of both the survival and recovery of a listed species in the wild by reducing the reproduction, numbers, or distribution of that species" (USFWS and NMFS 1999e, 31872). Adverse modification is defined as an alteration that "appreciably diminishes the value of critical habitat for both the survival and recovery of a listed species." By these definitions the agencies need to compare the likelihood of a species survival and recovery with and without the proposed action to establish jeopardy, and to compare the value of critical habitat with and without the proposed action to establish adverse modification.

In practice, however, the agencies seldom take that approach, and their consultation handbook lays out a different chain of logic. The handbook directs the agencies to consider the status of the species, the environmental baseline, the effects of the action, and cumulative effects to determine whether the species is likely to survive and recover (USFWS and NMFS 1999e). It does not say what the agencies should do after summing up those factors. If the species is not expected to survive and recover, how much must the action under consultation contribute to that failure before it is considered jeopardy? Or, less likely, if the species is expected to survive and recover, does it matter how much modification occurs to the species' remaining habitat? Analysis of adverse modification of critical habitat is further complicated by two circuit courts invalidating the regulatory definition, as discussed previously.

In addition to offering opinions on jeopardy and adverse modification, the USFWS and NMFS must issue an incidental take statement authorizing a given level of take associated with the proposed action. Where the action involves habitat modification (for example, a grazing allotment), the agencies must determine what level of take will be associated with the habitat modification. Although such a determination must be made based on scientific analyses, it is very difficult for scientists to quantify a species' response to habitat alterations, especially smaller-scale changes in habitat.

This is an area in particular where science is inadequate to answer the questions asked. Agencies often lack information to predict the effect an action is likely to have on a listed species. Furthermore, risks are generally cumulative and assessing the effect of each individual action on species status is exceedingly difficult. Finally, threats come from many different actions in different sectors, forcing the agencies to make a choice about how much of the conservation burden should fall on a given sector (box 10.1).

The Role of Science in Agency Practice

The variety of agency action considered in section 7 consultations is extremely diverse, as are the species affected. We offer a few examples in box 10.1 to draw lessons from agency practice.

BOX 10.1 Examples demonstrating the role of science in implementing section 7 limitations on federal actions under the Endangered Species Act

Example 1: Addressing Scientific Uncertainty

The manner in which inevitable scientific uncertainty is incorporated into section 7 consultations is key to using science to inform sound decisions. In the high-profile case of Bureau of Reclamation operations on the Klamath River Basin water management project, the National Research Council was brought in to help resolve what many characterized as a scientific dispute (Cooperman and Markle 2003). The NRC's final report (National Research Council 2004a) highlights several recommendations aimed at reducing the uncertainty in the biological conclusions by the the two agencies that the Bureau's proposed actions will not jeopardize the listed species. Recommendations include the following: (1) the U.S. Fish and Wildlife Service and the National Marine Fisheries Service are urged to complete recovery plans for the two species that should identify how research and monitoring will support species recovery and facilitate identification of what actions are allowed under section 7 and 10 consultations, (2) scientists should be allowed sufficient time to publish key research findings in peer-reviewed scientific journals, (3) a diverse team of "cooperators" should be convened for designing ecosystem-based management actions that have local support for implementation, and (4) experiments should be conducted to test the effectiveness and feasibility of specific remediation strategies (National Research Council 2002b, 2004a).

In another example, NMFS was thwarted in an attempt to deal with uncertainties associated with future allocation of necessary conservation actions among sectors in the Columbia River Basin, home to twelve species of endangered salmon and steelhead whose migrations are affected by operation of the power system. In 2000, NMFS issued a biological opinion on operation of the Federal Columbia River Power System (NMFS 2000a). To explain how it allocated the conservation burden, NMFS and the other federal agencies involved presented a conceptual recovery plan (NMFS 2000b) describing the necessary assumptions about continued harvest restrictions into the future if the sum of impacts on listed fish was to avoid jeopardy. This opinion was invalidated by a district court finding that the agency improperly relied on assumed future actions that were not "reasonably certain to occur" (National Wildlife Federation v. NMFS 2003), leaving in question the ability of the agencies to consider the "big picture" when section 7 biological opinions have implications for allocation of take.

Example 2: Considering Actions in Isolation

For many species it is the cumulative effect of many actions that have led to their imperilment and it is difficult for the Services in a section 7 consultation to make the case that a single small action, when added to the many other small actions, jeopardizes the species' continued existence. In the case of water withdrawals from the Columbia River, NMFS did issue a jeopardy opinion to the Corps of Engineers on the basis that Columbia River flows were already below species' needs in many years, the cumulative impact of withdrawals contributed to those low flows, and there was no mechanism in place to limit future withdrawals. Even though the withdrawal under consideration was very small compared to overall flows in the Columbia, NMFS concluded the proposed action would jeopardize Columbia River salmon and steelhead because of the cumulative effect of past and future withdrawals (NMFS 1998). This decision stirred considerable controversy in the Basin, leading Washington's Department of Ecology to appeal to the NRC, asking the NRC to review the science supporting flow levels in the Columbia. Although the question put to the panel was framed in terms of the incremental risk posed by a very small incremental degradation in flows, the panel resisted being drawn into answering the narrow question. In its preliminary findings, the panel appears to support the analysis that because flows currently are inadequate, even small increases in water withdrawals will increase risk (National Research Council 2004c).

Advancing the Role of Science

The agencies need to provide clear guidance regarding general standards for jeopardy and adverse modification. The U.S. Fish and Wildlife Service and National Marine Fisheries Service could also provide clearer guidance on individual species, for example on identifying critically low population levels, viable population levels, and allowable levels of take. Standards should allow for scientific information to be taken into account along with the policy considerations.

As with all sections of the act, a life-cycle framework for estimating the potential effects of an action on species status would appear to be the best way to adequately address the question posed in section 7. Whether that life-cycle framework is quantitative or qualitative is less important than adopting a life-cycle perspective. In general, because of the inherent scientific uncertainty in estimating the biological consequences of numerous, small-scale actions, section 7 consultations should be treated as experiments that are monitored and adjusted as needed over time (see box 10.1).

The Science Underlying Limitations on Private Actions

The Endangered Species Act prohibits any person from taking a member of a listed species (sec. (a)(1)(B); box 10.1). Take is defined broadly to include harm, and harm can include destruction of habitat to the extent it actually injures or kills individual animals. Science comes into play when a party seeks an exception to the take prohibition under section 10 (habitat conservation plans, or HCPs) or section 4(d). Regardless of the legal avenue, the standard is similar—the proposed take cannot result in jeopardy to the species' continued existence or the destruction or adverse modification of its habitat.

The Role of Science in Agency Practice

The U.S. Fish and Wildlife Service and National Marine Fisheries Service face the same challenges in permitting take that they face in consultations with federal agencies. However, consultations between federal agencies are relatively fluid and can be reinitiated when circumstances change or new information becomes available. Private parties, on the other hand, often seek a long-term commitment from the two agencies. In an effort to encourage more landowners to protect endangered species, the USFWS and NMFS adopted a series of policies offering assurances that agreements with the federal government would be lasting, for example through the "No Surprises" rule (USFWS and NMFS 1998) and safe harbor agreements (USFWS 1999f, 1999g, 2001, 2003h; Bean et al. 2001).

Advancing the Role of Science

The opportunities for improving the use of science under sections 10 or 4(d) are similar to those under section 7—that is, if the U.S. Fish and Wildlife Service and National Marine Fisheries Service encourage transparent evaluation of the cumulative effects of actions, in light of the overall effect of other actions throughout a species' life cycle, better decisions under these sections of the act should result.

Under sections 7 and 10 (and also under section 4(f), recovery planning, discussed below) three key ecological relationships must be established: (1) landscape-level processes that drive environmental factors imperiling a species, (2) relationships between critical environmental factors and species status, and (3) effects of actions that can directly or indirectly affect species status. To establish these relationships with certainty will require years of scientific study. Meanwhile, identifying data or information critical to such estimates will improve current decision making (e.g., Burgman 2005). Scientifically designed monitoring and adaptive management of habitat conservation plans is also desirable but currently absent from most (Kareiva et al. 1998).

The Science Underlying Recovery Planning

The Endangered Species Act requires the U.S. Fish and Wildlife Service and National Marine Fisheries Service to adopt recovery plans for listed species (table 10.1) but does not specify a time frame within which plans must be completed. A recovery plan is expected to describe the biological conditions necessary for recovery of the species, or the state under which the species can be delisted. Recovery plans do not have any regulatory effect, but they can be used to coordinate and guide the agencies' decision making in section 7 and 10 consultations or in issuing take permits across a species' range. The act has minimal requirements for recovery plans: they must specify objective, measurable criteria for delisting, specific actions that will achieve those objectives, and an estimate of the time and cost involved in completing the actions.

The Role of Science in Agency Practice

Science has a clear role in determining the objective, measurable criteria that will lead to delisting. It should also be used to identify factors limiting recovery and determine the biological consequences of site-specific management actions aimed at recovering the species.

The National Marine Fisheries Service provides a general recovery planning document that outlines principles for plan development and content (NMFS 1992). Subsequently, NMFS wrote a document providing additional guidance on specific technical issues concerning recovery planning for the twenty-six listed ESUs of Pacific salmon (McElhany et al. 2000; Ruckelshaus et al. 2002b). It addresses several fundamental questions, including (1) What was the historical population structure of an ESU? (2) What are the characteristics of a viable population for each of the historically independent populations in an ESU? (3) What are possible configurations (which might differ from historical conditions) of the spatial distribution, risk status, and diversity characteristics of populations across a viable ESU? and (4) What actions are needed for recovery of an ESU? Answers to questions 2 and 3 provide viability criteria for populations and ESUs, and analyses underlying question 4 allow for evaluation of alternative actions and their predicted effects on population and ESU status.

The U.S. Fish and Wildlife Service approaches recovery planning differently than the National Marine Fisheries Service. Rather than establishing species-based viability criteria and identifying which actions can achieve those criteria, the USFWS focuses technical analyses in recovery planning on threats to species viability and the actions needed to alleviate them. Most plans describe recovery criteria in qualitative rather than quantitative terms, although listed species whose recovery plans contained quantitative criteria were more likely to be improving (Gerber and Hatch 2002).

Because of the complexity of predicting cumulative effects of any recovery actions, the National Marine Fisheries Service is incorporating scenario planning into its estimates of the likely effects of habitat, hatchery, and harvest management actions on the population status of listed salmon (Ruckelshaus et al. 2002b). Land- and water-use scenarios are being elicited from watershed councils in addition to climate projections, providing greater confidence in the proposed recovery plan.

Advancing the Role of Science

The science underpinning recovery plans and their implementation needs improvement (Clark et al. 2002). Given the current state of knowledge, science is best used to evaluate the relative merits of alternative actions rather than to provide "the answer." Collaboration with policy and planning staff who will influence implementation of actions is important (Rinkevich and Leon 2000; Wondolleck and Yaffee 2000; Brick et al. 2001; Yaffee 2006). Given the uncertainty of recovery efforts, management actions should be treated as experiments that are monitored with vigilance (Boersma et al. 2001; Crouse et al. 2002).

The need for more basic natural history information for informing decisions under the ESA cannot be overstated. What constitutes a reproductively isolated group of individuals for a given species? In which habitats does a species occur throughout its life cycle, and what are its survival rates in alternative habitat types? What is the relative reproductive success of pairings between alternative life history types (table 10.1)?

Conservation scientists have called for greater attention to multispecies and ecosystem effects in recovery plans (USFWS and NMFS 1994b; Miller 1996). The potential importance of such community and ecosystem-level effects to species recovery is great, as illustrated by north Pacific whaling effects on sea otters in Alaska (Springer et al. 2003), ecological functions provided by grizzly bears (Pyare and Berger 2003), and predation by Caspian terns (*Sterna caspia*) on juvenile salmon in the Columbia River (Roby et al. 2003). How to incorporate community- or ecosystem-level effects in a recovery plan is not clear, and Clark et al. (2002) caution that multispecies plans may in fact reduce the focus on individual species to the detriment of their conservation status.

Finally, clearer agency guidance on what constitutes "acceptable" risk would improve recovery planning, as would clearer explanation of how uncertainty in biological conclusions is accounted for in decisions and whether there are differences between jeopardy and recovery standards.

How Can Scientists Improve ESA implementation?

The contributions of academic and agency science to ESA implementation have been unevenly distributed among topical areas. Quantitative analyses to identify units for conservation and to estimate species viability (or, conversely, risk of extinction) have received the lion's share of attention in the scientific literature (fig. 10.1). These methods are not without controversy but are relatively well tested and many of their limitations have been discussed (Waples, this volume; Boyce 1992; Akçakaya et al. 1999; Coulson et al. 2001; Brook et al. 2000, 2002; Ellner and Fieburg 2003). Unfortunately, due to a lack of data, such quantitative approaches are useful for only a small fraction of rare, threatened, or endangered species.

The science of characterizing degrees of imperilment using qualitative approaches also has improved since 1973 (e.g., IUCN 1994; Akçakaya et al. 2000; NatureServe 2003), and greater attention to these methods would be helpful in ESA decisions for a majority of the species considered (Keith et al. 2004; McCarthy et al. 2004).

Analytical methods to address the remaining questions asked in the ESA implementation process have barely emerged in the scientific literature (fig. 10.1). In particular, the science underlying identification of the effects of actions on species status lags far behind. Such analyses are needed to address questions under sections 7 and 10 (i.e., do these actions significantly reduce the species' like-

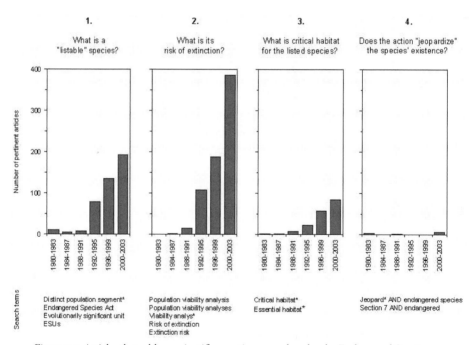

Figure 10.1. Articles that address scientific questions posed under the Endangered Species act, published between 1980 and 2003 and appearing in the ISL Web of Science's Science Citation Index Expanded Database. Search terms pertaining to each science question are listed below each panel.

lihood of survival and recovery?), section 4(b) (i.e., what habitat quantities and qualities are necessary for the survival and recovery of the species?), and section 4(f) (i.e., what actions are sufficient to achieve species viability criteria?). The needed research is challenging, time consuming, and difficult to generalize across species and locations. Especially lacking are empirical or analytical studies of the effects of specific actions on particular life stages and population dynamics.

Communication between scientists and decision makers is critical. Simple in concept, interaction between the groups is complicated in practice by the different worlds they inhabit—scientists can say "I don't know" and acknowledge that some scientific questions require years to answer, while decision makers must act within the limited time frames mandated by the Endangered Species Act, often on the basis of incomplete information. This can lead to frustration on both sides. We believe that the effort to communicate is well worth the trials involved (Ruckelshaus et al. 2002b). Previous studies have highlighted the need for help from conservation scientists that allows decision makers to more effectively link basic biology or ecology to management decisions (Floyd 2001; Clark et al. 2002). Approaches such as those developed under decision theory (Clemen 1996; Burgman 2005) and multicriteria mapping (Arrow and Raynaud 1986; Bana e Costa 1990) are potentially useful, but we found no examples applying these tools in decision making under the Endangered Species Act.

Science can have a significant impact on decisions made under the ESA as long as it isn't relied upon to be the sole arbiter in decisions (Doremus 1997; see Yaffee 2006). Scientists need to clearly explain to decision makers how science can (and cannot) inform their choices. Scientists and decision makers should be willing to participate in public forums where data, analytical approaches, and assumptions can be openly discussed. It is a rare manager of endangered species who will communicate through forums to which scientists are accustomed, such as the published literature (e.g., Rosenberg 2002). If scientists are free to interact with policy- and decision makers in processes designed to encourage open exchange, the result will be a clearer understanding of the need for an appropriate role of science in solving species protection challenges.

It is critical that discussions between scientists and policy makers and those involving the public clearly state the scientific basis for a result and any additional policy determinations brought to bear in making a decision under the act. To improve scientific credibility and agency decision making, scientists and decision makers must clearly distinguish between facts and assumptions and how each drives the results. If they fail to do so, laypersons will challenge the facts, rather than question the assumptions.

Because the act poses biological questions that almost always must be answered with imperfect information, scientists should encourage implementation of alternative actions as experiments. Furthermore, carefully estimating what we can learn from experiments before launching into controversial sets of actions is well worth the effort (e.g., Paulsen and Hinrichsen 2002), as is carefully monitoring the results. In the end, to enhance protection of species under the Endangered Species Act, biologists must get involved. Such involvement is not without potential costs (e.g., Halpern and Wilson 2003), but conducting sound research is not enough to protect a species if the results from a beautiful biological study sit in a journal, unread.

We thank Krista Bartz for conducting the analyses for and producing figure 10.1. Michael Bean, Frank Davis, Mike Ford, Dale Goble, Jeff Hard, Linda Jones, Jim Lecky, Marta Nammack, Mark Plummer, Mike Sissenwine, Russ Strach, John Stein, and Usha Varanasi provided helpful comments on this chapter and greatly improved its message.

I I Distinct Population Segments

Robin S. Waples

In reflecting on how the U.S. Endangered Species Act (ESA) has dealt with bio-diversity issues over the past thirty years, it is instructive to review the collection of fifty-seven papers in the 1988 volume by Wilson entitled *Biodiversity* (1988b). Anchored in time midway between enactment of the ESA in 1973 and the present (2006 and counting), Wilson's volume provides a snapshot of the issues related to biodiversity that occupied conservation biologists during the first half of these three decades. The vast majority (over 80 percent) dealt with higher levels of biological organization (species or ecosystems), while only two (less than 4 percent) dealt exclusively with diversity at the population level. In sharp contrast, the last decade and a half has seen an explosive interest in conservation of intraspecific diversity (Rojas 1992; Nielsen 1995; Hughes et al. 1997; Ceballos and Ehrlich 2002). A harbinger of this interest appeared in Wilson's *Biodiversity* volume in the paper by Ehrlich (1988), who argued that the loss of populations within species was at least as important a problem as the loss of entire species. Much of the recent interest in intraspecific diversity has focused on the concept of *evolutionarily significant units* (ESUs; Ryder 1986), and a variety of approaches to defining ESUs have been proposed (Waples 1991; Dizon et al. 1992; Vogler and DeSalle 1994; Moritz 1994; Bowen 1998; Crandall et al. 2000).

This chapter considers how these ESA approaches might compare if each were applied to a common conservation problem—how to define conservation units of Pacific salmon (*Oncorhynchus* spp.) from northwestern North America. These species have already been the subject of a large-scale application of biological principles to a real-world problem in applied conservation biology—identifying units that can be considered "species" under the Endangered Species Act. This body of work, based on the ESU framework developed by Waples (1991, 1995), provides a context for evaluating how different the outcomes might be if any of the other most popular ESU approaches were applied to Pacific salmon (see Ford 2004 for a brief example of this type of analysis for one species). Results of this exercise provide insights that may be relevant to conservation efforts for a wide range of species, both within and outside the aegis of the Endangered Species Act. A general discussion of the strengths and weaknesses of the various ESU approaches can be found elsewhere (Fraser and Bernatchez 2001).

Background on Pacific Salmon

The term "Pacific salmon" is used here to include seven North American anadromous salmonids in the genus *Oncorhynchus*. The five "traditional" species of Pacific salmon—pink (*O. gorbuscha*), chum (*O. keta*), coho (*O. kisutch*), sockeye (*O. nerka*), and chinook (*O. tshawytscha*)—all die after spawning; in contrast, rainbow trout (*O. mykiss*; the anadromous form is known as steelhead) and cutthroat trout (*O. clarki*) can spawn more than once. *O. mykiss, O. clarki,* and other western trout species were formerly considered to be members of the genus *Salmo*, which includes Atlantic salmon and brown trout.

Biology

Pacific salmon have a complex life history that involves spawning and rearing in freshwater streams or lakes and migration (as smolts) to the ocean for growth and maturation in the more productive marine environment. Migratory pathways differ but may include thousands of kilometers in the ocean as well as up to 3,000 kilometers upstream in freshwater. Age at *smoltification* and maturity, timing of juvenile *outmigration*, season of adult entry into freshwater (referred to as *run timing*), and other life history traits vary among species and among populations within species (Groot and Margolis 1991; Waples et al. 2001). Pacific salmon are justifiably renowned for their ability to home accurately to their natal stream. Opportunities for substantial reproductive isolation, together with environmental differences among habitats and a complex life history that requires precise execution of a long sequence of events, have led to a high degree of local adaptation (Ricker 1972; Taylor 1991). Perhaps the best general demonstration of the importance of local adaptation for Pacific salmon is the failure of the vast majority of stock transfer attempts within the historic range of the species to result in new populations (Withler 1982; Wood 1995). Thus, in general Pacific salmon populations are not exchangeable, at least on human time frames.

In spite of the strong homing tendency, some level of natural straying does occur in Pacific salmon, generally into nearby populations (Quinn 1993). Pacific salmon tend to show an isolation by distance pattern of genetic differentiation, provided that distance is measured via a stream network and not as the crow flies. Sharper genetic discontinuities are associated with some geographic features or historic lineages. Pacific salmon populations are linked in a hierarchical metapopulation network, with interactions between the various hierarchical levels occurring on different temporal scales. Thus, larger geographic/population units may be linked by significant gene flow only on evolutionary time scales.

Evolutionarily Significant Units and the Endangered Species Act

When the first petitions for ESA listing of Pacific Northwest salmon were filed in 1990, they invoked the provision in the act (sec. 3(15)) that allows listing not only of taxonomic species and subspecies, but also *distinct population segments* (DPSs) of vertebrates such as salmon. At that time, neither agency responsible for implementing the ESA (the U.S. Fish and Wildlife Service [USFWS] and the National Marine Fisheries Service [NMFS]) had formal guidance for how to interpret the DPS provision in the act. To address this need, Waples (1991) developed a framework stipulating that a salmon population (or group of salmon populations) would be considered a DPS if it represents an evolutionarily significant unit of the taxonomic species. In this framework, a population unit must satisfy two criteria to be considered an ESU: (1) reproductive isolation, and (2) evolutionary significance. Isolation need not be absolute; it must only be strong enough to allow evolutionarily important differences to accrue in different units. The "significance" criterion is met if the population unit contributes substantially to ecological/genetic diversity of the species as a whole—that is, to its evolutionary legacy. Waples (1995, 9) defined the evolutionary legacy as "genetic variability that is the product of past evolutionary events and that represents the reservoir upon which future evolutionary potential [of the species] depends."

The National Marine Fisheries Service adopted Waples's ESU approach for salmon as a formal policy in 1991 (NMFS 1991). After addressing the initial petitions, NMFS proactively initiated a series of comprehensive status reviews (1994) and used the policy framework to identify ESUs in all seven species of Pacific salmon from Washington, Idaho, Oregon, California, and parts of southern British Columbia (Weitkamp et al. 1995; Hard et al. 1996; Busby et al. 1996; Gustafson et al. 1997; Johnson et al. 1997, 1999; Myers et al. 1998). Reviewing a broad geographic range provided a context for interpreting local patterns of variation, and applying the same approach across seven species, thus providing opportunities to learn from congruent patterns of relationships as well as from species-specific ones. Abundant molecular genetic data are available for Pacific salmon, and these data, together with information from tagging studies and inferences about natural barriers, were the primary factors used to assess reproductive isolation. Traits that are evolutionarily significant must have a genetic basis and be adaptive, or potentially adaptive, so life history variation was carefully evaluated for the second ESU criterion. However, since most life history traits can be affected by environmental as well as genetic factors, ecological features of the habitat (as a proxy for different selective regimes) were also considered important.

Figures 11.1 to 11.3 illustrate how these three types of information have been used in ESU determinations for salmon. Ecological data were used to identify twelve major ecological-geographic provinces within the study area (fig. 11.1). Although some diversity occurs within provinces, differences among provinces in environmental conditions (and hence local selective pressures) are much more substantial. Ecological features had a strong influence on ESU determinations, particularly when changes in life history or genetic traits were

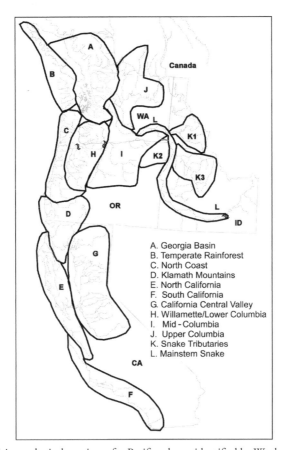

A. Georgia Basin
B. Temperate Rainforest
C. North Coast
D. Klamath Mountains
E. North California
F. South California
G. California Central Valley
H. Willamette/Lower Columbia
I. Mid - Columbia
J. Upper Columbia
K. Snake Tributaries
L. Mainstem Snake

Figure 11.1. Major ecological provinces for Pacific salmon identified by Waples et al. (2001).

congruent with the ecological boundaries (thus providing, respectively, corroboration of evolutionary significance or independent evidence for strong reproductive isolation).

In coho salmon, inferences about ocean ecology are possible based on a two-decade time series of adult size (fig. 11.2). Two patterns are apparent among geographic regions, indicating either a genetically based population difference or substantial environmental differences that can be expected to exert strong selective pressures for local adaptations: (1) Puget Sound populations, but not those from other areas, showed a 50 percent decline in adult size over two decades; and (2) coastal Oregon populations all showed a sharp decrease in adult size in 1983, presumably reflecting the unusually strong El Niño event in 1982.

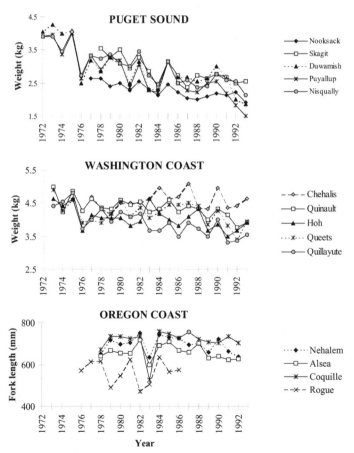

Figure 11.2. Temporal variation in adult size (weight measured in in-river fisheries or length of natural spawners) of coho salmon from populations in Puget Sound and the Oregon and Washington coasts. Source: Weitkamp et al. (1997).

Populations from the Washington coast showed no decline in size during this period, while those in Puget Sound showed a more modest decrease in 1984, a year later. These results indicate substantial variation in the ocean ecology of coho salmon, and this information was important in demonstrating that populations from the three areas met the second criterion to be considered separate ESUs.

Figure 11.3, which depicts genetic relationships among four lineages of chinook salmon from the Columbia River basin, demonstrates how genetic, life history, and geographic information can be integrated into a single analysis.

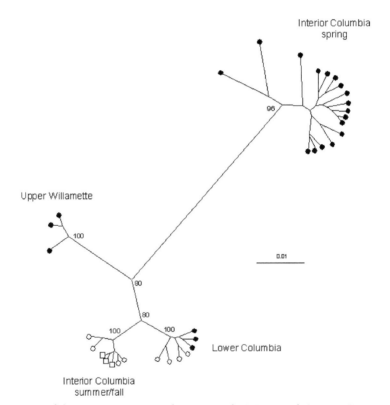

Figure 11.3. Life history variation mapped onto a tree depicting population genetic structure of Columbia River chinook salmon, based on pairwise genetic distances (Cavalli-Sforza and Edwards [1967] chord distance) among populations. Each population is represented by a symbol indicating the peak run timing (time of entry of adults into fresh water on their spawning migration): solid circle = spring; open square = summer; open circle = fall. Support for the four major genetic lineages (two from the interior Columbia River basin, east of the Cascades, and two from west of the Cascades) is indicated by numbers at nodes (percentage of one thousand bootstrap replicates having the identical tree topology). Modified from Waples et al. (2004).

The coherent genetic-geographic groups provide evidence for strong reproductive isolation—the first ESU criterion. Two clusters of populations are restricted to the interior Columbia Basin (east of the Cascades; Provinces I–L in fig. 11.1), and the other two (Lower Columbia and Willamette) are found only west of the Cascades. The four lineages are all in separate ESUs, and the two interior lineages have been further subdivided into ESUs based on geographic isolation and life history and ecological differences among the provinces. In the interior Columbia, all spring-run populations occur in a genetic lineage that is very divergent from all summer and fall-run populations, but spring- and fall-run populations in the lower Columbia River share a common genetic lineage. In the lower Columbia, the run-timing differences thus do not reflect ancient divergence and were considered to represent diversity among populations within a single ESU—consistent with the approach taken with traits showing evidence for parallel evolution (see discussion below).

A total of fifty-eight ESUs/DPSs have been identified in the seven Pacific salmon species (table 11.1), with the number of ESUs per species ranging from two to seventeen. About half of the salmon ESUs are listed as threatened or endangered "species" under the Endangered Species Act (see http://www.nwr.noaa .gov for a current tabulation). Some of the differences among species in number of ESUs are the result of biological differences in the degree of population differentiation and some are explained by geographic distribution (e.g., pink and chum salmon are primarily northern species with relatively few populations in the study area and therefore are represented by fewer ESUs). If these ESU

TABLE 11.1 Number of evolutionarily significant units and major components of diversity in each species of Pacific salmon

| Species | *Number of major diversity groups* | | | | |
	Ecology	*Life history*	*Genetics*	*Total*	*ESUs*
Pink	2	1	2	5	2
Chum	4	1	2	7	4
Sockeye	4	6	9	19	7
Coho	6	1	2	9	7
Chinook	11	7	10	28	17
Steelhead	11	7	7	25	15
Cutthroat	6	2	3	11	6
Total:	44	25	35	104	58

Sources: Major diversity groups for ecology, life history, and genetics were defined by Waples et al. (2001).

designations have successfully accomplished their intent, they represent population units that follow essentially independent evolutionary trajectories over time frames of evolutionary relevance (hundreds or thousands of years). Most salmon ESUs include populations with diverse genetic, ecological, and life history traits, but in general the differences among populations within ESUs are substantially less than differences among ESUs.

Nonsalmonid Distinct Population Segments

Beginning in the 1970s, distinct population segments of vertebrates have been defined under the Endangered Species Act using a wide variety of criteria. Most of these DPS determinations were made by the U.S. Fish and Wildlife Service for terrestrial species such as grizzly bears, bald eagles, and alligators. A desire for guidelines that would produce more consistent and predictable results motivated the effort to develop a joint USFWS-NMFS policy on interpreting the DPS language in the act, but it was not until 1996 that such a policy was actually finalized (USFWS and NMFS 1996e). The joint policy is used to identify distinct population segments of vertebrate species other than salmon, while the National Marine Fisheries Service continues to use the more detailed and specific ESU policy for Pacific salmon. Although the joint policy does not use the term *ESU*, it is also based on two criteria—discreteness and significance—that closely parallel those in the salmon ESU policy. Since 1996, the two agencies have used the joint policy to make DPS determinations for a number of nonsalmonid species, including the gray wolf (USFWS 2003b), Sierra Nevada bighorn sheep (USFWS 1999b), cactus ferruginous pygmy-owl (USFWS 1997a), barndoor skate (NMFS 2002a), white marlin (NMFS 2002b), and Puget Sound killer whale (NMFS 2005b).

Alternative ESU Definitions and Application to Pacific Salmon

Several other frameworks for defining ESUs have been suggested. These frameworks differ with respect to their underlying philosophy as well as the relative importance they place on different measures of population distinctiveness.

Phylogeography

Dizon et al. (1992) proposed an approach to defining conservation units based on principles of *phylogeography* (concordance of genetic lineages with geography) developed by Avise (1989). Dizon et al.'s framework is designed to handle pairwise comparisons of populations or population units, and their examples are drawn primarily from cetaceans. Population units are compared along two axes: adaptive divergence and reproductive isolation. The authors recognized that, in most cases, practical applications would require use of proxies. They considered distributional data the most suitable proxy for the isolation axis, whereas population response (demographic and behavioral data), phenotype (primarily morphological data), and genotypic data can be useful proxies for adaptation. Each comparison falls into one of four quadrants defined by scores on the two axes: category 1—high scores on both axes; category 2—high on adaptation, low on isolation; category 3—high on isolation, low on adaptation; category 4—low scores on both axes. Dizon et al. did not identify fixed cutoffs between high and low scores on each axis but did provide rough guidelines. Strong reproductive isolation is indicated by physical barriers to dispersal and evidence that the two population units do not intermingle, while mitochondrial DNA (mtDNA) sequence differences greater than 1 percent suggest likely adaptive differences. Firm cutoffs for defining ESUs were not proposed; instead, evidence for stock distinctiveness and evolutionary significance increases as one moves from category 4 to category 1.

COMPARISON WITH OTHER APPROACHES
Dizon et al.'s two axes are roughly comparable to Waples's two ESU criteria (reproductive isolation and contribution to evolutionary legacy), but the proxies are used a bit differently. Dizon et al. use molecular genetic data to make inferences about adaptive divergence, whereas Waples's framework places more emphasis on life history and ecology as proxies for adaptation and uses genetic data primarily as an indication of the strength of reproductive isolation.

APPLICATION TO SALMON
Salmon spawn in discrete freshwater areas that might be judged to meet Dizon et al.'s geographic isolation criterion, but some level of straying occurs, so nearby populations are generally not completely isolated. Furthermore, in the migration corridor and especially in the ocean, fish from many populations commingle over large geographic areas. It seems likely that pairwise comparisons of populations from distant geographic areas would meet the Dizon et al. criteria for a high score on the isolation axis, but this would not be true for comparisons involving populations in closer geographic proximity.

Scoring the adaptation axis would also present challenges. Many salmon populations show behavioral or phenotypic differences on the scale of those described in the appendix of Dizon et al. as evidence for genetic discontinuities. On the other hand, very few comparisons of salmon populations would meet the only quantitative criterion for this axis: greater than 1 percent sequence divergence at mtDNA. If phenotypic/behavioral data were weighted most heavily, most population comparisons would yield high scores on the adaptation axis (hence categories 1 or 2), and a large fraction of existing salmon populations might be considered distinct population segments. Conversely, if mtDNA data were weighted most heavily, most comparisons would yield low adaptive scores (hence category 3 or 4), and the distinct population segments would likely be restricted to the seven named species (table 11.2).

One result seems clear: some salmon population groups would fall into category 2 (strong adaptive differences but little geographic separation), which Dizon et al. and Avise (1989) considered to be a rare combination for most

TABLE 11.2 Application of alternative approaches to defining conservation units of Pacific salmon under the Endangered Species Act

Approach	Number of salmon DPSs[a]	Typical number of populations per DPS
Waples 1991 (ESU = DPS)	58	20–30[b]
Dizon et al. 1992		
If mtDNA heavily weighted	~10	hundreds
If demography/phenotype heavily weighted	~1,000	one
Vogler and DeSalle 1994	7	hundreds
Moritz 1994		
If ESU = DPS	7	hundreds
If MU = DPS	~1,000	one
Bowen 1998		
Using criterion 1 (vicariance) = DPS	a few	a few
Using criteria 2/3 (behavior/ecology) = DPS	~1,000	one
Using criterion 4 (polytypic) = DPS	7?	hundreds?
Using criterion 5 (chromosomal) = DPS	0?	
Crandall et al. 2000		
If only case 1 or 2 = DPS	~10	hundreds
If "distinct population" = DPS	~1,000	one

Note: Results for Waples' method are empirical data current through 2003; estimates for the other methods are best guesses based on likely application of published criteria. A DPS (distinct population segment) is considered a "species" under the ESA. In this analysis, a "population" is defined as described in McElhany et al. (2000) and is roughly equivalent to a "stock." The geographic area considered is Washington, Oregon, Idaho, California, and parts of southern British Columbia, and the seven species are listed in table 11.1.

[a]Gustafson et al. (unpublished data) have identified approximately one thousand separate populations of Pacific salmon in the geographic area under consideration here.

[b]For examples of population identification within salmon ESUs, see http://www.nwfsc.noaa.gov/trt/trtnews.htm.

species. Category 2 would apply to odd- and even-year pink salmon, which often spawn in the same stream in alternative years but are completely isolated reproductively to the extent that they exhibit outbreeding depression when artificially crossed (Aspinwall 1974; Gharrett and Smoker 1991), and to stream- and ocean-type chinook salmon, which can spawn in nearly adjacent areas in the interior Columbia River basin but are separated by large genetic and life history differences (Utter et al. 1995; Waples et al. 2004).

Monophyly of mtDNA

Moritz (1994) proposed what has become one of the most commonly used frameworks for identifying evolutionarily significant units. His approach is simple: ESUs are population groups that exhibit reciprocal monophyly in mtDNA along with substantial frequency differences in nuclear DNA. This criterion in essence requires that all members of one group carry mtDNA haplotypes that are not found in any individual from outside the group (and vice versa). Because Moritz intended his ESUs to complement (rather than replace) traditional taxonomy, formally recognized species are automatically considered ESUs and do not have to meet the reciprocal monophyly criterion. Moritz recognized that his approach would not encompass all units that might be legitimate focus for conservation efforts, so he also proposed recognition of *management units* (MUs), which are populations that do not show reciprocal monophyly for mtDNA but which have "significant divergence of allele frequencies." Management units represent functionally independent populations, are logical units for population monitoring and demographic study, and, ideally, would be managed in a way that promotes conservation of more inclusive ESUs.

COMPARISON WITH OTHER APPROACHES
Moritz's approach differs considerably from the previous two by focusing exclusively on molecular genetic data, primarily mtDNA. This focus was intentional, as Moritz argued that ancient lineages (identified by molecular genetics) are irreplaceable, whereas adaptive differences are more ephemeral on evolutionary time scales and can be regenerated more easily.

APPLICATION TO SALMON
Use of Moritz's criterion to define ESUs of Pacific salmon would be straightforward—no intraspecific population groups identified to date meet the reciprocal monophyly criterion, so no ESUs would be identified within any of the seven taxonomic species. Conversely, most populations or stocks of Pacific salmon would meet Moritz's criteria to be considered MUs, as statistically significant

allele frequency differences are routinely found even between nearby spawning aggregations (e.g., Teel et al. 2000). Therefore, application of Moritz's approach would either lead to recognition of no salmon DPSs other than the taxonomic species (if his ESU = DPS), or many more than are currently identified (if his MU = DPS) (table 11.2).

Phylogenetic Species Concept

In the view of Vogler and DeSalle (1994), tokogenetic lineages (ones that might still be exchanging genes) are not suitable for consideration as separate conservation units; that should be reserved for genetically isolated (phylogenetic) lineages. Accordingly, they proposed that ESUs be defined based on principles of the *phylogenetic species concept* (PSC; Nelson and Platnick 1981; Cracraft 1983). Although several variations of the PSC have been proposed, all are based on the premise that species are distinct entities that are diagnosable based on one or more characters—that is, every individual in taxon A shares one or more characters not found in any individual in taxon B, and vice versa. Vogler and DeSalle proposed that the term ESU be restricted to entities that are completely diagnosable based on one or more characters (e.g., genotypic, phenotypic, behavioral) believed to have a genetic basis.

COMPARISON WITH OTHER APPROACHES
In its focus on diagnosability, Vogler and DeSalle's approach is similar to Moritz's, except that it would recognize ESUs based on any heritable character, not just mtDNA. In theory, many of the characters considered in evaluating salmon ESUs (e.g., morphological or life history traits) could also form the basis of ESU determinations under Vogler and DeSalle's framework.

APPLICATION TO SALMON
Application of the Vogler and DeSalle approach to salmon would yield results similar to those of Moritz's (table 11.2). Although many salmon populations differ in mean values of eligible traits, few if any meet the diagnosability criterion when species-wide ranges of these traits are considered. For example, run-timing diversity is extensive in most salmon species, including chinook salmon (Healey 1991; Myers et al. 1998). Within any particular population, individuals return to spawn over a period of perhaps four weeks to four months (fig. 11.4). Although many pairs of populations have nonoverlapping distributions of run timing (e.g., Hoko and Willamette; Pistol and Nooksack), collectively North American chinook salmon can return to spawn during every month of the year. Thus, no population has a run timing that doesn't overlap with that of some other populations, and none would be completely diagnosable—not even

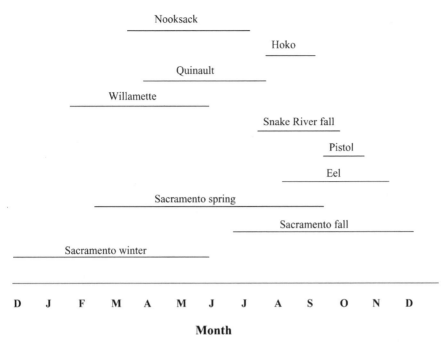

Figure 11.4. Variation in run timing in selected chinook salmon populations. Width of line indicates duration of run timing for each population. Some population pairs have nonoverlapping run timing, but this trait is not diagnostic for any single population when considering all other populations in the species. Source: Myers et al. (1998) and unpublished data.

the Sacramento River winter-run population, which is considered to have "unique" run timing.

Geminate Evolutionary Units

Bowen (1998) discussed the relevance for conservation of both evolutionary history and future evolutionary potential. He felt that Waples's (1995) definition of "evolutionary legacy" (cited above) captured the importance of both factors but that when put into practice the various ESU definitions had focused primarily on the former and had not effectively considered the latter. To address this shortcoming, Bowen proposed a new concept, that of the *geminate evolutionary unit* (or GEU). In Bowen's view, recognizing GEUs would afford conservation recognition and status to units that might play an important role in future speciation events.

Although identifying GEUs is challenging, Bowen suggested several criteria that might be useful: (1) recent isolation by vicariant events (e.g., marine species isolated by closing of the Isthmus of Panama near the end of the Pliocene); (2) behavioral barriers to gene flow, such as breeding at different times of the year; (3) ecological speciation—invasion of a new habitat or niche with novel selective pressures can lead to rapid divergence from the parent population; (4) polytypic species characterized by a high diversity in morphological, ecological, or genetic traits; and (5) morphological differentiation (especially that associated with chromosomal duplications or rearrangements) coupled with minimal divergence at molecular markers.

COMPARISON WITH OTHER APPROACHES

Bowen views the GEU as a complement to, rather than a substitution for, ESUs defined by other criteria. Although in principle the National Marine Fisheries Service ESU approach is both backward- and forward-looking, Bowen is correct that in application the primary focus has been on identifying components of diversity that are the result of past evolutionary events. Waples (1995) argued that this focus was appropriate because of the difficulty in identifying which particular populations will play a significant future role in evolution.

APPLICATION TO SALMON

To evaluate how his framework might apply to Pacific salmon, we can consider Bowen's criteria individually:

1. The most recent major vicariant event for Pacific salmon was the series of Pleistocene glaciations that fragmented populations, leading to separate glacial refugia (McPhail and Lindsey 1986). In the past ten thousand years, at least some of these vicariant separations have broken down. Some populations have been isolated much more recently by anthropogenic factors, such as dams or habitat degradation and fragmentation, but it is not clear whether Bowen would propose that such units be considered GEUs. A few peripheral populations (e.g., Snake River sockeye salmon, and steelhead in Southern California) may be undergoing a more natural process of isolation due to climate change and range constriction, and these would appear to be the best candidates to meet Bowen's first criterion.

2 and 3. Behavioral barriers to gene flow, such as differences in run or spawn timing, are common in salmon, so a large number of populations would meet this criterion. However, expression of these traits in salmon is known to be influenced by environmental as well as genetic factors, so the evolutionary significance of the differences cannot easily be evaluated without detailed information or experiments. Even if the differences weren't genetically based, however, they would appear to meet Bowen's third criterion (i.e., expansion into a new niche with different selective regimes).

4. All Pacific salmon species are polytypic, showing considerable variation in morphological, ecological, and genetic traits. A recent compilation (Waples et al. 2001) of major components of diversity (ecology, life history, genetics) in Pacific salmon found that the number of major diversity categories ranged from a low of five in pink salmon and seven in chum salmon to a high of twenty-five in steelhead and twenty-eight in chinook (table 11.1). Would all of these species, or only the most diverse, meet Bowen's criterion to be considered polytypic? If the criterion was met, would the whole species be considered a GEU, or would various subcomponents be separate GEUs?

5. Salmon are ancestrally tetraploid (Allendorf and Thorgaard 1984), so all extant populations share this feature. Some intraspecific variation in chromosome number does occur (e.g., Thorgaard 1983), but there is no evidence that variation in chromosome number leads to rapid reproductive isolation, as would be expected of units that meet this criterion.

In summary, a few peripheral populations in some species might meet Bowen's first criterion to be considered ESUs, but most are already considered ESUs. Still, identifying such populations as GEUs might call attention to population units that otherwise would be lumped in larger, more inclusive ESUs. A large number of populations would appear to meet Bowen's second and/or third criteria to be considered GEUs in their own right, whereas few if any would meet the fifth criterion (table 11.2),

Exchangeability

In reaction to Moritz (1994) and others who consider only molecular genetic markers for defining ESUs, Crandall et al. (2000) proposed a framework designed to place equal emphasis on adaptive diversity. They felt the ESU debate was too constrained by the either-or question, "Is it an ESU or not?" Instead, they outlined a framework involving eight separate cases, each reflecting different levels of evidence for genetic and ecological exchangeability. Exchangeability is assessed currently as well as historically.

Evaluation of ecological exchangeability focuses on traits believed to have a genetic basis. The ultimate criterion is whether a population can be moved to another geographic area and occupy the same ecological niche. In practice, various proxies are used for this criterion because direct tests of exchangeability are rare. Evidence for lack of genetic exchangeability can include occurrence of unique alleles, low estimates of gene flow, or genetic divergence concordant with geographic barriers. The proposed gene flow criterion (number of migrants per generation [Nm] less than one) corresponds to a measure of genetic divergence of approximately $F_{ST} = 0.2$. Crandall et al. (2000) did not specify a time scale for historical analyses, noting instead that the appropriate time frame would vary depending on the conservation issue and data at hand.

The eight cases are described by different patterns in a 2 × 2 matrix, with each cell represented by either a plus sign (+) (evidence to reject exchangeability) or a minus sign (–) (null hypothesis of exchangeability is not rejected). The left column represents genetic exchangeability and the right column ecological exchangeability; the top row represents current status and the bottom row historical conditions.

COMPARISON WITH OTHER APPROACHES

Crandall et al.'s (2000) framework is similar to that of Waples and Dizon et al. in that it focuses on both adaptive and isolation factors but provides more alternative scenarios. It also explicitly considers both historic and current characteristics of populations, which Moritz (1994) accomplishes to some extent by considering MUs as well as ESUs. Crandall et al. provide a separate management recommendation for each case.

APPLICATION TO SALMON

As most salmon populations do not appear to be ecologically exchangeable (direct test = transplants), they would have a plus (+) in the upper right sector. Conversely, F_{ST} values for most Pacific salmon are less than 0.1, suggesting Nm is greater than 2 (twice as high as Crandall et al.'s criterion). Most genetic differences among salmon populations are not diagnostic, and unique alleles, if present, usually occur at relatively low frequencies. Therefore, most salmon populations would receive a minus (–) for current genetic exchangeability. The stream- and ocean-type chinook salmon populations in the interior Columbia River basin (fig. 11.3) and many sockeye salmon populations from the Pacific Northwest (Winans et al. 1996) have F_{ST} values in the range 0.15–0.2, and these population groups might therefore score a plus (+) on the genetic exchangeability axis.

Lacking any clear guidance regarding a historical time frame, I will assume for the purposes of this example that "historical" represents conditions near the end of the Pleistocene, when the last episode of glaciation was ending but before salmon had expanded into the areas freed by receding glaciers (e.g., virtually all of British Columbia, Puget Sound, and parts of the upper Columbia River basin). In the bottom row, therefore, populations from areas subject to glaciation would have a minus (–) (or perhaps a blank) in both cells. Historic exchangeability of populations not directly affected by glaciation is largely speculative.

Taken together, the above considerations suggest that most salmon populations would fall into one of the following cases (current status/historical status):

+,+/+,+ (case 1; lack of exchangeability currently and historically). This might apply to the divergent chinook salmon lineages and at least some sockeye populations.

−,+/+,+ (case 3; recent loss of genetic distinctiveness). This might apply to ancient lineages that experienced some level of mixing following post-glacial dispersal. Possible examples include chinook salmon in British Columbia (Beacham et al. 2003; Waples et al. 2004) and inland and coastal subspecies of *O. mykiss.*

−,+/−,+ (case 5b; exchangeable genetically but not ecologically, both currently and historically). This is probably the most common situation for salmon populations.

−,+/−,− (case 6; recent evolution of ecological divergence). Evidence exists for repeated, parallel evolution (see discussion below) of some life history traits in Pacific salmon, perhaps over relatively short evolutionary time frames. However, it is difficult to distinguish differences that have evolved recently in isolation from differences that result from a long-term balance between divergence opposed by ongoing gene flow.

Like Dizon et al., Crandall et al. did not provide specific thresholds to be considered an ESU; in fact, they suggested that the term *evolutionarily significant unit* be abandoned, pointing out that various authors have used the term to represent each of the eight cases they identified. Crandall et al. (2000) recommend treating case 1 as long-separated species and cases 3, 5b, and 6 as distinct populations. However, there is no indication that they intended this latter term to equate to "distinct population segments" under the Endangered Species Act. It is reasonable to assume that any salmon populations falling in case 1 would be considered at least DPSs (if not full species) under the ESA, but these would be relatively few. On the other hand, if case 5 and 6 populations were also considered DPSs, there would be a large number of salmon DPSs (table 11.2).

Parallel Evolution

A phenomenon that complicates efforts to define conservation units is *parallel evolution*—the repeated evolution of the same trait (generally, a morphological or life history trait). Pacific salmon provide ample evidence for parallel evolution of life history traits. For example, in *Oncorhynchus nerka* repeated evolution of a freshwater resident form (kokanee) has occurred from the anadromous form (sockeye) (Taylor et al. 1996); in *O. tshawytscha* repeated evolution of run-timing differences has occurred among chinook salmon populations in coastal basins (Waples et al. 2004); and in *O. mykiss* parallel evolution has been documented for two life history traits: run-timing differences (summer-run populations presumably evolving from the more common winter-run; Busby et al. 1996) and anadromy/residency (the resident form [rainbow trout] apparently having evolved repeatedly from the anadromous [steelhead] form; Docker and Heath 2003). Parallel evolution of life history traits has also been described in a wide range of other taxa (e.g., Rundle et al. 2000; Briscoe 2001; Nosil et al. 2002), so how this topic is dealt with in defining conservation units is of general relevance.

In Pacific salmon, the different life history forms typically are more closely related to the opposite form in the same drainage than to the same form in another drainage. For example, summer steelhead from the South Fork Umpqua River are more closely related to nearby winter-run steelhead than to summer steelhead from other river basins. This general pattern of evolutionary relationships is shown schematically in figure 11.5, panel 1. Three different schemes for identifying conservation units are consistent with these evolutionary relationships (panels 2A–C), with the schemes differing in the degree to which populations are lumped within conservation units. It is not possible to determine which of these approaches is "best" based on biology alone. Based on congressional and legal guidance regarding the Endangered Species Act, life history variants believed to result from parallel evolution have generally been considered to be part of the same Pacific salmon ESUs (Busby et al. 1996; Myers et al. 1998). As most salmon ESUs contain populations from multiple river drainages, they typically follow the pattern shown in panel 2C.

It is not entirely clear how parallel evolution would be considered under the other ESU scenarios. Presumably the different life history types would be considered ESUs by Vogler and DeSalle or Moritz only if they achieved diagnosability or reciprocal monophyly. In Pacific salmon, the observed genetic differences among populations with different life history types are generally much less than this threshold (for example, Waples et al. [2004] found a mean F_{ST} of only about 0.01 for comparisons of spring and fall chinook in the same coastal basins). However, the separate forms presumably represent local adaptations and probably are not ecologically exchangeable, at least in human time frames. Therefore, application of the approaches of Dizon et al., Bowen, or Crandall et al. could lead to identification of conservation units that follow the pattern shown in figure 11.5, panel 2A. If Moritz's MU criteria were applied to salmon, the result would probably also follow this pattern. It is possible that one or more of the ESU approaches might "downgrade" the differences resulting from parallel evolution, resulting in a pattern that followed panel 2B in figure 11.5, but whether this would be the case is not easy to determine from published criteria.

ESUs and the Continuum of Biological Diversity

Except for Waples (1991, 1995), none of the ESU approaches considered above was designed specifically to conserve biological diversity under the legal frame-panel 1

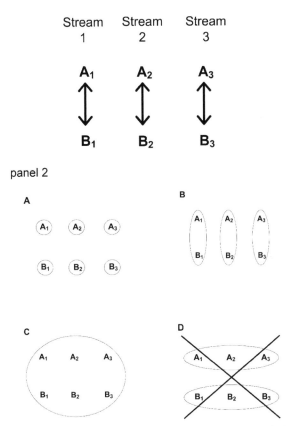

panel 2

Figure 11.5. Schematic diagram of parallel evolution of life history traits and ESU delineation. Pairs of populations occur in three different geographic areas (e.g., different river basins). Within each area, the same two life history types are found (A and B). In Pacific salmon, genetic data (e.g., Waples et al. 2004) indicate that, in general, A and B within an area are more closely related than either is to the same form in a different area (panel 1; genetic relationships indicated by arrows). Three different approaches to defining conservation units (ESUs) are consistent with this pattern of evolutionary relationships: each population a separate ESU (panel 2A); each river basin a separate ESU (panel 2B); or the entire system a single ESU (panel 2C). One approach that would not be consistent with the evolutionary relationships would be to create an artificial ESU uniting all the type-A populations and another uniting all the type-B populations (panel 2D).

work of the Endangered Species Act. In particular, none of the other approaches have attempted to define the ESA term "distinct population segment" in a biological framework. Therefore, when we ask the question, How many salmon DPSs would there be under an alternative framework?, the answer will of necessity be speculative.

Nevertheless, it is clear from the above analysis that application of several published ESU approaches would lead to widely divergent outcomes for Pacific salmon. The number of salmon DPSs identified would range from none or virtually none beyond the seven taxonomic species (Vogler and DeSalle; Moritz, assuming his ESU = DPS), to a few in some species (Crandall et al., assuming only case 1 or 2 = DPS; Dizon et al. if mtDNA is most heavily weighted as a proxy; Bowen under criterion 1) to very many (Moritz, assuming his MU = DPS; Dizon et al., assuming demographic and phenotypic data are heavily weighted; Crandall et al. if each of their "distinct populations" is considered to be a DPS; Bowen under criteria 2 or 3) (table 11.2). Thus, only for the Vogler and DeSalle approach is the outcome clear: as expected, application of the phylogenetic species concept would not be useful for recognizing diversity of Pacific salmon below the species level. For each of the other approaches, the number of conservation units recognized as "species" under the ESA could range from few or none to a large number, depending on how the criteria are interpreted. (Moritz [pers. comm., October 2003] has clarified that he did not intend that his MUs be equated with DPSs.)

One interesting result of this analysis is that it does not seem likely that any of the other approaches would result in ESUs/DPSs of approximately the same geographic scale as currently recognized salmon ESUs. Instead, the units would either be larger (perhaps only one for each of the seven taxonomic species) or much smaller (with a large fraction of local populations or stocks being recognized as separate DPSs) (table 11.2). That is, the other ESU approaches would appear to focus conservation attention at either of the two extremes in the continuum of biological diversity—the taxonomic species or the local population. Between these two extremes, however, there typically exist several additional levels of biological diversity in Pacific salmon—each of which has potential relevance for conservation. For example, it is possible to identify at least eight separate hierarchical levels in *O. mykiss* from the Oregon coast:

    1 Species (*O. mykiss*)
      2 Subspecies (*O. mykiss mykiss*) (coastal)
        3 ESU (Oregon coast)
          4 Gene Conservation Group (mid- and North Coast)
            5 Major River Basin (Umpqua River)
              6 Major tributary (South Fork Umpqua River)
                7a Life history form (resident)
                7b Life history form (anadromous)
                  8a Life history form (summer run)
                  8b Life history form (winter run)

Level 8 is generally considered a "population" or "stock," which is a natural unit for routine fishery management. The National Marine Fisheries Service has identified level 3 as a unit (Oregon coast ESU) that it believes is biologically meaningful and also consistent with the legislative and legal framework of the ESA. In contrast, application of other published approaches would appear to result in recognition of salmon DPSs at either extreme of this continuum of diversity (i.e., either levels 1–2 or 7–8).

The Oregon coast ESU covers a relatively large geographic area (coastal streams from Cape Blanco to the Columbia River—about 500 kilometers of coastline) and includes a substantial number of largely independent populations. Collectively, however, these populations share genetic, ecological, and life history traits that distinguish Oregon coast steelhead from those from other areas (Busby et al. 1996). The State of Oregon has made a systematic effort to identify major components of salmon diversity within Oregon (Kostow 1995) and recognizes three *gene conservation groups* of *O. mykiss* along the Oregon coast that are nested within the Oregon coast ESU. The State of Washington (Busack and Shaklee 1995) has also used biological criteria to define hierarchical levels of diversity within its salmon species, generally at smaller scales than ESUs.

How might these alternative ESU frameworks play out if applied to species other than salmon? Although it is beyond the scope of this chapter to consider such a question in any detail, some general observations can be made. Salmon have a natural proclivity for hierarchical population structure, fostered by the hierarchical design of stream networks and the complicated life cycle that lends itself to strong local adaptations. Still, many other species have complex population structures and more than one level of diversity below the taxonomic species, and if the analysis here is correct, patterns of diversity not at either extreme of the continuum might be overlooked in many of the commonly used approaches for defining ESUs.

Whether this is a desirable result is not a question that can be answered by science alone. The merits of any particular conservation approach can be evaluated properly only in the context of the goals one is trying to accomplish. Deciding where on the continuum of biological diversity to focus conservation efforts involves a trade-off between various societal goals. Defining DPSs and hence ESA species on a very fine scale (e.g., the level of a local population or stock) could provide legal protection for units that might otherwise receive little attention. This approach also could provide increased flexibility in recovery planning—for example, by allowing delisting of local populations that recover faster than others. On the other hand, it likely would lead to recognition of a very large number of ESA "species," with attendant increases in regulatory and administrative burdens for the agencies and the public alike. Some recovery options might be precluded if each subunit were required to be maintained in complete isolation of other subunits. If almost every biological population were a separate DPS/ESU, it would also be difficult for the U.S. Fish and Wildlife

Service and the National Marine Fisheries Service to determine how best to prioritize allocation of scarce resources for conservation. Finally, if DPSs were recognized on too fine a scale, there would be a risk of conferring ESA protection on units that would not persist in nature over evolutionary time frames—in which case the ESA would be attempting to preserve a rather ephemeral product of evolution.

Defining ESUs and DPSs to be more inclusive would alleviate many of these concerns and is arguably more consistent with the direction from the U.S. Senate that the two agencies use the ability to list vertebrate populations "sparingly" (96th congr., 1st sess., 1979, senate report 151). However, defining ESUs on too coarse a scale also has societal and biological costs. Under an extreme lumping scenario, distinctive populations might be overlooked and lost without triggering ESA protection. Flexibility would also be reduced, as the entire DPS must be listed or delisted as a unit. Larger and more inclusive DPSs would also be more likely to include a diverse and heterogeneous collection of local populations, which can greatly complicate extinction risk analysis and recovery planning. Defining conservation units on a large scale is most likely to yield successful results if other mechanisms exist to address diversity among the subunits.

Identifying conservation units is only the first step in a conservation program, and it might not even be necessary. Many feel that the ultimate goal should be the conservation of "normal" evolutionary processes (Rojas 1992; Bowen 1999; Crandall et al. 2000; Fraser and Bernatchez 2001; Moritz 2002; Naeem et al., this volume). According to this view, the focus on defining conservation units is somewhat unfortunate because it puts too much emphasis on identifying (and therefore conserving) specific types, when in reality evolution is a dynamic process, and population traits in evidence today might not even be adapted to current conditions, let alone be adaptive in the future (see Lomolino, this volume). Less consensus exists regarding how best to accomplish the goal of conserving evolutionary processes. The concept of ecosystem-based management has a certain cachet, because by conserving whole ecosystems one would by definition also be conserving many natural biological processes. Nevertheless, this concept remains poorly defined and few examples exist in which it has been applied to real-world conservation problems.

Moritz (2002) suggested that overall conservation goals can be achieved through attention to two major axes of diversity: long-term or vicariance (the focus of his 1994 paper) and adaptive divergence (emphasized in particular by Crandall et al. 2000). These two axes correspond closely to the two ESU criteria of Waples (1991, 1995) and the two axes of Dizon et al. (1992). According to Moritz, the vicariance axis is best considered as an index of representativeness (of unique evolutionary lineages), whereas the adaptation axis relates most directly to population fitness and persistence. In the view of Moritz (2002), a biologically sound conservation strategy would include a focus both on products of evolution (representation of divergent lineages, because these units cannot be replaced if lost) and evolutionary processes (which should allow the more ephemeral products of adaptive divergence to be regenerated naturally).

Since the legal framework of the Endangered Species Act is organized around protection of units that can be considered ESA "species," an emphasis on defining conservation units is unavoidable. Within this legal framework, it is still possible to make important contributions toward conserving evolutionary processes, as illustrated by experience with Pacific salmon. The overall approach to defining salmon ESUs follows Aldo Leopold's sage advice: unless you have a perfect understanding of how a complex system works, save all the pieces if you tinker with it (Leopold 1953). If most or all salmon ESUs are conserved (so the thinking goes), then adequate diversity will remain for the future evolutionary trajectory of the species to unfold largely unaffected by humans. These considerations have also informed ESA recovery planning for Pacific salmon, where regionally based technical teams are developing new methods to address the considerable genetic, ecological, and life history diversity that exists within most salmon ESUs (for example, see the Northwest Salmon Recovery Planning Web site at http://www.nwfsc.noaa.gov/trt/index.html) (Ruckelshaus and Darm, this volume). If recovery plans can be developed that conserve the essential fabric of this diversity, ample raw material should remain for the processes of evolution to act on in the future. This dual focus both on products and processes of evolution is consistent with the conservation strategy proposed by Moritz (2002).

ESU determinations for salmon were based on work by many people, especially Peggy Busby, Rick Gustafson, Jeff Hard, Orlay Johnson, Jim Myers, and Laurie Weitkamp. This chapter benefited from comments by Brian Bowen, Keith Crandall, Andy Dizon, Mart Gross, Craig Moritz, Mike Scott, and three anonymous reviewers on an earlier draft, and by help from Jean Cochrane and Marta Nammack. Kathleen Neely provided figure 11.1 and David Teel figure 11.3.

12   Hybrids and Policy

Susan M. Haig and Fred W. Allendorf

Hybridization (the interbreeding of individuals from genetically distinct populations, regardless of their taxonomic status) is the double-edged sword of conservation biology. On one hand, increased rates of hybridization because of human activities have led to the extinction of populations and species in plant and animal taxa throughout the world (Rhymer and Simberloff 1996; Allendorf et al. 2001). On the other, hybridization is an important and natural part of the evolutionary process. Thus, hybridization between isolated populations can be an important tool for recovery (Mansfield and Land 2002). However, it has been difficult to develop conservation policies that treat the problems caused by increasing anthropogenic hybridization and at the same time recognize the important evolutionary role of natural hybridization.

How the Endangered Species Act (ESA) should treat hybrids has been a topic of intense debate since its passage in 1973 (see box 12.1). The word "hybrid" does not occur in the definition of "species" in the ESA (sec. 3) nor are hybrids considered anywhere in the act. In fact, hybrids are not considered in endangered species legislation of any other nation (Haig, unpublished data) with the exception of the Biodiversity Act recently adopted by the Republic of South Africa (Republic of South Africa Act No. 8, 2004). In this chapter, we review the history of discussions related to listing hybrids under the Endangered Species Act, outline current legislation that may particularly address this issue, and explore new approaches to resolving this debate.

History of Hybrid Issues Related to the Endangered Species Act

A brief perspective on the terms and concepts related to hybrids may be useful prior to a discussion of policy (box 12.2 and fig. 12.1). The term "hybridize" has been used to mean very different types of matings, hence clarifying definitions is also critical for clear and informed consideration. Understanding and addressing conservation needs and management of hybrids has also become

---

BOX 12.1 Time line for events related to hybrid issues in the federal Endangered Species Act

1973	Passage of the Endangered Species Act: no mention of hybrids
1977	U.S. Department of the Interior defines "wildlife" to include hybrids in the Endangered Species Act
1977, 1983	U.S. Solicitor states that hybrids are not protected under the Endangered Species Act
Pre-1990	U.S. Fish and Wildlife Service discourages conservation efforts for hybrids because it felt doing so "might not help and could hinder recovery of endangered taxon"
1990	U.S. Fish and Wildlife Service states that "rigid standards should be revisited because the issue of hybrids is more properly a biological issue than a legal one"
1996	U.S. Fish and Wildlife Service and National Marine Fisheries Service propose an intercross policy for protection of hybrids under the Endangered Species Act
2000	U.S. Fish and Wildlife Service and National Marine Fisheries Service render policy on controlled propagation of captive populations
Present	Proposed intercross policy has not been approved or disapproved

---

more important as rates of hybridization increase due to increasing human encroachment on habitats and translocations of taxa (Allendorf et al. 2001).

Hybrid Policy

Four years after passage of the Endangered Species Act, hybrids became a controversial topic that has continued to this day (box 12.1). In May 1977, the U.S. Department of the Interior's Office of the Solicitor issued the statement that "because it defines 'fish or wildlife' to include any offspring without limitation, the act's plain meaning dictates coverage of hybrids of listed animal species. The legislative history buttresses this conclusion for animals and also makes clear its applicability to plants" (U.S. Department of the Interior 1977a). However, response from the U.S. Fish and Wildlife Service (USFWS 1977b) indicated that "since the Act was clearly passed to benefit endangered species, . . . it must have meant the offspring of two listed species and was not meant to protect a hybrid where that protection would in fact cause jeopardy to the continued existence of a species." The solicitor responded in August 1977 (U.S. Department of the Interior 1977c; reaffirmed in 1983; U.S. Department of the Interior 1983), stating that "Congress did not intend the Endangered Species

BOX 12.2 Definitions of hybrids and hybrid events

Admixture.	The production of new genetic combinations in hybrid populations through recombination.
Genetic mixing.	The loss of a formerly distinct population through hybridization.
Hybridization.	Interbreeding of individuals from genetically distinct populations, regardless of the taxonomic status of the populations.
Hybrid swarm.	A population of individuals that all are hybrids by varying numbers of generations of backcrossing with parental types and mating among hybrids.
Hybrid taxon.	An independently evolving, historically stable population or group of populations possessing a unique combination of heritable characteristics derived from two or more discrete parental taxa.
Hybrid zone.	An area of contact between two genetically distinct populations where hybridization occurs.
Intercross.	All crosses between individuals of different "species" as defined under the Endangered Species Act (i.e. taxonomic species, subspecies, and distinct population segments of vertebrates).
Introgression.	Gene flow between populations whose individuals hybridize.
Proportion of admixture.	The proportion of alleles in a hybrid swarm that come from each of the hybridizing taxa.
Pure population.	A population in which there has been no hybridization and therefore contains only individuals from the parental species.

Act of 1973 to cover hybrids of listed species" because he had learned that there was the potential for a listed species to be harmed by hybridization. Overall, the USFWS's early position was to "discourage conservation efforts for hybrids between taxonomic species or subspecies and their progeny because they do not help and could hinder recovery of endangered taxon." In 1990, the USFWS issued a statement that "rigid standards should be revisited because the issue of hybrids is more properly a biological issue than a legal one" (U.S. Department of the Interior 1990).

There was critical response from the scientific community regarding this approach to hybrids. In a 1991 paper, O'Brien and Mayr pointed out that invaluable biological diversity would be lost if the Endangered Species Act did not

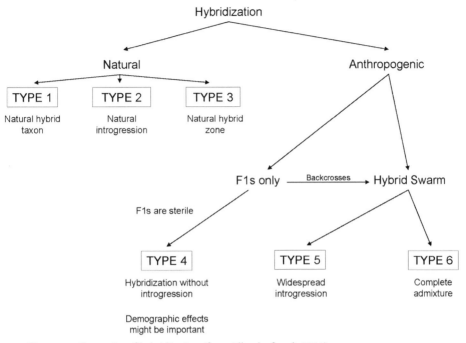

Figure 12.1. Categories of hybridization (from Allendorf et al. 2001).

protect some subspecies or populations that interbreed (e.g., Florida panther, *Puma concolor coryi*), or taxa derived from hybridization (e.g., the red wolf, *Canis rufus*). Further, Grant and Grant (1992) pointed out that few species would be protected by eliminating protection for any species interbreeding since so many plant and animal species interbreed to some extent.

Intercross Policy

In 1996, the U.S. Fish and Wildlife Service and the National Marine Fisheries Service (NMFS) drafted an intercross policy (USFWS and NMFS 1996f) that would have set guidelines for the possible protection of hybrids in response to the need for an updated policy. They used the word "intercross" instead of "hybrid" to try to avoid concerns that had accumulated with the term "hybrid." The policy would have included within the listing of a taxon

> "hybrid" individuals that more closely resemble a parent belonging to a listed species than they resemble individuals intermediate between their listed and unlisted parents. The Services propose to add to their joint regulations the terms "intercross" and "intercross progeny" and indicate

the inclusion of intercross individuals within the original listing action for the parent entity.

The proposed policy is intended to allow the Services to aid in the recovery of listed species by protecting and conserving intercross progeny, eliminating intercross progeny if their presence interferes with conservation efforts for a listed species, and fostering intercrossing when this would preserve remaining genetic material of a listed species. The proposed policy would only sanction these actions where recommended in an approved recovery plan, supported in an approved genetics management plan (which may or may not be part of an approved recovery plan), implemented in a scientifically controlled and approved manner, and undertaken to compensate for a loss of genetic viability in listed taxa that have been genetically isolated in the wild as a result of human activity. (USFWS and NMFS 1996f, 2)

Flexibility, adaptability, and guidelines in different situations were the key benefits of this policy. Thus, the two agencies could eliminate intercross progeny if their presence interfered with conservation efforts for a listed species as well as foster intercrossing where required for conservation. However, there was concern that the policy was worded in terms of individuals and not populations and that it did not address the issue of natural hybridization (Don Campton, USFWS, pers. comm.). This policy has never been formally adopted. However, it was also never formally withdrawn, and thus its adoption may be possible.

Controlled Propagation Policy

In 2000, the USFWS and NMFS adopted a new policy regarding controlled propagation of species listed under the Endangered Species Act (USFWS and NMFS 2000c). Overall, this policy provides clear authorization and latitude for cautiously tackling difficult situations related to genetic rescue. The policy specifically addresses the issue of hybrids in the following way:

Based on sound scientific principles to conserve genetic variation and species integrity. Intercrossing will not be considered for use in *controlled propagation* programs unless recommended in an approved recovery plan; supported in an approved genetic management plan (if information is available to develop such a plan, and which may or may not be part of an approved recovery plan); implemented in a scientifically *controlled* and approved manner; and undertaken to compensate for a loss of genetic viability in listed taxa that have been genetically isolated in the wild as a result of human activity. Use of intercross individuals for species conservation will require the approval of the FWS Director or that of the NMFS Assistant Administrator, in accordance with all applicable policies. (USFWS and NMFS 2000c, 56921)

This policy was principally initiated to protect aquatic organisms from disease when being transferred among captive facilities but was also to prevent, unless specifically necessary, situations such as that of captive propagation and release of the peregrine falcon (*Falco peregrinus*) in the 1970s and 1980s (Cade and Burnham 2003). When eastern peregrine falcons had declined to only a very few individuals, plans were implemented such that birds released from captivity were combinations of seven subspecies originating from the western United States, boreal Canada and Alaska, Aleutian and Queen Charlotte Islands, Scotland, Chile, Australia, and Spain. While these releases did represent a highly diverse gene pool and the birds were successful (Barclay and Cade 1983; Cade and Burnham 2003), it might not be the best approach in other situations.

Another example stems from a headwater population of topminnow (*Poeciliopsis monacha*) (Vrijenhoek 1996). The species had lost all detectable heterozygosity because of a population bottleneck caused by drought and was being outcompeted by a sympatric asexual hybrid taxon from the same genus. Experimental replacement of thirty females with females from a downstream population that had high heterozygosity restored the original heterozygosity and the competitive ability of the sexual population. Sadly, the same did not occur for the now extinct dusky seaside sparrow (*Ammodramus maritimus nigrescens*). This subspecies was down to its last few males and the U.S. Fish and Wildlife Service failed to support crossing of these males with individuals from other closely related subspecies, arguing pure dusky seaside sparrows could never be created (James 1980). Its extinction occurred shortly thereafter.

Similar issues must be sorted out for an upcoming decision on the fate of the Micronesian kingfisher from Guam (*Todiramphus cinnamomina cinnamomina*). These birds were extirpated from Guam as a result of the brown tree snake (*Boiga irregularis*) introduction in World War II (reviewed in Haig and Ballou 1995) and are now in captive-rearing facilities on the U.S. mainland and Guam. Captive breeding has not been as successful as hoped, and thus current considerations include crossbreeding the Guam birds with birds from the Micronesian island of Pohnpei (*T. c. reichenbachii*). These hybrids may be interspecific or intraspecific depending on genetic work underway (Haig, unpublished data), but in either case, they could be protected if approved under the controlled propagation policy.

Potential Solutions in Existing Legislation

There are a variety of legislative means by which hybrids can receive protection under the Endangered Species Act.

Listing Hybrid Species of Natural Origin

Currently, the U.S. Fish and Wildlife Service considers stable, self-sustaining species of *natural hybrid origin* eligible for full protection under the Endangered Species Act (A. Hecht, USFWS, pers. comm.). However, it can be difficult to distinguish between natural and anthropogenic hybridization. The alternative is either to not allow protection of natural hybrids or to protect anthropogenic hybrids that could contribute to extinction of parental species and waste limited resources available for conservation.

One example where hybrid taxa could be listed is the case of hybrids between blue-winged warblers (*Vermivora pinus*) and golden-winged warblers (*V. chrysoptera*). The two species cross and produce viable offspring (e.g., Brewster's or Lawrence's warblers; Gill 1980) however, the golden-winged warbler is declining throughout its range (Confer and Knapp 1992). Given that it is not possible to detect the genetic makeup of the hybrids, it is important to protect these closely related taxa lest we lose all genetic material from the golden-winged warbler. Similarly, the Pecos sunflower (*Helianthus paradoxus*) was listed as threatened only after greenhouse experiments and molecular analyses showed that it was a true species but with hybrid origin (USFWS 1999a). Conversely, recent evidence indicating that the endangered Lloyd's hedgehog cactus (*Echinocereus lloydii*) was a hybrid not evolving independently of its parental species resulted in a delisting (USFWS 1999d).

Similarity of Appearance

An infrequently used provision in the Endangered Species Act may be useful in resolving some situations regarding hybrids. Section 4(e), the "similarity of appearance" clause, can be used when two taxa are so similar that the listed taxon could face further decline or loss of viability without protection of the nonlisted taxon:

> The Secretary may, by regulation of commerce or taking, and to the extent he deems advisable, treat any species as an endangered species or threatened species even though it is not listed pursuant to section 4 of this Act if he finds that (A) such species so closely resembles in appearance, at the point in question, a species which has been listed pursuant to such section that enforcement personnel would have substantial difficulty in attempting to differentiate between the listed and unlisted species; (B) the effect of this substantial difficulty is an additional threat to an endangered or threatened species; and (C) such treatment of an unlisted species will substantially facilitate the enforcement and further the policy of this Act.

Thus, it is a device to prevent listed species from being taken or traded un-der the guise of similarly appearing unlisted species. It can be looked upon as a way of shifting the burden of proof from USFWS law enforcement agents hav-ing to prove that a particular individual is protected to a suspect having to prove that it is not.

The U.S. Fish and Wildlife Service has only used section 4(e) seven times (USFWS 1983c, 1987, 1990a, 1991b, 1992, 1996c, 1997b). The National Marine Fisheries Service has never used it (M. Nammack, NMFS, pers. comm.). However, when used, it is invoked in cases where the listed species closely resembled a nonlisted species, making the listed taxa more vulnerable to "take." For example, all *Puma concolor* are protected in Florida so that no one would kill a Florida panther and claim it had escaped from a roadside zoo where other *P. concolor* subspecies are held in captivity (USFWS 1991b). All desert tortoises (*Gopherus agassizii*) are protected in the Mojave desert to avoid people picking up individuals from the listed Mojave population and claiming they were from the nonlisted Arizona population (USFWS 1990a). And American alligators (*Alligator mississippiensis*) are now protected (USFWS 1987). Take is prohibited, except by state permit, so there is regulated trade. Additional exam-ples include the bog turtle (*Clemmys muhlenbergii*; USFWS 1997b), American black bear (*Ursus americanus*; USFWS 1992), and peregrine falcon (USFWS 1983c).

Implementing similarity of appearance protection under section 4(e) re-quires a formal rule-making procedure: listing in the *Federal Register*, public comment period, and final rule in the *Federal Register*. Similarity-of-appearance species are included on the list of threatened and endangered species as similarity-of-appearance-threatened or similarity-of-appearance-endangered. Under section 4(e), species are prohibited from intentional "take" as well as pro-tected by trade restrictions. They do not, however, receive protection under other sections of the act that address habitat protection.

Sections 4(e) may be an effective tool in many circumstances with hybrids. For example, six species or subspecies of western trout in the genus *On-corhynchus* are listed under the ESA. All of the listed taxa are threatened by hybridization with introduced rainbow trout (*O. mykiss*). Morphological iden-tification of these hybrids is extremely difficult and sometimes impossible (Al-lendorf et al. 2004). Protecting hybrids between the listed taxa and rainbow trout could be a helpful management tool under some circumstances.

A similar situation has recently arisen in the case of hybridization between the threatened Canada lynx (*Lynx canadensis*) and unlisted bobcats (*L. rufus*; Schwartz et al. 2004). Taxa can be difficult to identify in the field and because hunters use traps that are left unattended (e.g., snare traps), animals can be killed before they are identified. Thus trapping bobcats in areas where lynx and lynx-bobcat hybrids occur might result in unnecessary "take" of lynx. Therefore, implementation of section 4(e) for bobcats and the hybrids could provide a cushion for the lynx population to recover.

Finally, capturing hybrid trout in a similarity-of-appearance listing might be useful in some situations. This would be analogous to the similarity-of-appearance listing for all black bears in the range of the Louisiana subspecies.

Migratory Bird Treaty Act

An alternative to invoking the Endangered Species Act in hybrid cases involving birds is the Migratory Bird Treaty Act of 1918 (MBTA; Act of July 3, 1918), which, with a few exceptions, protects 99 percent of all North American bird species. The benefit of using the MBTA is that hybrids are included in the definition of species and are protected automatically and the ESA's extensive listing process can be bypassed. However, protection under the MBTA does not carry the stiff penalties exacted by the ESA. Thus, depending on the situation, the MBTA may be a more desirable route to pursue for prosecutors.

An example is the case of hybridization between northern spotted owls (*Strix occidentalis caurina*) and barred owls (*S. varia*) (Haig et al. 2004). Here, the issue was how to prosecute individuals who "take" hybrids when the hybrids can be difficult to differentiate in the field from ESA-listed northern spotted owls. Haig et al. suggested prosecuting under the Migratory Bird Treaty Act because they felt it was better to avoid going through the ESA listing process for similarity of appearance, especially when the number of violators would probably be minimal. And because the hybrids are deleterious to the recovery of spotted owls, there was no reason to afford them the special protection they would be given under section 4(e).

Convention on International Trade of Endangered Species of Wild Fauna and Flora

Parties (i.e., countries from around the world) to the Convention on International Trade of Endangered Species of Wild Fauna and Flora (CITES) have long struggled with the issue of hybrid protection in international trade. Overall, hybrids are considered protected under this agreement. However, there are important caveats regarding treatment of plants and animals (boxes 12.3 and 12.4). For animals, the concern is mostly that hybrids might prove detrimental to survival of the listed species. For example, trade and subsequent release of hybrid parrots (family: Psittacidae) and falcons (family: Falconidae) has been particu-

BOX 12.3 Treatment of animal hybrids by the Convention on International Trade in Endangered Species of Wild Fauna and Flora (CITES)

THE CONFERENCE OF THE PARTIES TO THE CONVENTION CONCERNED that trade in hybrids of species included in the Appendices should be controlled in order to support the controls on trade in the species included in Appendices I and II determined that:

a) Hybrids may be specifically included in the Appendices but only if they form distinct and stable populations in the wild;

b) Hybrid animals that have in their recent lineage one or more specimens of species included in Appendix I or II shall be subject to the provisions of the Convention just as if they were full species, even if the hybrid concerned is not specifically included in the Appendices;

c) If at least one of the animals in the recent lineage is of a species included in Appendix I, the hybrids shall be treated as specimens of species included in Appendix I (and shall be eligible for the exemptions of Article VII when applicable);

d) If at least one of the animals in the recent lineage is of a species included in Appendix II, and there are no specimens of an Appendix-I species in such lineage, the hybrids shall be treated as specimens of species included in Appendix II; and

e) As a guideline, the words "recent lineage", as used in this Resolution, shall generally be interpreted to refer to the previous four generations of the lineage;

RECOMMENDS that, when Parties are considering the making of non-detriment findings, in accordance with Article III, paragraph 2 (a), or Article IV, paragraph 2 (a), for specimens of hybrids that are subject to the provisions of the Convention, they take into account any potential detriment to the survival of the listed species.

larly problematic (CITES Secretariat 1996, 14). Conversely, issues are more complex in plants where hybrid issues have been particularly focused on orchids and cacti (box 12.4). The potential for artificial propagation and hybridization in plants makes enforcing CITES very difficult because taxa identification may only be possible via molecular methods. In summary, CITES may provide protection for some hybridizing taxa for which international trade is a major threat but is not the answer to having an ESA hybrid policy.

BOX 12.4 Treatment of plant hybrids by the Convention on International Trade in Endangered Species of Wild Fauna and Flora (CITES)

THE CONFERENCE OF THE PARTIES TO THE CONVENTION determines that

a) Hybrids shall be subject to the provisions of the Convention even though not specifically included in the Appendices if one or both of their parents are of taxa included in the Appendices, unless the hybrids are excluded from CITES controls by a specific annotation in Appendix II or III (see annotation °608 in the Interpretation of Appendices I and II); and

b) Regarding artificially propagated hybrids:

i) plant species or other taxa listed in Appendix I shall be annotated (in accordance with Article XV) if the provisions relevant to the most restrictive Appendix are to apply;

ii) if a plant species or other taxon listed in Appendix I is annotated, an export permit or re-export certificate shall be required for trade in specimens of all artificially propagated hybrids derived from it; but

iii) artificially propagated hybrids derived from one or more unannotated Appendix-I species or other taxa shall be regarded as being included in Appendix II and entitled therefore to all exemptions applicable to artificially propagated specimens of species listed in Appendix II.

Issues to Consider

The challenge in developing an effective hybrid policy is to identify consistency in solutions to issues while recognizing that the first step to a good solution for any particular hybrid situation is identification of the specific underlying issue. Resolving the following issues may simplify crafting an effective hybrid policy: (1) Should hybridized populations be included as part of the unit considered for listing? (2) Should hybrids be protected that are not part of the listing unit? (3) How much protection is needed or warranted?

Considering Hybridized Populations for Listing

Should hybrid populations be listed? is an important and difficult question because the issues raised range from cases with natural and limited introgression, natural hybrid zones, and situations where hybridization is not a substantial threat to the persistence of the candidate taxon, to cases where anthropogenic forces are causing or significantly accelerating introgression. In general, hybrids should be excluded if introgression can be stopped or limited. However, there are situations where we risk losing all remaining genetic material from a swamped taxon. The problem is that by the time this has happened, the swamped entity may be largely subsumed into something that does not itself meet the definition of threatened or endangered such as in the Mexican duck (*Anas "diazi"*). It was delisted because there was so much introgression with mallards (*A. platyrhynchos*) that it was not a distinguishable species (USFWS 1978a). It can be difficult to distinguish between natural and anthropogenic hybridization; nevertheless, this distinction is of primary importance. Without it, the alternatives for hybrid policy are either to not allow protection of natural hybrids or to protect anthropogenic hybrids that could contribute to extinction of parental species and waste limited resources available for conservation.

Treatment of hybridized populations has been especially problematic for westslope cutthroat trout (WCT, *O. clarki lewisi*). The U.S. Fish and Wildlife Service received a formal petition in 1997 to list westslope cutthroat trout as threatened throughout its range (USFWS 2002b). The agency concluded that listing the species as threatened was not warranted because of its widespread distribution and current status of its overall population (USFWS 1999h). However, a subsequent legal suit argued that this finding was incorrect because it included populations hybridized with rainbow trout in the WCT population considered for listing. The court ruled that the listing determination for westslope cutthroat trout was not based on the best available science and ordered the USFWS to reconsider whether to list the species as threatened after taking into account the prevalence of hybridization (USFWS 2002b).

How hybrids are treated in this case has important implications for whether the species should be listed. If hybrids between westslope cutthroat trout and rainbow trout (*O. mykiss*) are considered to be part of the WCT listing unit, then the listing unit almost certainly does not warrant protection under the Endangered Species Act because of its widespread distribution. However, if only WCT populations without introgression from rainbow trout are considered to be westslope cutthroat trout, then the listing unit would more likely warrant protection under the ESA because of its limited distribution and rapid continued decline. Hitt et al. (2003) found that introgression with rainbow trout is spreading rapidly in WCT populations.

Morphological detection of hybrids between westslope cutthroat trout and other trout has not been found reliable (Allendorf et al. 2004). Nevertheless, the Reconsidered Finding for an amended petition to list the westslope cutthroat trout as threatened throughout its range relied upon morphological criteria to identify it (USFWS 2003f). The finding also concluded that populations

containing 20 percent or less admixture with rainbow trout determined by molecular techniques would be considered westslope cutthroat trout. Thus the petition to list was denied (USFWS 2003f).

This finding is inconsistent with earlier USFWS findings. For example, the
comparable finding with the Rio Grande cutthroat trout considered populations to be part of the listing unit only if they contained less than 1 percent
introgression with either rainbow or another subspecies of cutthroat trout
(USFWS 2002a). Protection of populations that appear to be westslope cutthroat trout morphologically but contain up to 20 percent admixture from
rainbow trout also protect sources of spreading hybridization and will likely
lead to the continued rapid decline of westslope cutthroat trout.

Protection of Nonlisted Hybrids

Often, information is obtained following the listing of a taxon that reveals hybridization of a listed taxa with another. Several factors need to be considered
when assessing the potential value of a hybridized population. One is how
many pure populations of the taxon remain. The smaller the number of pure
populations, the greater the conservation and restoration value of any hybridized population. In addition, the greater the phenotypic (behavioral, morphological, etc.) differentiation between the hybridized population and remaining pure populations, the greater the conservation value of the hybridized
population, because it may represent greater evolutionary potential. Another
factor to consider is whether the continued existence of hybridized populations
poses a threat to remaining pure populations. The greater the perceived threat,
the lower the value of the hybridized population.

Determining Adequate Protection Levels

The degree of protection needed for hybrids clearly depends on the situation.
Currently, taxa listed under section 4(e) are primarily protected from take but
are not provided habitat protection under ESA section 7. Further, ESA violations carry heavy fines and potential incarceration—not insignificant punishment. Thus, as is often the case for enforcement of the ESA, decisions must be
made on a case-by-case basis. However, the full complement of protections afforded by ESA should be available, if necessary, in hybrid situations.

Conclusion

In this chapter, we outlined the history of efforts to include protection of hybrids in the Endangered Species Act, potential current solutions, and issues to

consider in future amendments to the act. Clearly, establishing an effective policy regarding hybrids will not be simple given the variability of situations. Thus, developing a flexible policy will be key to its appropriateness and effectiveness in resolving key conservation dilemmas. Perhaps the most important feature of an effective policy would be a requirement that biological justification for the treatment of hybrids be included in any recovery or management plan involving hybrids.

We thank Elise Elliott-Smith (USGS Forest and Rangeland Ecosystem Science Center) for performing searches for international hybrid legislation information and are grateful to Steve Chambers (USFWS), John Fay (USFWS), Anne Hecht (USFWS), Marta Nammack (NMFS), Mike Schwartz (U.S. Forest Service), and Robin Waples (NMFS) for many conversations related to hybrids and the Endangered Species Act. We also thank Mike Scott for inviting us into this Pandora's box!

I3 Critical Habitat

J. Michael Reed, H. Resit Akçakaya, Mark Burgman, Darren Bender,
Steven R. Beissinger, and J. Michael Scott

The U.S. Endangered Species Act (ESA) requires that *critical habitat*—areas essential to the persistence or recovery of a species or population—be identified and protected (Goble and Freyfogle 2002). Despite apprehension that requiring critical habitat designation at the time (or within a year) of listing under the ESA would reduce the rate at which species were listed, this does not appear to have happened (Greenwald et al., this volume; Suckling and Taylor 2006). In fact, critical habitat has been designated for only a fraction of listed species (Scott et al. 2006). Reasons for the poor rate of designation include concerns that it provides little additional protection to species (e.g., Hoekstra et al. 2002a, but see Suckling and Taylor 2006) and that sufficient data to determine critical habitat are not available. One problem is lack of a systematic framework for determining critical habitat using various types and amounts of data.

There are two key steps to determining critical habitat. The first is to characterize habitat requirements of a species based on its ecology and life history. Ideally, this is achieved by identifying variables that contribute to presence, density, and demography in different landscapes. The end product is a set of quantitative, functional relationships that predict presence or abundance. When sufficient data are lacking, descriptive habitat preferences based on known occurrences of the species are used to identify habitat requirements and elicit structured opinions from experts.

The second step is to evaluate how different amounts and configurations of habitat affect survival or recovery of the species. In making this determination, different scenarios for the amount and configuration of habitat under protection, and/or characteristics of the population inhabiting that area, are compared to each other and to a criterion, a threshold, or a critical level that embodies an acceptable risk of decline or loss. Again, when sufficient data are lacking, expert opinion can be used, cautiously, to evaluate risks of different scenarios for protecting critical habitat.

The Endangered Species Act mandates designating critical habitat based on the best available scientific data (Ruckelshaus and Darm, this volume). Data availability differs by species, which in turn affects the approach used for determining suitable and critical habitats (Karl et al. 2002; Scott et al. 2002). Models are the primary means of assessing habitat relationships and predicting consequences of habitat change (Wiens 2002). Ideally, sufficient data are needed to effectively determine if the designated habitat would support a viable population. However, often we cannot wait for these data to be collected. As Ruckelshaus and Darm (this volume) point out, logistics of model selection and development for determining critical habitat can be daunting.

In this chapter, we discuss a hierarchical approach to predicting species occurrence and designating critical habitat appropriate for the type and amount of data available to managers.

A Multilevel Framework for Predicting Species Occurrence

Mapping species distributions involves estimation, since it is not feasible to observe presence or abundance of a species across a wide area and because available habitat expands and contracts over time in response to succession and disturbance. Furthermore, individuals might be absent from suitable habitat or occupy suboptimal habitat because of population size, social interactions, historic events, or current pressures. Therefore, mapping species occurrence is an exercise in prediction. Predictive models take many forms, but in the context of mapping species occurrence, three are fundamental: *expert models, empirical models,* and *statistical models.*

Expert models rely on knowledge, experiences, and judgment of biologists with expertise in the distribution of a particular species. Although occurrence data are often the basis for defining the predicted occurrence of a species, expert-based maps can possess qualitative and arbitrary elements. They usually define the extent of occurrence of a species or population and are often binary, meaning they show where a species should or should not occur. Range maps published in taxonomic field guides typify this approach.

Empirical models take a quantitative, geographic approach to defining suitable habitat for a species. They infer occurrence from empirical relations describing habitat suitability, usually through use of land cover and other biophysical geospatial data layers entered into a geographic information system (GIS). Empirical models employ two broad approaches. The first, habitat suitability indices (HSIs), describe the suitability of habitat variables, usually subjectively, by experts. They require a priori weighting of individual empirical relations between suitability and habitat characteristics for each GIS layer, such as vegetation type and elevation. GIS layers are combined and analyzed spatially to define suitable and unsuitable habitat for the species. The second approach uses presence-only information together with GIS layers to create geographic or climatic "envelopes" that transcribe potential habitat (e.g., Elith 2000). In both approaches, various grades of suitability (e.g., high, medium, low) can be modeled, meaning that occurrence becomes a probabilistic prediction, in contrast to expert models. An example is occurrence models developed by the U.S. Gap Analysis Program for a wide range of vertebrate species (Scott et al. 1993).

Statistical models are similar to empirical models in that they infer species occurrence through its association with habitat variables. These models also require use of GIS and geospatial data. Statistical models of occurrence are distinguished from empirical models by the incorporation of numerical or statistical analyses that associate probability of occurrence with habitat resources or other features (e.g., mapped distributions of prey resources). Statistical models take many forms and use different approaches, including multivariate distance and factor analysis methods (Carpenter et al. 1999; Hirzel and Metral 2001), general linear models, general additive models, resource selection functions (Boyce et al. 2002; Manly et al. 2002), and machine learning methods (Elith 2000; Elith and Burgman 2003).

Each modeling approach has advantages and disadvantages. Expert-based models are attractive because they do not require extensive geographic data or a GIS, nor do they require quantitative analysis of species occurrence data. Hence, expert models can be thought of as "data informed" but not "data reliant." However, these models may be subject to biases of expert(s), and the method may have low repeatability.

Empirical models are quantitative and repeatable and hence might be viewed as more scientifically rigorous than expert-based models. However, habitat suitability indices depend on expert judgment, and although more explicit than expert models they still are susceptible to subjectivity and bias. They also may be difficult to perform if expert group consensus is required. Envelopes tend to be biased, overpredicting potential habitat (estimating more habitat than is available) (Burgman and Fox 2003). Empirical and statistical approaches require accessible GIS data relevant to the species, and models may be sensitive to data quality (Edwards et al. 1996; Ferrier et al. 2002).

Statistical models are the least subjective and least biased, relying solely on statistically derived relations between observations of presence/absence or abundance and habitat variables to map a probability surface of occurrence. This process is repeatable and scientifically defendable. These methods, however, can require considerable expertise in statistical analysis. When presence/absence data are lacking, *pseudoabsences* may be generated using a range of algorithms from a random selection of points to more complex methods of inference (Zaniewski et al. 2002). Alternatively, a multivariate technique may be used that is designed to work specifically with presence-only data (Hirzel and Metral 2001).

A Proposed Multilevel Framework for Designating Critical Habitat

The strengths and weaknesses of each model dictate the approach best suited to a particular situation. For example, if species location and geospatial data are not available, the expert model may be favored. Alternatively, if a higher level of scientific rigor must be achieved, and data are available, empirical or statistical methods may be favored. Generally, one can view the models as representing positions along a continuum of increasing repeatability and rigor, from expert to empirical to statistical, at the cost of increasing analytical complexity and reliance on data. Thus, the degree of scientific rigor is constrained by the burden of data requirements and analytical capability.

We advocate a multilevel framework for achieving the highest-possible levels of scientific rigor (fig. 13.1). Our framework is based on the simple principle that any predictive modeling exercise should begin at the lowest achievable level (i.e., expert model) and build scientific rigor as the data and capabilities of organizations and their personnel allow.

Expert-based approaches provide a foundation for building models of species occurrence grounded in biological expertise and are therefore defendable in

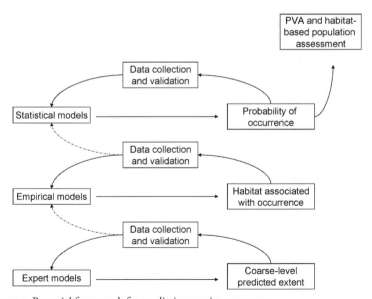

Figure 13.1. Potential framework for predicting species occurrence.

their own right. Over time, experts can identify specific areas of uncertainty where additional data are needed. Thus, the process of making expert maps need not be a static, one-time exercise. Rather, modeling should proceed in an iterative fashion, making use of new data to allow for continual revision, refinement, and independent validation. As with any model, expert models are most accepted when confronted and validated with independent data.

Validating expert models with independently collected data also allows the establishment of databases that accommodate empirically based occurrence models. Like expert models, empirical models can be made transparent and defendable if uncertainties are represented explicitly in functions and on maps (Burgman et al. 2001). Validation data can be used to develop empirical relations between occurrence and habitat suitability. Empirical modeling, like expert modeling, should be an ongoing process; independent data collection and validation are necessary for determining map accuracy and subsequent revisions.

The process of validating empirical models provides additional biological data to construct statistically based models and to represent model uncertainties mathematically and visually (Elith et al. 2002). Observations of species presence/absence used in validation also can be used to build statistical models. Further, the process of creating empirical models facilitates the statistical approach because empirical models provide a guide to which variables are likely to determine the distribution and abundance of the species and the forms of statistical relations they must likely accommodate. For example, the relationship between a habitat variable (e.g., elevation) and a species' occurrence may be quadratic, rather than linear, with a peak in suitability at intermediate values (e.g., a species occupying habitats only at intermediate elevations). Knowledge of the functional relation between a species' habitat and its occurrence is necessary for constructing appropriate models, and, fortunately, this information is often provided from empirical models of species occurrence, such as habitat suitability models.

Statistical models also require validation with independent data before their accuracy can be judged, although this practice seems to be accepted as necessary when using statistical approaches for modeling species occurrence (Boyce et al. 2002). Additional data can be incorporated easily into subsequent runs of the statistical model. As the extent and sample size of data grow, so does model completeness and accuracy (tables 13.1 and 13.2).

Identifying Suitable Habitat Using Logistic Regression

It is common for researchers and resource managers to have location information for a target species, such as those found in breeding bird atlases

TABLE 13.1 Making predictions with available data

Data type	Uses for data
Expert information, collateral data, allometric relationships, qualitative trends	Guess N (current or target population size), develop conceptual model
Information from cell above, plus single count (census in one time step)	Estimate N
Information from two cells above, plus counts over time (census in multiple time steps)	Scalar model (estimate N, trend)
Information from all cells above, plus life history information (censuses include data on stage, age, sex)	Structured model (estimate survival, reproduction, N, trends)
Any of the above with spatial data	Same models with spatial structure (e.g., habitat-based population viability analysis)

Note: Data are provided in sequence from least to most required.

TABLE 13.2 Deriving statistical models from available data

Data type	Derived habitat models
Map(s) and experts	Habitat suitability index
Locations only	Minimum convex polygons, alpha hulls, kernels
Locations and maps of variables	+ climate envelopes, multivariate distance methods, canonical correlation analysis
Locations and random (available) locations and maps	Resource selection function
Presence/absence (used and unused locations)	General linear model (logistic regression), general additive model
Abundance/absence and maps	General linear model (Poisson regression), general additive model
Habitat dynamics	Landscape models (new in recovery context)
All data types	Decision trees, neural networks, genetic algorithms

Note: Data types are presented in increasing order of data need and model complexity.

(e.g., Robbins and Blom 1996), even if data on the quality of occupied habitat and detailed observations on demography are not available. From this, one can quantify variables that might be important to a species, such as elevation, slope, ground cover, and overstory species. Data should be at least taxon specific— meaning they vary by type of species: amphibian versus herbaceous plant versus beetle—but often they are species specific, for instance a known habitat requirement such as salty soils or a den site.

The goal is to use a statistical procedure to distinguish habitat features important for species presence as a means of identifying other sites with similar characteristics that might be suitable for the species. Logistic regression is a statistical procedure that uses data from multiple independent variables (habitat variables in our example) to distinguish between two alternatives (here, suitable versus nonsuitable habitat) (Hosmer and Lemeshow 2000; Scott et al. 2002). Logistic regression can be used with model selection criteria, such as Akaike's Information Criterion, to evaluate a suite of potential models and generate predictions of habitat occupancy by combining inference from multiple models or model averaging (Burnham and Anderson 2002).

Logistic regression requires presence/absence data, but often only observations of species presence are available—usually because more effort is required to identify sites where a species is absent (Reed 1996). Determining the status of cryptic species (for instance, those that are nocturnal, small, or subterranean except when flowering or fruiting) is particularly difficult (e.g., Bibby et al. 2000). Although observed absences are preferred, another solution is to generate pseudoabsences, randomly selected points where presence has not been determined (Klute et al. 2002; van Manen et al. 2002).

The eastern timber wolf is an endangered subspecies of the gray wolf that has been reduced to less than 3 percent of its range outside of Alaska (Mladenoff et al. 1999). A large carnivore with a strong social structure, it lives in packs whose territory can cover 30 to 180 square miles (50–300 square kilometers). Wolves declined throughout their range primarily because of habitat loss from logging, agriculture, and human settlement (Fritts and Carbyn 1995). An extensive database was gathered from radio-collared animals, which provided details of habitat use and ecology. A geographic information system was used to add landscape features of habitat use to the distributional data, providing a platform to infer the potential importance of large-scale habitat features for occupation or avoidance of sites by wolves. Features studied included human population, deer (prey), and road densities. Data were gathered from seventeen to twenty-one wolf packs and compared to fourteen similarly sized, randomly selected sites a minimum distance from known wolf habitat. Logistic regression results showed a number of significant variables such as land ownership class and human population, with the most important variables being road density and fractal dimension (an index of patch-boundary complexity relative to patch size). This model was then used to identify amount and spatial distribution of suitable wolf habitat in the region. Model validation and improvement is ongoing (D. Mladenoff, pers. comm.).

Using Population Viability as a Criterion for Critical Habitat Determination

The second step in designating critical habitat requires determining whether a particular size and configuration of habitat is sufficient for survival or recovery of the species; such analyses implicitly relate population size and connectivity to measures of viability. The question, How much is enough? as applied to population size and habitat configuration, is perhaps the most difficult problem for the science of conservation biology to answer. First, targets for risk in the form of extinction rates, population size or number of populations, and time horizons must be identified. Then analyses must be conducted to accurately and precisely assess extinction risk from different levels and configurations of habitat. This is the classic "minimum viable population size" problem (Shaffer 1981), which created the field of population viability analysis (Beissinger 2002).

Defining a Viable Population

Viability can be defined as the chance (probability) of species persistence or recovery to a predetermined level. Thus, a viable population is one that has a high probability of long-term persistence or of increasing to a predetermined level. *Population viability analysis* (PVA) is an assessment of risk of reaching some threshold (such as extinction) or projected growth for a population, either under current conditions or those predicted for proposed management. PVAs have ranged from qualitative, verbal processes without models to spatially explicit, stochastic simulation models (Boyce 1992; Burgman et al. 1993), but recently only quantitative, data-based models are considered to be PVAs (Ralls et al. 2002; Reed et al. 2002).

Concerns about appropriate use of population viability analysis have been expressed elsewhere (Taylor 1995; Beissinger and Westphal 1998; Ralls et al. 2002; Reed et al. 2002) and should be reviewed by anyone attempting a PVA. Alternative methods of making conservation decisions, however, are often less able to address uncertainty and may be less transparent about their reliability (Brook et al. 2002; Akçakaya and Sjögren-Gulve 2000). Stochastic (probabilistic) results of PVA have been evaluated by comparing predicted declines with observed declines of corresponding populations (Brook et al. 2000). Although PVA models can predict short-term dynamics in an unbiased manner, their ability to precisely and accurately forecast the chance (i.e., likelihood) of extinction is much weaker unless the population is growing or declining very rapidly (e.g., Ludwig 1999; Belovsky et. al. 1999; Brook et. al. 2000; Fieberg and Ellner 2000). The likelihood of extinction usually cannot be tested directly with field measurements, but secondary predictions from PVA models can be compared with patterns observed or measured in the field (e.g., McCarthy and Broome 2000; McCarthy et al. 2001).

For application to determining critical habitat for threatened species, viability should be defined in terms of an acceptable probability and time frame, and an agreed definition of persistence (e.g., a population size or rate of change). There are few purely scientific reasons to select particular levels for these parameters; their values are a function of the level of risk aversion or attitude toward risk and uncertainty. They can be based on previous applications or precedence, or on rule-based criteria used to assess threat categories. For example, the International Union for the Conservation of Nature and Natural Resources (IUCN 2003) criteria define a species as "vulnerable" if it has 10 percent probability of extinction within one hundred years. If the goal is species recovery, then a threshold should be defined based on a historical or other socially acceptable level of abundance (box 13.1).

There are also a few technical considerations. For example, probabilities very close to 0 or 1 are difficult to estimate, so "high probability" cannot be defined as 100 percent or a value very close to it. Very long term predictions tend to be uncertain because errors in models are propagated with each time step (usually a year) and the future itself is often full of unanticipated events that are not incorporated into the model. Thus, there is a trade-off between the relevance of long-term predictions and the relative certainty of short-term predictions, so multiple time horizons might be examined with lower levels of risk tolerance for shorter time frames (Ralls et al. 2002). Finally, population dynamics are difficult to predict at low population sizes due to Allee effects, so higher thresholds for persistence are both more precautionary and technically more feasible. For example, viability of a long-lived vertebrate might be defined as the probability that population size will stay above fifty mature individuals for the next fifty or one hundred years.

Determining Viability

Viability of a population or species depends on many factors and interactions among them. These factors can be grouped into four broad classes:

BOX 13.1 Biological and Nonbiological Decisions in Recovery Planning

Setting recovery criteria for endangered species, such as number of viable populations, minimum number of individuals, or minimum distribution of individuals across a region, requires that both biological and nonbiological decisions be incorporated into the process.

Biological Decisions

Defining species, subspecies, populations, and (infrequently) individuals
Defining the management landscape
Identifying threats to population persistence
Identifying sources of relevant data

Nonbiological Decisions

Establishing a time frame for recovery
How far into the future should you evaluate viability? We recommend at least twenty generations *and* one hundred years. Our feeling is that a time frame of at least twenty generations *and* one hundred years would be needed.
Determining the degree of acceptable risk in long-term persistence
How certain should you be that your recovery goal will be effective? The greater the desired certainty, the larger the required population (and therefore more habitat saved) and the more accurate predictive modeling data must be. We recommend at least 90 percent certainty of greater than 90 percent probability of long-term persistence.
Deciding what type of risk to minimize
There are two types of relevant statistical errors (Reed 1996): *Type I error* concludes a species is endangered when it is secure. The cost of being wrong means spending money to recover species not at risk (worse economically). *Type II error* concludes that a species is secure when it is endangered. The cost of being wrong means species could be lost by subsequent actions (worse biologically). One cannot minimize both types of error, so compromise must agree on the acceptable level of risk for both types.

Population size and structure, including the number of individuals; distribution to stages and subpopulations; density of individuals; and trends in population size and structure

Habitat, including quality; amount; and spatial configuration

Demography, including survival; fecundity; dispersal rates, including spatial variation, temporal trends, and fluctuations; breeding system; and sex ratio

Relationships between demographic rates and habitat and between demographic rates and population size

Thus, measures such as population size, population growth rate, or area of habitat capture only a portion of the factors that affect viability. See Ruckelshaus and Darm (this volume) for further discussion.

Using Viability as a Criterion

Viability can be defined as long-term survival of the species, so it is an appropriate end point for designating critical habitat. More important, viability implicitly integrates factors that determine persistence and recovery, namely habitat quality (e.g., the abundance of food resources, levels of contaminants, presence of predators), demography (survival, reproduction, variability, density dependence in survival and reproduction), and spatial characteristics of both habitat and the target species. If a given habitat does not support a viable population, population viability analysis can be used to present alternate management scenarios that create critical habitat, such as changes in the spatial configuration of the habitat, habitat improvement, and increasing connectivity through, for instance, habitat corridors.

Viability can be used as a criterion in designating critical habitat by calculating and comparing viability of the species under different scenarios for the area and spatial configuration of the habitat that would be protected under alternative critical habitat designations (fig. 13.2). Scenarios are ranked in comparison to one another and compared with the viability criteria.

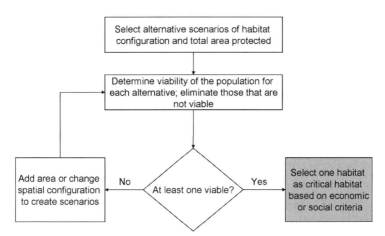

Figure 13.2. Using population viability analysis to compare alternative scenarios for designating critical habitat.

Incorporating Habitat into a Viability Assessment

Incorporating habitat into a viability assessment requires a quantitative description of the habitat (see table 13.2). Habitat models describe suitability of the land as habitat for a particular species. Suitability is usually based on locational information or presence/absence data occurrence or sightings but also can be based on variables such as fecundity.

There are various methods of estimating the habitat model outlined above, each with differing demands for data and technical expertise (table 13.2). The resulting model is one step used to create a map of the species' habitat (fig. 13.3) Habitat models can be validated by estimating them with data from half of the landscape and using them to predict the suitability of locations where the species has been observed in the other half (e.g., Akçakaya and Atwood 1997), or with new field data (e.g., Elith 2000).

A habitat model can be incorporated into viability assessment by basing components of the PVA model, or alternative scenarios, on the amount of and connections between habitats, or on maps of habitat (Akçakaya 2000; fig. 13.3). These components can include spatial structure of the model (number and location of subpopulations), dispersal rates among subpopulations, as well as population-specific model parameters such as population size, carrying capacity, survival rate, and fecundity. Thus, habitat-based population viability analyses have the potential to integrate demographic and habitat models. These models can be used to determine whether a given configuration of habitat is more likely to support a population with a low risk of decline and/or a high probability of recovery than some alternative configuration.

In many landscapes, habitats for most species change over time due to natural processes, such as disturbances and succession, and human activities, such as

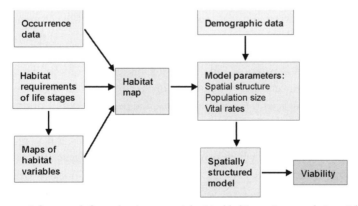

Figure 13.3. A framework for evaluating potential critical habitat using population viability analysis (Akçakaya and Atwood 1997; Elith 2000).

forestry and urban growth. Such changes can be incorporated into viability assessments by linking habitat-based demographic models with landscape models (Akçakaya 2001). Species that live in fragmented landscapes and depend on temporary habitat patches are especially sensitive to both habitat and population dynamics. Viability of such species depends on the balance between the rate of appearance and spatial arrangement of patches and the reproductive capacity of the species. Thus, the only way to assess viability of such species is to consider both habitat dynamics and population dynamics simultaneously.

Caveats to Population Viability Analysis

Population viability analysis is a model, and like all models the assumptions that underlie it should be kept in mind when interpreting results. Consequently, it is important to consider how to translate the results of a population viability analysis into on-the-ground habitat designation (cf. box 13.1). One should not merely take the minimum viable population size and associated habitat; focus on the minimum has long been criticized in the field of conservation biology. Issues of particular importance include problems associated with errors in model structure and data availability, and the stochastic nature of population dynamics. There are many sources of information on—and growing scientific discussion about—accounting for uncertainty in a population viability analysis (e.g., Burgman et al. 1993). None of the methods, however, make quantitative predictions about the minimum population size needed to ensure a suitably low risk of loss. Although not likely significant when comparing differences among reliable, quantitative solutions, and although eliminating risk entirely is not possible, the problem is exacerbated by the difficulty of accurately determining population sizes of some species (Peery et al. 2003).

So, what can be done? Emerging consensus advocates a conservative approach, perhaps taking some value at the high end of a confidence interval. The Marine Mammal Protection Act of 1994 (Act of April 30, 1994) specifies a target population size two-thirds above that of the predicted viable population.

Even if a PVA is practical and a sufficient buffer is placed on viability estimates to reduce uncertainty risk, population size and associated critical habitat might still be insufficient. An ecosystem may require more than a minimum viable population of the target species to create a viable ecosystem. Soulé et al. (2003) introduced the concept of highly interactive species, a new manifestation of keystone species, which play key roles in species interactions and nutrient cycling. Although the concept of a viable ecosystem is not new (e.g., Conner 1988; Loreau et al. 2002; Lomolino, this volume), the idea is not well developed, and sufficient data and methods to determine population sizes needed to maintain ecosystem services and processes are lacking. Soulé et al.

(2003) and Peery et al. (2003) offer examples of how species interactions within a community and the population sizes required to maintain them might be determined.

These arguments support the idea of being generous in initial critical habitat designation and of over- rather than underestimating needed area because of uncertainty, and they describe the asymmetric consequences of being wrong (cf. Reed 1996). An error in one direction could result in species extinction while an error in the other direction could result in loss of resources and opportunities. How large beyond the estimated critical population size this should be is unknown.

Conclusion

Inadequate data to securely determine critical habitat will be a continuing problem. Obviously the more data available, the better will be the proposed designation. A variety of data sources exist, including censuses, surveys, mark-recapture studies, published and gray literature, expert opinion, and occurrence data from Natural Heritage databases. Even data from related species or species with similar habitat requirements can sometimes be used.

In this chapter, we suggested a framework for selecting models to fit available data, but assessment of model effectiveness depends on the question asked. Recovery planning is often about exploring or ranking management options, and in such cases it is more appropriate to instead assess relative risks, which require less precision (Beissinger and Westphal 1998; McCarthy and Broome 2000; McCarthy et al. 2001). Even with insufficient data, a preliminary model is useful for identifying data gaps and research priorities, organizing available information, and focusing discussions. Ultimately, the best evaluation comes from long-term monitoring data and population viability reevaluation to determine if designated critical habitats are supporting viable populations and are expected to do so in the foreseeable future.

Part III Conservation Policy and Management

The theme of this volume, "conserving biodiversity in human-dominated landscapes," is the focus of part 3. The traditional tools of set-aside strategies, focus on federal lands, prohibitory actions, and last-minute interventions are, we believe, insufficient to realize the full promise of the act's purpose to "provide a means whereby the ecosystems upon which endangered species and threatened species may be conserved" (Act of December 28, 1973).

Set-aside strategies have resulted in a system of protected areas not representative of the ecological or geophysical diversity of the country and are often too small to maintain evolutionarily viable populations for many species or even minimally viable ones for larger species. Thus lands adjacent to protected areas are important components of our conservation landscape. They provide habitat in which threatened and endangered species may move from one protected area to another in response to seasonal and climatic changes. With adjustments in our land use practices (Rosenzweig 2006; Brosi et al., this volume), our working landscapes, both on land and in water, provide not only the necessities for a healthy economy and a prosperous people but also vital habitat for wildlife, either as travel corridors for species to move between traditional reserve areas or as areas to reproduce, feed, and rest.

Making the American working landscape hospitable to endangered species will require new tools (Bean 2006; Thompson 2006), new partnerships (Scott et al. 2006, chap. 2), and new attitudes (Swain 2006). Existing tools tend to be useful to developers and those with large financial resources (Thompson 2006; Sunding, this volume). Those with fewer resources and those with process-oriented businesses such as ranching and farming have fewer tools and incentives available to them (Thompson 2006; Bean 2006; Shogren, this volume).

The chapters in this part complement many in the companion volume, *The Endangered Species Act at Thirty: Renewing the Conservation Promise.* In chapter 14, Jason Shogren discusses the benefits and costs to society of implementing the act, while in chapter 15 David Sunding reminds us that landowners incur costs when threatened and endangered species are present. Rozensweig's (2006) reconciliation-ecology premise that we must do a better job of protecting species at risk in the areas where we live work and play is explored in greater depth in chapters 16, 17, and 18 by Tom Scott and his coauthors, Brosi and colleagues, and Timothy Beatley. They discuss the importance of agricultural, urban, and working landscapes to wildlife, including threatened and endangered species. Armsworth et al. extend this discussion in chapter 19 to marine environments, while in chapters 20 and 21, Jessica Fox and her colleagues and Geoffrey Heal, respectively, provide detailed analysis of tools available to developers to meet the legal hurdles in areas with species at risk.

Together, these chapters suggest a new approach to protecting endangered species by working across political and scientific boundaries to recover species that are threatened and endangered and to prevent others from becoming endangered.

I4 Benefits and Costs

Jason F. Shogren

The Endangered Species Act of 1973 (ESA) provides benefits to and imposes costs on the citizens of the United States. Benefits are captured by the market and nonmarket gains that arise today and in the future by avoiding the consequences of species extinction (Norton, this volume; Callicott, this volume). Costs are measured by the foregone opportunities due to restrictions on property because of ESA listings, designation of critical habitat, and recovery plans. From an economics perspective, three questions need to be addressed:

- Have the net national benefits (i.e., benefits minus costs) of the ESA been positive or negative over the last three decades?
- If we disregard the benefit side, has the ESA, as currently designed and implemented, been at least cost-effective in achieving the stated regulatory goals?
- Will the future benefits of species protection exceed the costs of the ESA?

Economists define efficiency as a policy that creates the greatest positive net benefits for society today and into the future. No one knows whether the ESA has been *efficient* today and whether it will be efficient in the future. Many economists agree, however, that the current ESA structure has not been cost-effective under the perverse incentives built into section 7 (jeopardy) and section 9 (taking). These sections do not necessarily align the incentives of private landowners with the act's goal of preserving all species (see Innes et al. 1998; Donahue 2005). Landowners should not be penalized for having prime habitat or rare species on their lands (Burnham et al. 2006; Swain 2006), but any compensation scheme is complicated by the fact that landowners have private information on how they personally value these species (Shogren et al. 2006).

Economics cannot answer the efficiency question because we do not have a national estimate of the private and social benefits or the costs of the act. Estimating the private benefits derived from species protection (e.g., commercial use, consumptive use, and recreation) using tangible market prices is possible but has not been done at a national level. In contrast, estimating social benefits is more challenging because one is trying to determine preferences for protecting species and related services they do not directly use or perceive as valuable. Quantifying these values at a national level has not been attempted. Even if such values are eventually estimated, inherent limits to valuation methods restrict their use in policy.

No one has estimated at a national level the difference in actual economic growth with the Endangered Species Act versus potential economic growth without it. What would the U.S. economy have looked like without the ESA? One needs this counterfactual baseline to determine the potential per capita costs imposed by the act in terms of lost consumption or wealth. At best, we have regional and local studies, and these suggest that the impact of the act is a transfer of wealth rather than a loss of wealth (see Brown and Shogren 1998; Sunding 2005).

Economists argue that wealth spent here is not spent somewhere else and that an ESA policy that accounts for behavior and incentives would provide more species protection for less cost. But questions of overall efficiency are frequently less important in policy debates than concerns over the redistribution of wealth. The ESA epitomizes the classic question of diffuse social benefits and concentrated private costs; about half of the listed endangered species have 80 percent of their habitat on private land. These landowners complain that the costs of complying with the ESA are too great.

Supporters of the ESA, however, argue these private costs are not decisive in species protection because these services are irreplaceable—the benefits of these services are priceless. Preservationists argue that species habitat has other uses than just for human financial gain and that landowners are free to pursue private profits only so long as they also behave as responsible social citizens. Because by definition land and species habitat are already in public service, all land uses should be designated as "harm-preventing" rather than "public-good-providing." As Sagoff (1997, 845) notes: "the conviction that the freedom to wring the last speculative penny from one's land is of a piece with one's most fundamental civil, political, and personal liberties seems to be grounded less on argument than on assumption." By these arguments the implied benefits of the ESA goals are inestimable and the efficiency of the act is best evaluated in terms of cost-effectiveness.

In this chapter, I briefly consider what economists know about the benefits and costs of the Endangered Species Act. In general, the literature has focused on specific case studies rather than a broad general evaluation of the act (see, for example, National Research Council 2005, a report on valuing ecosystem services). Politicans are the final decision makers, but as Dales (1968) has suggested, they are staking their political futures on their ability to accurately assess what the public wants and as a result are perhaps better able to assess the benefits and costs of their actions than experts. Understanding ESA benefits and costs can help frame future ESA debates by identifying the elements that inflate costs with no additional benefits. Given real budget constraints, identifying and defining the benefits and costs of species protection and their distribution helps illustrate how to use criteria and analyses that permit discrimination among species (Shogren et al. 1999).

ESA Benefits

The potential private and social benefits of the Endangered Species Act derive from the prevention of species extinction. Private benefits derived from species protection include commercial use, consumptive use, and recreation. Commercially, the possibility of new pharmaceutical products derived from plant and animal tissue, including from endangered species, is being explored. Examples include the drug vincristine, derived from a rare plant called "rosy periwinkle" (*Catharanthus roseus*) and used to treat leukemia, and taxol, derived from the Pacific yew (*Taxus brevifolia*) and used in ovarian cancer treatment. Some maintain that we need to save the totality of the world's variety of genetic and biochemical resources because no one knows exactly where the next breakthrough to cure cancer might come from. With new and future breakthroughs in biotechnology, preserving all parts of nature makes sense because it is hard to anticipate all potential future beneficial uses of rare species. By this logic, keeping all species serves as "ecosystem insurance" that transfers the wealth from the good state of the world today to the potentially bad state of the world tomorrow.

While no substitute exists for biodiversity as a whole, measuring commercial value requires insight into substitution possibilities and the marginal contribution that each species makes toward a new and useful product. The expected marginal value of a species equals the expected payoff from testing it times the probability that all other species fail to provide the desired product. If one species substitutes for another in potential market success, the marginal value of an extensive genetic exploration declines as the odds increase that a firm will find a profitable species quickly.

The value of some species is enhanced by introducing prior knowledge of their greater potential (Rausser and Small 2000); the associated cost is to reduce the value of other species. By this model, a firm pays a premium for exclusive access to relevant information, which in turn creates an incentive to preserve ecological resources to charge access fees.

It will be some time before economics links up with ecology to understand human–species and species–species interactions well enough to measure accurately the marginal value product of any one species contributing to a market good. Along these lines, Finnoff and Tschirhart's (2003a, 2003b) development of the General Equilibrium Ecosystem Model is providing useful insight into how to disentangle each species contribution to the economic and ecological system.

Estimating the commercial benefit of commercially and recreationally harvested species is relatively straightforward. Angler and hunting expenditures amounted to about $60 billion in 1996 (USFWS and NMFS 1996c). According to a 2004 report by the National Oceanic and Atmospheric Association, marine recreational fishing supported some three hundred and fifty thousand jobs and generated $30.5 billion in economic impact to the nation. Commercial and recreational salmon fishing in the Pacific Northwest helps support sixty thousand jobs and over $1 billion in personal income in the regional economy (Irvin 1995).

Ecotourism—for example, the $200 million California whale-watching industry—is another economic benefit. Global ecotourism expenditures have been estimated at $90–$200 billion in 1988, with about 15 percent spent in the North America (Filion et al. 1994). But ecotourism is also unlikely to save all endangered species: not many endangered or threatened insects or fungi will qualify for preservation on these grounds.

Estimating the social value of endangered species protection presents a greater challenge. Contention centers on trying to put a monetary value on social preferences for protecting species today and in the future. We know that endangered species contribute—albeit a small proportion relative to abundance or biomass—to the social goods that affect human well-being, including "the regulation of climate, floods, disease, wastes, and water quality; cultural services such as recreation, aesthetic enjoyment, and spiritual fulfillment; and supporting services such as soil formation, photosynthesis, and nutrient cycling" (Millennium Ecosystem Assessment 2005a, 19). The primary economic tool to measure social values is the public opinion survey, known as *contingent evaluation survey* or *stated preference method*, which uses a set of questions to put a monetary value on personal preferences. This method is contentious because respondents are only answering a survey rather than facing their own budget constraints and spending their own money.

Many valuation studies focus on a single species, usually a well-known megavertebrate such as grizzly bears (*Ursus arctos horribilis*), wolves, and eagles. These studies do not address important ecological complementarities since high-profile carnivores depend on the existence of other, lower-profile species. In theory, an implicit value of these other components of the ecosystem could be retrieved (Crocker and Tschirhart 1992).

Economic values for endangered and threatened species have typically been estimated using a willingness-to-pay approach. Researchers have estimated a range of willingness to pay for individual species as low as $6 for a striped shiner (*Luxilus chrysocephalus*) and as high as $95 for the northern spotted owl (*Strix occidentalis caurina*) (Loomis and White 1996).

Studies vary considerably by geography and method. For example, examining the Mediterranean monk seal (*Monachus monachus*), Langford et al. (1998) showed that Greek households place a nontrivial dollar value on preserving the monk seals. Their study is similar to most other surveys in eliciting one species' value rather than examining the linkages of certain species and examining the entire habitat.

In contrast, Carson et al. (1994) estimate the value for speeding up recovery of four species in California (bald eagle [*Haliaeetus leucocephalus*], peregrine falcon [*Falco peregrinus*], kelp bass [*Paralabrax clathratus*], and white croaker [*Genyonemus lineatus*]) and find from a dichotomous choice survey that the average individual is willing to pay around $63 in a one-time lump sum tax to expedite the recovery process. Walsh et al. (1990) examined twenty-six species in Colorado using an open-ended survey and found that Colorado residents were willing to pay $58 as a one-time lump sum tax to protect all these species.

Jakobsson and Dragun (1996) conducted a mail survey to Victorian residents in Australia concerning their willingness to pay to avoid either a decline in a number of endangered species (flora and fauna) or the loss of Leadbeater's possum (*Gymnobelideus leadbeateri*). The results show that the conservation value of the Leadbeater's possum is less than those values for the conservation of all endangered flora and fauna, suggesting that respondents value one individual endangered species significantly less than a collection of endangered species. Reaves et al. (1999) considered both species and their habitat. Overall, they found across each treatment all mean willingness-to-pay values to preserve the woodpecker and restore its habitat are statistically different from zero; the average person would pay about $10.

Overall, people say they will pay a nontrivial dollar value to preserve and protect endangered species, whether alone or in aggregate. If one summed the stated preferences from various endangered species surveys as a rough measure of benefits, the average person would pay about $1,000 to protect eighteen different species. Multiplying $1,000 by the number of U.S. households suggests they would pay over 1 percent of the national gross domestic product to preserve less than 2 percent of the endangered species, a suspiciously high number for some observers. The literature is moving toward a more thorough recognition of the complementarity and substitution effects across species and habitat that can critically matter when valuing a species (Brown and Shogren 1998).

Many benefits from endangered species are not provided to us today; rather, they will be provided to future generations. Asking people in 2006 to assess how people in 2016 will value species is a sketchy business given we have little clue as to available substitutes that are key to all valuation studies. More available substitutes for what people need in the future imply lower values for the species of today. People today may value the flexibility that future generations will have when more species still exist, but this does not necessarily translate into how those in the future will think about the problem. We can make assumptions but we cannot, with any degree of accuracy, assign future generations' economic values to them from today's perspective. The safest presumption is that people in future will prefer good events over bad events, however they are defined in the future.

ESA Costs

Many anecdotal stories exist about how the Endangered Species Act has restricted opportunities to capture rents or develop land, but these do not really capture the costs of the act. If it simply works to transfer wealth from one party to another it is not an economic cost, which as defined by economists would imply a decrease in the size of the overall economic pie. Here we use the concept of *opportunity cost* as our best measure of the potential drag on the economy. Opportunity costs capture the foregone opportunities due to restrictions on the use of property because of listings, designation of critical habitat, and recovery efforts. Opportunity costs include the reduced economic rents from restricted or altered development projects, agriculture production, timber harvesting, minerals extraction, recreation activities, wages lost by displaced workers who remain unemployed or who are reemployed at lower wages, lower consumer surplus due to higher prices, and lower capital asset value. For example, the Bonneville Power Administration estimated that its expenditure on salmon conservation was about $350 million in 1994 (1 percent of 1994 revenues), of which about $300 million represented the opportunity cost of lost power revenues (National Research Council 1995).

The assessment by Brown and Shogren (1998) still holds today—no one has estimated at the national level the difference in actual economic growth with the Endangered Species Act and potential economic growth without it. Although one study considered the association between the ESA and national economic growth, it did not estimate national opportunity costs (Meyer 2001). Based on an econometric analysis of economic growth trends in all fifty states between 1975 and 1990, Meyer argued the act has not been detrimental to economic development since a negative relationship was not found between ESA listings and either construction employment or gross state product. For example, Alabama with seventy listed species had a booming economy, while Louisiana with twenty-one listings did poorly. But without some measure of opportunity costs, these results cannot lead one to conclude that the ESA has not been a drag on the national economy. Crellin (2002) considers how the act affected housing prices in three counties in the state of Washington. Using a reduced form regression, Crellin finds that if at least four endangered species are present in an area, there is a substantial decline in the price of single-family homes.

The impact of the ESA is likely to be less than that estimated for environmental regulation on air and water quality and global climate change policy, which is estimated to reduce the U.S. economy by about 0.2–1 percent annual gross domestic product (Jorgenson and Wilcoxon 1990; Shogren and Toman 2000). One could take the position that if we measured GDP properly—along the lines of the green accounting proposed by, say Nordhaus and Tobin (1972)—then ESA regulation could well have increased, rather than decreased, GDP.

Opportunity costs have been estimated for a few high-profile, regional ESA conflicts such as the northern spotted owl. One study estimated that an owl recovery plan that increased the survival odds to 91 percent for about 1,600 to 2,400 owl pairs would decrease economic welfare by $33 billion (1990 dollars), with a disproportionate share of the losses borne by the regional producers of intermediate wood products, a relatively small segment of the population (Montgomery et al. 1994). If the recovery plan tried to push the goal to 95 percent survival odds, costs increased to $46 billion. Another study estimated the short-run and long-run opportunity costs to Washington and Oregon of owl protection at $1.2 billion and $450 million (Rubin et al. 1991). Short-run costs included the value of timber foregone plus the additional costs of displaced workers—estimate ranged from 13,272 lost jobs by 1995 to over 28,000 by 2000. Long-run costs included the value of the timber foregone, as displaced workers found other positions at similar wages.

Opportunity costs have also been estimated for critical habitat designation in the Virgin River basin in Utah for the woundfin (*Plagopterus argentissimus*) and Virgin River chub (*Gila seminuda*), and in the Colorado River basin for the razorback sucker (*Xyrauchen texanus*), humpback chub (*Gila cypha*), Colorado pikeminnow (*Ptychocheilus lucius*), and bonytail chub (*Gila elegans*) (Brookshire et al. 1994, 1995). Three conclusions emerge: First, the difference in total economic output with and without critical habitat designation is relatively small, in other words, 0.0016 percent of the present value of the baseline stream of output for Washington county (Utah) (see also Suckling and Taylor 2006); similar results hold for earnings income, tax revenues, and employment. Second, the impact of critical habitat designation is not evenly distributed across the states in the basin as streamflow requirements may negatively impact recreation, electric power production, and future consumptive use in some states but enhance these activities in other states. And third, the potential national impacts of the designation are negligible.

Opportunity costs also exist with public programs—resources devoted to endangered species could have been spent on something else, something viewed as potentially more valuable to the general public. The General Accounting Office reported on fifty-eight approved recovery plans, finding that thirty-four had a total-cost estimate for carrying out the recovery, twenty-three had cost estimates for the initial years of recovery, and one had a cost estimate for one part of a twelve-part plan (GAO 1995). The thirty-four total-cost estimates range from $145,000 in 1994 for the White River spinedace (*Lepidomeda albivallis*) to about $154 million in 1991 for the green sea turtle (*Chelonia mydas*) and loggerhead sea turtle (*Caretta caretta*); the total estimated cost for the thirty-four species is approximately $700 million. For the twenty-three plans with initial three-year estimates, costs range from $57,000 in 1990 for the Florida scrub jay (*Aphelocoma coerulescens*) to $49.1 million in 1991 for the black-capped vireo (*Vireo atricapilla*); the three-year total costs for the twenty-three species is over $350 million. For the "high-priority" actions, the total estimated cost is about $223 million for three years.

Economists have estimated what federal and state agencies have spent on endangered species protection between 1989 and 1996. Expenditures increased to about $270 million in 1996 from $44 million in 1989, a small figure relative to total government expenditures of over $1.4 trillion (Dawson and Shogren 2001). Limited budgets and political realities also create conflicts within ESA recovery plans, in which over 50 percent of expenditures go to ten vertebrates. These species and their 1993–96 expenditures are northern spotted owl ($55.8 million), red-cockaded woodpecker ($38.7 million), bald eagle ($25.2 million), desert tortoise (*Gopherus agassizii*) ($22.8 million), Colorado pikeminnow ($22.5 million), marbled murrelet (*Brachyramphus marmoratus marmoratus*) ($16.9 million), gray wolf (*Canis lupus*) ($13.8 million), peregrine falcon ($13 million), whooping crane (*Grus americana*) ($10.7 million), and razorback sucker ($10.6 million).

If opportunity costs cannot be estimated, actual expenditures on the transaction costs of dealing with habitat conservation plans might serve as a lower bound on costs. The private ESA transaction costs include the time and money spent applying for permits and licenses, redesigning plans, and legal fees. Again national estimates do not exist. As a crude comparison, the transaction costs are estimated to be between 30 and 70 cents on the dollar for Superfund (the Comprehensive Environmental Response, Compensation, and Liability Act—CERCLA) (Dixon 1995). It is unlikely the Endangered Species Act has generated transaction costs of the same magnitude, but with an estimated 900,000 acres captured each year by urban expansion, ESA conflicts and transaction costs may increase quickly.

Sunding (this volume) provides a good example on the costs of development.

Conclusion

We have all heard that the Endangered Species Act either generates countless benefits to society or imposes never-ending costs on landowners. Both arguments have some merit—species protection provides society with private and social benefits; species protection makes old practices more expensive. If the benefits are assumed to be infinite, the question is whether we can meet the desired targets cost-effectively. If potential substitutes exist for certain species as defined by a human dimension, the question is to measure both the benefits and costs of the ESA. In the end, the key is to understand whether the act imposes true economic loss (i.e., a shrinking economic pie) rather than a transfer of wealth from traditional economic sectors to other sectors (i.e., a reallocation of the pie from say agriculture to recreation).

Regardless, framing the ESA debate in cost-benefit terms remains useful for two reasons. First, the framework serves to create a benchmark against which we can judge other demands of a fixed public budget such as education and health care. The argument to protect species "at whatever cost" sounds hollow when your own property or land is excluded from the set of options. Second, economics is a discipline of scarcity, just like conservation biology. The more we can connect the mindsets of the two groups to understand each other's definitions of values and opportunity sets the better we can manage our species and preserve our wildness.

15 Economic Impacts

David L. Sunding

This chapter considers the economic costs of endangered species regulation, focusing on the market for new housing. Housing is a dominant urban land use and the homebuilding industry is an economically significant one. Indeed, the average U.S. household spends well over half of its income on the related goods of housing and automobiles. The analysis illustrates how endangered species regulation affects the process of real estate development, leading to delays, cost increases, and reduced output. A final section offers concluding comments about the role of economics in endangered species protection and summarizes lessons from a case study.

This chapter does not attempt a comprehensive assessment of the costs and benefits of the Endangered Species Act. Rather, it provides a detailed look at the costs of regulation as viewed from the perspective of a significant industry. By illuminating the cost implications of habitat protection, it may be possible to develop cost-effective approaches that avoid excessive impacts while still affording protection to vulnerable species.

The Development Process and Regulation of Land Use Changes

The process of real estate development is highly variable and project dependent. Nonetheless, it can be divided into several distinct phases. In the planning and initiation phase, the development team is assembled, major hurdles are identified, and overall project objectives are assessed. Next, the feasibility of the project is considered through an assessment of market conditions, local and regional governmental objectives, availability and cost of financing, and potential project sites. Typically, land will be optioned by the end of this phase at the latest. The commitment phase of the development process involves land assembly, preparation and negotiation of environmental documents, assembly of materials needed for other regulatory approvals, preparation of documents needed for financing, and finalization of the project design. This phase culminates when the developer obtains the needed financing and regulatory approvals. The developer then moves on to project construction and operation.

Real estate development is a complex undertaking; following is a discussion of six factors that affect real estate development and the economic analysis of endangered species regulations.

Development is subject to multiple, uncoordinated regulatory processes. The land development process is subject to a complex web of federal, state, and local regulations. These regulatory processes are largely uncoordinated and have differing objectives, but the outcome of one permitting process can affect the others. A federal regulation meant to reduce the size or configuration of a housing project, for example, will require the developer to alter the application to the local agency. The result will be an increase in permitting costs.

Another implication of uncoordinated regulatory processes is that land development can be subject to multiple environmental regulations, and for more than one endangered species. The cumulative effect is likely to be larger than the sum of individual effects. Unless habitat associations are perfectly correlated across species or targeted amenities, adding regulations increases the amount of land set aside for conservation and increases permitting costs.

ESA regulation can be a signal that increases the cost of local regulation. Federal regulation of endangered species may affect the treatment of the project at the local level through a signaling effect. Regulators operate under uncertainty and may be risk averse. A federal designation may raise concerns about negative environmental impacts and lead the local agency to adopt a more conservative perspective on the development project. The response of a local agency to critical habitat designation may vary depending on local sensitivities to environmental protection and economic development, as well as the extent of knowledge on the part of local agencies and the public.

That ESA regulation increases the signaling effect of critical habitat designation suggests the following:

- The less informed the local agency is about the local environment, the more likely critical habitat designation will increase the difficulty of permitting
- The more a community emphasizes environmental protection over economic development, the stronger the impact of critical habitat designation on local approval
- The higher the actual risk posed by development, the stronger the impact of critical habitat designation

Critical habitat designation has an economic cost, even on lands with no federal nexus, and may affect severity of treatment and delay approvals at the local level. The delay effect will be larger in cities and counties with a more constrained permitting capacity.

Numerous physical constraints can influence site selection. Site selection can occur before or after the developer evaluates local market conditions. This process is often exhaustive since many factors must be considered. The National Association of Home Builders has developed a list of over a thousand factors to be considered before acquiring land for development. Those that make a site suitable for development include

- Zoning and growth-control regulations
- Location and neighborhood
- Size and shape
- Accessibility and visibility
- Environmental conditions
- Legal constraints
- Placement of utilities

Although an area may appear to have sufficient vacant land available for development, only a portion of those lands will satisfy previously stipulated conditions allowing development. Imposing additional regulation of land use changes through the Endangered Species Act may reduce the stock of land available for development in a region, reduce the regional stock of housing and other goods, and create unintended consequences on other resources (such as agriculture) and local planning processes.

Development is sequential in space and with regard to the regulatory queue. Leapfrog development can be problematic when local governments seek to confine development within defined boundaries. Nonsequential development requires utilities, roads, and other infrastructure to be extended longer distances, thereby increasing project costs. Thus, land away from the urban boundary may be at best an imperfect substitute for land on the boundary that is set aside for habitat protection.

Local governments have limited capacity to process permit applications and usually consider them in the sequence in which they would like the area to evolve. Developers interviewed for this study recalled instances where they were forced to wait long periods, in some cases several years, for a local government to work through its backlog of applications for projects that were closer to the city center.

Project delays can be costly to developers, consumers, and others. Regulation can significantly delay completion of a project, imposing potentially large costs on the developer, consumers, and others affected by project completion.

Consider the costs of delay on one component of land development expense: the cost of acquiring land. The developer typically acquires land for the project in three steps: a "free-look" period, a period in which the developer has locked up the land with an option to purchase, and closing. Developers usually acquire an option to purchase early in the process.

The ultimate decision to assemble land and construct a project is the result of many factors. If environmental regulation requires a redesign of the project or simply delays receipt of needed permits, overall project costs can increase significantly. For example, if environmental regulation reduces the number of allowable units in a project, then the developer may need to redesign the entire project, reconsider the financial analysis, and rework financing.

Beyond increasing development costs, delay can reduce societal benefits from development in other ways. Delay reduces the present value of the developer's return on investment and the final consumers' enjoyment of the product. In extreme cases, delay can lead to bankruptcy if the developer is highly leveraged; to relocation of key industries away from the region as they search for needed facilities; and to increases in costs of related infrastructure development—cost often borne by cities or counties, or financed by surcharges on residential development.

The development process requires sufficient financial and human capital. In general, housing can be expensive for two reasons: (1) Land is expensive; this explanation is consistent with the neoclassical Alonso-Muth-Mills framework taught to every graduate student in urban economics. (2) Supply is artificially restricted through zoning and other regulation; comparing different measures of the value of land in housing can confirm this. One approach to measuring land value would be to calculate the value of land implied by hedonic regressions of housing price on lot size and other characteristics. This is the intensive margin value of land. Another approach is to compare new home prices to the costs of construction and development. The difference is akin to the extensive margin value of land, or how much a unit of land is worth with a house on it.

In the neoclassical approach to urban growth and land markets of Alonso-Muth-Mills, the intensive and extensive margin values of land should be the same. This approach essentially argues that housing is expensive because land is expensive. However, if zoning and other growth controls are important determinants of housing prices because they artificially limit construction, then the intensive and extensive margin values of land may be quite different.

Various studies of housing prices and land values suggest that the American housing market can be divided into three broad categories. In the first, home prices are roughly equal to the cost of construction and development. This is the largest category and includes areas of rapid growth on the urban fringe where land is abundant and inexpensive. In the second, housing is priced below the cost of construction (Glaeser and Gyourko 2002). These areas are primarily central cities in the Midwest and Northeast such as Detroit and Philadelphia where there is almost no growth. In the third, housing prices exceed construction and land costs; Glaeser and Gyourko report that hedonic estimates of land values are as little as one-tenth their extensive margin value in these areas, providing strong evidence for the importance of regulation in determining the price of housing.[1] This category is perhaps the most interesting with respect to environmental regulation of land use changes in that it is already highly distorted. Additional regulations can potentially impose large incremental costs since new housing is already rationed.

Modeling Development

When the supply of housing is restricted, ESA regulation has great potential to alter its equilibrium price. Let the demand for new housing in a region be given by $P = D(Q)$. Typically, housing development is "lumpy" in the sense that much or all of new development in a region is contained within a single project, or at least built by a single developer. For this reason, regional and project-level impacts of regulation are highly related. Figure 15.1 shows the basic model of environment regulation. The preregulation quantity of development occurs at Q_0,

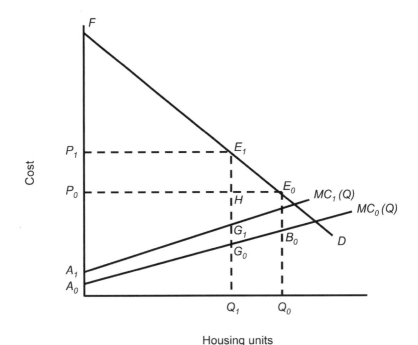

Figure 15.1. Impact of ESA regulation on housing development.

reflecting the fact that land at the project location earns some quasi rents. The gap between the market price of new housing and the marginal cost of construction and development reflects the scarcity value of land.

As discussed above, environmental regulation increases the marginal cost of home building because the developer must expend resources to get through the permitting process, redesign the project if necessary, and perform off-site mitigation. The postregulation marginal cost is denoted MC_1. The second effect of environmental regulation is to reduce the output of the project in an attempt to minimize on-site impacts. This effect is captured in the reduction in project output from Q_0 to its postregulation level, Q_1. An important consequence of the reduction in supply is that the price of new housing increases from P_0 to P_1. This change in price transfers wealth from consumers to developers and landowners.

The welfare effect of these two types of impacts can be seen in figure 15.1. The preregulation level of consumer and producer surplus is given by the area $FE_0B_0A_0$. Its postregulation level is $FE_1G_1A_1$. Consumers certainly lose from the regulation, but the effect on producers is ambiguous since marginal cost goes up, quantity produced goes down, and price increases.

The third effect of ESA regulation is to delay completion of the project. The loss from delay is potentially quite large and has been generally overlooked in the economic literature on regulation and permitting. The surplus concepts in figure 15.1 are net present values since housing is a durable good. Thus, the costs of delay involve the total amount of surplus lost from the failure to build during the period of delay, the length of this period, and the rate of interest. The cost of a one-period delay in completing the project is essentially the area of total surplus $FE_1G_1A_1$ multiplied by the rate of interest.

An example can illustrate data requirements, suggest how to calculate welfare losses, and demonstrate the potential range of welfare impacts. Consider a thousand-unit housing project proposed on a 250-acre parcel, implying a gross density of four units to the acre (typical for suburban Southern California). Suppose that the market price of the new homes is $250,000 and the constant marginal cost of development and construction (exclusive of land assembly costs) is $200,000 per housing unit.

Environmental regulation of the proposed land use change impacts the development in three ways: The cost of development is increased by $6,000 per unit, the number of homes is scaled back to nine hundred, and completion of the project is delayed by one year. Under the assumption of a unitary demand elasticity, application of the impact framework shows that the price of housing rises to $275,000. The total welfare loss is $28.5 million, over half of which results from delay.

An interesting extension of this example is to consider the implicit cost of conservation by permitting. If the end result of the permitting process is to prohibit development on one-tenth of the total acreage of the project, then the $28.5 million-dollar welfare loss should be divided by the 25 acres preserved by government oversight. Viewed this way, the cost of conservation by permitting exceeds $1 million per acre. Another way to calculate the implicit cost of conservation is to divide the total welfare loss by the total acreage of the project. This approach is also reasonable, especially if the developer is forced to perform off-site mitigation for environmental values lost by construction. Under this approach, the welfare loss should be divided by the entire 250-acre footprint of proposed development, implying that the per-acre cost of conservation is over $100,000.

ESA and the Housing Industry: The Case of the Coastal California Gnatcatcher

The general framework described above can be used to measure the costs of endangered species regulation on housing projects. For example, we can estimate costs imposed on the housing industry for 495,795 acres in Los Angeles, Orange, Riverside, San Bernardino, San Diego, and Ventura counties within the boundaries of proposed critical habitat for the California gnatcatcher.

The six-county region encompassing the gnatcatcher critical habitat is one of the largest centers of population growth and economic activity in California and the United States. According to decennial census estimates, the region grew by more than 2.1 million people (13 percent) between 1990 and 2000, and the number of households in the region grew by 540,000 (9 percent).

As the supply of housing tightens in the region, houses have become less affordable, particularly near the coast where land scarcity has led to dramatic price increases. For example, in the first quarter of 2001 the National Association of Home Builders estimated that only 27 percent of the homes sold in San Diego were affordable to a family of four earning the median income ($56,900) (SANDAG 2001). Projections developed by the California Department of Housing and Community Development indicate that Los Angeles and Orange counties lack sufficient land to accommodate the projected housing demand by 2010 and the agency predicts that San Diego and Ventura counties will run out of developable land around 2020 (Landis and Smith-Heimer 2000).

Table 15.1 displays basic socioeconomic characteristics for each of these units. Based on 2000 estimates, at present there are more than 2.5 million people, 846,566 households and 816,167 jobs located in the census tracts that intersect gnatcatcher critical habitat. Coastal regions are more densely settled and large centers of economic activity.

Interregional disparities in housing costs, income, and commute times are also evident. In coastal regions near units 3, 6, and 8, median home values in some census tracts are as high as $1 million, and higher in a few cases. These prices reflect in part the high costs of land in a region where land availability is highly constrained and also reflect the affluence of some communities in these units. Median income is high near the coastal critical habitat units in Los Angeles, Orange, and San Diego counties, with numerous census tracts reporting median household incomes greater than $100,000. Numerous census tracts near critical habitat units in Riverside County report average commute times of more than forty minutes one way and, while there is variability among median incomes and home values within regions, household income and home values are generally lower in the inland regions.

Since designation of critical habitat for the gnatcatcher will affect future urbanization in the six-county region, it is important to gauge the nature and extent of planned growth. Forecasts of population, households, and employment for the region are generated by two federally designated metropolitan planning agencies for Southern California: the Southern California Association of Governments (SCAG) and the San Diego Association of Governments (SANDAG).

Census-tract-level projections indicate that the population will grow by more than 1.1 million people (45 percent) in the 321 census tracts that encompass the gnatcatcher critical habitat. This surge in population will drive a commensurate increase in the number of households in the region. SCAG and SANDAG estimates predict that more than 376,000 houses will be built in the area that encompasses the critical habitat. Of these new housing units, over 124,000 will actually be built within gnatcatcher critical habitat (table 15.2; see Sunding and Arnold 2003 for full details on the method used to allocate growth to critical habitat areas).

As discussed in the previous section and presented graphically in figure 15.1, the effect of ESA regulation on housing projects is threefold. First, it increases the marginal cost of development. Second, it can place some land off-limits to development; from a project viewpoint, this effect is best expressed as a reduction in the number of housing units constructed. Third, it requires developers to obtain needed approvals from the federal government, which can delay completion of projects and cause losses to consumers and producers.

Calibrating an ESA impact framework requires that we specify how the presence of the gnatcatcher impacts residential housing projects. To do so, we use survey evidence taken from single-family housing projects in Southern California affected by the gnatcatcher, focusing on three types of impacts: the out-of-pocket costs incurred by the developer to obtain needed approvals, the reduction in the output of the project caused by the gnatcatcher, and the delay in completing the project.

TABLE 15.1 Socioeconomic characteristics of coastal California gnatcatcher (*Polioptila californica californica*) critical habitat units

Unit	Unit name	Number of intersecting census tracts[a]	Population[b]	Households[c]	Employment[d]	Median household income[e] ($)	Median new home price[f] (SF) ($)	Median new home size[g] (SF) (sq. ft.)	Average commute[b] (mins)
1	South San Diego County	44	202,185	67,440	59,182	60,218	424,439	2,275	28
2	Upper San Diego River and El Capitan linkage	6	33,508	13,429	8,410	56,513	410,207	1,845	35
3	North San Diego County Multi-species Habitat Conservation Plan	72	385,442	141,527	194,756	61,011	609,331	2,691	28
4	Fallbrook Naval Weapons Station	7	66,940	16,184	47,818	44,482	477,995	2,661	27
5	North County subarea of the multispecies habitat conservation plan for unincorporated San Diego County	20	179,567	54,714	77,953	55,271	311,680	2,313	30
6	Southern Orange County/northwestern San Diego County	17	205,123	67,949	92,565	88,754	598,051	2,492	31
7	Central/Coastal Natural Community Conservation Plan subregions of Orange County	27	220,855	74,827	86,792	87,277	672,544	2,372	29

8	Palos Verdes Peninsula subregion	19	118,898	42,323	23,508	94,917	1,393,305	3,781	31
9	East Los Angeles County; matrix Natural Community Conservation Plan subregion of Orange County	34	291,794	92,659	92,600	72,509	436,161	2,489	32
10	Western Riverside County MSHCP	45	728,934	237,927	185,413	55,972	293,193	2,377	34
11	San Bernardino Valley Multi-species Habitat Conservation Plan	6	86,883	25,368	18,019	63,568	308,402	2,399	36
12	East Los Angeles County linkage	13	110,968	30,938	31,578	62,729	779,879	3,701	32
13	Western Los Angeles and Ventura counties	34	239,006	77,996	76,266	73,466	528,120	2,770	32
	Total	321	2,528,189	846,566	816,167	68,250	400,835	2,144	31

Sources: Census 2000 tract-level population, household, and employment estimates from socioeconomic forecasts provided by the Southern California Association of Governments and the San Diego Association of Governments; Census 2000 data from Census 2000 summary file 3 data tables, published by the U.S. Census Bureau; GIS data for critical habitat designations provided by the U.S. Fish and Wildlife Service; GIS data for census tracts from TIGER/Line data compiled by U.S. Census Bureau; single-family-home transactions compiled by DataQuick; and home price indices used to inflate past sales are calculated using Conventional Mortgage Home Price Index for Metropolitan Statistical Areas, published by Freddie Mac.

a–hTotals may not be additive due to rounding and overlap.

eEqual to the median household income from intersecting census tracts. Income is reported in 1999 dollars.

f,gMedian home prices and square footage estimates are based on new home sales reported by DataQuick. Estimates include homes built in 1997 or later. Prices of homes sold prior to 2003 were adjusted into 2003 dollars using the Conventional Mortgage Home Price Index for Metropolitan Statistical Areas, published by Freddie Mac.

hCalculated as the aggregate commute time for workers older than age sixteen divided by total individuals older than age sixteen who did not work at home.

TABLE 15.2 Allocation of new housing to critical habitat units

Unit	Unit name	Number of intersecting census tracts[a]	Projected household increase by 2020[b]	New housing allocated to critical habitat designations[c]	% of total new housing allocated to critical habitat designations
1	South San Diego County	44	44,801	10,961	8.83
2	Upper San Diego River and El Capitan linkage	6	3,767	80	0.06
3	North San Diego County Multi-species Habitat Conservation Plan	72	48,155	18,066	14.56
4	Fallbrook Naval Weapons Station	7	2,669	7	0.01
5	North County subarea of the multispecies habitat conservation plan for unincorporated San Diego County	20	25,930	2,371	1.91
6	Southern Orange County/northwestern San Diego County	17	19,720	17,082	13.76
7	Central/Coastal Natural Community Conservation Plan subregions of Orange County	27	13,740	3,103	2.50
8	Palos Verdes Peninsula subregion	19	4,734	541	0.44
9	East Los Angeles County; matrix Natural Community Conservation Plan subregion of Orange County	34	22,886	4,936	3.98
10	Western Riverside County Multi-species Habitat Conservation Plan	45	165,204	37,289	30.05
11	San Bernardino Valley Multi-species Habitat Conservation Plan	6	16,392	5,713	4.60

12	East Los Angeles County linkage	13	2,944	1,147	0.92
13	Western Los Angeles and Ventura counties	34	45,906	22,815	18.38
	Total	321	376,627	124,110	100.00

Sources: Census 2000 tract-level population, household, and employment estimates from socioeconomic forecasts provided by the Southern California Association of Governments and the San Diego Association of Governments; GIS data for critical habitat designations provided by the U.S. Fish and Wildlife Service; GIS data for census tracts from TIGER/Line data compiled by U.S. Census Bureau; single-family-home transactions compiled by DataQuick; and home price indices used to inflate past sales are calculated using Conventional Mortgage Home Price Index for Metropolitan Statistical Areas, published by Freddie Mac.

a—Totals may not be additive due to rounding and overlap.

c—Household estimates based on 1990 census tracts in the SCAG region, and 2000 census tracts in the SANDAG region. Estimates may differ slightly from Census 2000 estimates.

Several case studies help illustrate the value of these parameters:

- *Project A* Approximately $5 million in mitigation and transaction costs for a 200-acre site, not including the lost value of property devoted to on-site mitigation. The land supported 1,200 residential units, implying per-unit mitigation costs of $4,166 per unit.
- *Project B* A 268-unit residential project. Mitigation costs alone were $1.5 million, implying per-unit mitigation costs of $5,597.
- *Project C* A 193-unit residential project. Gnatcatcher concerns delayed completion of the project by twelve months and resulted in the loss of eighteen units.
- *Project D* The Central/Coastal Natural Community Conservation Plan. This plan includes a mitigation bank component authorizing developers to "buy into" the mitigation provided at a cost of $50,000 per acre. At a density of six units per acre, a typical number for Orange County, cost per unit is $8,333. This "buy-in" feature of the plan was approved by the U.S. Fish and Wildlife Service and presumably constitutes the agency's estimate of a reasonable cost to mitigate for endangered species impacts.

The U.S. Fish and Wildlife Service is assessing the impact of the gnatcatcher listing on housing projects in Southern California. This work has been carried out largely through a review of biological opinions and other evidence (Economic and Planning Systems, pers. comm., October 2003). Consistent with these findings, the permitting, redesign, and mitigation costs resulting from the gnatcatcher listing can be set at $4,000 per housing unit, project delay at twelve months, and the reduction in project output at 10 percent. To calculate losses in profit and consumer surplus resulting from delay, a discount rate of 5 percent is used.

By using a partial equilibrium model of the housing market in the 321 census tracts comprising critical habitat for the gnatcatcher, the economic costs of the listing can be calculated based on the framework presented in the last section. The model calculates changes in housing output and prices, and of consumer, producer, and landowner welfare resulting from the listing, within the proposed critical habitat.

Table 15.3 shows economic impacts of the gnatcatcher listing disaggregated by critical habitat unit and sector. Total impacts are largest in units 3 ($908 million), 6 ($871 million), 13 ($713 million), and 10 ($669 million). These units have high median home prices and a large percentage allocation of new households to critical habitat. Impacts are lowest in units 4 ($166,000) and 2 ($2.1 million) due to the small amount of growth anticipated in these areas. Taken together, these figures indicate that the impact of the gnatcatcher listing on the housing sector will exceed $4.2 billion for the period 2003–20.

TABLE 15.3 Allocation of impacts to critical habitat units

Unit	Unit name	Economic costs of housing market regulation ($)
1	South San Diego County	373,026,641
2	Upper San Diego River and El Capitan linkage	2,093,444
3	North San Diego County Multi-species Habitat Conservation Plan	908,069,175
4	Fallbrook Naval Weapons Station	166,821
5	North County subarea of the multispecies habitat conservation plan for unincorporated San Diego County	101,083,662
6	Southern Orange County/northwestern San Diego County	870,824,022
7	Central/Coastal Natural Community Conservation Plan subregions of Orange County	203,082,118
8	Palos Verdes Peninsula subregion	40,098,993
9	East Los Angeles County; matrix Natural Community Conservation Plan subregion of Orange County	210,268,508
10	Western Riverside County Multi-species Habitat Conservation Plan	668,546,608
11	San Bernardino Valley Multi-species Habitat Conservation Plan	94,503,144
12	East Los Angeles County linkage	52,532,840
13	Western Los Angeles and Ventura counties	712,681,176
	Total	4,236,977,153

Between 2003 and 2020, the total footprint of new housing in the area of gnatcatcher critical habitat is less than 30,000 acres, or roughly 6 percent of the total amount of critical habitat proposed (Landis et al. 2000). Thus, the economic cost of the gnatcatcher listing is close to $150,000 per developed acre, and costs exceed $400,000 per developed acre in 18 of 321 census tracts. This range of values is consistent with the simulation results of the previous section and provides a good illustration of why the Endangered Species Act has generated such controversy. Analysis of census-tract-level impacts also suggests, for example, that 70 percent of all housing market losses from the gnatcatcher listing—over $3 billion in current dollars—could be avoided by eliminating protections on just 3 percent of its habitat (or 50 percent of the 6 percent of land slated for development by 2020). Assessment of whether this is a sensible reform depends on the biological value of this fraction of habitat.

Other factors can be added to this basic model. For example, restricting the supply of new homes should increase the price of existing homes. However, this effect is a transfer between the current and future owners of these homes and thus it nets out of the welfare calculation. Nonetheless, this is an important consideration from a political point of view and is, in fact, the impetus for much zoning regulation.

Yet another factor would be the value of open space created by the endangered species regulation. The value of this open space may increase home values by increasing the stock of local amenities, thereby stimulating demand. In general, the willingness to pay for open space will depend heavily on its quality, location, and accessibility. In the example of the gnatcatcher, it is doubtful that the value of open space will rise above $4 billion. Regulation of the 30,000 acres of anticipated housing development will create roughly 3,000 acres of open space according to the parameters of the impact model. The value of this open space would have to exceed $1 million per acre to eliminate all costs of the gnatcatcher protections. Such an outcome is highly unlikely, but generally the value of open space created reduces the economic cost of ESA regulations.

Conclusion

The case of the gnatcatcher illustrates that the economic impacts of ESA regulation can be highly localized and dependent on the pattern of development. More than 90 percent of the land designated as gnatcatcher critical habitat is not expected to be developed in the next twenty years, and all impacts are concentrated on the small fraction of land that is projected to be developed. Growth patterns are influenced in turn by physical constraints on developable land, the amount and location of preexisting development, competing non-urban uses, and local zoning ordinances and growth controls (including a limited capacity of local agencies to process applications for changes in land use).

Because the economic impacts of ESA regulations are not uniform over space, there may be great value in investments in knowledge about the landscape. ESA regulations can slow the development process and increase costs, placing burdens on developers and landowners, and, especially, on consumers. If the federal government were to obtain more detailed knowledge about the occurrence and needs of endangered and threatened species, it may be possible to focus protection in areas where there are likely to be small economic costs.

Analysis of ESA regulation costs shows that traditional measures of economic cost, such as the cost of preparing and negotiating a permit, can seriously understate the actual impacts. In areas where land is scarce, regulation that further restricts development can cause significant increases in the price of housing and other outputs. These price increases are borne primarily by consumers since the change in price transfers welfare from consumers to developers and landowners.

Another lesson taken from the case study is that project delays are a primary and significant source of the economic cost of ESA regulations. Delay imposes losses on all participants in the development process because there are no compensating price changes to redistribute losses. In simulations performed in other studies, delay has been shown to account for over half the economic costs of environmental regulations pertaining to land use changes. The costs of delay can be reduced by speeding up the government's decision-making process, perhaps through special assessments on development with the revenues earmarked for environmental agencies.

16   Land Use Planning

Thomas A. Scott, Linda Fernandez, and Michael F. Allen

The 1973 Endangered Species Act (ESA) has come to be used as a federal land use planning law, altering the process of suburban development in cities across the western United States (Sullivan and Scott 2000). This unplanned authority evolved through court interpretation of ESA intent (Batt 1995) and because the absolute prohibitions of the ESA are ideally suited to stop or leverage land development projects (Scott et al. 1995; Platt 1996). The resulting conflicts have been used as evidence of ESA hegemony (Thornton 1991; Sunding, this volume) and the failure of species-specific conservation (Jasny et al. 1997).

We argue that conflicts over application of the Endangered Species Act are symptoms of a broader conflict over land use along the wildland-urban interface, fueled by demand for housing and the rapid transition from wild to suburban landscapes. The act became a nexus for resolving suburban sprawl, not because it protected species, but because it could stop land development until the fate of wildlands was settled. From a broader perspective, the ESA stablized land use planning in hyperbolic real estate markets and forced regional planning in areas of sprawl.

In this chapter we discuss the impact of the Endangered Species Act in Southern California, an area rich with endangered species and also one of the fastest-growing urban areas in the United States.

Land Use Conflicts in the Wildland-Urban Interface

Most conflicts over the Endangered Species Act can be traced to our continuing inability to reconcile laws of wildlife and land use, which diverged early in our country's history when the framers of the U.S. Constitution gave control of wildlife to states and rights associated with land and resource use to private landowners. However, as long as Americans considered wildlands boundless, they would support only limited state and federal action regulating the destruction of wildlife habitat on private property (see Goble et al. 2006).

As recently as the 1980s, land use and resource agencies mostly pursued independent policies, and interagency coordination concerning wildlife, including endangered species, was rare. For example, in Southern California it was illegal to capture or handle Stephens' kangaroo rats (*Dipodomys stephensi*) without a special permit from the California Department of Fish and Game. However, by issuing soil-grading permits within the species' habitat, the county of Riverside in effect permitted landowners to indiscriminately kill this state-listed endangered species. As the complexity of the urban-wildland interface increased, the applications of local land use policies versus state and federal wildlife laws became even more haphazard.

The primary forum for discussing wildland conversion in California is the California Environmental Quality Act (CEQA), which requires project proponents to disclose habitat conversions but has no authority to resolve them (Fulton 1999). It does allow suits and injunctions if its protocols are not followed, potentially stalling a project until the proponents go bankrupt.

Early applications of the Endangered Species Act to private land were ambiguous, but, beginning in the 1980s protection under the ESA for habitat on private lands gradually increased (Goble, this volume), and the two-hundred-year-old separation of wildlife management and land development ended. Neither land use nor wildlife laws provided solutions to problems along the interface until 1982, when the ESA was amended to allow for the use of habitat conservation plans. It seems clear, however, that many of the problems attributed to use of the ESA were part of a broader conflict over land use in California well before the act was invoked.

The Need for New Land Management Options

In 2002 California's single-family detached-housing industry was worth over $65 billion (U.S. Census Bureau 2005). From 1970 to 1990, the Southern California counties of Riverside, Orange, and San Diego added over 1.4 million single-family detached houses, with more than 700,000 houses built in six years (fig. 16.1) (Scott and Sullivan 2000). Land development followed transportation corridors, generating constellations of suburbs across an urban-wildland gradient, with thousands of miles of edge between housing and habitat (Scott et al. 1995). California uses land use laws to control sprawl, but in some instances their flexibility has been exploited by market forces to override land use controls, especially in rural communities ill-equipped to deal with rapid suburban growth (Daniels 1999).

The rush to build housing created a new problem for developers: well-educated, politically active homebuyers began to populate the wildland-urban

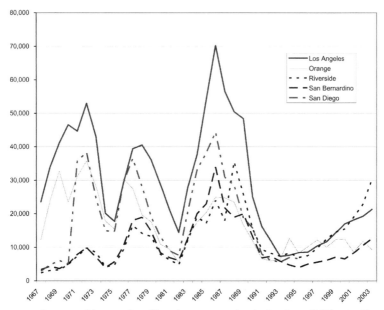

Figure 16.1. Boom-and-bust cycles of housing construction in Southern California. Housing permits for Southern California counties oscillate between rapid upswings that overwhelm planning agencies (1982–87) and downswings that reduce their staff (1987–92). (Data from SCAG Socioeconomic Database established by the Southern California Association of Governments, Community Division.)

interface, demanding protection for their lifestyles and investments (Sullivan and Scott 2000; Standiford and Scott 2001). Growth control advocates failed to slow suburban construction (Warner and Molotch 1995) but became a political force in local communities. The demand for single-family detached homes drove investors to find exemptions, special plans, and ways to circumvent growth ordinances and land use restrictions (Jonas and Wilson 1999).

Habitat Conservation Plans

By the late 1970s, land developers recognized that the Endangered Species Act could be invoked to stop or delay the development process, potentially destabilizing the housing construction industry. Timing and certainty are critical elements in suburban development, affecting costs, profits, and bankruptcies (Sunding, this volume). Land developers sought to resolve the uncertainty created by the ESA and helped develop in habitat conservation plans (HCPs). HCPs provided land developers a flexible tool for avoiding conflict and forced an open discussion of these amenity values, accepting their validity but limiting their impact in negotiated settlements.

The HCP process began to reintegrate wildlife into land governance. In Southern California, committees of stakeholders formed in San Diego, Orange, and Riverside counties, typically at the prompting of the development community (Jasny et al. 1997; Hood 1998). Although habitat conservation plans were conceived by the development community, very few were undertaken in the 1980s because the process was unpredictable, potentially costing a great deal of time and money with no guarantee a permit would be issued. But with hundreds of rare and endangered species in Southern California, nearly all housing projects faced the prospect of developing serial HCPs. A precedent had been set with the San Bruno Mountain Habitat Conservation Plan, which addressed three, and possibly more, listed species (County of San Mateo Planning Commission 1982), but it was ten years before multiple-species HCPs would be proposed.

Multispecies Habitat Conservation Plans

In the early 1990s, the Irvine Ranch Company proposed that California develop a regional system to preserve endangered species and to resolve all ESA section 9 issues with one permit agreement. The company appealed to then-governor Pete Wilson to create a state-level process that would provide multiple 10(a) permits from the U.S. Fish and Wildlife Service. State staffers used the political support of the development community to create the California Natural Community Conservation Planning Act (Jasny et al. 1997; Manson 1994). Under an agreement with the U.S. Department of the Interior (4[d]) rule, the State Resources Agency assumed control of multispecies habitat conservation plans (MSHCPs) in California with federal oversight. It provided a state framework and funding for the development of bioregional plans for habitat protection. The Natural Community Conservation Planning (NCCP) program process was voluntary and open to any scale of land unit from single properties to counties and cities.

Early MSHCP processes had no set structure, and both land developers and wildlife groups lobbied hard on behalf of their own interests. For the first time, however, all groups interested in wildlife protection and real estate development were operating under the same system of policy and law. Multispecies habitat conservation plans became the common platform for resolution of wildlife and land development issues. Land developers were the primary beneficiaries; other stakeholders (e.g., environmentalists, agriculturalists, conservationists, trade groups, elected officials, and home owners) became reactive elements, attempting to recalibrate multispecies habitat conservation plans in a muddled democratic process.

Landowners within these jurisdictions could opt out of MSHCP agreements but in doing so had to find their own means of avoiding ESA restrictions as they converted wildlands. Local community groups resisted multispecies habitat conservation plans (Jonas and Wilson 1999) but recognized their potential for cost sharing and for applying regional solutions to local problems. Conservationists were initially suspicious that the regulatory certainty provided to developers would not be matched by long-term certainty for species persistence (Hood 1998; Sullivan and Scott 2000). This concern, however, was outweighed by the perception that multispecies habitat conservation plans could be used to protect unlisted species and unique ecosystems that lacked listed species.

Regional planning may be the only way to efficiently manage for species persistence in fragmented landscapes, such as those in Southern California (Noss et al. 1997). Multispecies habitat conservation plans provide a mechanism to protect key habitat areas while allowing development to continue within the framework of community goals (Jonas and Wilson 1999).

This is not to say that multispecies habitat conservation plans are without risks. An ill-conceived plan could be a one-time process that irreparably damages wildlife conservation and/or causes unnecessary costs in land development. The Interior Department's "No Surprises" policy is a particularly poignant example of this controversy (Kostyack 1998). Conservation groups argued that the Southern California firestorms in 2003 were not adequately addressed in the San Diego and Riverside multispecies habitat conservation plans (Bond and Bradley 2004). These fires consumed 26,779 acres of threatened California gnatcatcher (*Polioptila californica californica*) habitat, 5,389 acres of endangered mountain yellow-legged frog (*Rana muscosa*) habitat, and 3,055 acres of endangered least Bell's vireo habitat. However, fires are considered to be either an unforeseen circumstance, which is the permittee's responsibility to fix, or they are fall under the administrative "No Surprises" rule. In the latter case, the federal government makes up any shortfall in species persistence caused by incomplete information in the 10(a) permits. Multispecies habitat conservation plans potentially pass management costs from land developers to the public because no economic disincentive exists for inadequate preparation of such a plan by local governments and land developers.

Multispecies habitat conservation plans now overlay all wildlands south and east of metropolitan Los Angeles (fig. 16.2). The Endangered Species Act became a regulatory stick, driving voluntary habitat conservation, multilevel government cooperation, and regional land use planning. Plan proponents found that the momentum of multispecies habitat conservation plans often resolved broader land development, a simplification that saved time and increased certainty for land developers. The voluntary nature of MSHCP participation remains a critical element for almost all plans.

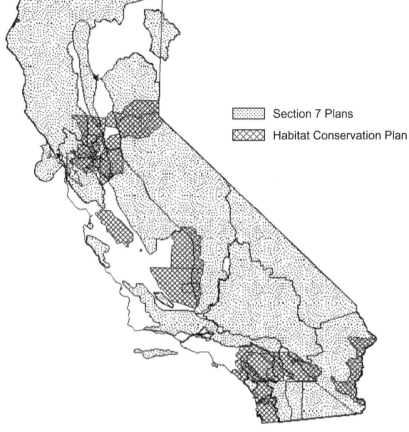

Figure 16.2. Multispecies bioregional planning under the Endangered Species Act in California. Approximately 84 percent of the state's area is affected by the ESA, prompted by federal section 7 consultations (77 percent; stipple) or ESA habitat conservation planning (15 percent; crosshatch). (Compiled from original MSHCPs and Section 7 planning documents, T. Scott unpublished data.)

Economic Consequences of the Endangered Species Act on Land Use

The economic impact of the Endangered Species Act on land development must be viewed within the context of broader land use constraints. Property rights do not exist without government sanction and protection, and the responsibilities that come with that protection should not be viewed as economic externalities. Courts have always honored the right to develop land but have also upheld zoning, covenants, nuisance laws, and other restrictions protecting the rights of other citizens (see Platt 1996). Despite popular claims of landowner sovereignty, constraints imposed by the land regulations (including the ESA) have been upheld by U.S. Supreme Court (e.g., *Babbitt v. Sweet Home*; see Platt 1996). The exceptions have been limited to cases where a government-sponsored change in zoning destroyed all property values after purchase (e.g., *Lucas v. South Carolina Coastal Council*; see Daniels 1999).

The discovery of an ESA-listed species may alter the economic expectations of a landowner by prohibiting changes in property use. This superficially resembles the *Lucas* decision; however, attempts to change land use designations are not protected under the Fifth Amendment anymore than speculations and investments are protected in the stock market. A gray area of law exists when an otherwise approved use of land is blocked by section 9 after a resident species is listed. This special case typically applies to single-home construction on small parcels (less than 5 acres), often with inexperienced landowners who have difficulty negotiating agency requirements.

Large-scale land development companies, in contrast, are neither naïve nor uninformed. Their projects often require complex permitting and special-plan amendments to county general plans. Since 1982, the cost of housing construction has routinely included negotiated settlements for section 9 constraints (Sullivan and Scott 2000). Under sections 7 and 9 of the act, petitions generate costs associated with assessment of the ESA nexus, planning solutions for *incidental take* of listed species, HCP implementation, and long-term HCP management.

In the eastern United States, most landowners have assumed the costs and risks of habitat conservation plans. In the West, Congress began a precedent of government-sponsored HCPs by spending millions of dollars to help timber companies address the issue of the northern spotted owl (*Strix occidentalis caurina*) (Lint and Martin 2005). When the Irvine Ranch Company initiated statewide community conservation planning in Southern California, it prompted the State Resources Agency to launch a multimillion-dollar program in conservation planning.

Initially, county governments were reluctant to use their limited resources in ESA planning, but by the year 2000 most NCCPs were implemented by city and county governments using public funds. More important, a wide array of state and local agencies contributed personnel and logistical resources (e.g., data, GIS analyses) to multispecies habitat conservation plans. Conservation groups, despite their doubt about the MSHCPs, donated thousands of hours of volunteer time to develop such plans. Since then, three of the four costs associated with habitat conversion permits (assessment, planning, long-term management) have shifted from land developers to the public agencies. The fourth cost, plan implementation, is borne by both land developers and public agencies, but in many cases, core elements of the plans are paid for with state or federal resources.

Western Riverside County Multi-Species Habitat Conservation Plan

In 1989, the county of Riverside took the lead in first developing the Stephens' Kangaroo Rat Habitat Conservation Plan (Riverside County Habitat Conservation Agency 1996; USFWS 1996d). The Stephens' kangaroo rat was listed as endangered in 1989 (USFWS 1988), primarily because its habitat was coincidental with most suitable land for development in Riverside County (Feldman 1995). The county assumed the risks and costs of getting a section 10(a) permit for all potential land developers with kangaroo rat problems. The plan was heavily subsidized by the Metropolitan Water District and other agencies that needed permits for incidental take of Stephens' kangaroo rat to complete water and transportation projects. These agencies drove the process, purchasing the habitat reserves that formed the core plan. It is unclear if the plan would have been viable without these reserves and the commitment of management funds by county, state, and federal governments.

Developers bought coverage under a county 10(a) permit to convert kangaroo rat habitat into housing. They paid a development fee per housing unit. In effect, landowners were now free to remove a public resource (kangaroo rats) from their land if they paid the county to take care of the consequences. Most public facilities such as dams, sewer treatment plants, schools, and roads provide efficient services through economy of scale, efficient management, and coordinated logistics. To permit applicants, however, paying a capital facility fee for a sewer hook-up seemed reasonable; paying for the right to remove kangaroo rats, did not. Environmental groups also contested the fee, charging that as a negotiated settlement rather than a calculation of actual cost of land acquisition, it was too low (Dan Silver, pers. comm.). They also charged that because developers were not required to fund a management endowment, agencies assumed preserve management costs.

Land developers benefited from the Stephens' Kangaroo Rat Habitat Conservation Plan because it limited landowner responsibilities for management of an endangered species. Furthermore, the limit was not set solely by the habitat needs of the species but was negotiated as a balance between public good and private rights. In the end, the plan restricted the extent of lands designated to protect the public good (kangaroo rat habitat persistence), without restricting land development in Riverside County. The county used eminent domain to condemn a few parcels it needed to fulfill the 10(a) permit requirements, but even this taking was designed to protect the rights of other landowners who wanted to use the county's 10(a) permit to convert wildlife habitat to housing.

In 1993, Riverside County implemented a multispecies habitat conservation plan to permit the incidental take of the wide number of rare species found in the county. In 2004 the Western Riverside County Multi-Species Habitat Conservation Plan was signed by county, state, and federal officials, protecting 146 species. The plan was part of an overall growth proposal seeking to maintain the region's wildlife and quality of life as the population doubles to 3 million by 2020 (Southern California Association of Governments 2001).

The plan provided economic flexibility and economy of scale for participating cities, limited the exposure of developers to ESA costs, and provided environmentalists with a mechanism for funding wildland preserves. It also allowed fourteen cities to consolidate permit review by federal agencies, jointly allocate open space, and receive transportation funds. More important, it reestablished local government sovereignty over land development and open space. Developers avoided high transactions costs, delays, and uncertainty in permitting and mitigation from joint rather than independent action. David Hayes, former deputy secretary of the Department of the Interior, cited the $30 million plan as an example of the "No Surprises" policy, which assures developers that once they comply with a habitat conservation plan they will not face further building restrictions or fees (Fisher 2004).

The 1.2-million-acre MSHCP area includes 500,000 acres for preservation and 700,000 developable acres. The preserve increases the probability of actual protection of habitat and benefits from economies of scale and scope as pooled resources over time means the cumulative amount pays for a larger amount of protected habitat. The 500,000 preserved acres comprise 350,000 acres of existing public land and 153,000 acquired acres. Federal grants and state matching funds totaling $19 million in 2003 have also been instrumental in land acquisition. County funds were used to acquire part of the 153,000 acres. These public sector contributions make up a significant portion of the cost of habitat protection.

The burden of paying for remaining MSHCP acquisitions (about 80,000 acres) is shared. Developers pay a uniform mitigation fee to offset impacts of their development project on habitat for endangered species. For example, the rates are $1,800 per single-family home, $10,816 per acre for commercial construction, and $7,780 per acre for industrial development. These can be compared to the higher transportation impact fee of $6,650 per home, $7.81 per square foot of commercial construction, and $1.45 per square foot of industrial development (David Taussig and Associates 2003). Thus, developers receive reduced permitting costs and the market value of their development is increased by provision of open space. The underlying demand for housing and amenities (such as open space) has led to an increase in retail price of houses. The development impact fee can be thought of as parallel to preferential taxation used in the past through the California Land Conversion Act in order to retain land in agricultural or open space through reduced taxes. The taxes are based on use value of capitalized rental income rather than on market value. Economists cite greater efficiency in a flat, uniform rate for impact fees than in fees based on the actual impact of development on the margin. Impact fee programs lead to up-front payment by developers to help acquire habitat for endangered species. The fees are used to improve public goods and therefore generate a variety of amenity values for existing and new residents.

Nevertheless, some legal rulings have rejected equating impact fees with marginal impacts in the context of "takings" (Patterson 1999). The use of im-pact fees for operation and maintenance costs has been questioned (Ihlanfeldt and Shaughnessy 2002), suggesting that developers may avoid the cost of species persistence despite it being a guiding tenet of habitat conservation plans.

Enhancing Economic Incentives

Open space, whether public or private, is highly valued. There is public demand for wildland habitats, albeit as open space, strong enough to generate revenue to ensure such habitat is acquired and maintained. Data on the price and demand for housing is used in the hedonic pricing method for valuing habitat. The premise is that home buyers place value on the public-good improvements asso-ciated with impact fees. Recent hedonic modeling on this topic by Ihlanfeldt and Shaughnessy (2002) finds that in Dade County, Florida, a $1 increase in fees generates a $1.60 increase in prices of new and existing houses. This finding suggests that home buyers value public good benefits derived from fees by more than their costs. Thorsnes (2002) finds that new 1-acre subdivision lots close to forest preserves in Grand Rapids, Michigan, sold for $5,800 to $8,400 more than those farther away. He contends that this reflects higher amenity values provided by the preserve. Similar results were derived by Irwin (2002) in a study in central Maryland. She finds that preserving open space near residential areas increased residential land prices by $2,500 to $4,500 per acre. The study also revealed that higher values accrued when open space was preserved by private owners through conservation or agricultural easements. Bluffstone and Fazeli (2002) found that residents of Redlands, California, were willing to pay ap-proximately $54 per household per year to establish a 15,000-acre multiuse state park in San Timoteo Canyon.

These surveys indicate general support for ESA habitat values and its pub-lic benefits, for developers who generate higher value by complying with regu-latory requirements, and for flexible solutions that accommodate housing and amenities simultaneously. Between 1986 and 2000, 671 local land use initia-tives were considered by incumbent voters in California and in 2000 sixty percent approved limits on growth (Carrigg 2002). Virginia-based Avalon Bay Communities was forced to abandon its 378-unit Scripps Ranch project in northern San Diego County because of massive local opposition (Strickland 2001). Growth control may increase land rents, but part of the increase is capitalized as amenity values. Overall, developers benefit from multispecies habitat conservation plans through significant pubic subsidies that reduce private costs along with increases in home market values associated with open space preservation.

From a mechanistic perspective, multispecies habitat conservation plans can allow larger, contiguous tracts of habitat to be awarded higher conservation credit value. If credits earned within an MSHCP permit are auctioned and traded among developers in a credit market, then incentives will be based on the dynamics of price, parcel by parcel. Higher value of quality habitats could be recognized and captured explicitly; developers and landowners would act accordingly to capitalize on land amenities of such contiguous habitat. This would allow valuation of the spatial changes at the margin in rents; flat rather than averaged fees would be levied to all developers, since flat fees often fail to cover infrastructure costs, such as water and electric utilities for development with dispersed housing patterns.

Conclusion

The Endangered Species Act has been an effective policy lever to induce regional planning for suburban wildlands. The broad language of the act has allowed it to expand its authority as court decisions clarify its powers. Given the history of wildlife law in the United States and the fortuitous timing of the act, it is unlikely another regulation could have achieved this goal. Land developers have played an active role in modifying the ESA; some prohibitions have eventually worked in the favor of developers through multispecies habitat conservation plans (Jonas and Wilson 1999).

Economic consequences of the Endangered Species Act on land development include time, risk, and monetary costs to developers. Multispecies habitat conservation plans streamline local permitting processes. ESA-related costs are only a portion of the costs of land development, and the amenity value created by MSHCP reserves compensates land developers by increasing value in market price and demand for housing. ESA costs to land development are a result of a broader resistance to wildland conversion, which would likely manifest itself in some form in the absence of the ESA. Furthermore, multispecies habitat conservation plans have distributed the costs of the act in the same manner that many infrastructure costs are distributed among local, state, and federal governments.

Section 2(b) of the Endangered Species Act states that "The purposes of this Act are to provide a means whereby the ecosystems upon which endangered species and threatened species depend may be conserved." Exurban ecosystems were headed for inadvertent destruction without the ESA, because Americans could not agree on the set of values to protect along the wildland-urban interface, if they even saw the conflicts. Winton Churchill's quote, "The Americans will always do the right thing . . . after they've exhausted all the alternatives," is a fitting explanation for the lack of integrated management in ecosystems along the interface. Without the ESA the right things would have been done too late, because problem recognition lagged so far behind the juggernaut of suburban development.

17 Arbitrage and Options

Geoffrey Heal

The Endangered Species Act (ESA) is one of the most important pillars of environmental conservation in the United States, and arguably one of the most controversial. The operation of the act has evolved substantially since its inception in 1973. The ESA was originally administered in an economically inefficient fashion, a failing that was bad economics and bad politics, but the last two decades have seen more imaginative and flexible approaches to its implementation, with the introduction of habitat conservation plans, natural community conservation plans, mitigation banking, and safe harbor agreements (Brown and Shogren 1998; Noss et al. 1997; Czech and Krausman 2001). These have undoubtedly made attainment of the act's goals less costly and softened its impact on landowners, particularly private landowners (see Bean and Wilcove 1997; Polasky and Doremus 1998). But have they compromised the effectiveness of the act from a conservation perspective? Where will such developments lead if pursued to their fullest extents? Do they represent a good model for the evolution of species and habitat conservation?

This chapter focuses on mitigation banking, an approach which, although widely used and growing in acceptance, has rarely been the subject of a thorough analytical study melding economic and ecological concepts. We develop an analytical model of mitigation banking and safe harbor agreements in the context of the ESA and use this as a vehicle to study the impact of such measures on the conservation of species and its economic cost.

Mitigation banking was introduced in the Clean Water Act of 1972. It allows developers to use threatened and protected habitat provided they mitigate by ensuring conservation in perpetuity of a compensating amount of equivalent habitat elsewhere, as determined by the appropriate conservation authority. Compensation can be flexible; for example, agencies can require that more than 1 acre of land be set aside elsewhere to compensate for the use of one of the original acres, and a developer may conserve more equivalent land than required to sell at a later date to other developers. The process of creating equivalent conserved land in excess of immediate requirements to hold for future sale to others who need to mitigate, is known as mitigation banking and is now a well-developed practice.

A more complex version of mitigation banking is also applied under the Endangered Species Act. International Paper (IP) and the U.S. Fish and Wildlife Service, for example, have used mitigation banking to protect the endangered red-cockaded woodpecker (*Picoides borealis*), which nests in forests owned by the company. The USFWS and International Paper agreed on a target number of breeding woodpecker pairs that the company would protect to comply with the Endangered Species Act; by meeting or exceeding this number, the company is free to use its land without additional restriction (Bayon 2002; Bonnie 1999; Bonnie and Bean 1996). Further, the agreement states that surplus breeding on the land can be "banked"—used by the company to offset ESA requirements for red-cockaded woodpeckers elsewhere. Because International Paper can sell its "surplus" woodpeckers to other landowners, the company has an economic incentive to encourage the presence of endangered species on its property. The company estimates that it can sell banked credits for breeding pairs for about $100,000 per pair. If several pairs can nest on each acre, the value of land for breeding woodpeckers greatly exceeds its value as a source of timber.

The extension of mitigation banking to species conservation has several potential advantages: it reduces the cost of ESA compliance for landowners and provide them with clear financial incentives to encourage conservation (see Fox et al., this volume, for an overview of species conservation banking). However, the idea has not yet been investigated or modeled in depth.

In this chapter, I propose that mitigation banking of species, paired with safe harbor agreements, can benefit landowners by reducing the burden of ESA requirements. By encouraging populations of endangered species on land not zoned for development, and "banking" the increase, landowners can benefit from the presence of endangered species but still retain the right to develop land otherwise restricted by ESA regulations.

A Model of Mitigation Banking

The simplest case of mitigation banking involves an exchange of land, or habitat. In this case, we assume an extant area of habitat (H_0) that is valuable and deserving protection. The U.S. Fish and Wildlife Service, under pressure to open the area to development, determines that an amount $\underline{H}$ must be conserved, and that the difference, $[H_0 - \underline{H}]$, can be sold for development. In addition, more of the initial area H_0 can be sold if an equivalent amount of currently unpreserved similar habitat is irreversibly preserved: this is the banking provision.

We further assume that a unit of similar habitat elsewhere is deemed equivalent if it is F times the area of the amount to be developed. The factor F is set by the management authority (the USFWS) on the basis of ecological considerations. F need not be constant, depending on the distance between the new land and the original habitat, and the similarities (or dissimilarities) of such characteristics as their soil, vegetation, and species supported. But because we are not explicitly modeling these characteristics, we take F to be a constant without a loss of generality. To make matters simpler still, we take F to be 1.

There is a demand for land for development in the original habitat. The demand curve is described by $P = f(S)$ where S is the amount supplied and P is the amount developers are willing to pay for an extra unit: clearly P is decreasing in S. Absent any mitigation, the supply of land for development would be $[H_0 - \underline{H}]$ and the market price would be $P = f(H_0 - \underline{H})$. Mitigation allows the supply of land for development to be increased by the amount of land available for mitigation. But mitigation has a cost: the land to be banked must be purchased and set aside. As more equivalent land is purchased and set aside the cost of finding such land will rise: we assume the cost curve of land for mitigation is $C(M)$ where C is the cost of an extra unit and M is the amount used for mitigation. At a market price of P per unit of land, therefore, the total supply is the amount of the initial area allowed to be used for development $[H_0 - \underline{H}]$ plus the amount supplied for mitigation at a market price of P, which is the value of M given by $C(M) = P$. Hence, we have a market equilibrium with mitigation when the price is such that demand and supply are equal, so that

$$f(H_0 - \underline{H} + M) = C(M)$$

Figure 17.1 shows this diagrammatically. $[H_0 - \underline{H}]$ is the amount of the original space made available for development, a supply made available inelastically. To this is added the supply from mitigation banking, $C(M)$. The supply curve intersects the demand curve at price P_2, which is lower than the price P_1 at which the market would clear in the absence of mitigation banking. So the impact of the banking provision is to lower the cost of development and increase the supply of land for development without the target habitat falling below $\underline{H}$. The precise amount by which these changes occur depend on the slope of the curve $C(M)$, which in turn depends on the amount of equivalent land available, its cost, and the factor F—a higher value for F will increase the cost of mitigation and raise the slope of $C(M)$. Thus, ecological factors will affect the equilibrium price and the amount of development, and final equilibrium is a function of both economic and ecological considerations.

Mitigation Banking with Species

We extend the simple model from the previous section to endangered species as illustrated by the example described earlier in the chapter of International Paper

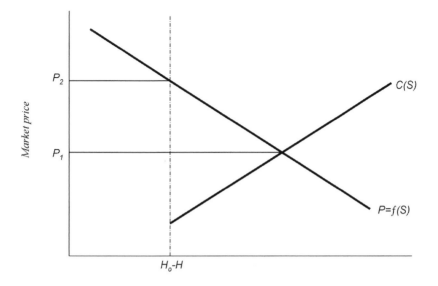

Supply for land development

Figure 17.1. Equilibrium in the market for land without (P_1) and with (P_2) mitigation.

and the red-cockaded woodpecker. To do so, we must identify the factors contributing to the population size, namely, area of available habitat, denoted by H, and the resource input. In this case, International Paper established nesting sites where they did not naturally occur. Other examples include protecting endangered species from nonnative predators. (e.g., the Australian company Earth Sanctuaries Ltd.; De Alessi 2003) or controlling or modifying some aspect of the physical environment for their benefit (e.g., Wildlands Inc. manipulates surface water levels to maintain vernal pool wetlands for endangered fairy shrimp and other target species in a mitigation bank in California; see http://www.wildlandsinc.com/).

Let R denote the monetary value of the resources used to support the endangered species, understanding that the nature of the support offered to different species may vary. Thus, the current population, B, is a function of H and R: $B = f(H,R)$. B is clearly an increasing function of both H and R: it might be linear in H so that if H is doubled with no change in R then the population will double in equilibrium. In this case, B, as a function of both variables, shows increasing returns. If B increases in both inputs, then we can support the same population with less land if we use more resources, implying a land-resource trade-off that is formalized in the function $f(H,R)$. This is illustrated by the isoquants of the function, curves in the $H-B$ plane that join alternative combinations of H and B that can support a given population. Figure 17.2 illustrates a

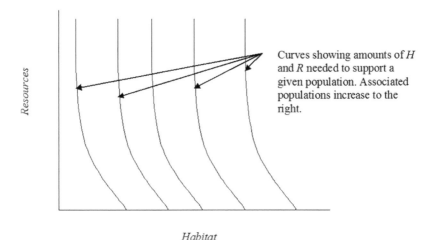

Curves showing amounts of H and R needed to support a given population. Associated populations increase to the right.

Habitat

Figure 17.2. Isoquants of the population support function B = f(H, R).

possible form for these. Habitat is measured horizontally and resources vertically. The slope up and to the left shows that as we supply more resources a given population needs less habitat. There is, we assume, a minimum area of habitat needed by any population and this is the vertical asymptote of the corresponding isoquant.

Now suppose that in this context we introduce a mitigation banking system of the type used for woodpeckers, outlined above. Specifically, there is a current population B_0 that must be preserved. Any land use is possible provided the population remains intact. Initially, no resources are devoted to supporting this population and the habitat used is H_0. Figure 17.3 shows that some land can be released if we move up and to the left along the isoquant corresponding to the initial population, making it a reasonable response for the landowner, who would invest in supporting the population and reducing the amount of land that it needs, releasing the excess land for development. The landowner will invest in support until the marginal cost of releasing land this way just equals its market price.

An additional feature of species mitigation banking mentioned above is that if the population rises above B_0, then the excess over B_0 entitles the landowner to release more land for development or to transfer to another landowner the right to use previously restricted land for development. If land is used for development on the basis of a population increase, then the higher population must be maintained but otherwise the landowner is under no obligation to maintain the larger population. This feature is known as a *safe harbor agreement*: it assures landowners that they won't be penalized by promoting the growth of an endan-

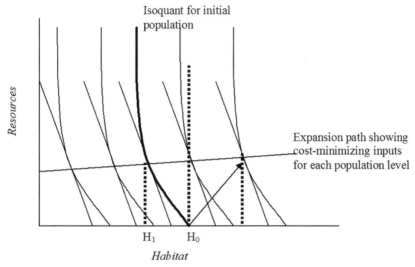

Figure 17.3. A landowner's choice under mitigation banking and safe harbor agreements.

gered species. An important parameter is the rate at which the landowner is allowed to release land for development, or to entitle others to do this, as the population of the endangered species increases.

Figure 17.3 allows us to see geometrically the options facing a landowner who undertakes mitigation banking with safe harbor agreements. The axes, as before, are the amounts of habitat and resources devoted to the support of an endangered population, with larger populations corresponding to curves further to the right. Initially, the landowner allocates habitat H_0 to the species, and no resources, so that the population corresponds to the curve cutting the horizontal axis at H_0: call it population B_0. The straight lines tangent to the isoquants are budget lines—they show alternative combinations of resources and habitat that can be purchased for a fixed cost, and their slopes are equal to the price ratio of resources to land. The least-cost combination of land and resources that will support a given population occurs where a budget line is tangent to the isoquant, and the line that connects all such tangencies is the expansion path shown in the diagram.

The least-cost support of population B_0, therefore, is to reduce land input from H_0 and raise resource input until the point of tangency between the H_0 isoquant and a budget line is reached: this isoquant is shown in bold in the figure. This leads to a drop in the amount of habitat used from H_0 to H_1, an amount now available for development while maintaining an intact population. Alternatively, the landowner could increase the population supported and bank the increase, hoping to sell it to others. By maintaining the amount of habitat constant and raising the allocation of resources to a point on the expansion path, the landowner could generate a bankable population increase and indeed could generate an even larger population increase by moving in the direction of the arrow from H_0 and allocating more habitat and resources to produce a larger bankable surplus. Which would a landowner choose, in order to maximize profits?

We use L to represent the area of land that can be released from ESA restrictions in exchange for a one-unit population increase. L is clearly a variable central to this analysis, but has been discussed only infrequently in the literature. Profits are given by

$$\pi = LP[B(H, R) - B_0] - R - P[H - H_0] \qquad (17.1)$$

In this expression the term $[B(H,R) - B_0]$ describes the population excess after allocation of habitat and resources, $B(H,R)$ over the initial level and thus is the amount available for banking. LP is the market value of the land that can be released as a result and thus represents the value of the banked population. Profit is calculated by subtracting from this the resources allocated and also the market value of the habitat used (which could be negative if habitat is released and $H < H_0$). Choosing H and R to maximize profits gives as first-order conditions

$$\frac{\partial B}{\partial H} L = 1 \quad \text{and} \quad \frac{\partial B}{\partial R} LP = 1 \qquad (17.2)$$

Using these results we can perform elementary comparative static analysis to determine how the allocation of land and resources to the endangered species changes as the parameters L and P are altered.

Suppose that L, the amount of land released when the population increases, is raised. How will the profit-maximizing value of H change? In other words, what is $\partial H / \partial L$ when the landowner is a profit-maximizer? Assuming that the marginal product of habitat decreases as habitat increases, this is positive: an increase in L, more generous terms for land bankers, will raise the amount of habitat allocated to supporting the endangered species. The same is true of the effect of an increase in L on the choice of resources R: assuming diminishing returns to resources alone, a higher L leads to more resources allocated to the endangered species. An increase in the price of land P acts in the same way, increasing the resources allocated to the species. This reflects the fact that by using land of low market value to breed the endangered species and thus release high-value land to the market, the owner of the low-value land can appropriate some of the value of land zoned for development. The banking of the endangered species becomes a vehicle for arbitrage between two different land markets.

In the analysis above, we assumed a single price of land in equation (17.1), meaning that the price at which land can be sold as a result of mitigation banking is the same as the cost to the landowner of using his own land. This was not the case for International Paper. The company owned land zoned for forestry whereas neighboring landowners owned land zoned for development. The Endangered Species Act applied equally to all, prohibiting activities that threatened woodpeckers on either type of land, but the value of releasing land zoned for development from ESA restrictions was obviously much greater than that of releasing land whose only permitted use was forestry. In such a case, there are two land prices: P represents land for development and P_0 represents the opportunity cost to the landowner of using his own land, with $P > P_0$. Profits are given by

$$\pi = LP[B(H, R) - B_0] - R - P_0[H - H_0] \tag{17.3}$$

and the first-order conditions for a maximum are

$$\frac{\partial B}{\partial H} LP = P_0 \quad \text{and} \quad \frac{\partial B}{\partial R} LP = P_0 \tag{17.4}$$

In this case, both the amount of land and the amount of resources allocated to supporting the population will increase with an increase in the ratio P/P_0, which indicates the market price of land for development compared to the opportunity cost of land to the landowner (assuming that the landowner's land is not zoned for development).

Now assume that there is a spontaneous increase in the population of the endangered species, from B_0 to B_1. The growth in population means that some land can be released for development, but to offset this the higher population requires more land and resources to support it. The landowner will presumably support the extra population if the value of the land released exceeds the cost of land and resources needed to support the population increase. Formalizing this observation requires that we specify how much land can be released as a result of a unit increase in population, a critical variable in the economic analysis. The amount of land released when one new population unit is realized is denoted by L. We use $H_0(B)$ to represent the amount of land needed to support a population of B when no additional resources are provided, so that

$$B = f(H_0, 0)$$

There is a cost to supporting a higher population because more resources and land are needed. The minimum cost of supporting a population of B when the market price of land is P is given by the cost function

$$C(B, P) = Min_{f(H,R) \geq B} [PH + R]$$

which corresponds to the locus of points of tangency between a budget line and an isoquant in figure 17.3. The profit a landowner makes from the sale of land when the population rises by one unit is therefore

$$\pi = PL - \frac{\partial C(P, B)}{\partial B}$$

where $\partial C/\partial B$ is the marginal cost of a population increase. Because the landowner is not required to support the population increase unless in his or her interest to do so under a safe harbor agreement, profit from the increase is the maximum of this and zero:

$$\pi = Max \left\{ PL - \frac{\partial C}{\partial B}, 0 \right\}$$

This clearly shows that a safe harbor agreement acts to give the landowner a call option on the profits from population growth.

Conclusion

Mitigation banking has been used successfully to reduce the impact of species conservation on land markets and to provide a mechanism for compensating landowners for the removal of land from the development market. The critical issue is whether the correct terms are set for compensation: what type, where, and how much land will mitigate the loss of one unit of the designated habitat. These decisions affect the economic outcome in the obvious ways—restricting choices raises the market price and vice versa. Ecologically these decisions may be detrimental if they lead to conservation of areas and patterns of habitat insufficient to support the threatened and endangered populations they seek to help.

Applying mitigation banking to species is a more complex undertaking. Figure 17.3 and equations (17.1) and (17.2) suggest that mitigation banking can release land for development while preserving a species' population intact and also can provide landowners with the incentive to increase species' populations, particularly when the opportunity cost to the landowner of allocating land to the endangered species is below the market price of land zoned for development. Mitigation banking effectively allows the landowner to arbitrage between markets via the "endangered species bank." In other words, finding endangered species may be in the landowner's interest since, if the land is not zoned for development, the landowner can access some of the premium from development by facilitating development by others.

Finally, the option value conveyed by safe harbor agreements introduced under the Endangered Species Act allows landowners to support and bank an increased population when advantageous for them to do so. The ESA together with the mitigation banking provision act to redistribute wealth away from owners of land zoned for development that is restricted by the ESA and toward landowners whose property cannot be developed but who can "bank" endangered species on their property and sell the excess. Under this scenario, wealth is redistributed among landowners, but as a group they neither increase nor lose significant wealth.

18 Conservation Banking

Jessica Fox, Gretchen C. Daily, Barton H. Thompson Jr., Kai M. A. Chan,
Adam Davis, and Anamaria Nino-Murcia

Market-based environmental regulations emphasize incentives and efficiency in the provision of vital public goods such as clean air, clean water, and biodiversity protection. Because individuals can be expected to act in their perceived self-interest, solutions that reward production or conservation of public goods are a practical addition to the more traditional approach of catching and punishing those who fail to comply with standards. The Millennium Ecosystem Assessment (2005b) recently expressed encouragement for market-based systems, such as conservation banking, as one tool for "taking natures value into account" and achieving a more sustainable future. The release of federal guidance for establishing conservation banks indicates the growing support for strategies that encourage proactive protection of vital ecosystem services. In this chapter, we consider the history, status, and potential of conservation banking.

Similar to their purchasing wetland credits from a wetland mitigation bank, landowners can purchase species credits from a conservation bank to offset project-specific impacts to threatened and endangered species. As recently described, a conservation bank is "a parcel of private property that is conserved and managed in perpetuity under a conservation easement for the benefit of rare species" (Fox and Nino-Murcia 2005, 997). The party that holds the easement is granted credits by a federal or state agency for the land's species and habitat value. A bank owner may use or sell the credits within a predesignated service area to address mitigation required by state and/or federal law (USFWS 2003g). Theoretically, conservation banking reduces piecemeal mitigation approaches by consolidating projects into large, biologically functioning reserves and is "attractive to landowners and land managers because it allows conservation to be implemented within a market framework, where habitat for listed species is treated as a benefit rather than a liability" (USFWS 2003g, 1). In the following sections, we discuss the critical variables that determine whether this theory will hold in practice.

Potential Benefits of Conservation Banking

The structure and limitations of the Endangered Species Act are key to under-standing the potential benefits of conservation banking. Sections 9 and 10 form the nucleus of the ESA's regulation of private property. As interpreted by the U.S. Fish and Wildlife Service (USFWS), section 9(a)(1) proscribes any "significant habitat modification or degradation" that "actually kills or injures wildlife by significantly impairing essential behavioral patterns, including breeding, feeding, or sheltering" (ESA sec. 7(a)(1); *Code of Federal Regulations* 50:17.3). Under section 10(a), however, a landowner who wishes to develop or use land in ways that might incidentally violate section 9 can obtain an *incidental take permit* from the agency (ESA sec. 10(a)). To obtain a permit, the landowner must prepare a *habitat conservation plan* (HCP) that, among other require-ments, "minimizes and mitigates" the impacts of the land use "to the maximum extent practicable" and ensures that the land use will not "appreciably reduce the likelihood of the survival and recovery of the species in the wild" (ESA sec. 10(a)(1)(B)).

Despite its considerable reach in protecting habitat, section 9 suffers several major limitations. First, it prohibits only *affirmative* actions that modify or de-grade habitat. Under section 9, the U.S. Fish and Wildlife Service can prevent a landowner from building a new residential subdivision in prime habitat but can neither require a landowner to improve habitat so that it better supports an en-dangered species nor require protection of habitat from exogenous risks such as exotic species or fires. Second, under both the agency's regulations and federal court decisions, section 9 does not enjoin the development or degradation of *potential* habitat. Unless the U.S. Fish and Wildlife Service can show that mem-bers of a listed species are living on a particular parcel of land, it cannot use sec-tion 9 to regulate the land's use. The "mere potential for harm . . . is insuffi-cient" to trigger section 9's prohibitions (*Arizona Cattle Growers Association v. U.S. Fish and Wildlife Service* 2001). Finally, section 9(a)(1) does not regulate private land that is the habitat of an endangered or threatened *plant* but applies only to endangered fish and wildlife (and, by regulatory extension, to threat-ened fish and wildlife). The Endangered Species Act relegates endangered plants to section 9(a)(2), which prohibits the removal or destruction of plants on pri-vate lands only when in "knowing violation" of state law.

The U.S. Fish and Wildlife Service can apply its authority under sections 9 and 10 to address some of these limitations. When a property owner seeks an incidental take permit to develop habitat, for example, the agency can use a habitat conservation plan to require the property owner not only to preserve some of the habitat but also to improve and manage it for long-term species support. In an HCP, the agency can also require the property owner to preserve and improve other lands that have greater long-term potential as habitat for the species at risk (whether or not the land is currently active habitat) or that provide habitat for a broader set of species (including endangered or threatened plants). There are limits to this authority: the Endangered Species Act, as noted, requires property owners to minimize and mitigate their impacts only "to the maximum extent practicable," and the U.S. Fish and Wildlife Service cannot require property owners to protect land that has no mitigation value for the impacted species (e.g., land that is potential habitat only for plants or other unrelated species). The agency nonetheless can and frequently does exercise its authority over the modification of actual habitat to seek habitat improvements, long-run management, and the protection of unregulated lands.

Protecting species through individual habitat conservation plans has its drawbacks, however. First, the agency cannot act until a landowner applies for an incidental take permit and negotiates the terms of a habitat conservation plan. While the agency is waiting for a permit application to be filed, the owners of potential habitat may develop or otherwise adversely modify their land without risk of punishment. Land development in the region may increase the commercial value of potential reserve land, increasing the cost of assembling a reserve. Current habitat, moreover, may naturally change to the detriment of listed species. If the listed species abandon the property as a result, the landowner is free to develop the property without violating the Endangered Species Act.

Second, individual habitat conservation plans generally result in small, disconnected, and uncoordinated reserves. Even if the U.S. Fish and Wildlife Service works from a master blueprint to prioritize lands reserved for each species, lands that are set aside in connection with individual HCPs also depend on which lands are available for sale at the time each HCP is developed. Also, land use changes between HCPs may isolate lands set aside by prior HCPs.

Finally, protecting species through habitat conservation plans is expensive and time consuming. Each individual permit applicant must negotiate the terms and conditions of a mitigation reserve and then acquire, improve, and maintain the relevant land, entailing considerable administrative costs. Once initial land for a reserve has been purchased, moreover, the reserve value of the remaining land increases; owners of the remaining land may be tempted to hold out for large sums when later permit applicants seek to complete the overall reserve by purchasing their land. This problem parallels the difficulties that large developers encounter when word of their development plans escapes before they have purchased all of the needed acreage.

Conservation banking overcomes these drawbacks of habitat conservation plans. Attracted by the economic prospect of selling conservation credits in the future, landowners or entrepreneurs are willing to assemble reserves now. In some cases, large property owners may offer to create conservation banks on their existing lands. In others, developers may acquire and assemble reserves from third parties. Unlike a property owner seeking an incidental take permit for a specific project, the bank developer can take advantage of real estate opportunities when they arise (e.g., a large parcel of potential habitat that has suddenly come on the market). Regardless of how banks are assembled, conservation banking speeds up protection efforts, allowing protection and improvement of habitat before permit applications are filed. Conservation banking also allows the U.S. Fish and Wildlife Service to work with bank developers to design more cohesive and effective reserves than the piecemeal results of HCP-by-HCP efforts. Finally, conservation banking engenders economies of scale in the acquisition, improvement, and operation of reserves, and it helps avoid the potential holdout problem created when reserves are assembled parcel by parcel.

Conservation banking should provide other benefits as well, including those associated with the allowance for trading. In theory, for example, conservation banking should enable more effective conservation at a lower total social cost, allowing high-value development without net loss to threatened and endangered species. Bank developers have an incentive to find ways to generate as many credits as possible on a single piece of property, which should theoretically translate into greater benefits for the listed species (assuming the credits reflect improved habitat rather than political negotiations or influences). And bank developers have an incentive to find ways to do so at the lowest possible cost. They may invest in research to find new techniques for maximizing the conservation value of their banks (e.g., improved methods of habitat management) and for reducing costs (e.g., bundling species protection with other commercially valuable ecosystem services, such as improved water quality and carbon sequestration, which hold economic value via other market-based credit trading systems).

By increasing flexibility and reducing compliance costs, conservation banking may also reduce political opposition to the Endangered Species Act. By simplifying and shortening the HCP process and reducing the cost of implementation, conservation banks can mitigate political resistance. In the case of multiple species impacts, the strategic design efforts required for multispecies HCPs makes the use of conservation banks especially compelling. By establishing a pool of credits under one agreement, transaction costs are lessened (on a per credit basis), bank location is simplified (because it is not constrained to the exact specification of impact size), and revenue can be received for any extra credits sold. From the perspective of the credit buyer, banks simplify the mitigation process by allowing the purchase of credits that were previously approved by the U.S. Fish and Wildlife Service.

Regulatory Provisions Governing Conservation Banking

Conservation banks originated in California as part of the State's efforts to develop regional and subregional habitat conservation plans through its Natural
Community Conservation Planning (NCCP) program. The NCCP program
contemplated permitting development in a region in return for the creation of a
large reserve system. A key problem was determining how to assemble and pay
for the reserves prior to habitat owners seeking to develop their land. Legal and
political restrictions, however, made public financing infeasible, so conservation
banking was used to encourage entrepreneurs to create the reserve systems.

On April 7, 1995, the California Resources Agency released the first formal
policy guidance for species conservation banks (California Resources Agency
1995). California's "Official Policy on Conservation Banks" anticipates that
banks can generate credit through preserving, enhancing, restoring, and/or creating habitat. The policy requires bank developers to "permanently" protect the
bank reserves "through fee title or conservation easement" (p. 1, item 4) no later
than upon the first sale of a credit in the bank. The policy encourages developers to vest long-term management responsibilities in a government resources
agency or "qualified non-profit organization, although a private entity may be
an acceptable long-term manager" (p. 2, item 7). To ensure the bank's long-
term viability, the policy requires bank managers to provide a "sufficient level of
funding with acceptable guarantees (e.g., cash, letters of credit, public charity,
public funding mechanisms" (p. 2, item 6). The policy also mandates annual reports and requires the bank to guarantee government access to the property for
inspections and quality assurance. The other basic details of a bank (e.g., size,
geographic boundaries, and the terms and transferability of bank credits) are
left to agreement with the appropriate governmental agencies, such as the U.S.
Fish and Wildlife Service and the state Department of Fish and Game. It is stipulated, however, that banks must be of sufficient size to be "ecologically self-
sustaining" or else "part of a larger conservation strategy that has a reasonable
expectation of being accomplished" (p. 1, item 3) Since 1995, California has
approved over thirty conservation banks under this policy.

Hawaii is the only other state to address conservation banking explicitly. In
1997, the Hawaii legislature included an HCP process in its own endangered
species act and provided that HCPs could include "habitat banking" (*Hawaii
Revised Statute* sec. 195D-21(b)). The legislature, however, defined the term
narrowly to mean the purchase by a property owner seeking to develop the
habitat of listed species of "another property on which those affected species are
found for purposes of preserving those species" (*Hawaii Revised Statute* sec.
195D-2). The Hawaii legislation thus does not specify whether habitat conservation plans can rely on banks in which there is no transfer of property rights or

which involve habitat where listed species are not currently found. Other than in this definition, moreover, the Hawaii legislation provides no guidance on the terms or conditions of a "habitat bank."

Although the federal Endangered Species Act does not mention conservation banking, the general provisions of section 10 appear to implicitly authorize the U.S. Fish and Wildlife Service to approve conservation banks as part of the agency's general authority over habitat conservation plans. Individual field offices of the agency have approved conservation banks since the mid-1990s without any official agency guidance. No one has mounted a legal challenge to these banks, and it is unlikely that any challenge mounted would succeed.

In May 2003, the agency issued a publication, "Guidance for the Establishment, Use, and Operation of Conservation Banks" (USFWS 2003g; Bauer et al. 2004) anticipating their broad use. According to the guidance, banks can be used not only in conjunction with habitat conservation plans but also to meet section 7 requirements and as part of candidate conservation agreements with assurances. Many of the provisions of the USFWS guidance document are similar to those of the California policy document, albeit far more detailed. The USFWS guidance document, for example, authorizes banks to be created through various means, including habitat acquisition, protection, enhancement, and creation, as well as "prescriptive management of habitats for specified biological characteristics." The guidance also provides that habitat be conserved and managed "in perpetuity" (p. 2) and that the price of credits includes funding for long-term management and protection (in the form of a nonwasting endowment).

Mechanics of Conservation Banking

Conservation banks are individually designed through a collaborative process between the bank sponsor, the U.S. Fish and Wildlife Service, and, in some cases, the state wildlife agency. The success of banks in both ecological and economic terms will depend on specification of the bank's objectives; determination of the credit type, credit currency, and methodology for calculating both availability of credits within the bank and incurring debits outside the bank; establishment of the service area within which credits can be traded; provision for long-term management; and monitoring and enforcement.

In a narrow sense, *bank objectives* are simply to mitigate legally permissible impacts on threatened or endangered species, as defined under the Endangered Species Act. We might hope, however, that conservation banks would go beyond ensuring no net increase in extinction risk, which is implied by the term *mitigation*. In the ideal, they would promote the goal of the Endangered Species

Act to "reduce the likelihood of extinction—or conversely, increase the probability of survival—to a safe level" (Bean and Dwyer 2000, 10539).

The species and habitats in question are specified by the *credit type*. For example, the Pleasanton Ridge Conservation Bank in Livermore, California, sells credits for the California red-legged frog (*Rana aurora draytonii*) and the Alameda whipsnake (*Masticophis lateralis euryxanthus*). In theory, wetland banks further differentiate credits based on whether the habitat was preserved as original habitat, restored to something resembling its natural condition, or created *de novo*. It remains to be determined if conservation bank agreements will consistently include this type of distinction. Most agreements to date establish credits only for preserved original habitat (although some improvements to preserved habitats have occurred in conservation banking—including erecting fences, conducting controlled burning, managing invasive species, and grazing). In contrast to wetland banking, the emphasis of conservation banks has been on preserving, rather than creating or restoring, habitat.

The *credit currency* refers to the metric by which the credit type is quantified: namely, acres of suitable habitat, or numbers of individuals or breeding pairs of the species supported by the bank. In the latter case, all individuals may count or, in other instances, only breeding pairs or groups may count. To date, banks approved in California and elsewhere exhibit a mixture of currencies with a preference for acres.

The issue of currency is especially complex when the credits differ from the currency of debits. For example, a developer in Southern California was required to mitigate the anticipated impacts of a project in terms of breeding pairs of California gnatcatchers (*Polioptila californica californica*), yet the banks in the area had been required to establish credits in terms of acres. The U.S. Fish and Wildlife Service would not allow the project to be mitigated with the available bank credits, prompting protest on the part of the bank owner. The California Department of Fish and Game resolved the issue by assigning conversion ratios between currencies, in other words, between numbers of individuals or breeding pairs and acres.

The *number of credits* is based on the quality and extent of habitat or population size. When a bank is first established, biological surveys are conducted to document the extent of appropriate habitat available and the abundance of breeding pairs or groups. In order for banks to increase the number of credits approved, they generally must add additional acres of suitable habitat to the bank. In cases where banks are based on numbers of individuals (whether breeding or not), if a biological survey shows an increase in numbers of individuals, additional credits may be awarded by the U.S. Fish and Wildlife Service. By contrast, we are not aware of a case where the numbers of credits awarded to a bank that was abiding by the terms of the banking agreement was reduced based on a biological survey showing a decrease in habitat quality or number of breeding pairs. Even when the sweeping fires of 2003 burned several large banks in San Diego, including about 1,300 acres of the Cornerstones Conservation Bank and a large portion of the 2,377-acre Crestridge Conservation Bank, the number of credits was not reduced. According to banking agreements, "banks will not be held responsible for offsetting acts of nature . . . such as floods, earthquakes, or fires" or natural fluctuations in species populations (USFWS 2003g, 14, 19). However, if a bank owner does not meet its habitat maintenance responsibilities, the U.S. Fish and Wildlife Service can assume management of the bank and/or reduce the number of approved credits.

In cases where habitat is improved through investments by the bank, the agency has awarded credits on a rolling basis, increasing over time as the habitat is progressively improved. An example of this is the East Plum Creek Conservation Bank, which was awarded 25 percent of the total possible credits once the property was committed to conservation purposes, 50 percent once groundwater levels were controlled, and the remainder once successful restoration of vegetation was documented. This is analogous to the credit-awarding system for many wetland banks arising from restoration.

A *conservation easement* must be placed on the property where the bank is established. This easement is required by the U.S. Fish and Wildlife Service in order for the banking agreement to be signed and for credits to be sold. The easement must be in perpetuity and the land must be maintained to support its original conservation purpose as stipulated in the banking agreement, "regardless of the future status of the species for which the bank was initially established" (USFWS 2003g, 2). In some cases, bank owners have passed the ecological management responsibility for the property to another organization that has the expertise to manage the site appropriately over the long term. In practice, the conservation easement is often placed on the property at the same time that the first credits are sold. Because the easement must be placed before the banking agreement is finalized, credits are technically sold prior to the banking agreement being signed.

The *service area* refers to the geographic area or areas within which credits can be bought and sold. Impacts on threatened and endangered species must occur within the service territory of the bank in order for the bank credits to be used. Service area decisions may be influenced by the proximity of other banks that offer credits for the same species. The federal guidance suggests that the species recovery plan inform service area decisions. The guidance does not state a preference for how service territories are defined, however, and gives equal weight to ecological and jurisdictional criteria: "In general, the Service Area of a conservation bank is identified in the bank agreement and defines the area (e.g., recovery unit, watershed, county) in which the bank's credits may be used to offset project impacts" (USFWS 2003g, 8). Thus, some service areas are delimited by ecological considerations, while others are defined by county or state lines and may include land not recognized in the species recovery plan as being important to the long-term survival of the species. Moreover, many threatened and endangered species lack a completed recovery plan to guide the service area decision.

Because service area determines the number of eligible buyers of a bank's credits, this factor has a great impact on the "thickness" of the market for mitigation credits. Since market thickness (the volume of trading) has such crucial implications for a market's ability to function properly and deliver the cost savings of ideal markets (Salzman and Ruhl 2001), this factor is a crucial element in conservation banking design.

An *endowment fund* is established for each bank by the terms of the banking agreement. The nonwasting endowment fund must cover the annual operation and maintenance of the bank, including the biological and administrative needs. The fund should be large enough to provide the necessary income from interest without depleting the base fund. In California, many banks have used the property analysis record developed by the Center for Natural Lands Management to estimate the size of the endowment required to manage the bank in perpetuity. In general, banking agreements will require a portion of each credit sale to be deposited into the endowment fund until the necessary balance is reached. In addition to providing the means for the bank manager to maintain the conservation value of the bank, the fund is also intended to provide the financial assurances to the U.S. Fish and Wildlife Service to allow it to manage the bank in the event that the bank owner cannot meet the obligations of the banking agreement.

Some bank owners manage their own endowment funds and are responsible for documenting the balance of the funds to the U.S. Fish and Wildlife Service and the other parties signatory to the banking agreement. In California many endowments are held by the California Department of Fish and Game. More generally, endowments are held by a USFWS-approved, nonprofit organization or government agency. Bank owners, many of whom are experienced business professionals, may be more likely to invest in risky funds with higher yields, while public agencies may be more likely to select low-risk, low-yield funds. Bank owners are generally allowed to use the interest on the account to manage their banks while leaving the principal untouched. The federal guidance states that low-interest rates may require larger endowments to generate the necessary funds for bank management (USFWS 2003g). This indicates that there is an option for bank owners to invest in higher-interest (and riskier) accounts, which will generate the operation and maintenance funds from a smaller base fund. Because the guidance does not specifically stipulate who will hold the endowment, the door is left open to bank-specific decisions. Like service territory, this decision can have a significant impact on the financial outcome of a bank because it determines the size of the base fund required and can affect both credit prices and future profits.

Current Status of Conservation Banking

Fox and Nino-Murcia recently reviewed species-credit trading activities in the United States (Fox and Nino-Murcia 2005). While there are seventy-six species-crediting agreements, only thirty-five are official conservation banking agreements (as of December 2003). The conservation banks range in size from 25.3 to 10,400 acres (10.2 to 4,210 hectares) and officially protect habitat for twenty-two threatened and endangered species with many other common and rare species actively using the sites. Ninety-one percent of banks define credits on area of habitat (versus breeding pairs). Sixty-five percent of the banks have a credit ratio of one credit to 1 acre, with 11 percent of banks being awarded more credits than acres and 24 percent awarded fewer credits than acres.

Since Fox and Nino-Murcia completed their study, many additional banks have been approved throughout the United States, and in 2005 the Sacramento office of U.S. Fish and Wildlife Service reports a backlog in reviewing the growing stack of new agreements (Jerry Bielfeldt, conservation banking coordinator, pers. comm.). The release of federal guidance is likely contributing to banking's growing popularity, particularly outside of California, which has seen the majority of banking activity (as of 2003, twenty-nine of the thirty-five banks were in California). The U.S. Fish and Wildlife Service is considering a Web-based tracking system for conservation banks, which will likely lead to a more robust credit trading market by aligning credit buyers and sellers.

Case Study: The Hickory Pass Ranch Conservation Bank

In 2000, Jacquelyn and David Johnston, owners of 3,000 acres of undeveloped and ecologically important property in central Texas, explored options for generating revenue from the land while maintaining its conservation value and their ownership (David Johnston, pers. comm., July 31, 2003). Johnston initially estimated that he could make twice as much by selling conservation credits for golden-cheeked warbler habitat as by selling development rights to the land in the form of conservation easements. Johnston approached the Austin field office of the U.S. Fish and Wildlife Service with the idea and soon began negotiations over the Hickory Pass Ranch Conservation Bank. The bank, located in Burnet and Travis counties in Texas, supports critical breeding habitat for the federally endangered golden-cheeked warbler (*Dendroica chrysoparia*).

The banking agreement took about two years to establish from the time of original conception and about one and a half years from when the agency became involved. Because federal guidelines had not been released by the agency and there was no state guidance, the Austin USFWS field office used California's state guidance as a model.

Johnston temporarily quit his law practice to focus on establishing the bank. He hired an environmental attorney to help negotiate with the U.S. Fish and Wildlife Service and environmental consultants to prepare the biological information. He estimated the costs of establishing the bank at about $200,000 and determined that they would sell credits for less than the ranch's market value if he sold it to developers but more than the market value of a conservation easement. The required endowment fund took the longest to negotiate and required a deposit of $250 per credit sold, adjusted annually for inflation. By the end of four years, a required minimum of $310,000 was to be deposited in the endowment.

Johnston agreed to set up a scientific advisory board to help manage the land, including members of the U.S. Fish and Wildlife Service, Environmental Defense, a environmental consulting firm, and Texas A&M University. In particular, Dr. Keith Arnold, professor of ornithology and curator of birds at Texas A&M Cooperative Wildlife Collection, designed a program that will bring biology students to the bank to study and contribute their knowledge to the management of the ranch.

This multiuse bank allows some hunting and other activities compatible with the primary objective of supporting golden-cheeked warbler populations. Credits are sold for $5,000 each (2003 U.S. dollars); over four hundred credits have been sold to both public and private entities. The maximum potential credits that could ever be sold is three thousand. The currency for this bank is one credit per acre of habitat.

As illustrated by this case study, setting up a conservation bank requires tremendous commitment from the bank sponsor. In spite of this personal commitment, conservation banking's contribution to species conservation remains an open question. The potential for conservation banking to mitigate harm to endangered species will depend on several key factors discussed below.

Factors Influencing the Economic Success of Conservation Banking

Because banking is an incentive-based mechanism, property owners will generally require relatively certain economic rewards in order to establish banks on their land. Naturally, one of the primary factors determining the economic success of a bank is the ability to sell credits. A bank's ability to sell credits depends on the U.S. Fish and Wildlife Service aggressively enforcing the Endangered Species Act. However, USFWS enforcement of these mitigation requirements varies and may depend upon funding, staff resources, political pressures, and conflicting regional goals. When mitigation credits are not in sufficient demand due to either a lack of impacts to the species in question or a lack of USFWS-enforced mitigation requirements, associated banks will not be successful financially. The value of species credits is also undermined in cases where the agency allows the payment of an in-lieu fee to serve as an alternative to the purchase of credits from a bank.

The U.S. Fish and Wildlife Service must take steps to assure bank owners that it will not impede the selling of credits unduly. In California, some bank owners have suggested that once an easement is in place on a property, agencies regard the land as conserved and seek to conserve new sites rather than direct credit buyers to banks with unsold credits (Bean and Dwyer 2000; Fox and Nino-Murcia 2005). For conservation banking to become a national strategy for protecting species, the U.S. Fish and Wildlife Service must assure bank owners that this will not happen.

Ultimately, financial success will depend on a range of factors, including the number and value of credits, demand for credits, requirements of the endowment fund, and the cost of establishing the banking agreement. While it is the owner's burden to ensure the financial success of the bank, the agency has multiple opportunities to reduce the number of uncertainties involved. In practice, the potential to receive significant financial benefits from banking is promising. Credit prices have reportedly ranged from $3,000 for 1 acre of San Joaquin kit fox (*Vulpes macrotis mutica*) to $125,000 for a breeding pair of least Bell's vireo (*Vireo bellii pusillus*) (Fox and Nino-Murcia 2005). Despite significant potential for improvement, many banks across the United States are already enjoying impressive financial rewards (Fox and Nino-Murcia 2005).

Factors Influencing the Ecological Success of Conservation Banking

For many threatened and endangered species, avoiding the path to extinction would require interventions hardly imaginable from biophysical, let alone political, perspectives. The key challenge is that the amount of suitable habitat required to ensure the long-term survival of such species is often far more than that presently available, a problem compounded by ongoing global change (Rosenzweig 2003b). Interventions necessary to ensure long-term survival include (1) greatly increasing the amount and quality of primary habitat available to increase population sizes and ranges to more secure levels (through protection of existing habitat and restoration of former habitat); (2) greatly increasing the amount and quality of primary and secondary habitats available to facilitate range shifts in response to anthropogenic and natural global change; and (3) greatly reducing the magnitudes and rates of anthropogenic global changes other than habitat modification (e.g., changes in hydrological cycles, fire regimes, the nitrogen cycle, the biotic community associated with invasive species, and climate).

In light of this backdrop, conservation banks might best be thought of as development tools rather than conservation tools per se. Conservation banks can fiddle at the margins of the threats faced by threatened and endangered species, but they will not change significantly the fundamental outlook (i.e., the degree of threat) for the species they target—at least not directly. Moreover, conservation banking will only happen—and would be more lucrative—in areas where there is development pressure. Indeed, its very use may imply an increase in extinction risk.

One way conservation banking can alter the fundamental outlook for species is through its ability to foster an attitude that conservation and development can be harmonized and thereby strengthen the political will to protect threatened and endangered species. The question therefore becomes—given the inherent limitations of conservation banking relative to the magnitude of the extinction problem—what ecological considerations are important for optimizing the use of this tool?

Extinction Risk and Credit Ratios

The Endangered Species Act prohibits activities that increase extinction risk, providing the underlying motivation for conservation banking. Yet extinction risk is difficult to estimate, except in the trivial case where risk is extremely high. The empirical basis for understanding extinction risk is poor because decadal-scale population dynamics have been documented for only a few dozen of the world's species. Fortunately, conservation banking involves trading relative risks, and extinction risk is easier to measure in relative than absolute terms. Nevertheless, great uncertainty remains. For instance, how overall extinction risk of a threatened or endangered species will be affected by any particular conservation banking transaction is highly uncertain and will remain so for the foreseeable future. Furthermore, because many threats go unrecognized, extinction risk is generally underestimated by current approaches.

Even species with stable and apparently robust population sizes can suddenly collapse to extinction. For instance, the bay checkerspot butterfly (*Euphydryas editha bayensis*)—one of the world's few species with well-studied dynamics—was thought secure in its seemingly large (1,200-acre) Jasper Ridge Biological Preserve. Yet it declined to extinction because of two changes whose impacts were not initially appreciated and which were exogenous to the management of the preserve: habitat loss nearby, which wiped out important populations and their potential colonists, and increasing climatic variability (Ehrlich and Hanski 2004).

Mitigating this uncertainty and bias will require great care in selecting credit ratios and it argues for ratios considerably higher than the conventional 1:1 ratios. High credit ratios would also help to balance other threats involved in banking. For example, it appears that a landowner who enters into a banking agreement can take advantage of episodic increases in the population on his or her land by selling additional credits. Effectively, landowners can benefit from natural increases in populations but cannot be harmed by natural decreases. Clearly, this asymmetry is a recipe for trading-associated slippage, since credits from natural variation can be used to offset habitat-destructive "take." A similar logic applies to trading based on habitat: generally only occupied habitat requires mitigation, but appropriately managed habitat can yield credits even if unoccupied. Just as population abundances fluctuate, so does habitat occupancy. Since natural variation is a prevalent component of population dynamics, it provides further impetus for some form of insurance. Other possible insurance mechanisms include taxation of transactions, the purchase and retiring of credits, and the locking away of suitable habitat. A countervailing consideration is that any insurance mechanism might discourage banking activity, preventing trades that would actually benefit the species of concern.

Ecological Fungibility

There is ongoing debate regarding the ecologically optimal credit currency. In cases of species whose population abundances are difficult to estimate, or fluctuate dramatically on their own, it may be best to use a currency based on habitat area. This merely trades one type of uncertainty for another, however, as it is notoriously difficult to assess the suitability or quality of habitat for a species in question.

In the case of trading individuals for individuals, another important consideration is the implications of trades for genetic diversity. Particular populations, or combinations of populations, might retain much more genetic diversity than others (Waples, this volume). Along the same lines, the spatial context of a population is a crucial concern. In many cases, connected populations will be favorable, but in others, isolated populations would be advantageous (e.g., Earn et al. 2000).

In the case of trading individuals for habitats, securing existing populations involves less uncertainty over the short term—you know you've got what you want in your hand. Long-term survival will hinge on securing good habitat (large areas that can support breeding populations over a range of future eco-logical dynamics) and managing it appropriately. The need for bank owners to manage habitat in perpetuity is a benefit of conservation banking, but it must be weighed against the various difficulties in assessing habitat quality based on initial assessment of population abundance of the target species. First, one-time assessments are prone to great uncertainty. Second, the habitats most crucial to the survival of a species may not support the highest mean population sizes but rather the most consistent (if smaller) population sizes (Armsworth and Rough-garden 2003). Third, factors thought unrelated to habitat quality may cause population decline—and extinction in key habitat or temporary population in-crease in marginal habitat. This occurred in the case of the bay checkerspot but-terfly, for instance, taking more than two decades of intensive research to dis-cover that topographic heterogeneity is perhaps the most important contributor to habitat quality (which had previously been measured on the basis of habitat size and density of plant resources) (Ehrlich and Hanski 2004). Another point in the case of trading individuals for habitats is that the distribution of other species of concern should be factored into the decision of what and how to trade in order to optimize the benefits of conservation investments.

In the case of trading habitat for habitat, three issues stand out. First, mea-suring differences in habitat quality can be difficult, as mentioned above. Sec-ond, both the benefits and costs of spatial aggregation of habitat should be con-sidered when assessing habitat quality. Potential costs include reduced habitat variety (if there is spatial covariance in habitat features), higher correlation of climatic risks, and greater risk of spread of fire, invasive species, epidemics, or other threats (Diamond et al. 1976; Simberloff and Abele 1976). Third, other species of existing or potential conservation concern should be taken into ac-count. If habitat loss was the principal cause of endangerment of the species in question, then it is highly likely that many other species associated with the same habitat are endangered as well (whether or not their status has been stud-ied, or addressed by the Endangered Species Act). Concerns of other species are especially pertinent when management activities for increasing credits of a species involve increasing only the limiting factor of that species (such as the nesting holes for a particular bird species).

Conclusion

Market-based environmental mitigation strategies such as conservation bank-ing will likely play an important role in reducing anthropogenic impacts to global ecosystems. The potential for conservation banking to assign a real, fun-gible, dollar value to endangered species is powerful, providing the basis for rec-onciling historic conflicts between business and conservation. Private property owners might no longer fear the discovery of rare animals on their land. In fact, some savvy entrepreneurs will seek opportunities in such discoveries. Although a number of crucial ecological issues remain unresolved, conservation banking may yet overcome economic and social hurdles, releasing effective endangered species protection from the paralysis of political conflict.

This chapter was greatly improved by discussions with and critical comments from Paul Armsworth, Michael Bean, Paul Ehrlich, Geoff Heal, and Joan Roughgarden.

19 Working Seascapes

Paul R. Armsworth, Carrie V. Kappel, Fiorenza Micheli,
and Eric P. Bjorkstedt

Marine species are being listed under the Endangered Species Act with increasing frequency and this trend can be expected to continue (Armsworth et al. 2006). The taxonomic focus of marine listings is also diversifying (Armsworth et al. 2006). Despite long-held assumptions that life history characteristics of some marine species render them less vulnerable to extinction, anthropogenic impacts to marine ecosystems have imperiled a growing number of species. In this chapter, we review both the threats endangering marine species and some of the strategies being employed to mitigate those threats.

Listing decisions reveal the relative importance of different threats across taxonomic groups and ecosystems (Kappel 2005). Although many threats facing marine organisms are not unique to the seas, their relative importance differs from those faced by terrestrial species. For listed marine, estuarine, and diadromous species the most commonly identified threat is overexploitation (including targeted harvest, bycatch, and indirect effects), which threatens 81 percent of marine, estuarine, and diadromous listed species (Kappel 2005). Habitat degradation ranks second and is listed as a threat to 76 percent of vulnerable marine species, followed by pollution at 61 percent (Kappel 2005). In contrast, Wilcove et al. (2000) found that habitat impacts topped the list of threats to terrestrial and freshwater species, while invasive species and pollution ranked second and third. As for terrestrial species, habitat degradation is the most frequent threat to many estuarine and diadromous species (Kappel 2005).

Two other efforts to list marine species at risk of extinction, the IUCN Red List of Threatened Species (IUCN 2003) and the American Fisheries Society

---

The views or opinions expressed or implied are those of the authors and do not necessarily reflect the position of the National Marine Fisheries Service.

list of fish stocks at risk from extinction (Musick et al. 2000), provide interesting comparisons to the set of species listed as endangered, threatened, or as species of concern under the Endangered Species Act (see Armsworth et al. 2006; NMFS 2002d). Where they intersect in their taxonomic and spatial coverage, the three lists generally agree on the species and subspecies that are most vulnerable. However, each list was created for a distinct purpose and each used different criteria to assess extinction risk. Disparities between lists may therefore reflect gaps in coverage of candidate species, differences in assessment criteria, or different assessment outcomes for particular species.

Over 80 percent of the threatened marine species on the red list were included, at least in part, under IUCN (World Conservation Union) criterion A, or in other words because they had undergone large declines in relative abundance in a limited time period (IUCN 2003). Application of this criterion to marine species is controversial (Musick 1999; Powles et al. 2000; Hutchings 2001). The critical question concerns how large a proportional decrease in abundance a marine species can support before it is at risk of extinction. For example, the central/southern population of the rockfish bocaccio (*Sebastes paucispinis*) has undergone a 96 percent decline in spawner abundance off the California coast but at the same time there are estimated to still be 1.6 million fish of age one (NMFS 2002e).

The American Fisheries Society (AFS) recently published its first recognized list of distinct population segments (DPS) of marine fish at risk of extinction in North America (Musick et al. 2000). The list includes marine, estuarine, and diadromous fish but does not cover Pacific salmonids. It includes 151 distinct population segments from seventy-nine species that are vulnerable to local extirpation; twenty-two of these species are vulnerable to global extinction because all of their population segments are listed. The American Fisheries Society also lists species if they undergo sufficiently large declines in abundance. But unlike the IUCN criterion, which is applied consistently across all species, the society first estimates intrinsic rates of increase of each species and then applies different thresholds for assigning threatened status to species that fall into different resilience classes (Musick 1999).

The IUCN and AFS lists are based on simple quantitative criteria that are applied consistently across species; they do not rely upon the detailed, case-by-case assessments required for federal listings. These lists, then, are perhaps most useful for flagging particular species that may warrant further scrutiny and for identifying common characteristics of those species that are most vulnerable. A petition is required before a species is considered for listing under the Endangered Species Act and, therefore, only a subset of the species considered by the IUCN and AFS have been examined by the National Marine Fisheries Service.

The ESA assessment process, however, is more rigorous for those species that are evaluated.

Threats to Marine Biodiversity

The threats to marine species have recently been reviewed at length by the Pew Oceans Commission (2003) and the U.S. Commission on Ocean Policy (2004). In this section, we specifically examine the implication of different threats both for endangered species and for the likelihood of additional listings in the future.

Fishing

Impacts of overfishing predate all other anthropogenic stressors of coastal ecosystems (Jackson et al. 2001). The importance of fishing as a risk factor contrasts with the relatively low ranking of excessive harvest as a threat to terrestrial species in the United States (Wilcove et al. 2000). In part, this reflects the fact that ocean fisheries are the last permitted market harvest of wild animals (Goble, this volume).

Fishing has both direct and indirect impacts on marine species. Target species experience direct fishing mortality, which can cause shifts in the age, size, sex, social, and genetic structure of populations (National Research Council 1999b). Top predators are the preferred targets of many fisheries and thus suffer the most pronounced losses (Pauly et al. 1998; Myers and Worm 2003). Populations of large-bodied species can be less resilient to overexploitation because they often are slow to mature and exhibit low fecundity. Of the seventy-nine species identified by the American Fisheries Society as containing at least one vulnerable distinct population segment, forty-eight are estimated to have low intrinsic rates of increase; these include a number of sharks, sturgeons, rockfish, and larger groupers (Musick et al. 2000). Mixed-species fisheries present a particular threat to low-productivity species because catches of more productive stocks continue to support fishing while less resilient populations collapse (Huntsman 1994; Musick et al. 2000).

Bycatch is listed as a threat to 42 percent of marine and estuarine endangered, threatened, and species of concern (Kappel 2005). Bycatch mortality was identified as the primary factor behind declines leading to listing of smalltooth sawfish (*Pristis pectinata*) (NMFS 2003b) and remains a critical threat to listed populations of leatherback (*Dermochelys coriacea*), Kemp's ridley (*Lepidochelys kempii*), and olive ridley (*L. olivacea*) sea turtles (NMFS 2002d). Based on catch data and observer programs from around the world, a recent assessment estimated that over two hundred thousand loggerhead turtles (*Caretta caretta*) and fifty thousand leatherbacks may have been taken in pelagic longline fisheries in 2000 (Lewison et al. 2004).

Aquaculture

Aquaculture operations have multiple impacts on marine ecosystems (Goldburg et al. 2001). Individuals that escape from aquaculture facilities can damage wild stocks through competition, by introducing novel diseases and parasites, and by diluting the gene pool if interbreeding occurs. Atlantic salmon (*Salmo salar*) are extinct throughout the United States in all but eight rivers in Maine (Musick et al. 2000), where they are listed as endangered (USFWS and NMFS 2000d). Escaped aquaculture fish of the same species, but of distinct, and often European genetic origin, can comprise over 80 percent of the individuals in rivers in Maine (USFWS and NMFS 2000d). Furthermore, a novel and lethal virus, *infectious salmon anemia*, which was first detected in aquaculture sea pens in New Brunswick, has now been detected in escapees and wild fish in nearby rivers (USFWS and NMFS 2000d). Atlantic salmon are also farmed on the West Coast; here, too, individuals have escaped and are now breeding in British Columbia reaches (Volpe et al. 2000) where they might present a new threat to Pacific salmon and steelhead.

Habitat Destruction

Roughly 45 percent of endangered and threatened species depend on coastal habitats (Glomb 1995). These habitats are being lost to coastal development. Species like the tidewater goby (*Eucyclogobius newberryi*), which was listed as endangered in 1994, depend on shallow coastal lagoons and estuaries and are threatened by filling of wetlands, dredging, breaching of coastal lagoons and diversion of freshwater flow (Lafferty et al. 1996). The key silverside (*Menidia conchorum*) and mangrove rivulus (*Rivulus marmoratus*), both listed as species of concern, are threatened by the loss of mangrove habitats (Gilbert 1992). Of the marine, estuarine, or diadromous ESA species affected by habitat degradation, 85 percent use fresh or brackish water or land for some part of their life cycle, bringing them in contact with coastal development and altered landscapes; all forty listed diadromous species are affected by habitat degradation (Kappel 2005). Fully marine species are also directly and indirectly impacted by habitat degradation (Kappel 2005). Offshore, the action of some fishing gears, such as scallop dredges and otter trawls, radically increases the frequency and magnitude of disturbances to sensitive benthic habitat structures (Watling and Norse 1998; Koslow et al. 2000).

Water Diversion and Flow Modification

Alterations of fresh water and tidal flows are significant threats to diadromous and estuarine species. Diadromous stocks depend on water quality, sufficient in-stream flows, and particular substrate characteristics within the streams and rivers they utilize, all of which may be impacted by terrestrial human activities. Construction of upstream dams can impede spawning by inhibiting access to spawning sites or reducing in-stream flows to the point at which rivers or estuaries become uninhabitable. Impacts other than hydropower development are also important. For example, the totoaba (*Cynoscion macdonaldi*), a federally listed endangered fish that inhabits Mexican Gulf of California waters depends on the Colorado River delta for spawning. However, outflows in the delta have effectively ceased because of diversions for crop irrigation and municipal water needs (Dalton 2003). Channelization and dredging reduce complexity of streambeds, tidal creeks, and estuaries and can destroy spawning, foraging, and refuge habitats. For example, sandbars that restrict tidal flow into coastal lagoons and estuaries are often breached to create boat access and harbor facilities. The resultant increase in flow, scouring and erosion, and salinity can have major impacts on lagoon and estuarine communities, as has been the case in Elkhorn Slough, California, since creation of a direct opening to the ocean in 1947 (Caffrey et al. 2002).

Pollution, Sedimentation, and Run-off

Marine pollution comes from both catastrophic and chronic sources. There were 8,700 oil spills of over 1,000 gallons in U.S. waters between 1973 and 2000 (one every twenty-eight hours) and 30 of these were of more than 1 million gallons (U.S. Coast Guard 2001). Spills associated with the extraction and transportation of petroleum, however, constitute only a small fraction of the petroleum entering the sea as a result of human activities. Fully 85 percent of these inputs come from diffuse sources associated with petroleum consumption in cars and private boats, and from run-off from paved areas (National Research Council 2003b). Chemical pollutants, such as PCBs, DDT, and other organic contaminants, accumulate in the tissues of top predators, sea turtles, and seabirds, and may interfere with health and reproduction (NMFS 2002d). Plastic debris and other garbage is a major threat to sea turtles that ingest it or become entangled (NMFS 2002d). Estuaries and shallow coastal waters are becoming increasingly eutrophic due to run-off of agricultural fertilizers and waste products. The resulting increase in nitrogen can lead to explosive growths of algae, some of which are toxic (Burkholder at al. 1992). The hypoxia that accompanies these algal blooms causes radical shifts in community structure; pelagic organisms are displaced and there is a selective loss of benthic organisms

(Rabalais and Turner 2001). Threatened Johnson's seagrass, (*Halophila johnsonii*), the only listed marine plant, is restricted to a small area on the east coast of Florida, where its survival is jeopardized by siltation, eutrophication, and altered water quality (NMFS 2002d). Approximately 40 percent of U.S. estuaries exhibit high eutrophication conditions, with the Gulf of Mexico and mid-Atlantic coast most severely affected (Bricker et al. 1999).

Invasives

Nonindigenous species are arriving on our coasts at an accelerating rate. Commercial shipping is the primary vector for marine invasives. Planktonic organisms, including larvae of many species, are transported inside ships' ballast water tanks (National Research Council 1996b). These species can radically alter ecosystem interactions and outcompete or prey upon native species. The San Francisco Bay is currently home to at least 234 exotic species (the origins of 125 more are uncertain); a new species is introduced to the bay every fourteen weeks (Cohen and Carlton 1998). In some of the bay communities, nonindigenous species comprise 40–100 percent of common species, 97 percent of the total abundance of organisms, and 99 percent of the biomass (Cohen and Carlton 1998). Some are spreading to other estuaries and sites along the coastline.

To date there has been little evidence that interactions with marine invasive species lead to native species extinctions (Carlton 1993). A few examples, however, suggest that such impacts may be more common than previously thought. For example, *Spartina alterniflora*, an East Coast native cordgrass, was introduced to the Pacific coast where it spreads and hybridizes with *S. foliosa*, a West Coast native. Genetic evidence shows that *S. alterniflora* and the hybrid dominate invaded marshes while *S. foliosa*'s abundance plummets (Ayres et al. 1999). In another case, the decline of a native mussel species (*Mytilus trossulus*) was masked by the invasion of a visually indistinguishable nonnative (*M. galloprovincialis*); the decline may have been linked to competition with the invader (Geller 1999). Within its coastal lagoon habitat, the tidewater goby is threatened by competition with and/or predation by introduced fish, crayfish, and clawed frogs. The U.S. Fish and Wildlife Service critical habitat designation for this fish prescribes removal of all exotics from its critical habitat and the prevention of new introductions (USFWS 2000).

Disease

The spread of disease, which may also be facilitated by global shipping and navigation, threatens many native species (Harvell et al. 1999). For example, withering syndrome has led to a die-off of black abalone (*Haliotis cracherodii*), now a species of concern (NMFS 2004b), and may also restrict recovery prospects for endangered white abalone (*H. sorenseni*) and pink (*H. corrugata*) and green (*H. fulgens*) abalone, which were recently added to the species of concern list (Hobday and Tegner 2000; NMFS 2004c, 2004d). The elkhorn coral (*Acropora palmata*) and the staghorn coral (*Acropora cervicornis*) are now on the species of concern list following declines of 80–98 percent from 1970s abundance associated with the outbreak of white band disease among Caribbean populations in the late 1970s and early 1980s (Gladfelter 1982; McClanahan and Muthiga 1998). In another example, fibropapillomatosis, a sometimes-fatal disease that causes tumors on the skin and eyes, is a major threat to green (*Chelonia mydas*), loggerhead, Kemp's ridley, and olive ridley sea turtles, and is thought to be the main roadblock to recovery of Hawaiian populations of green sea turtles (NMFS 2002d).

Stressors of marine species also act indirectly, as in the case of the eelgrass limpet (*Lottia alveus alveus*), which was lost from the Atlantic Ocean basin in the 1930s after beds of the seagrass (*Zostera marina*), upon which it lived, succumbed to a disease (Carlton 1993). The seagrass retreated to brackish water refugia, but the limpet, whose physiology could not tolerate reduced salinity, could not follow and was extirpated.

Climate Change

The effect of climate change on ocean conditions remains uncertain. Many species, however, are finely adapted to ocean conditions for migration and dispersal. Changes in these conditions could destroy critical dispersal pathways and interrupt the timing of consumer-resource dynamics (Fields et al. 1993). Warmer ocean temperatures from the late 1970s through the mid-1990s associated with a quasi-cyclic shift in oceanic regime are thought to have contributed to poor recruitment of bocaccio and other rockfish along the California coast (MacCall and He 2002; Armsworth et al. 2006). Rising ocean temperatures can also interact with diseases to increase their impacts on populations (Harvell et al. 1999). For example, withering syndrome, which affects black and perhaps other species of abalone, is present at low levels in the population at all times but seems to increase mortality during El Niño events, which bring warm water (Friedman et al. 1997). Coral reef ecosystems are thought to be particularly vulnerable to the effects of climate change. Increased water temperatures, ocean acidification, and storm frequency and severity due to global climate change could adversely impact coral populations through increased bleaching, reduced calcification rates, more frequent physical disturbance, and pathogen outbreaks (Fields et al. 1993; Pittock 1999; Knowlton 2001).

Conservation Strategies

Given the variety of stressors of marine ecosystems, a suite of conservation strategies is required. For our purposes, it is useful to distinguish between those conservation measures intended to protect or restore particular endangered species from more general conservation strategies. The former management approaches clearly fall within the mandate of the Endangered Species Act, but the latter may not.

Endangered Species Protection

For some direct threats to endangered marine species, where takings are easily delineated and causal relationships are apparent, the necessary remedial measures are obvious; they would include, for example, the prohibition of directed fishing and development projects or polluting activities that threaten critical habitats. For many threats, however, causal linkages are uncertain and the involvement of many stakeholders dilutes personal responsibility. These more diffuse threats will be best managed by improving marine resource management and conservation in general.

When localized threats are involved, a useful strategy for protecting species is to designate sensitive habitat areas as reserves. At present, however, U.S. marine reserves are both few in number (there are around thirty fully protected areas in U.S. waters [Palumbi 2002]) and small (many are less than 2 square kilometers in area [Halpern 2003]). Generally, these reserves have been established opportunistically and have not been designed to meet specific biological goals such as the protection of federally endangered species.

The presence of critical habitat would provide compelling reasons for instituting local closures of exploitative activities. To date, multiple areas containing endangered species have been identified and targeted for restriction of some human activities (e.g., seasonal trawling closure in Steller Sea Lion Protection Areas, Gulf of Alaska). A comparison, however, of maps of critical habitat and species protected area sites for listed species (available from http://www.mpa .gov/) with maps of fully protected marine reserves (Palumbi 2002) indicates that none of the protected areas established for listed species is a fully protected reserve.

A growing body of evidence indicates that endangered marine species would benefit if their habitats were designated as reserves. Reserves studied in East Africa contain greater numbers of rare species than nearby fished areas (McClanahan and Arthur 2001). Halpern (2003) documented that biomass of fish and invertebrates was on average 192 percent greater within reserves than in fished areas, while densities, average size, and diversity were 91, 31, and 23 percent greater respectively. Long-term studies of control and reserve sites on two Philippine islands provide some of the best evidence that protection can rebuild depleted populations within reserve boundaries (Russ et al. 2003, 2004). This work also supports the hypothesis that reserves can increase abundance in immediately adjacent habitat areas through the spill-over of biomass across reserve boundaries. Although estimates of increased egg production within reserves suggest that larval spill-over may also occur, there is little empirical evidence yet that reserves enhance recruitment over large spatial scales (Palumbi 2002). For threatened, highly migratory species, reserves can offer benefits if they are designed to protect critical life stages and habitats, including spawning aggregations, and nesting and foraging areas. Finally, reserves can serve as a form of insurance for vulnerable species should regulations being implemented in the broader seascape fail. For example, it is hoped that the newly created Channel Islands reserves provide such insurance for the conservation measures intended to help rebuild bocaccio elsewhere (NMFS 2002e; Armsworth et al. 2006). Unfortunately, many threats to marine ecosystems, such as pollution, invasive species, and climate warming, cannot be excluded and a reserve will offer little protection against them.

In many instances, threats to endangered species occur throughout working seascapes. Localized management measures, such as marine reserves, therefore cannot provide sufficient protection on their own. Instead, regional-scale management approaches that make endangered species protection compatible with the continued operation of exploitative activities must be implemented. The search for such approaches forms part of an ongoing culture change in fisheries management (Fluharty 2000). Traditional, single-species management techniques are complemented by considerations of the ecosystem-level impacts of fishing. For threatened and endangered species to benefit from this change, fishery managers must move beyond considering only the most commercially valuable stocks. Many endangered marine species either were never economically important or are no longer so because of their scarcity (Huntsman 1994).

A concrete example of managing exploitation while protecting endangered species in a working seascape is provided by fishery management plans for Alaskan ground fish stocks. These plans are tailored to minimize the risk of further jeopardizing the endangered western distinct population segment of Steller sea-lions (*Eumetopias jubatus*). A thirty-year decline of 64 percent led to listing the entire U.S. Steller sea-lion population as threatened in 1990. The western population segment, however, continued to decline steadily and was listed as endangered in 1997 (NMFS 1997). Competition with the groundfish fisheries for important prey sources has been suggested as a possible threat to this top predator because population declines partially correlate with growth of those fisheries (Pascual and Adkison 1994; NMFS 1997). The fishery management plans for groundfish seek to protect sea lions through regional-scale conservation measures that include seasonal restrictions to disperse fishing effort in space and time and a requirement that fish stocks be maintained at or above minimum abundance levels. The plans also employ more localized measures, which include many small-scale fishing closures around important sea-lion rookeries and haul-outs (NMFS 2003c).

Recent technological advances in marine management make enforcement of seascape-scale fishery regulations more straightforward. For example, vessel monitoring systems are now mandatory in many fisheries. The U.S. Ocean Commission recently called for the installation of these systems to be a prerequisite for any commercial vessel to receive a fishing permit under a federal fishery plan (U.S. Commission on Ocean Policy 2004). These systems allow managers to determine when and where fishing is occurring, and they support the enforcement of marine reserves, time-area closures, and other spatially structured management strategies. In 2001, a prosecution based exclusively on data from such a monitoring system succeeded for the first time, when a New England scallop fisherman was fined for repeatedly entering areas closed to protect spawning groundfish (NOAA 2001).

For some endangered marine species, such as white abalone (*Haliotis sorenseni*), prohibitive management measures alone are unlikely to prevent extinction, and restoration efforts are urgently needed (Armsworth et al. 2006). Unfortunately, the science of restoration ecology in marine environments is in its infancy. There have been, however, some encouraging early success stories, such as the successful reestablishment of populations of the endangered tidewater goby in California (Lafferty et al. 1996).

Marine Biodiversity Conservation

Although the Endangered Species Act has typically been aimed at single-species conservation, the act states that its purposes "are to provide a means whereby the ecosystems upon which endangered species and threatened species depend may be conserved, [and] to provide a program for the conservation of such endangered species and threatened species" (sec. 2(b)). Since 1994, NMFS and USFWS policies have required consideration of impacts to ecosystems when making decisions regarding listed species. As noted in the cooperative policy agreement, "species will be conserved best not by a species-by-species approach but by an ecosystem conservation strategy that transcends individual species" (USFWS and NMFS 1994b, 34274). Thus, the wording of the act and the implementing policies can benefit overall marine biodiversity by requiring the protection of ecosystems and their natural processes in the course of species protection.

Ancillary benefits will be conferred on other species that share habitats protected for listed species. For example, programs to remove invasive species from critical habitat of listed species, as called for in the critical habitat designation for the tidewater goby (USFWS 2000), could benefit whole ecological communities by reducing local impacts of invaders. Similarly, regulations and technologies that reduce bycatch of listed species may also reduce bycatch of other, unlisted species. Interdependencies among listed species also suggest that improvements in the status of one species can enhance recovery prospects for others. Salmon runs, for example, provide an important conduit of marine nutrients into diffuse stream networks and lake systems throughout the Pacific Northwest (Gende et al. 2002). The recovery of salmon populations thus could provide cascading benefits and also improve the prospects of threatened bull trout (*Salvelinus confluentus*) (Peery et al. 2003). The Endangered Species Act has the potential to support broader marine biodiversity conservation either directly, through ecosystem-based management approaches to endangered species conservation, or indirectly, through side-benefits of species-based management.

Conclusion

Endangered species protection and biodiversity conservation take place within different cultural and institutional contexts for marine and terrestrial systems. Unlike the terrestrial realm, there is no large, established system of reserves in the marine environment. Development of an ecologically effective network of such reserves should be pursued as one critically important component of integrated seascape management. On their own, however, marine reserves do not offer a panacea (Norse et al. 2003). Policy makers must also look beyond reserves to protect endangered marine species and to manage marine ecosystems sustainably because many species need protection throughout the broader seascape and some threats are most effectively tackled at their point of origin rather than their point of impact.

In looking beyond reserves, we again note that the marine environment differs from the terrestrial. Lands outside reserves have been privatized and the conflict is with private landowners. The marine environment, on the other hand, to some degree remains a commons and the conflict is with the perceived right of individuals to exploit the seas free from regulation. Common-property issues are most difficult for highly migratory species that leave the Exclusive Economic Zone. The recent petition to list Atlantic white marlin (*Tetrapturus albidus*) illustrates this problem: the United States is responsible for only 5 percent of the total mortality of this species, most of which is due to bycatch by international longline fleets.

Marine conservation is also inhibited by widely held beliefs that stocks cannot be overfished and that the oceans' ability to absorb pollution is unlimited. In part, this syndrome may reflect the myopia of each new generation of resource users, which sets up a shifting baseline, or more accurately a declining one, against which the status of marine ecosystems is judged (Pauly 1995; Jackson et al. 2001). The growing number and diversity of marine species facing an immediate risk of extinction belies these assumptions. Marine species are being imperiled as a direct result of anthropogenic impacts to marine ecosystems. Conservation action is urgently needed to protect these species. When integrated with other statutes (Armsworth et al. 2006), the Endangered Species Act provides an important policy framework both to support and to mandate these actions.

20 Agricultural and Urban Landscapes

Berry J. Brosi, Gretchen C. Daily, and Frank W. Davis

The future of biodiversity, and the benefits it supplies society, will be dictated largely by what happens in human-dominated, working landscapes (Daily 2001; Daily et al. 2001). This is because reserve networks alone are unlikely to protect more than a tiny fraction of Earth's biodiversity over the long run. Reserve networks are (and are likely to remain) too small, too isolated, and too subject to climatic and other change to protect more (Daily 2001; Rosenzweig 2003b). Nonreserve "countryside"—land dedicated primarily to farming, grazing, forestry, gardening, landscaping, urban parks, and other types of human enterprise—is thus critical to biodiversity in augmenting the habitat area and connectivity, and the range of ecological conditions, represented by reserves (Daily et al. 2003).

Countryside is also critical to the supply of ecosystem services and the stream of societal benefits derived from ecosystems and their biodiversity (Daily 1997). These include the renewal of soil fertility, purification of drinking water, control of floods, pollination of crops, stabilization of climate, and provision of beauty, serenity, and inspiration. Because many of these services are supplied on local and regional scales, their delivery hinges on the capacity of countryside species and ecosystems to generate them—in the midst of human enterprise (Hughes et al. 1997; Luck et al. 2003). The provision of globally supplied services, such as carbon sequestration for climate stability, also hinges on countryside because the global nature reserve system will never be large enough to ensure adequate supply.

Currently there is little scientific basis for assessing trade-offs between production of conventional commodities and provision of ecosystem services, for the range of alternative management systems and landscape configurations. Such a basis is urgently needed because rapid intensification of land use is closing the window of opportunity for retaining and enhancing the value of countryside worldwide (e.g., Krebs et al. 1999; Donald et al. 2001; Tilman et al. 2001b).

In the early development of conservation science and practice in the United States, countryside was not the focus of much attention, whether in the context of protecting diverse native biotas or ecosystem services. Caricaturing only slightly, traditional conservation was guided by the notion that the world comprises two types of places: natural habitat and human-created nonhabitat (e.g., Cronon 1995). The logic was that organisms evolved tightly tuned to their native habitats; that few, therefore, are able to exploit areas devoted to human enterprise; and that those few do not merit attention, at least from a conservation standpoint. The conservation strategy that followed from this logic was to secure as nature reserves the biggest and most (bio)diverse set of sites possible—and to restore and maintain this fleet of arks in an increasingly hostile sea of development (Daily 2003; Rosenzweig 2003b). Now a growing array of innovative science and policy efforts aim to expand the focus of conservation attention to include not only nature reserves but human-dominated, working landscapes as well (Margules and Pressey 2000; Daily 2001; Daily and Ellison 2002; Haila 2002; Millennium Ecosystem Assessment 2003).

These developments bring into focus a critical set of longstanding issues. What is the capacity of countryside habitats and landscapes to support biodiversity? What types and levels of other ecosystem services, besides biodiversity conservation, could be supplied by countryside habitats? What practical measures could enhance the capacity of countryside to sustain biodiversity and ecosystem services?

This chapter addresses the first of these major questions. First we review briefly the emerging scientific framework for understanding conservation value of countryside, by which we mean the capacity of habitats and landscapes to support biodiversity, unless stated otherwise. (In general, ecosystem service values other than sustaining biodiversity remain too poorly characterized to bring into our analysis and discussion.) Second, we summarize the conservation value of countryside in the context of the federal Endangered Species Act. Third, we present a new database analysis of the potential conservation value of countryside habitats in California, with special emphasis on legally threatened and endangered species.

Countryside Biogeography: Toward a Scientific Framework

Resource management disciplines, including forestry, agriculture, and rangelands management, have long focused on managing landscapes for both biodiversity and ecosystem services (wildlife, timber, forage, water quality, etc.). However, the mainstream conservation community has only recently begun to integrate this valuable, but fragmented, body of knowledge to develop a holistic scientific basis for assessing the relative biodiversity conservation value of alternative production regimes and landscape configurations. Although many elements of understanding exist, these are just now being unified in a general predictive framework, called "countryside biogeography" (Daily 1999). In this framework, the potential distribution, abundance, conservation, and restoration of biodiversity in countryside are a function of several basic factors relating to both habitat and organisms. Major habitat drivers include landscape configuration, disturbance regimes, and ecological history; important organismal factors include the reproductive and dispersal capacities of species in such habitats. The degree to which populations can persist and thrive depends on the rates and directions of change in these basic factors. Subsumed within these factors are complex species interactions, such as those between pathogens and their hosts.

The immaturity of countryside biogeography is evident even in the European Union, where extensive human-dominated countryside was created long ago, where its associated biodiversity has been the subject of detailed inquiry, where farmland is the land cover upon which many threatened species depend most (e.g., Tucker 1997), and where roughly 20 percent of farmland is presently under environmentally sensitive management (e.g., Pienkowski 1998). In the Netherlands, for instance, over twenty years of biodiversity management schemes on farmland have yielded little perceptible benefit. The diversity of plants and abundance of target bird species is no higher on fields under management agreements than on those under conventional management (Kleijn et al. 2001).

Although farmers abided by their agreements, conservation goals were not achieved because of poorly understood constraints on the conservation and restoration of biodiversity at both landscape and local scales. Potentially important constraints involve the atmospheric deposition of nitrogenous and sulfuric compounds, the dispersal and seed bank dynamics of plants, and the nesting cues used by birds (Bakker and Berendse 1999; Kleijn et al. 2001; D. Kleijn, pers. comm. to G. Daily, December 3, 2002). In the case of floristic diversity, for instance, it is possible that farmers' reductions of local fertilizer inputs (intended to foster greater native plant diversity) were overwhelmed by widespread atmospheric deposition of nitrogen. An alternative possibility is that enrolled farms did have suitable conditions but that seed sources were too few and far away to enable colonization of suitable sites. Yet another possibility is that the biodiversity-friendly farming practices are working, only more slowly than expected, so that in another two decades of continuing these practices the desired benefits might be realized.

Elucidating the response of populations and species to changing landscape composition and configuration is not simple. For instance, relationships between bird populations and attributes of agricultural landscapes in the United States are rarely consistent across species (Murphy 2003). The same is true across higher taxonomic groups. In Costa Rica, nocturnal moths respond to landscape attributes very differently than diurnal butterflies in spite of the two having similar ecological and evolutionary attributes (Daily and Ehrlich 1996). Moreover, interactions between the same species may vary greatly, from mutualistic in some habitats to commensal or antagonistic in others (Thompson and Cunningham 2002).

In spite of the complexities inherent in assessing conservation value of countryside, several general principles have emerged from recent work in both tropical and temperate regions. First, there is no substitute for native habitats. Many species (generally up to 50 percent, and a much higher fraction in some tropical groups of organisms) occur nowhere else, or have spatial distributions that extend beyond native habitat elements only in small halos (Daily 2001; Ricketts et al. 2001).

Second, the conservation value of countryside is highly variable. Countryside that retains even relatively small cover of native habitat (about 15 percent) and a diversity of land covers can have tremendous conservation value, supporting a diverse native fauna at least over a period of decades following major habitat alteration (Estrada et al. 1997; Maestas et al. 2002; Matlock et al. 2002; McNeely and Scherr 2002; Horner-Devine et al. 2003; Daily et al. 2003; Maestas et al. 2003). Landscapes under extensive monocultures of annual crops have lower conservation value, supporting less than 10 percent of the native biota (McNeely and Scherr 2002). In many places, hunting compromises the conservation potential of a countryside, especially for mammals and birds (e.g., Daily et al. forthcoming). And the long-term sustainability of diverse countryside biotas is a critical, open question.

Third, rapid intensification of land use threatens to close the window of opportunity for retaining or enhancing the conservation value of countryside at relatively low cost (e.g., Pain et al. 1997; Pienkowski 1998; Krebs et al. 1999; Donald et al. 2001; Tilman et al. 2001b). In southern Costa Rica, for instance, ongoing removal of mature trees and of vegetation borders between agricultural plots (hedgerows, living fences) could reduce the diversity of the avifauna in the deforested countryside by at least 40 percent (Hughes et al. 2002). Arresting and reversing some of these trends could create tremendous conservation benefits and possibly confer economic benefits in the form of various ecosystem services, such as landscape stabilization, flood control, improved water quality, climate stabilization, pollination, and pest control.

Countryside and the United States Endangered Species Act

In the United States, a tremendous amount of biodiversity occurs on privately owned land, much of which was converted from wilderness to countryside decades or even centuries ago. Only one-third of populations of both federally listed and imperiled species are found on federal lands (Groves et al. 2000). Private lands harbor at least one population of more than half of all legally protected species and two-thirds of federally listed species. Nearly 10 percent of imperiled and federally listed species are restricted entirely to private lands.

Private lands in the United States are undergoing rapid land use changes. From 1982 to 1992, for instance, over 2.47 million acres (1 million hectares) of pasture lands were converted to residential and industrial development, roads, and shopping centers. Over the same period, nearly 988,422 acres (400,000 hectares) of privately owned wetlands were developed, despite a national policy of "no net loss."

Urban areas occupy a relatively small fraction of the U.S. land surface but support a disproportionate share of endangered plant species. Twenty-two percent of the known occurrences of federally listed endangered plant species are in urban areas—only 8.4 percent of the U.S. land area but where half of all Americans live (Schwartz et al. 2002). Several factors contribute to this pattern, including habitat loss and fragmentation, the association of urban areas with high-biodiversity environments such as coastal habitats and valley floors, and relative survey effort, which is greater in urban than rural areas. Whatever the cause of the pattern, the high density of endangered plant species in urban areas highlights the importance of developing novel conservation strategies in densely settled areas where large preserves are precluded (see Beatley, this volume).

Conservation Value of Urban and Agricultural Lands in California

California is a major testing ground for the Endangered Species Act. An estimated twenty-nine plant species and fifty-four animal species have gone extinct in California since European settlement. Urban development and agricultural and grazing activities appear to be major causes of extinction for twenty-two of the fifty-four animal species (California Department of Fish and Game, cited in Tennant et al. 2001). As of June 2003, eighty animal species are federally listed as endangered in California (20.6 percent of U.S. total) and another forty are listed as threatened (30.1 percent of U.S. total). Similarly, 137 California plant species are listed as federally endangered (22.9 percent of U.S. total) and another 48 are listed as threatened (32.7 percent of U.S. total). Conflicts between urban and agricultural development and endangered species have spawned numerous subregional Natural Community Conservation Planning (NCCP) programs and habitat conservation plans (HCPs) for multiple species (Fulton 1999). Statewide, at least 104 HCPs have been approved covering over

5,536,000 acres (2,240,390 hectares), or 5.5 percent of the state's land area (USFWS 2005).

California's human population is currently growing by roughly 0.5 million per year and is projected to reach 58.7 million by 2040 (California Department of Finance 2002). To meet projected 2020 demand for new housing, California home builders would need to construct an average of 220,000 additional housing units every year. Much of the development is expected to occur on agricultural lands (Landis and Reilly 2002). Areas projected for rapid population growth such as southern coastal California, the San Francisco Bay Area, the southern San Joaquin Valley, the western Mojave Desert, and the foothills of the Sierra Nevada already support relatively high densities of threatened and endangered species, and mitigating the loss of endangered species habitats is one of the major hurdles to continued land and water development in those regions (California Department of Fish and Game 2005).

Given recent trends, one could project that many of California's urbanizing landscapes will eventually resemble coastal Southern California, in which an archipelago of highly managed reserves, many established to protect endangered species, must function in a matrix of high-density urban and suburban development. To what extent could appropriately designed and managed urban and agricultural lands relieve the demand for new large biodiversity reserves and enhance the long-term conservation capacity of existing reserves? Is it possible to maintain some native species on relatively intensively developed landscapes thereby easing the conflict between conservation and land development and reducing the perceived economic impact of the Endangered Species Act in California?

Many rare and threatened plant species in California occur in urban or urbanizing areas (Schwartz et al. 2002). However, few native plant species are strongly positively associated with urban development or agriculture. The CALFLORA database lists only 34 of 6,300 native taxa that are either weedy and associated with disturbed areas (and thus likely to thrive in urban settings) or are considered agricultural weeds (Calflora 2005). Many of California's federally listed plant species are narrow habitat specialists associated with unusual substrates (e.g., serpentinite or spodosolic sands), limiting conservation options (Pavlik 2003). Furthermore, many native plant species require fire, flooding, or other disturbances that are difficult to manage in densely settled areas. On the brighter side, many plant populations are able to persist in relatively small areas and thus might be accommodated with relatively modest set-asides combined with appropriate management and/or restoration activities.

Relatively few native animal species favor urban habitat but a sizeable number can persist in remnant habitat fragments depending on fragment size and isolation (Soulé et al. 1992), habitat division by roads or other features, and levels of human activity in habitat remnants (Buechner and Sauvajot 1996). Arthropod communities in urban areas are dominated by exotic species, and native species richness increases with fragment size (Suarez et al. 1998; Bolger et al. 2000). Native bird species can be very sensitive to fragmentation due to higher nest predation, parasitism (e.g., from cowbirds), and invasion by exotic species (Soulé et al. 1992). Thus the landscape pattern of urbanization (extent of edge or linking corridors) can be an important determinant of extinction risk (Bolger et al. 1997a; Morrison and Bolger 2002).

Similar patterns have been shown for small mammals and reptiles (e.g., Buechner and Sauvajot 1996; Bolger et al. 1997b; Fisher et al. 2002). Medium-sized carnivores such as bobcats and coyotes can persist in surprisingly urbanized settings, in part by modifying their diets and behavior, but they suffer elevated mortality on roads (Tigas et al. 2002). Mountain lions require at least an order of magnitude more natural habitat and demand an altogether different conservation strategy of extensive wildland areas and corridors (Crooks 2002). Taken together, studies of native animals in urban habitats suggest that large and/or well-connected areas of native habitat (that include extensive interior areas free from edge influence) must be part of any long-term conservation strategy but that even densely settled urban and residential areas continue to harbor some native biodiversity and with appropriate land planning and management the number of viable species can be expanded (see Beatley, this volume).

California agriculture is a $30 billion industry that occupies roughly 25 million acres (about 10 million hectares, or about 25 percent of the state's land area) and encompasses a wide range of products and climatic settings. Much of the loss of biodiversity in California can be attributed to land conversion, wetland drainage, water diversions, pesticides, and exotic species associated with the state's enormous agricultural enterprise (Jensen et al. 1993). Agriculture's negative impact on biodiversity has likely increased in recent decades as agricultural practices have intensified (Benton et al. 2003). Agriculture has been pitted against endangered species conservation in many areas of California, particularly over water diversions and wetland losses. At the same time, farmland conservation in urbanizing areas has been promoted not only as a means of sustaining regional agricultural production and providing open space but also of providing wildlife habitat.

There is little doubt that California farmlands can harbor many native animal species. For example, despite extensive modification, the Central Valley continues to be a major flyway for migratory birds, and the valley's farmlands provide important habitat for both migratory and resident shorebirds and waterfowl (Shuford et al. 1998; Czech and Parsons 2002; Elphick and Oring 2003). Retaining even small habitat remnants, especially riparian habitats, in agricultural landscapes can have a large positive effect on native animals. Such remnants can sometimes reduce the impacts of agricultural pest species by promoting biological control agents (e.g., Nicholls et al. 2001), and organic farmers are increasingly retaining untilled areas along field margins for this purpose. Some endangered species may also be compatible with agriculture with modest habitat set-asides. For example, the endangered San Joaquin kit fox can persist in farmlands so long as there is a suitable prey base and untilled areas are available for denning (Williams et al. 1998). Farmers, too, may realize important economic benefits from set-asides, such as for pollination services (Kremen et al. 2002).

CWHR Database Analysis

To explore the importance of urban and agricultural habitat in the context of the Endangered Species Act, we analyzed new, comprehensive databases on vertebrate species and land cover use in California. We posed two questions: What is the conservation value of urban and agricultural habitats for vertebrates in California? And what is this value for legally protected vertebrates in the state?

We used the California Wildlife Habitat Relationships (CWHR) database (California Department of Fish and Game 2002) and the land use and land cover dataset from the California GAP Analysis project (Davis et al. 1998). The CWHR is a comprehensive database of all 675 California terrestrial vertebrates (birds, mammals, amphibians, and reptiles) and their habitat affinities. Information is included on fifty-seven primary terrestrial and freshwater habitats most of which are divided into "stages" or subclassifications. Ordinal values (none, low, medium, high) for reproduction, cover, and feeding are given for all combinations of species and habitats; we converted these values into integers (0 to 3) for our analysis. We queried the CWHR database along two major axes throughout our analysis: species status (legally protected versus nonprotected) and habitat association (native habitat type, urban, or agricultural).

Species Richness by Habitat

To assess the relative contribution of habitat factors and habitat area (i.e., to ensure that our habitat-focused results were not artifacts of species-area relationships), we ran regressions of species richness (as the dependent variable) as a function of total habitat area and average area per habitat polygon (based on GAP land cover data). Both relationships were nonsignificant, with low correlation coefficients (total habitat area: r-squared = 0.0031, p = .683; average area of habitat per polygon: r-squared = 0.030, p = 0.387).

Native habitats have the greatest aggregate species richness, followed by agricultural habitats, then urban habitats (fig. 20.1). These trends hold for

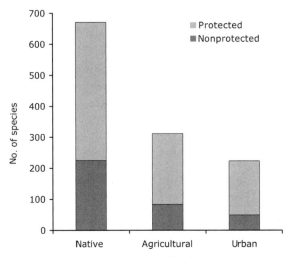

Figure 20.1. Species richness by habitat group and legal protection category. (Data from California Department of Fish and Game 2002; Davis et al. 1998.)

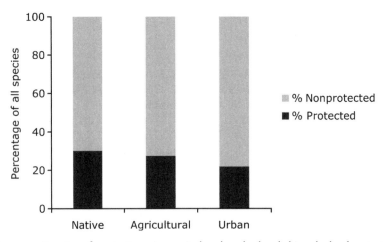

Figure 20.2. Fraction of species in native, agricultural, and urban habitats by legal protection category. (Data from California Department of Fish and Game 2002; Davis et al. 1998.)

protected species as well, both in absolute numbers and percentages of protected species (fig. 20.2). Agricultural habitats have significantly fewer species than native habitats (*t*-test assuming unequal variance, $p = 0.0003$; fig. 20.3b). Urban habitat has higher species richness than the average agricultural or native habitat, partly because there is only one broad urban classification but also

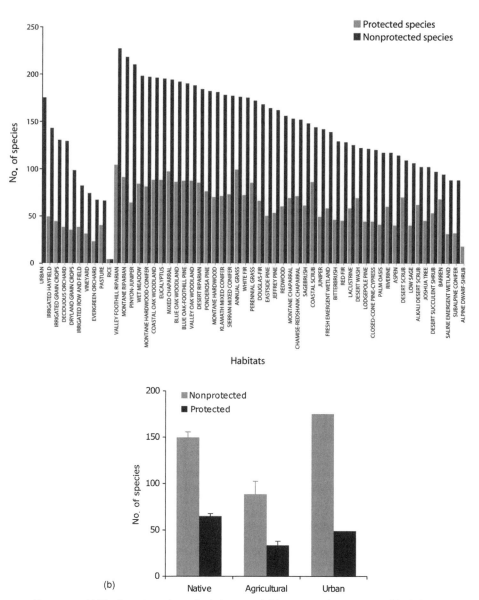

Figure 20.3. (a) Total species richness by habitat; and (b) species richness averaged by habitat group. (Data from California Department of Fish and Game 2002; Davis et al. 1998.)

because that single habitat classification covers a large range of bioclimates (discussed below in "Potential Biases of the CWHR Database").

Species Habitat Associations

The differences in habitat association between protected and nonprotected species are statistically significant (chi-squared, $p < 0.0001$, fig. 20.4). The largest differences are found in species that occur either in native habitat only or in all three habitat groups (i.e., agriculture, urban, and native habitats). Nonprotected species are more likely to occur in all three habitat groups (31 percent versus 18 percent for protected species), while protected species tend to occur in native habitats only (60 percent versus 42 percent for nonprotected species).

Four of the 675 nonaquatic vertebrate species in California occur exclusively in agricultural or urban habitats or their combination. Of these four species, all are capable of flying and dispersing widely, and three are either introduced or their ranges have expanded to include California; these species are the bronzed cowbird (*Molothrus aeneus*), the Inca dove (*Columbina inca*), and the ringed turtle dove (*Streptopelia risoria*). The remaining species, the big free-tailed bat (*Nyctinomops macrotis*), is a California Species of Special Concern and has been found in California only in urban areas of San Diego County, where it most likely does not breed; its normal home range is limited to Texas, New Mexico, and Arizona (California Department of Fish and Game 2002). Despite the lack of human influence during most of the evolutionary history of the California fauna, almost half (46 percent) of terrestrial vertebrates utilize agricultural habi-

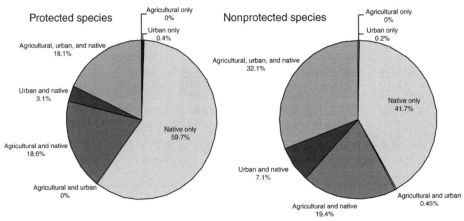

Figure 20.4. Overlap of species richness by habitat groups for protected and nonprotected species.

tats, and a full third (33 percent) make use of urban habitats to fulfill some life history requirement.

Factors Affecting Species Habitat Associations

We also examined habitat associations in relation to taxonomic class (bird, mammal, amphibian, or reptile), migratory behavior (long-distance migrators, local migrators, unpredictable migrators, and nonmigrators), volancy (flying versus nonflying animals), and species origin (native versus introduced). These factors are clearly interrelated; for example, taxonomic class is related to volancy because almost all birds fly while no reptiles or amphibians do. Generally, species groups with greater dispersal ability tend to use agricultural and urban habitats more than low-dispersal species groups (table 20.1). We found significantly different patterns of habitat association across all of the factors examined except species origin. Although introduced species are more likely to use agricultural and urban habitats than native species, the difference is not statistically significant given the small number of introduced vertebrates.

Flight ability is strongly associated with increased use of urban and agricultural habitats, presumably because more mobile organisms can glean resources from a broader spectrum of habitats.

Habitat Value by Species

We tallied, for each species, the maximum value (0–3) of each habitat (across habitat stages) for reproduction, cover, and feeding; these values were then averaged across habitat classifications (native, agricultural, and urban). We used maximum values within each habitat to avoid overemphasizing the importance

TABLE 20.1 Species-based factors and patterns of habitat overlap

Factor	*Percentage in agricultural or urban habitats*				
Taxonomic class	Birds (%)	Mammals (%)	Reptiles (%)	Amphibians (%)	Chi-squared
	64	47	21	30	$\ll 0.0001^*$
Migration	Long-distance	Local	Unpredictable	Nonmigrators	Chi-squared
	64	65	46	41	0.0007^*
Volancy	Flying	Nonflying	Chi-squared		
	68	25	$\ll 0.0001^*$		
Species origin	Native	Introduced	Chi-squared		
	52	76	0.24 (NS)		

*p < 0.001; NS, not significant.

of habitat stages (subtypes) that are utilized less than others. We stratified this analysis by comparing values for legally protected and nonprotected vertebrates. In a three-way ANOVA, habitat group, species protection status, and life history requirement (i.e., reproduction, cover, and feeding) were all significant factors ($p < 0.001$ for all three, fig. 20.5). The interactions of habitat by protection status and habitat by life history requirement were also significant ($p < 0.001$ for both).

Native habitats have consistently high value for both legally protected and nonprotected species for reproduction, feeding, and cover. Agricultural habitats are less valuable for protected species than nonprotected ones and have greater

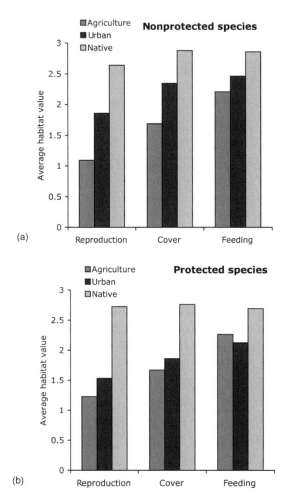

Figure 20.5. Maximum reproduction, cover, and feeding values by species and habitat, averaged across habitat groups, for (a) nonprotected species; and (b) protected species. (Data from California Department of Fish and Game 2002; Davis et al. 1998.)

feeding and cover value than reproductive value. Urban habitats were rated as more valuable than agricultural ones across species protection status and life history requirements, with the exception of feeding value for protected species. This may be due in part to the lower species richness in urban areas; the smaller set of species that exist in urban habitats may be better able to utilize them for a range of life-history requirements. Additionally, as already noted, migratory organisms extensively utilize agricultural habitats for only parts of their year (in particular for feeding), which in turn lowers the average score for other life history requirements for agricultural habitats. Finally, because urban habitats are defined more broadly than agricultural habitats, species have a broader range of resources and conditions in urban than in agricultural habitats. The differences between agricultural and urban habitats were smaller for protected species than nonprotected species.

Correlation of Reproduction, Cover, and Feeding Values

Based on average values by species and excluding species that do not occur in a given habitat group, agricultural habitats provide less value for reproduction on average than do native habitats (t-test, $p \ll 0.0001$; tables 20.2 and 20.3). In native habitats, reproduction, cover, and feeding are all positively correlated with correlation coefficients greater than 0.29, whereas in agricultural habitats, reproduction and feeding are slightly negatively correlated. Reproductive and

TABLE 20.2 Correlations of habitat values to species by different habitat groups

	Reproduction by cover	Cover by feeding	Reproduction by feeding
Native	0.68	0.55	0.29
Agricultural	0.42	0.48	−0.03
Urban	0.58	0.84	0.48

TABLE 20.3 Correlations of habitat values for legally protected and unprotected species

	Reproduction by cover	Cover by feeding	Reproduction by feeding
Nonprotected	0.26	0.49	−0.02
Legally protected	0.50	0.36	−0.10

cover values are more tightly correlated in species with legal protection than in unprotected species (p = 0.007), though differences in the correlations of cover with feeding and reproduction with feeding are not significantly different between legally protected and nonprotected species. We were somewhat surprised not to find stronger patterns in these correlations, as legally protected species are generally range-restricted and thus derive all their life history needs from a small set of habitats. However, this is certainly not true of all endangered species: marbled murrelets and sandhill cranes, among others, need very different habitats to fulfill different life history requirements, which would lead to low correlations of these requirements. Similarly, many nonendangered species utilize only a small range of habitats but still maintain large population sizes.

Taxonomic class, species origin, migratory behavior, and volancy all have a significant influence on the correlation of reproduction, cover, and feeding values within habitats (p < 0.001 for all twelve combinations—three correlations across four factors). The similarity of results is not surprising given that movement ability is probably the most important trait causing differences in all of the species factors except for species origin (as discussed above). The correlation of reproduction with feeding was much stronger in the lower-movement groups (reptiles and amphibians, nonmigratory species, etc.) than in groups with higher dispersal abilities. These patterns may in turn affect the patterns seen in differences among habitat groups (agricultural, native, and urban habitats) discussed above; for example, migratory waterfowl tend to make extensive use of agricultural areas for feeding but usually rely on native wetland habitats for reproduction. Interestingly, introduced species have higher correlations of reproduction, cover, and feeding than do native species; this may be in part because successful invaders also tend to be generalists who can use a given habitat for a range of life history requirements.

Potential Biases of the CWHR Database

The California Wildlife Habitat Relationships database is a valuable synthesis of information applicable to a wide range of uses. Like any information set, however, the CWHR database has inherent biases that are important to consider when interpreting the results of an analysis. The database is based on generalized range maps and expert models of habitat use and thus tends to overestimate the geographic and habitat distributions of vertebrates in California.

Species Habitat Models

Species habitat models are based in part on literature surveys as well as personal judgment and experience. Both sources may underestimate species' uses of urban and agricultural landscapes given that these habitat types are less studied by wildlife biologists. For example, in the CWHR database, only eight vertebrate species are listed as occurring in rice fields in any season of the year or stage of cultivation (including flooded fields). In contrast, the California Rice Commission states that 141 bird species, 28 mammal species, and 24 amphibian and reptile species utilize rice fields, including 30 legally protected species (California Rice Commission 1997). Scientists and groups other than rice cultivation advocates have also recognized the biodiversity value of rice cultivation, especially for migratory birds (e.g., Elphick and Oring 2003).

Habitat Definitions

In the CWHR database most "native" or "natural" habitats are relatively narrowly defined, whereas agricultural and urban habitat categories cover a much broader spectrum of land use and land cover. This concern is especially applicable to the "urban" habitat category, which includes a wide range of residential, commercial, and industrial uses.

Bioclimatic Ranges of Habitat Groups

Urban and agricultural habitats occur in nearly every bioclimate in the state, while most native habitats occur in only one or a few bioclimates. This bias could lead to relative overestimates of the conservation value of human-dominated landscapes. To examine this potential effect, we compared species richness in urban, agricultural, and native habitats at both countywide and statewide scales. Interestingly, and contrary to our expectation, we found considerably higher proportions of species richness occurring in agricultural and urban habitats on the countywide scales than we did in a statewide analysis. An average of 50 percent of species in each county occurred in urban habitats and 63 percent in agricultural habitats; statewide, 33 percent of species occur in urban habitats and 46 percent in agricultural habitats. This effect may be caused by restricted-range species that occur only in native habitats in only part of the state; when pooled at the countywide scale they represent a lower fraction of species richness than when pooled at the statewide scale. Put another way, the "turnover" (the proportion of species that differ) between two urban areas is probably low, while the species turnover between two native oak woodlands in different parts of the state is probably quite high. Therefore, we do not think the bioclimatic range of urban and agricultural habitats is a significant source of bias in the database.

Legal Protection of Subspecies and Populations

If a subspecies or population of any species is protected, the CWHR database counts the entire species as protected. This leads to overestimation of percentages of protected species occurring in any given habitat. Though other biases could affect these percentages as well, this problem is unidirectional. To estimate the magnitude of this bias, we analyzed the number of species protected at the subspecies and population levels using the Special Animals list of the California Department of Fish and Game (California Department of Fish and Game 2003) and found that there are approximately 87 protected subspecies out of 218 total legally protected species from the CWHR database (about 40 percent). Although some of these subspecies are the only representatives of their species in California, numbers or percentages of protected species occurring in any habitat should be interpreted as maximum values.

Generality of Our Results

In this analysis, we focused on terrestrial vertebrates because of the detailed and reliable information available on them, not because they are necessarily representative of ecological patterns for other taxa. Our analyses pointed out that species traits can be important correlates of survival in human-dominated habitats. For example, low vagility was clearly associated with lower likelihood of existence in working landscapes in our database analysis.

Research to Inform Policy

The conservation of biodiversity and ecosystem services, two goals of utmost importance for humanity, cannot be achieved with reserves alone. While many species (especially legally protected ones, which tend to be most sensitive) need relatively pristine habitats to persist, a surprisingly high proportion can survive and even thrive in human-dominated lands. The management of urban and countryside landscapes, which cover a large and increasing portion of the globe, will be a major determinant of biodiversity and ecosystem services in the future. We desperately need more scientific information about how to improve the biodiversity conservation potential of working landscapes and believe that this should be a priority for ecology and conservation biology.

Proactive conservation of nonlisted species must also be part of any meaningful biodiversity conservation strategy (Davis et al. 2006). This pertains to the Endangered Species Act but also intersects a broader range of local, state, and federal statutes that govern land and water use. In considering policy options and innovations, a major question in countryside biogeography concerns conservation trade-offs among different land uses. In our analysis of the CWHR database, agricultural habitat types on average are predicted to support more biodiversity than urban habitats despite the fact that urban habitats are defined more broadly and occur in a wider range of bioclimates than categories of agricultural land uses defined by the database. This general finding suggests that the conversion of farmland to residential or industrial uses (a large and increasing trend in the United States) generally diminishes biodiversity. However, farmlands and urban areas are highly variable land uses with similarly high variation in their ability to support biodiversity.

Given that native habitats usually have greater conservation value per acre than agricultural or urban ones, should we try to concentrate the spatial footprint of human-dominated lands thereby leaving more pristine habitats available for biodiversity? This may be a good conservation planning tactic in many cases, but "extensification" of agriculture or urban areas under certain scenarios may be a more economically efficient conservation strategy overall. Under what circumstances is it better to have smaller reserves combined with better management of human-dominated land instead of larger reserves set aside with less attention to conservation in surrounding lands? Understanding the ecological and economic trade-offs between different land uses is an important but understudied research topic for scientists and regional planners.

There are many ways to improve the conservation value of urban habitats, for example controlling pets and exotic species, installing wildlife under- and overpasses, and reducing nocturnal light pollution. However, to be effective in the long run, they must to be combined with other conservation measures that directly address critical life history and population biological parameters, such as reduction of population isolation through connections to reserves. The conservation value of urban habitat thus hinges on configurations of landscape-scale factors that can perhaps only be addressed through the combined efforts of conservation biologists and urban and regional planners. If these two groups would work together, biodiversity in urban landscapes could benefit tremendously. A potential means to jump-start these collaborations would be to integrate elements of each profession into the professional certification and education and training programs of the other.

There are also ways to reduce the impacts of agriculture to biodiversity: reducing agrochemicals, managing for heterogeneity (Benton et al. 2003), and minimizing disturbance of hydrological regimes. Several crop- or area-specific practices, such as flooding rice fields to enhance waterfowl habitat, are also well characterized. The challenge to countryside conservation efforts is in deciding which management techniques are appropriate and efficient when and where, and tipping the economic scales to favor their use. Efforts should focus on interventions that profit conservation in multiple ways, like the small riparian set-asides mentioned previously that could potentially yield proportionately large conservation benefits for their cost, including habitat connectivity and flood control, among others.

Much of the time, what is good for biodiversity is also good for people. Reducing the use of agricultural chemicals is good for human health; augmenting the habitat heterogeneity of urban and agricultural landscapes in many cases makes them aesthetically pleasing. Increasing the number of trees on residential lots can enhance property value as well as conservation value. Similarly, retaining or restoring riparian strips of native habitat in farmlands can potentially contribute to the ecosystem services of pest control, pollination, and flood abatement in addition to the biodiversity benefits they can confer. Finding these parallel benefits and making sure that they are included in cost-benefit analyses could be key in successfully moving countryside conservation into the policy domain (Daily and Ellison 2002).

2 1 Cities and Biodiversity

Timothy Beatley

To encourage cities to preserve biological diversity, we must counter the prevailing perception that biodiversity and cities have little to do with each other. Many think that cities have little nature, little direct connection to wildlife and biodiversity, and therefore are mostly irrelevant to the challenge of preserving biodiversity. Most popular images of biodiversity conservation involve efforts in places far removed from cities, whether conserving Florida panthers in the Everglades, returning California condors to the wild, or preserving tropical rain forests.

I challenge this perception in three ways. First, although the suggestion of biodiversity in cities may bring to mind only flocks of pigeons, cities are in fact host to substantial biodiversity. Second, many threats to species and biodiversity stem directly or indirectly from cities and urbanization. For example, habitat loss is increasingly a function of wasteful patterns of urban sprawl and its secondary impacts on water and air quality, and auto traffic. Third, cities are venues for highly consumptive lifestyles; urban populations import a tremendous amount of resources—energy, wood, water, and food—and generate substantial waste flows with enormous impacts on biodiversity, sometimes hundreds or thousands of miles away. What happens in cities can profoundly affect biodiversity elsewhere.

This chapter outlines key elements of a "cities and biodiversity" agenda and suggests possibilities for broader biodiversity preservation. It begins by identifying key roles that cities might play and ways in which cities and urban populations might work to protect biodiversity. It then examines two U.S. cities that demonstrate tools, techniques, and strategies for preserving biodiversity in urban settings. Finally, it discusses the lessons from these cases and more generally the obstacles, impediments, and challenges to implementing a meaningful urban biodiversity strategy.

Biodiversity as Urban Infrastructure and the Role of Urban Stewardship

Cities harbor more biodiversity than is commonly appreciated. London, for instance, is home to more than fifteen hundred species (Greater London Authority 2002). New York's Central Park alone is home to more than twenty-five hundred species and in 2002 was the site of discovery for an entirely new genus and species of centipede (American Museum of Natural History 2003).

City governments have a responsibility to serve as conscientious, careful stewards of urban biodiversity and to promote protection and restoration in the roles they typically play—landowner, regulator, builder, public service provider, and educator of the public. Much of the task at hand is to give biodiversity priority equal to other traditional functions and concerns of city government. A key step would be to increase the attention given to biodiversity in local and regional planning and decision making. More cities are preparing biodiversity plans, and this is an encouraging trend. The Greater London Authority, for instance, has recently completed a comprehensive strategy for the metropolitan area that places urban biodiversity on par with the city's other main strategic elements.

In some cases, urban habitats and urban ecological systems (or "green infrastructure") can replace engineered infrastructure. The City of Arcata, California, for example, owns a community forest that provides important recreational, stormwater, and water-quality services. Its restored marshlands serve as important habitat for migratory water birds as well as natural treatment of wastewater. In the New York City region, preservation of the last remaining pine barrens not only protects this special natural community but also protects a portion of the region's potable groundwater supply.

Good planning and stewardship of urban biodiversity require a deeper understanding of existing biodiversity and how urban projects and land use changes might affect it. One of the first tasks, therefore, is to inventory existing urban biodiversity. Many cities have used a volunteer process for this endeavor. For instance, in June 2003 in New York City's Central Park, volunteers organized a "BioBlitz" in which some 350 individuals, assigned to taxonomic groups, scoured the park over a twenty-four-hour period to inventory plant and animal life.

Knowledge of the biological heritage and patrimony of a city is essential to nurturing a new urban conservation ethic, and cities can play a special role in the process. For example, children and adults alike should be able to recognize a green darner dragonfly as easily as they recognize the logos for Target and Wal-Mart stores, and they should be as appreciative of seasonal bird migrations through the city as they are, say, of sporting events or the latest movie releases.

Cities can educate their inhabitants about urban biodiversity and nurture an ethic of stewardship in many ways, through school curricula, public education campaigns, and other public events.

Guiding Urbanization and Development to Protect Biodiversity

Urban sprawl is a significant threat to biodiversity and curtailing it should be a priority for cities. This can be done through land use measures that set aside key habitat areas and preserve essential ecological systems while steering new growth and development to sites where impacts to biodiversity are minimal. Growth management, smart growth, and brownfield redevelopment are all strategies that cities can pursue that help protect habitat and biodiversity while reducing energy consumption and pollution.

A litany of factors encourage sprawl (Orfield 1997) and while success has been mixed, cities like Portland, Oregon, and Vancouver, British Columbia, are positive models for promoting compact, land-efficient metropolitan areas. Vancouver, for instance, has achieved a compact urban form using strategies that steer development into town centers along the route of the SkyTrain, the region's elevated rail system. This urban compactness, along with regulatory controls on development in the surrounding "green zone," has done much to protect the region's biodiversity.

Although many contemporary threats to listed species result from suburban and exurban sprawl, the Endangered Species Act is silent on the issue of urban form and regional growth patterns. A major limitation of habitat conservation plans is that they rarely incorporate conservation strategies calling for growth containment or compact land use. Indeed, they more often accept prevailing land use patterns—typically, low-density sprawl (see Beatley 1994).

There are several important provisos in advocating compact cities as a biodiversity conservation strategy. First, care must be taken that existing biodiversity within cities is not further diminished. Steering new growth inward means new pressure on leftover or abandoned lands that may harbor significant biodiversity and provide other important environmental services. Analysis of the ecological value of sites proposed for redevelopment is an important step and careful distinctions must be made between sites within cities that can accommodate development and those that should be preserved or protected.

Second, habitat and ecologically important lands surrounding cities must also be protected. This can be accomplished using a variety of local land use conservation tools, such as transfer of development rights, conservation easements, and fee-simple acquisition; increasing numbers of cities and metropolitan areas have undertaken some form of open space or open lands acquisition program in recent years.

Ecological Retrofitting of Urban Landscapes to Support Biodiversity

Over time, as fewer opportunities exist to preserve undeveloped sites, the challenge in cities will be to restore and repair ecological systems that support biodiversity. This can happen in both large and small ways. At the city or metropolitan level, efforts can be made to restore rivers, wetlands, and forestlands. Cities like Tulsa, Oklahoma, have relocated homes and buildings from floodplains and made room for open space to foster natural river functions. Considerable restoration work has occurred along Washington, D.C.'s Anacostia River. Similarly, an ambitious plan has been unveiled to restore the Los Angeles River, presently little more than an engineered flood control structure. Many of these initiatives are nascent, but they illustrate a growing commitment by cities to improve the health and integrity of urban watersheds and ecological systems.

At the level of neighborhood and block, many restoration actions are possible. In cities like Seattle, streets are being reconceived as *green streets*—areas that serve as places for trees, gardens, and the collection and treatment of stormwater. Reducing the imperviousness of cities—the area of roads, parking lots, and rooftops—is a primary goal; many examples exist of cities working to "de-seal" their urban environments by replacing asphalt and cement with plantings.

New habitat can be created from unlikely gray spaces. Green rooftops, already common in Europe, are becoming increasingly popular in the United States. They serve many functions, such as retaining stormwater, sequestering carbon, improving the aesthetics of cities, and providing new habitat for birds and invertebrates. Chicago has retrofitted its city hall with a green rooftop containing some twenty thousand plants; monitoring by local volunteers is finding a remarkable and growing diversity of species living or visiting the roof—birds, spiders, grasshoppers, and other insects, and even native bees (Millett 2004).

We also find many examples of cities that encourage natural drainage through the use of "rain gardens" as an alternative to conventional stormwater management. In the Northwest, Seattle Public Utilities has undertaken an interesting initiative, the Street Edge Alternatives project. Several streets in older Seattle residential areas have been redesigned to conform to ecologically acceptable drainage patterns. One of the most dramatic examples is 2nd Avenue, where a conventional suburban-style street has been converted to a green, linear rain garden. On this street, some eleven hundred shrubs and more than one hundred evergreen trees have been planted. Monitoring shows that the volume of stormwater runoff coming from the site has been reduced by nearly 100 percent (Seattle Public Utilities n.d.). This approach also expands the avenue's pedestrian qualities and calms car traffic.

Habitat-Friendly Urban Design

A variety of building design and project features can be used to protect and restore biodiversity. Urban design guidelines and development codes can, for example, require on-site habitat restoration elements, or building placement and orientation to protect and incorporate habitat. The new Greenwich Millennium Village development, in London, for instance, incorporates an ecology park—a major restoration of wetland habitat along the Thames River —that restores ecological qualities found prior to major industrialization. It includes a series of walkways, blinds for wildlife viewing, and a nature center, all in close proximity to relatively dense urban housing.

New ecological developments that include few explicit wildlife or species conservation elements may do as much or more for biodiversity. A recent, and exemplary, case in point is the Beddington Zero-Energy Development, or BedZED. Built on recycled land within the existing urban fabric of London, this development relies on locally produced renewable energy (with south-facing flats that require little energy or heat to begin with) and a flow of materials coming from within a short radius on the project's location. Wood for the buildings (and also to burn in its combined heat and power plant) comes from nearby sustainably managed forests, including the Borough of Croydon, which may be the first city in the world actually certified as a sustainable forest.

Urban Management for Biodiversity

The management and operation of large cities has considerable implication for biodiversity conservation. City governments generate waste, air pollution, and water pollution; they purchase and consume resources that draw down biological wealth; they consume energy for their buildings and infrastructure; and they manage extensive portfolios of parks and recreation areas.

Cities can also be large landowners; their portfolios typically include neighborhood and regional parklands, ball fields, golf courses, recreational lands of various kinds, cultural and historic lands, and airports and utility corridors, as well as the land and spaces around many municipal buildings (such as city offices, schools, and municipal libraries). These properties offer direct opportunities to promote biodiversity. Some cities, for instance, have now severely restricted or curtailed the use of pesticides and herbicides on parks and recreation areas. In northern California, the City of Arcata has banned their use on all public parks and playing fields; Seattle has adopted a resolution in July 2002 to reduce the use of "persistent bio-accumulative toxins"; and San Francisco has adopted integrated pest management programs that have dramatically lowered the use of toxic chemicals.

Still other cities have taken steps to convert portions of traditional parklands to more natural, biodiversity-supportive areas. Chicago, for instance, has created more habitat for migratory waterfowl in its parks. Other urban park departments delineate no-mow zones and or mow less frequently to enhance habitat values as well as to reduce pollution, energy consumption, and other costs. Utilizing recycled or reclaimed water, eliminating or reducing fertilizer use, and planting only native trees and shrubs are other common urban land management methods.

Urban and suburban households can limit conventional turf-grass lawns and their substantial environmental impacts (Bormann et al. 1993). Public information campaigns and demonstration sites can promote natural landscaping and suggest ways to reduce the use of water, pesticides, and fertilizers. Some cities provide financial incentives to home owners and businesses to encourage planting native species, often specifically to reduce the high water consumption associated with conventional lawns. The OpenLands Project in Chicago works with corporations to use natural landscaping on their corporate campuses. Similarly, using funding from the U.S. Fish and Wildlife Service, Sears Roebuck significantly reduced maintenance costs by transforming the grounds of its Prairie Stone Facility to an ecologically valuable site.

Reducing the Biodiversity-Destructive Footprint of Cities

The recent footprint and metabolism study conducted for the city of London provides unusual insights into the impacts of cities on the biosphere. The flow of inputs and outputs needed to sustain London's population of 7.5 million is striking. Each year the city consumes 154,400 gigawatt hours of energy, producing 41 million metric tons of carbon dioxide. The city consumes nearly 28 million metric tons of materials for construction, including about 2.4 million tons of wood. London, moreover, requires almost 7 million metric tons of food each year, including 6,000 metric tons of coffee and 11,000 metric tons of tea.

Few footprint analyses or urban metabolism studies of this kind have been done for American cities, but we would expect their consumption habitats and demands for resources to be even greater. Chicagoans, for instance, consumed 22 billion kilowatt-hours of energy and emitted 24 million tons of greenhouse gases in 2000 (City of Chicago 2001). Projections suggest substantial increases in the future—some 27 billion kilowatt-hours will likely be consumed by 2010.

Few cities have addressed the problem of their large ecological footprints. I advocate an urban "supply line," where extra-local environmental impacts are actively avoided. To its credit, London is one of the few cities to attempt to

reduce or moderate the impacts of its resource demand on biodiversity—
regardless of where these impacts occur. In its voluminous Biodiversity Strategy,
London makes explicit connections between its large ecological footprint and
threats to biodiversity. "Few people realize that by pressing a switch in London,
one threatens the ecology of a bird of upland brooks, the dipper. Our high rate
of energy consumption also contributes to global warming, which is likely to
have major effects on biodiversity worldwide" (Greater London Authority
2002, 85). Policy 12 of the strategy states that "the mayor will encourage practices, and support existing effective initiatives, that reduce London's impact on
biodiversity elsewhere" (86). Moreover, it proposes the development of a "strategy for ethical trade, to discourage trading activity that damages biodiversity beyond London's border" (86).

Cities directly purchase a great many products and services and thus have
tremendous opportunity to make a positive difference. in this area. The Center
for the New American Dream in Tacoma Park, Maryland, operates a Procurement Strategies Program intended to encourage green procurement at state and
local levels. Its online database describes almost fifty local jurisdictions implementing some form of green procurement. Although one is struck by the estimated reduction in environmental impacts, in most cases there are also economic savings. For example, San Francisco's green building and energy
efficiency programs has saved an estimated $6 million (as of 1999) and reduced
greenhouse gasses by 80,000 tons (see www.sfenvironment.com/aboutus/inno-
vative/greenbldg/).

Many localities—particularly in Europe—are implementing green procurement policies. A number of cities, American and European, have adopted renewable energy goals and policies to ensure that at least a portion of a city's direct energy needs are supplied from renewable sources. Chicago's goal is for 20
percent of its power to come from renewable sources by 2006; Santa Monica,
California, purchases 100 percent of its power from renewable sources.

Cities can also exercise considerable influence over the purchasing practices
of other nongovernmental interests and actors. In European cities, it is common
for municipalities to require by contract that developers and builders of new
housing projects use lumber only from certified sustainably managed forests.
This approach has significant potential for growing cities and where redevelopment is occurring.

Urban school systems represent another opportunity to green the supply
lines. Some school districts have implemented schoolyard gardening programs
to produce some food on-site; others are seeking to purchase organic and locally
produced food for their cafeterias. Some European cities have mandated that
only organically grown foods are allowed in public facilities where food is
served, such as day-care facilities and community centers, and shade-grown
and/or fair-trade coffee is commonly served in municipal offices and cafeterias

(Beatley 2000). While such steps are partly symbolic, the potential to shape biodiversity-supportive product markets and to reduce the negative ecological effects of consumption are considerable.

City Building and Biodiversity

Sustainable or green building represents an increasingly promising way in which cities can protect biodiversity. Many cities have adopted some form of green-building policy, with tremendous momentum behind such initiatives. The U.S. Green Building Council's green building certification system, LEED (Leadership in Energy and Environmental Design), has done much to ease the way. Cities such as Seattle and Portland now require, for example, that all future public buildings and facilities achieve a minimum LEED certification standard.

Cities like San Diego are also setting high energy and environmental goals for their public buildings. The mayor has set a goal that the city be energy independent, and consequently, several city buildings are being retrofitted or designed to be super energy efficient and to incorporate solar energy. The city has also replaced 86 percent of it traffic lights with low-energy, light-emitting diodes, substantially reducing energy consumption and emission of greenhouse gases.

While not an exhaustive list, it does identify many areas in which cities can conserve biodiversity. The arsenal of tools and policies available is extensive, and urban conservation efforts hold promise for raising the quality of life for city dwellers, protecting public health, and promoting energy independence, in addition to protecting biodiversity.

Biodiversity Conservation in Two Urban Areas

We can demonstrate the potential for biodiversity conservation in urban areas as well as identify several key obstacles by examining the conservation and planning processes implemented by the cities of Seattle and Chicago. Their experiences demonstrate what can be achieved even in unlikely conservation settings. (See also Behan 2006 for similar efforts in Tucson, Arizona.)

Seattle and the Plight of Salmon

Salmon are an important symbol of the Pacific Northwest, but many species are at risk of extinction and seven have recently been listed under the Endangered Species Act. The listings astonished many residents, setting in motion a number of initiatives in the three-county Puget Sound region to address the problem. In the words of one report, "Never before has an urban economic hub been required to address an environmental issue of this magnitude" (King County 2002a).

Much of the impact in the Seattle/King County area stems from urbanization, including streams filled in and paved over, increased sedimentation, and degraded water quality as a result of urban runoff—in short, a fundamental alteration of the natural watersheds on which salmon depend. Increased water use and appropriation also significantly affect minimum in-stream flows. Driving this habitat alteration has been a substantial increase in human population; the region is predicted to grow from its present population of 3.5 million to 5.5 million by the year 2025 (as cited in Center for Maximum Potential Building Systems 2002).

A recent study found that even in restored urban streams, salmon quickly succumb to the toxic mix flowing in them. The study, conducted by the National Marine Fisheries Service, compared salmon mortality before spawning in a rural and an urban stream. Most of the coho salmon (*Oncorhynchus kisutch*) entering the urban stream died within hours, probably from a fatal combination of polycyclic aromatic hydrocarbons, insecticides, and other chemicals found in urban runoff. Although Seattle has spent millions on streams restoration efforts in recent years, a wider effort will be needed to address the sources of these pollutants (Stiffler and McClure 2003).

In response to the listings, a voluntary Tri-County Partnership was formed between King, Pierce, and Snohomish counties, as well as with other organizations and interests in the Puget Sound region. Short-term projects have included habitat acquisition, vegetation and riparian restoration work, and levee removal and redesign. Some were financed through a state salmon recovery fund. Much of the long-term recovery work will be guided by comprehensive watershed plans due for completion in 2005.

Local officials are also updating and strengthening local land use plans (required under Washington's Growth Management Act) to encourage future growth within existing cities and urbanized areas. An important component of this planning system is the requirement that local jurisdictions adopt critical areas ordinances. King County has proposed an ordinance that substantially strengthens the regulatory standards for wetlands and also fish and wildlife conservation areas. The ordinance would expand minimum streamside buffers and impose mitigation requirements for activities allowed to take place in critical areas. Though controversial among landowners and farmers, it holds considerable promise for reducing the ecological impacts of future development.

Seattle's salmon strategy is presented in *Seattle's Urban Blueprint for Habitat Protection and Restoration* (City of Seattle's Salmon Team 2001). The document summarizes threats to chinook salmon and its habitat and proposes regulatory and restoration actions. The city has since added inspectors and a fisheries biologist to its permit review staff to bolster enforcement of stormwater and erosion permitting and has strengthened its regulatory provisions, such as lowering thresholds for stormwater, issuing erosion control permits, and strengthening its controls on development in environmentally sensitive areas. Seattle also plans a major revision of its Shoreline Master Plan, required under the state's coastal management program, has made impressive strides in managing stormwater runoff, has actively promoted low impact development techniques and technologies, and has sponsored extensive public awareness and public education programs.

One of the most interesting debates centers on the feasibility of restoration of salmon streams in highly urbanized settings. One recent proposal is Initiative 80, the Seattle Creek Restoration Initiative. This proposal would mandate "daylighting" streams throughout the city. Advocates cite the example of Thornton Creek, a watercourse that runs under the Northgate Shopping Center, arguing that it should be day-lit, uncovered, and restored as a part of a major renovation and expansion of the shopping center.

Thornton Creek is one of forty Seattle creeks that have historically supported salmon, and one goal of Initiative 80 would be to restore salmon runs by requiring landowners and developers of large parcels to restore and uncover creeks; future development over buried creeks would be prohibited. The initiative would also impose new responsibilities on the City of Seattle, including compensating landowners for "takings," eliminating the use of pesticides and herbicides near waterways, and developing a long-term creek restoration plan. Seattle mayor Greg Nickels opposed the initiative, citing its expense and proposing his own more modest plan. Indeed, a study of the initiative by the City found that more than 15 percent of the land area would be affected by the initiative's requirements and that the cost to the City could range from half a million dollars to over $20 billion (City of Seattle 2002). The project has since been derailed by a recent legal decision citing that the proposed measure exceeded the scope of initiative power.

It remains to be seen whether watershed plans and other similar efforts in western Washington will be sufficient to save listed salmon; however, considerable efforts are underway throughout the state to redirect growth and curtail negative impacts of urbanization on sensitive aquatic habitats. Seattle's example has launched interesting and potentially far-reaching discussion about how far cities can and should go, including the promise of significant ecological "retooling," such as comprehensive stream daylighting and restoration, to support biodiversity.

Chicago: A City in a Regional Wilderness

Probably few residents of Chicago—a metropolitan region of almost eight million people—realize the extent of the biological diversity found there. For example, some seven million birds from 250 species pass through the city, which lies along the Midwest flyway, during winter and spring migration. But with more than twelve hundred local governmental jurisdictions in the area, government oversight of the landscapes harboring such biodiversity is fragmented and often ineffective.

Chicago Wilderness is a network of more than 160 conservation groups that envisions a "regional nature reserve" in the Chicago urban setting. The groups, formally known as the Chicago Wilderness Coalition, comprise public and private environmental and community organizations and agencies and receive substantial funding from the U.S. Fish and Wildlife Service and U.S. Forest Service. The coalition has led numerous efforts to document, restore, protect, and educate the public about the richness of the biodiversity in the Chicago region. It also seeks to preserve historical landscapes totaling more than 250,000 acres, including remnants of tall grass prairies, oak woodlands, swamps, dunes, and other habitats and species that existed before European settlement (Chicago Wilderness 2001).

Chicago Wilderness recently published a reference work entitled *Atlas of Biodiversity* (Chicago Wilderness 2001), which documents the richness of nature in the region, and also publishes educational videotapes, model school curricula, and a monthly magazine. The coalition has written a biodiversity recovery plan with comprehensive suggestions for regional land protection, management, and restoration and a "shared long term vision for the Greater Chicago region," which includes the idea of a "network of protected lands and waters" that will "preserve habitat for a complete spectrum of the living things that form the region's natural communities" (Chicago Wilderness 1999, 14). Key recommendations include improving management of existing protected areas, expanding the amount of land included in the protection network, protecting water quality in streams, lakes, and water bodies, expanding monitoring efforts, and increasing public awareness of biodiversity. The plan, which took two years to complete, also recommends that municipal governments (more than three hundred in the region) consider biodiversity protection and restoration in their planning decisions.

Chicago mayor Richard M. Daley has been a passionate advocate for urban greening, and under his leadership a number of important local actions have been undertaken, including extensive tree planting, urban habitat restoration, brownfield cleanup and redevelopment, and adoption of a new, tougher landscape ordinance. The most dramatic example of the mayor's commitment is the retrofitting of city hall with a green (living) rooftop. Other important initiatives have included a design competition for a model green home and initiatives to promote renovation and greening of the city's aging but unique stock of bungalow homes. In 1998, the City created a program called CitySpaces that creatively expands open and green spaces, for example, by removing pavement and "greening" schoolyards. A related program, NeighborSpaces, helps to convert vacant lots into community gardens and small neighborhood parks.

The City of Chicago also participates in the U.S. Fish and Wildlife Service's "Urban Conservation Treaty for Migratory Birds" (see http://birds.fws.gov/urbantreaty.html). The program promotes conservation treaties between the agency and participating communities, who receive money (to be matched locally) in exchange for developing and implementing bird conservation actions in their region.

Chicago mapped and classified migratory bird habitats and used them as a basis for a variety of projects, such as bird-friendly landscaping and habitat restoration work, and educating home owners about bird-friendly backyards. The City has also sponsored "Lights out Chicago" to turn off skyscraper lights that disorient and confuse birds during migratory periods. Its positive effects were documented in a recent study by the Chicago Field Museum, which determined that turning off lights and closing blinds resulted in an 83 percent reduction in bird deaths (Kousky 2004).

Chicago has also proposed a plan to clean up the 20-square-mile Calumet industrial area on the city's southeast side. Although the area is highly polluted from its industrial past, it harbors considerable biodiversity and has been described as having "the largest concentration of wetlands in the Midwest" (Abolt 2001). Plans include restoring 4,800 acres of the Calumet Open Space Reserve and setting aside additional open space. The City also hopes to build an environmental center and ultimately to set aside land for the production of renewable energy.

A nongovernmental, business-backed organization called Chicago Metropolis 2020 has more recently suggested an alternative growth plan for the Chicago region that calls for compact growth patterns, growth close to public transit lines, and protection and restoration of the region's "prairie reserves, woodlands, and wetlands" (Chicago Metropolis 2020 2003, p.23). The plan also identifies several "first steps," including coordination of land use and transportation policy, transportation improvements (e.g., bus rapid transit), expansion of housing options, and adjustments to the economic-incentive structure, such as a shared sales tax system.

Toward an Urban Biodiversity Conservation Agenda

As the previous examples suggest, cities can play several important roles in protecting and preserving biodiversity. First, because they directly impinge on habitat as they expand, and because sprawling development patterns wreak havoc on biodiversity, cities can protect remaining biodiversity by retaining undeveloped habitat, redirecting urban growth to brownfield and infill locations, and increasing building densities. Second, cities can protect remaining ecosystems by restoring and enhancing degraded habitat. And third, cities can work to reduce their ecological footprints, minimizing impacts on biodiversity locally *and* globally.

Implementing urban biodiversity conservation will require concerted effort to encourage collaborations and partnerships at a local level, leadership from larger jurisdictions, and governmental support from federal and state resource agencies. It will also require scientific data on both negative and positive consequences of urbanization, including restorative actions and projects to mitigate identified problems.

The greatest hope for protecting biodiversity in urban areas may come from enlisting the support of urban populations with their potentially large conservation constituencies. As the biodiversity recovery plan for the Chicago region notes (Chicago Wilderness 1999), a large urban population can represent an important political resource and serve as a potent force for protection and conservation. The preservation and restoration of biodiversity close to urban centers holds the promise that biodiversity will improve the quality of life for many residents and in turn may lend essential political and cultural support for the application of strong conservation measures elsewhere.

22 Conserving Biodiversity in Human-Dominated Landscapes

Dale D. Goble, J. Michael Scott, and Frank W. Davis

In 1973, UPC barcodes were used for the first time, OPEC doubled the price of crude oil, a cease fire was signed in Paris to end the war in Vietnam, *Roe v. Wade* was decided by the U.S. Supreme Court, the Watergate tapes were released, and an embattled President Richard M. Nixon signed the Endangered Species Act into law on December 23. At the time, the human population of the United States stood at roughly 212 million; since then, it has increased nearly 40 percent to almost 293 million (Doremus 2006) and the gross domestic product is now eight times greater (Census Bureau 2004).

Obviously, much has changed over the past thirty years, not the least of which is our understanding of how the natural world is put together. In 1973, many ecologists and wildlife biologists assumed ecosystems to be in quasi equilibrium in the absence of human or environmental perturbations. Perturb a system and it would eventually return to the same steady state. The Endangered Species Act reflects this model: remove the threat to species, its population will return to normal, and the act will no longer be necessary. The act was a statute predicated upon planned obsolescence. But the more ecologists have learned about complex ecosystem and population dynamics, the less confident we are in making such predictions based on the historical state of the system (Wallington et al. 2005). We have also come to realize the importance of landscape-scale patterns and processes, greatly extending the relevant space and time scales for effective conservation. Contrary to public expectations and political demands, species protection and recovery is neither straightforward nor inexpensive. But as Jane Lubchenko commented in her presidential address to the annual meeting of the American Association for the Advancement of Science in 1997, "All too many of our current environmental policies and much of the street lore about the environment are based on the science of the 1950s, 1960s, and 1970s, not the science of the 1990s" (Lubchenko 1998, 495).

The two volumes of *The Endangered Species Act at Thirty* look backward to evaluate the effectiveness of the act over its first three decades (Wilcove and

McMillan 2006; Scott et al. 2006, chap. 2; Goble, this volume; Svancara, this volume; Callicott, this volume; Norton, this volume) and also forward to suggest how it can be used as a cornerstone for conserving biological diversity in increasingly human-dominated landscapes (Davis et al. 2006; Bean 2006). The chapters in part 2 of this volume, for example, appraise the science of the 1990s and 2000s at both the large scale (Lomolino, this volume; Naeem et al., this volume; Naeem and Jouseau, this volume) and the small (Waples, this volume; Haig and Allendorf, this volume; Reed et al., this volume) and examine the current debate over how science should inform the policy decisions that the act necessarily raises (Doremus, this volume; Ruckelshaus and Darm, this volume). As the authors note, conserving biodiversity involves more than science. The landscapes are, after all, human dominated—and as such must be human managed. The chapters in part 3 evaluate the issues that human management raise, its costs and benefits (Shogren, this volume; Sunding, this volume), emerging mechanisms that may offer tools to reduce the conflict by shifting increasingly to incentives (Scott et al., this volume; Heal, this volume; Fox et al., this volume), and an assessment of the potential to conserve biodiversity across a variety of sea- and landscapes (Armsworth, this volume; Brosi et al., this volume; Beatley, this volume).

The numbers seem stacked against success: the listing process is stalled despite a backlog four to five times larger than the number of currently listed species, recovery activities are funded at less than 20 percent of identified costs, research management partnerships fall far short of what is needed, and implementation of the act is bogged down in the courts. To overcome these and other difficulties in the next thirty years, we must be more creative in choosing our mechanisms and adapting them to conserve the ecosystems that sustain us. Essential to this effort will be an effective science-policy partnership (Ruckelshaus and Darm, this volume; Doremus, this volume).

Conserving the nation's biological heritage will necessarily require revisioning the Endangered Species Act. Although legally enforceable mandates remain crucial to the conservation of biodiversity, the act must also become a tool for fostering the necessary conservation management. We must find a way to move from permitting to enabling, from top-down to bottom-up conservation planning and implementation, from preventing extinction to promoting recovery, from triage to keeping common species common. The act must become a tool that both prods and permits us to move away from the species-specific toward an ecosystem understanding of our place in this world. Just as wildlife biology has evolved into the interdisciplinary field of conservation biology, the Endangered Species Act must become a mechanism that encourages integration, not only across political jurisdictions—from county to state, tribal, and federal—but also across the public and private domains. Private landowners are also habitat owners and their role will become increasingly important over the next thirty years; there are also thousands of local organizations focused on meeting local conservation needs.

To achieve the purpose of the Endangered Species Act and "provide a means whereby the ecosystems upon which endangered species and threatened species depend may be conserved" (ESA sec. 2(b)) will require a broader vision than we have so far managed. Some of the steps are clear:

- We must confront the large backlog of unlisted but critically imperiled species. The increasing loss of habitat and the growing number of invasive species suggest that the number of these species will continue to grow.
- We must, therefore, intervene before a species is endangered if we are to have any hope of getting ahead of the at-risk curve.
- We need a system of protected natural areas representative of the ecological and geophysical diversity of the country—a vision of the American conservation landscape dating back to 1917 and perhaps earlier (Ecological Society of America 1926) but still unfulfilled (Scott et al. 2001). Statewide wildlife habitat conservation plans embody a federal, state, and local planning partnership and should contain much of the information to fill the gaps in America's conservation landscape.
- We must reconcile human actions with the biological needs of wildlife in our urban, suburban, and exurban landscapes because a reserve network is insufficient in itself. Rosenzweig (2006), Heal, Beatley, and Brosi (this volume) have identified some ways to reconcile human and wildlife needs on working landscapes. Adding to our difficulties is global climate change, which will shift species ranges in ways we do not fully understand (Root et al. 2003).
- We must be lighter on our feet so that we can respond to the changes.

Ultimately, we need a new land ethic—an objective that will require political leadership and will.

Contributors

H. RESIT AKÇAKAYA is Senior Scientist at Applied Biomathematics, where he works on models for ecological risk analysis, population viability analysis, integrating metapopulation and landscape dynamics, and incorporating uncertainty into criteria for threatened species. He has authored numerous publications, including three books and six software programs. He chairs the IUCN Red List Standards and Petitions Subcommittee and serves on the editorial boards of *Conservation Biology* and *Population Ecology*.

MICHAEL F. ALLEN is Director for the Center for Conservation Biology, Chair of the Department of Plant Pathology, and Professor in the Departments of Plant Pathology and Biology at the University of California, Riverside. He is a Fellow of the American Association for the Advancement of Science and the recipient of numerous distinguished awards. His research focuses on developing ecological monitoring systems.

FRED W. ALLENDORF is Regents Professor in the Division of Biological Sciences, University of Montana, and a Professorial Research Fellow at Victoria University of Wellington, New Zealand. He has authored numerous papers in the areas of evolution, population genetics, and conservation biology. He is a fellow of the American Association for the Advancement of Science and served as president of the American Genetic Association in 1997.

PAUL R. ARMSWORTH recently joined the University of Sheffield as Lecturer in Biodiversity and Conservation. Previously, he was a postdoctoral fellow in the Center for Conservation Biology at Stanford University. A theoretical ecologist, he holds Ph.D.s in mathematics and biology. His recent research examines the consequences of dispersal and recruitment dynamics in shaping reef fish populations and the economic efficiency of management alternatives for highly migratory stocks.

TIMOTHY BEATLEY is Teresa Heinz Professor of Sustainable Communities in the Department of Urban and Environmental Planning, School of Architecture, at the University of Virginia. His recent research has focused on sustainable communities and strategies to allow cities, towns, and regions to reduce their ecological footprints. His most recent work is *Native to Nowhere: Sustaining Home and Community in a Global Age.*

STEVEN R. BEISSINGER holds the A. Starker Leopold Chair in Wildlife Biology at the University of California, Berkeley, in the Department of Environmental Science, Policy, and Management. He is a fellow of the American Ornithologists Union and a member of the board of directors of the National Audubon Society. His research addresses issues of conservation, and behavioral and population biology of threatened and exploited species.

DARREN BENDER is Assistant Professor at the University of Calgary. He teaches in the Graduate Program of Geographic Information Science, Department of Geography, and holds an adjunct appointment in the Department of Biological Sciences. His current research explores the interface between biology and geography, particularly in the fields of landscape ecology, conservation biology, and ecological applications of geographic information science.

ERIC P. BJORKSTEDT is a research scientist with NOAA Fisheries (previously National Marine Fisheries Service) and an adjunct professor at Humboldt State University. His research focuses on biological and physical processes that influence recruitment and spatial structure of fish and invertebrate populations in coastal marine systems, and on the population dynamics and structure of anadromous salmonids. His recent work contributes to the scientific foundation of recovery planning for Pacific salmon and steelhead.

DONNA BREWER manages the conservation policy curricula for the U.S. Fish and Wildlife Service at its National Conservation Training Center in Shepherdstown, West Virginia. She has been involved with environmental conservation and endangered species issues for over thirty years, holding related positions with several state and federal government agencies.

BERRY J. BROSI is a doctoral student in conservation biology at Stanford University where he studies bee communities and pollination services in human-dominated landscapes in southern Costa Rica. He holds a master of environmental science degree from Yale University. He has conducted environmentally related fieldwork in New England, Mexico, Costa Rica, Brazil, Hawaii, and Micronesia.

MARK BURGMAN is Professor in the School of Botany at the University of Melbourne, Australia, where he teaches and conducts research in ecological modeling, conservation biology, and risk assessment. He holds a Ph.D. in ecology from the State University of New York at Stony Brook. He is author or editor of numerous articles and books, most recently, *Risks and Decisions for Conservation and Environmental Management.*

J. BAIRD CALLICOTT is Professor of philosophy and religion studies in the Institute of Applied Sciences at the University of North Texas. Best known as a contemporary exponent of Aldo Leopold's land ethic, he is author or editor of numerous journal articles and books on issues concerning environmental philosophy and ethics. He has served as president of the International Society for Environmental Ethics and as Bioethicist-in-Residence at Yale University.

KAI M. A. CHAN is Assistant Professor at the University of British Columbia and has been nominated for a Canada Research Chair. He holds a Ph.D. and a certificate in public policy from Princeton University, where he researched species diversification and environmental ethics. He was a senior fellow of scienceinpolicy.org and is a fellow of the Environmental Leadership Program.

GRETCHEN C. DAILY is Professor of Biological Sciences and Senior Fellow at the Center for Environmental Science and Policy at Stanford University. An ecologist by training, her current research investigates the future course of biodiversity loss, the resulting changes in the delivery of ecosystem services, and opportunities for biodiversity conservation. Her most recent work, coauthored with journalist Katherine Ellison, is *The New Economy of Nature: The Quest to Make Conservation Profitable.*

DONNA DARM is Assistant Regional Administrator for Protected Resources for NOAA Fisheries (formerly National Marine Fisheries Service) and is responsible for implementation of section 4 of the Endangered Species Act, and the Marine Mammal Protection Act, for the agency's Northwest Region. A graduate of the University of Washington Law School, she worked for five years at the State Department in Washington, D.C., where she was involved in international fisheries negotiations.

ADAM DAVIS is President of Solano Partners Inc., a consulting firm specializing in environmental economics and conservation finance. He also serves as editor-in-chief of *Ecosystem Marketplace*, as a collaborating scientist at the Stanford University Center for Conservation Biology, and as a member of the steering committee for the Aldo Leopold Leadership Program. He was the recipient of the Ecological Society of America's Corporate Award for 2002.

FRANK W. DAVIS is Professor in the Donald Bren School of Environmental Science and Management at the University of California, Santa Barbara, where he teaches and conducts research in landscape ecology and conservation planning. He holds a Ph.D. in geography and environmental engineering from the Johns Hopkins University. He is a fellow in the Aldo Leopold Leadership Program and member of the board of trustees of the Nature Conservancy of California.

HOLLY DOREMUS is Professor of Law and Chancellor's Fellow at the University of California, Davis. She is a Member Scholar of the Center for Progressive Regulation. She earned a Ph.D. in plant physiology from Cornell University and J.D. from the University of California, Berkeley, Boalt Hall. She has written extensively about endangered species and biodiversity protection as well as the intersection of science and natural resources policy.

LINDA FERNANDEZ is Associate Professor of environmental and resource economics in the Department of Environmental Sciences at the University of California, Riverside. Her research interests and publications include economic evaluation of policy options to abate marine invasive species, trade liberalization and transboundary air and water pollution, cross-media environmental regulations, and economics of policies to address urban sprawl and protection of habitat such as wetlands and open space.

JESSICA FOX is a senior scientist at EPRI Solutions Inc. in Palo Alto, Calif. She holds a master's degree in conservation biology from Stanford University and is an associate ecologist certified by the Ecological Society of America. She has conducted benchmark research in conservation banking and frequently presents her academic and practical experience with market mechanisms for ecosystem protection.

DALE D. GOBLE is Margaret Wilson Schimke Distinguished Professor of Law at the University of Idaho, where his teaching and research focus on the intersection of natural resource law and policy, constitutional law, and history. He has authored numerous articles and essays and is coauthor with Eric Freyfogle of *Wildlife Law: Cases and Materials* and *Federal Wildlife Statutes: Texts and Contexts.*

SUSAN M. HAIG is a wildlife ecologist at the U.S. Geological Survey Forest and Rangeland Ecosystem Science Center in Corvallis, Oregon; Professor of Wildlife Ecology at Oregon State University; and a research associate of the Smithsonian Institution. She has served as a recovery team leader and international coordinator for Piping Plover Recovery. Her current research addresses population structure and factors that affect endangered species viability, particularly in Pacific island species.

GEOFFREY HEAL is Paul Garrett Professor of Public Policy and Corporate Responsibility and Professor of Economics and Finance in the Graduate School of Business at Columbia University and Professor of International and Public Affairs in the School of International Affairs at Columbia University. He serves as director of the Union of Concerned Scientists and director of the Beijer Institute of the Royal Swedish Academy of Sciences. His research explores the interaction between society and its natural resource base and the management of risks by financial markets.

CLAIRE JOUSEAU is a doctoral student in Columbia University's Department of Ecology, Evolution and Environmental Biology. Her research explores the interface of community and ecosystem ecology and focuses on understanding the connections between community structure and the stability of ecosystem-level processes within the community. Her research involves midwestern tall-grass prairies and northeastern hardwood forest moss-microarthropod communities.

CARRIE V. KAPPEL is a graduate student in ecology at Stanford University's Hopkins Marine Station. Her research focuses on rare marine species, including spatial patterns in coral species diversity and rarity and its implications for reserve network design to the threats, as well as management of vulnerable marine species and habitats worldwide. She has also studied Caribbean coral reefs, California kelp forests, and rocky intertidal habitats.

MARK V. LOMOLINO is Professor in the Department of Environmental and Forest Biology at the College of Environmental Science and Forestry in Syracuse, New York. His research and teaching focus on biogeography and conservation of biological diversity. He is a cofounder and past president of the International Biogeography Society. He received the American Society of Mammalogists Award, and serves on editorial advisory boards for *Biological Conservation* and *Global Ecology and Biogeography.*

FIORENZA MICHELI is Assistant Professor of Biological Sciences at Stanford University, Hopkins Marine Station. She studies species interactions and species-habitat relationships in marine communities and the applications of community ecology to the conservation of marine ecosystems. She is a fellow of the Aldo Leopold Leadership Program, a member of the Monterey Bay National Marine Sanctuary research activity panel, and serves on the editorial board of *Conservation Biology*.

CRAIG MORITZ is Professor of integrative biology at the University of California, Berkeley. His research centers on the use of molecular approaches to study ecology and evolution, in particular the use of molecular markers to infer current and historical population processes at various spatial and temporal scales; the effects of historical changes in habitat on current distributions and diversity of faunas, with particular reference to rainforest biotas; and improving the use of molecular information in conservation biology and developing strategies that recognize evolutionary processes.

SHAHID NAEEM is Professor of Ecology at Columbia University and holds a Ph.D. from the University of California, Berkeley. He is recipient of the Buell and Mercer awards from the Ecological Society of America and is a fellow of the American Association for the Advancement of Science and the Aldo Leopold Leadership Program. He has published extensively on the environmental consequences of biodiversity loss.

ANAMARIA NINO-MURCIA is a senior associate on the extractives team at Business for Social Responsibility. She holds a master of science degree in earth systems from Stanford University, where she conducted undergraduate research to evaluate social forestry projects in rural India as investments in natural capital; her honor's thesis project involved a multidisciplinary analysis of species conservation banking in the United States.

BRYAN NORTON is Professor in the School of Public Policy, Georgia Institute of Technology. He has served on the Environmental Economics Advisory Committee of the U.S. Environmental Protection Agency Science Advisory Board, on the governing board of the Society for Conservation Biology, and on the board of directors of Defenders of Wildlife. He has authored numerous articles in several disciplines. His current research focuses on issues of sustainability theory.

J. MICHAEL REED is Associate Professor in the Department of Biology at Tufts University where he teaches conservation biology and conducts research on extinction risk and endangered species conservation, focusing in particular on fragmented landscapes, primarily of forest and wetland habitats. Currently, he is studying marsh birds and waterbirds in Hawaii and Massachusetts, and also vernal-pool breeding amphibians.

MARY RUCKELSHAUS is a research biologist with NOAA Fisheries (formerly National Marine Fisheries Service) in Seattle. She leads the salmon risk and recovery science group at the Northwest Fisheries Science Center and chairs the Puget Sound Technical Recovery Team. She serves as a trustee on the Nature Conservancy's Washington board, is a member of the conservancy's national science board, and is chair of the Science Advisory Board of the National Center for Ecological Analysis and Synthesis for the National Science Foundation.

J. MICHAEL SCOTT is Professor of Wildlife Biology at the University of Idaho, a research biologist with the U.S. Geological Survey, and Leader of the Idaho Cooperative Fish and Wildlife Research Unit. He has served as Director of the Condor Research Center for two years, and since 1986 has conducted research on endangered species and reserve identification, selection, and design.

THOMAS A. SCOTT is a natural resources specialist with University of California, Berkeley, and Associate Director for the Center for Conservation Biology at the University of California, Riverside. He holds a Ph.D. in wildland resource science from UC Berkeley; he was a Fulbright Research Fellow and the recipient of the Education Leadership award from the American Planning Association. His current research explores wildlife response to human activities along the wildland-urban interface.

JASON F. SHOGREN is the Stroock Distinguished Professor of Natural Resource Conservation and Management at the University of Wyoming. His research focuses on the behavioral underpinnings of private choice and public policy, especially for environmental and natural resources. In 1997, he served as the senior economist for environmental and natural resource policy on the Council of Economic Advisers in the White House.

DAVID L. SUNDING is professor of environmental and resource economics at the University of California, Berkeley. Previously, he served as a senior economist at President Clinton's Council of Economic Advisers. He serves on the Science Advisory Board of the National Center for Housing and the Environment and on a Science Advisory Board panel for the U.S. Environmental Protection Agency. His research focuses on environmental and natural resource economics, land use regulation, and water resources.

LEONA K. SVANCARA received her master of science degree in wildlife resources from University of Idaho and is currently working on a Ph.D. in natural resources. She is a spatial ecologist and data manager for the Inventory and Monitoring Program of the Upper Columbia Basin Network for the National Park Service.

BARTON H. THOMPSON JR. is Director of the Stanford Institute for the Environment and the Robert E. Paradise Professor of Natural Resources Law at Stanford Law School. He is author of *Environmental Law and Policy: Concepts and Insights* and of numerous articles on biodiversity policy and other environmental issues. Following law school, he clerked for Chief Justice William H. Rehnquist of the United States Supreme Court.

ROBIN S. WAPLES is a senior scientist with the Northwest Fisheries Science Center in Seattle. His research background is in population genetics and conservation biology. For over a decade beginning in 1990, he led efforts within the National Marine Fisheries Service to identify conservation units of Pacific salmon and steelhead, assess their status under the federal Endangered Species Act, and develop scientifically based recovery plans.

Notes

Complete references for the works cited in short form are given in the References section.

Preface

1. Virginia Albrecht (board member, National Center for Housing and the Environment), Maeveen Behan (assistant to county administrator, Pima County, Ariz.), Troy Bredenkamp (director, Congressional Relations, American Farm Bureau Federation), Jeff Eisenberg (director, Environmental Issues, National Cattlemen's Beef Association), John Kostyack (senior counsel and manager of wildlife conservation programs, National Wildlife Federation), James Kraft (senior vice president, general counsel, and secretary, Plum Creek Timber Company), Michael Mittelholzer (director, Air, Waste, and Wildlife Regulatory Affairs, National Association of Homebuilders), Dennis Murphy (University of Nevada-Reno, Biology Department), Kieran F. Suckling (president, Center for Biological Diversity), Mark L. Shaffer (senior vice president for programs, Defenders of Wildlife), and Hilary Swain (director, Archbold Biological Station).
2. Paul R. Armsworth (Stanford University, Department of Biological Sciences), Timothy Beatley (University of Virginia, Department of Urban and Environmental Planning), J. Baird Callicott (University of North Texas, Department of Philosophy and Religion Studies), Chris Costello (University of California, Santa Barbara, Donald Bren School of Environmental Science and Management), Ray Dacey (University of Idaho, Department of Business), Gretchen C. Daily (Stanford University, Department of Biological Sciences), Andy Dobson (Princeton University, Department of Ecology and Evolutionary Biology), Holly Doremus (University of California, Davis, School of Law), Peter Kareiva (The Nature Conservancy), Mark V. Lomolino (State University of New York, College of Environmental Science and Forestry), Craig Moritz (University of California, Berkeley, Department of Integrative Biology), Shahid Naeem (Columbia University), Bryan Norton (Georgia Institute of Technology, School of Public Policy), Stuart Pimm (Duke University, Nicholas School of the Environment and Earth Science), Steve Polasky (University

of Minnesota, Department of Applied Economics), William H. Rodgers Jr. (University of Washington School of Law), Michael L. Rosenzweig (University of Arizona, Department of Biological Sciences), Mary Ruckelshaus (National Marine Fisheries Service, Northwest Fisheries Science Center), Jason F. Shogren (University of Wyoming, Department of Economics and Finance), A. Dan Tarlock (Illinois Institute of Technology, Chicago-Kent College of Law), Barton H. Thompson Jr. (Stanford University School of Law), Robin S. Waples (National Marine Fisheries Service, Northwest Fisheries Science Center), and Steven L. Yaffee (University of Michigan, School of Natural Resources and Environment).

Chapter 2. Evolution of At-Risk Species Protection

1. The category is sufficiently flexible to be used to delay listing any species. A 1992 General Accounting Office report noted that 105 species had been in the warranted-but-precluded category for more than two years, and fifty-six of those for more than eight years (GAO 1992; Greenwald et al. 2006).

Chapter 9. Science and Controversy

1. See for example, *Predatory Mammals and Endangered Species: Hearings Before the Subcommittee on Fisheries and Wildlife Conservation of the House Committee on Merchant Marine and Fisheries* (U.S. Congress 1972).
2. The law does provide an exception for insect species that present an overwhelming threat to humans (ESA sec. 3 (6)).
3. Nonfederal actors are generally prohibited from "taking" listed animal species but can get a permit allowing incidental take that will not appreciably diminish the likelihood of survival and recovery of the species (ESA sec. 10(a)(2)(B)). Federal actors must ensure that their actions are not likely to jeopardize the continued existence of the species, which means they must not be expected to appreciably reduce the likelihood of survival and recovery[1] (ESA sec. 7 (a)(2); Code of Federal Regulations 50:402.02). Exemptions can be granted by the Endangered Species Committee, popularly known as the "God Squad" (ESA secs. 7 (e)–(o)), but the committee has only convened three times in thirty years.
4. For example, prior to the 2004 presidential election, the Union of Concerned Scientists released a statement signed by dozens of Nobel laureates and thousands of other scientists criticizing the Bush administration's use of science in policy decisions. The statement and list of signatories are available at http://www.ucsusa.org/global_environment/rsi/page.cfm?pageID=1320 (accessed May 6, 2005).

Chapter 15. Economic Impacts

1. Other approaches to the question of regulation and the price of new housing are to measure the relationship between zoning and density and to directly estimate the impact of zoning on prices. The problem with the latter approach is that zoning is very difficult to measure in a sensible way.

References

Abbitt, R. J. F., J. M. Scott, and D. S. Wilcove. 2000. The geography of vulnerability: Incorporating species geography and human development patterns into conservation planning. *Biological Conservation* 96:169–75.

Abolt, W. F. 2001. Statement to Subcommittee on Water Resources and Environment. U.S. House of Representatives. March 15. http://www.house.gov/transportation/water/03-15-01/abolt.html.

Act of June 4, 1897 (Organic Administrative Act of 1897). 30 *U.S. Statutes at Large* 34 (codified at 16 U.S.C. sec. 475).

Act of May 25, 1900 (Lacy Act). Chapter 553, 31 *U.S. Statutes at Large* 187 (codified as amended at 16 U.S.C. secs. 701, 3371–78).

Act of March 3, 1913 (Weeks-McLean Migratory Bird Act). Chapter 145, 37 *U.S. Statutes at Large* 828 (codified at 16 U.S.C. secs. 847–48).

Act of August 25, 1916 (National Park Service Organic Act and General Authorities Act). 39 *U.S. Statutes at Large* 545 (codified as amended at 16 U.S.C. secs. 1–20g).

Act of July 3, 1918 (Migratory Bird Treaty Act). Chapter 128, 40 *U.S. Statutes at Large* 755 (codified as amended at 16 U.S.C. secs. 703–4).

Act of February 18, 1929 (Migratory Bird Conservation Act). Chapter 257, 45 U.S. *Statutes at Large* 1222 (codified as amended at 16 U.S.C. secs. 715–715k).

Act of March 16, 1934 (Migratory Bird Hunting Stamp Act of 1934). Chapter 71, 48 *U.S. Statutes at Large* 452 (codified as amended at 16 U.S.C. secs. 718–718j).

Act of September 2, 1937 (Federal Aid in Wildlife Restoration Act). Chapter 899, 50 *U.S. Statutes at Large* 917 (codified as amended at 16 U.S.C. secs. 669–669i).

Act of June 8, 1940 (Bald Eagle Protection Act). Chapter 278, 54 *U.S. Statutes at Large* 250 (codified as amended at 16 U.S.C. secs. 668–668d).

Act of June 11, 1946 (Administrative Procedure Act). Chapter 324, 60 *U.S. Statutes at Large* 237 (codified as amended at 5 U.S.C. secs. 551–59).

Act of June 12, 1960 (Multiple-Use Sustained-Yield Act). 74 *U.S. Statutes at Large* 215 (codified at 16 U.S.C. secs. 528–31).

Act of May 28, 1963 (Land and Water Conservation Fund Act). 77 *U.S. Statutes at Large* 49 (codified as amended at 16 U.S.C. secs. 460L-11).

Act of September 3, 1964 (Wilderness Act). Public Law 88-577, 78 *U.S. Statutes at Large* 890 (codified as amended at 16 U.S.C. secs. 1131–36).

Act of October 15, 1966a (Endangered Species Preservation Act). Public Law 89-669, 80 *U.S. Statutes at Large* 926 (repealed 1973).

Act of October 15, 1966b (Refuge Administration Act). Public Law 89-669, 80 *U.S. Statutes at Large* 927 (codified as amended at 16 U.S.C. secs. 668dd–668ee).

Act of December 5, 1969 (Endangered Species Conservation Act). Public Law 91-135, 83 *U.S. Statutes at Large* 275 (repealed 1973).

Act of January 1, 1970 (National Environmental Policy Act). 83 *U.S. Statutes at Large* 852 (codified as amended at 42 U.S.C. secs. 4331–35).

Act of December 15, 1971 (Wild Free-Roaming Horses and Burros Act). Public Law 86-234, 73 *U.S. Statutes at Large* 470 (codified as amended at 16 U.S.C. secs. 1331–40).

Act of October 21, 1972 (Marine Mammal Protection Act). Public Law 92-522, 86 *U.S. Statutes at Large* 1027 (codified as amended at 16 U.S.C. secs. 1361–407).

Act of December 28, 1973 (Endangered Species Act). Public Law 93-205, 87 *U.S. Statutes at Large* 884. (codified as amended at 16 U.S.C. secs. 1531–43).

Act of July 12, 1976 (Endangered Species Act Amendments of 1976). Public Law 94-359, 90 *U.S. Statutes at Large* 911.

Act of April 13, 1976 (Magnuson Fisheries Conservation and Management Act). Public Law 94-265, 90 *U.S. Statutes at Large* 331 (codified as amended at 16 U.S.C. sections 1801–83).

Act of October 21, 1976 (Federal Land Policy and Management Act). 90 *U.S. Statutes at Large* 2744 (codified as amended at 43 U.S.C. secs. 1701–84).

Act of October 22, 1976 (National Forest Management Act). 90 *U.S. Statutes at Large* 2949 (codified as amended at 16 U.S.C. secs. 1600–16).

Act of October 25, 1978 (Public Rangelands Improvement Act). 92 *U.S. Statutes at Large* 1803 (codified at 43 U.S.C. secs. 1901–8).

Act of November 10, 1978 (Endangered Species Act Amendments). Public Law 95-632, 92 *U.S. Statutes at Large* 3751.

Act of September 25, 1979 (Energy and Water Development Appropriations Act). Public Law 96-69, 93 *U.S. Statutes at Large* 437 (codified at 40 U.S.C. secs. 174b-1).

Act of December 28, 1979 (Endangered Species Act Amendments). Public Law 96-159, 93 *U.S. Statutes at Large* 1225.

Act of November 16, 1981 (Lacey Act Amendments). Public Law 97-79, 95 *U.S. Statutes at Large* 1073.

Act of October 13, 1982 (Endangered Species Act Amendments). Public Law 97-304, 96 *U.S. Statutes at Large* 1411.

Act of October 7, 1988 (Endangered Species Act Amendments). Public Law 100-478, 102 *U.S. Statutes at Large* 2306.

Act of October 9, 1997 (National Wildlife Refuge System Improvement Act). 111 *U.S. Statutes at Large* 1254 (codified at 16 U.S.C. secs. 668dd–668ee).

Act of December 21, 2000 (Data Quality Act). Public Law 106-554, 114 *U.S. Statutes at Large* 2763.

Akçakaya, H. R. 2000. Population viability analyses with demographically and spatially structured models. *Ecological Bulletin* 48:23–38.

———. 2001. Linking population-level risk assessment with landscape and habitat models. *Science of the Total Environment* 274:283–91.

Akçakaya, H. R., and J. L. Atwood. 1997. A habitat-based metapopulation model of the California gnatcatcher. Modelo de metapoblación basado en el hábitat de *Polioptila c. californica. Conservation Biology* 11:422–34.

Akçakaya, H. R., M. A. Burgman, and L. R. Ginzburg. 1999. *Applied population ecology: Principles and computer exercises using Ramas EcoLab.* 2d ed. Sunderland, Mass.: Sinauer Associates.

Akçakaya, H. R., S. Ferson, M. A. Burgman, D. A. Keith, G. M. Mace, and C. R. Todd. 2000. Making consistent IUCN classifications under uncertainty. *Conservation Biology* 14:1001–13.

Akçakaya, H. R., and P. Sjögren-Gulve. 2000. Population viability analysis in conservation planning: An overview. *Ecological Bulletins* 48:9–21.

Aldred, J. 1994. Existence value, welfare, and altruism. *Environmental Values* 3:381–402.

Allen, R. P. 1952. *The whooping crane.* New York: National Audubon Society.

Allendorf, F. W., D. Bayles, D. L. Bottom, K. P. Currens, C. A. Frissel, D. Hankin, J. A. Lichatowich, W. Nehlsen, P. C. Trotter, and T. H. Williams. 1997. Prioritizing Pacific salmon stocks for conservation. *Conservation Biology* 11:140–52.

Allendorf, F. W., and R. F. Leary. 1988. Conservation and distribution of genetic variation in a polytypic species, the cutthroat trout. *Conservation Biology* 2:170–84.

Allendorf, F. W., R. F. Leary, N. P. Hitt, K. L. Knudsen, L. L. Lundquist, and P. Spruell. 2004. Intercrosses and the U.S. Endangered Species Act: Should hybridized populations be included as westslope cutthroat trout? *Conservation Biology* 18:1203–13.

Allendorf, F. W., R. F. Leary, P. Spruell, and J. K. Wenburg. 2001. The problems with hybrids: Setting conservation guidelines. *Trends in Ecology and Evolution* 16:613–22.

Allendorf, F. W., and G. H. Thorgaard. 1984. Polyploidy and the evolution of salmonid fishes. Pp. 1–53 in *The evolutionary genetics of fishes*, ed. B. J. Turner. New York: Plenum Press.

Alley, R. B., J. Marotzke, W. D. Nordhaus, J. T. Overpeck, D. M. Peteet, R. A. Pielke Jr., R. T. Pierrehumbert, et al. 2003. Abrupt climate change. *Science* 299:2005–10.

Alsea Valley Alliance v. Evans. 2001. 161 F. Supp. 2d 1154. U.S. District Court for the District of Oregon.

American Museum of Natural History. 2003. Central Park survey finds new centipede. *Center for Biodiversity and Conservation News*, January 29. New York.

Arizona Cattle Growers Association v. U.S. Fish and Wildlife. 2001. 273 F. 3d 1229. U.S. Court of Appeals for the 9th Judicial Circuit.

Armsworth, P. R., C. V. Kappel, F. Micheli, and E. P. Bjorkstedt. 2006. Marine species. Pp. 36–44 in *The Endangered Species Act at thirty: Renewing the conservation promise*, ed. D. D. Goble, J. M. Scott, and F. W. Davis. Washington, D.C.: Island Press.

Armsworth, P. R., and J. E. Roughgarden. 2003. The economic value of ecological stability. *Proceedings of the National Academy of Sciences of the United States of America* 100:7147–51.

Arrow, K. J., and H. Raynaud. 1986. *Social choice and multicriterion decision-making.* Cambridge, Mass.: MIT Press.

Aspinwall, N. 1974. Genetic analysis of North American populations of the pink salmon, (*Oncorhynchus gorbuscha*): Possible evidence for the neutral mutation-random drift hypothesis. *Evolution* 28:295–305.

Audubon, J. J. n.d. Ornithological biography. Reprinted in *The passenger pigeon*, ed. W. B. Mershon. 1907. New York: Outing. 28–31.

Avise, J. C. 1989. Gene trees and organismal histories: A phylogenetic approach to population biology. *Evolution* 43:1192–208.

———. 2000. *Phylogeography: The history and formation of species.* Cambridge, Mass.: Harvard University Press.

Avise, J. C., and W. S. Nelson. 1989. Molecular genetic relationships of the extinct dusky seaside sparrow. *Science* 243:646–48.

Ayres, D. R., D. Garcia-Rossi, H. G. Davis, and D. R. Strong. 1999. Extent and degree of hybridization between exotic (*Spartina alterniflora*) and native (*S. foliosa*) cordgrass (*Poaceae*) in California, USA, determined by random amplified polymorphic DNA (RAPDs). *Molecular Ecology* 8:1179–86.

Babbitt v. Sweet Home. 1995. 515 U.S. 687. U.S. Supreme Court.

Bakker, J. P., and F. Berendse. 1999. Constraints in the restoration of ecological diversity in grassland and heathland communities. *Trends in Ecology and Evolution* 14:63–68.

Balmford, A., A. Bruner, P. Cooper, R. Costanza, S. Farber, R. E. Green, M. Jenkins, et al. 2002. Economic reasons for conserving wild nature. *Science* 297:950–53.

Balvanera, P., G. C. Daily, P. R. Ehrlich, T. H. Ricketts, S. A. Bailey, S. Kark, C. Kremen, and H. Pereira. 2001. Conserving biodiversity and ecosystem services. *Science* 291:2047.

Bana e Costa, C. A. 1990. *Readings in multiple criteria decision aid.* Berlin: Springer-Verlag.

Barclay, J. H., and T. J. Cade. 1983. Restoration of the peregrine falcon in the eastern United States. *Bird Conservation* 1:3–40.

Barnes, R. S. K., and K. H. Mann. 1991. *Fundamentals of aquatic ecology.* Malden, Mass.: Blackwell Science.

Barrow Jr., M. V. 1998. *A passion for birds: American ornithology after Audubon.* Princeton, N.J.: Princeton University Press.

Barry, D. J. 1998. Keynote speech: Opportunity in the face of danger: The pragmatic development of habitat conservation plans. *Hastings West-Northwest Journal of Environmental Law and Policy* 4:129–33.

Bascompte, J., and R. V. Solé. 1996. Habitat fragmentation and extinction thresholds in spatially explicit models. *Journal of Animal Ecology* 65:465–73.

Baskin, Y. 1997. *The work of nature: How the diversity of life sustains us.* Washington, D.C.: Island Press.

Batt, K. D. 1995. Above all, do no harm: Sweet Home and section nine of the Endangered Species Act. *Boston University Law Review* 75:1177–231.

Bauer, M., J. Fox, and M. J. Bean. 2004. Landowners bank on conservation: The U.S. Fish and Wildlife Service's guidance on conservation banking. *Environmental Law Reporter* 30:10537–56.

Baumol, W. J. 1952. *Welfare economics and the theory of the state.* Cambridge, Mass.: Harvard University Press.

Bayon, R. 2002. A bull market in . . . woodpeckers? *Milken Institute Review* 4:30–39.

Beacham, T. D., K. J. Supernault, M. Wetklo, B. Deagle, K. Labaree, J. R. Irvine, J. R. Candy, K. M. Miller, R. J. Nelson, and R. E. Withler. 2003. The geographic basis for population structure in Fraser River chinook salmon (*Oncorhynchus tshawytscha*). *Fishery Bulletin* 101:229–42.

Bean, M. J. 2006. Second-generation approaches. Pp. 274–85 in *The Endangered Species Act at thirty: Renewing the conservation promise*, ed. D. D. Goble, J. M. Scott, and F. W. Davis. Washington, D.C.: Island Press.

Bean, M. J., and L. E. Dwyer. 2000. Mitigation banking as an endangered species conservation tool. *Environmental Law Reporter* 30:10537–56.

Bean, M. J., J. P. Jenny, and B. van Eerden. 2001. Safe harbor agreements. *Conservation Biology in Practice* 2:8–16.

Bean, M. J., and M. J. Rowland. 1997. *The evolution of national wildlife law.* 3rd ed. Westport, Conn.: Praeger.

Bean, M. J., and D. S. Wilcove. 1997. The private-land problem. *Conservation Biology* 11:1–2.

Beard, D., F. C. Lincoln, V. H. Cahalane, H. H. T. Jackson, B. H. Thompson, and C. Elliot, eds. 1942. *Fading trails: The story of endangered American wildlife.* New York: Macmillan.

Beatley, T. 1994. *Habitat conservation planning: Endangered species and urban growth.* Austin: University of Texas Press.

———. 2000. *Green urbanism: Learning from European cities.* Washington, D.C.: Island Press.

Behan, M. 2006. County conservation planning. Pp. 156–60 in *The Endangered Species Act at thirty: Renewing the conservation promise,* ed. D. D. Goble, J. M. Scott, and F. W. Davis. Washington, D.C.: Island Press.

Behnke, R. J. 1992. *Native trout of western North America.* Monograph 6. Bethesda, Md.: American Fisheries Society.

Beissinger, S. R. 2002. Population viability analysis: Past, present, future. Pp. 5–17 in *Population viability analysis,* ed. S. R. Beissinger and D. R. McCullough. Chicago: University of Chicago Press.

Beissinger, S. R., and M. I. Westphal. 1998. On the use of demographic models of population viability in endangered species management. *Journal of Wildlife Management* 62:821–41.

Belovsky, G. E., C. Mellison, C. Larson, and P. A. Van Zandt. 1999. Experimental studies of extinction dynamics. *Science* 286:1175–77.

Bengston, D. N., D. P. Fan, and D. N. Celarier. 1999. A new approach to monitoring the social environment for natural resource management: The case of U.S. national forests benefits and values. *Journal of Environmental Management* 56:181–93.

Bentham, J. 1789. *Introduction to the principles of morals and legislation.* Oxford: Clarendon Press.

Benton, T. G., J. A. Vickery, and J. D. Wilson. 2003. Farmland biodiversity: Is habitat heterogeneity the key? *Trends in Ecology and Evolution* 18:182–88.

Bibby, C. J., N. D. Burgess, D. A. Hill, and S. Mustoe. 2000. *Bird census techniques,* 2d ed. New York: Academic Press.

Bluffstone, R., and R. Fazeli. 2002. What is the value of a state park in the San Timoteo Canyon? Paper presented at the Second World Congress of Environmental and Resource Economics, Monterey, Calif., June.

Boersma, P. D., P. M. Kareiva, W. F. Fagan, J. A. Clark, and J. M. Hoekstra. 2001. How good are endangered species recovery plans? *BioScience* 51:643–49.

Bolger, D. T., A. C. Alberts, R. M. Sauvajot, P. Potenza, C. McCalvin, D. Tran, S. Mazzoni, and M. E. Soulé. 1997b. Response of rodents to habitat fragmentation in coastal Southern California. *Ecological Applications* 7:552–63.

Bolger, D. T., T. A. Scott, and J. T. Rotenberry. 1997a. Breeding bird abundance in an urbanizing landscape in coastal Southern California. *Conservation Biology* 11:406–21.

Bolger, D. T., A. V. Suarez, K. R. Crooks, S. A. Morrison, and T. J. Case. 2000. Arthropods in urban habitat fragments in Southern California: Area, age, and edge effects. *Ecological Applications* 10:1230–48.

Bond, M., and C. Bradley. 2004. *Impacts of the 2003 Southern California wildfire on four species listed as threatened and endangered under the federal Endangered Species Act.* Tucson, Ariz.: Center for Biological Diversity.

Bonnie, R. 1999. Endangered species mitigation banking: Promoting recovery through habitat conservation planning under the Endangered Species Act. *Science of the Total Environment* 240:11–19.

Bonnie, R., and M. J. Bean. 1996. Habitat trading for red-cockaded woodpeckers: Enhancing recovery, reducing conflicts. *Endangered Species Update* 13:7–9.

Bormann, F. H., D. Balmori, and G. D. Geballe. 1993. *Redesigning the American lawn: The search for harmony.* New Haven, Conn.: Yale University Press.

Bowen, B. W. 1998. What is wrong with ESUs? The gap between evolutionary theory and conservation principles. *Journal of Shellfish Research* 17:1355–58.

———. 1999. Preserving genes, species, or ecosystems? Healing the fractured foundations of conservation policy. *Molecular Ecology* 8:S5–S10.

Boyce, M. S. 1992. Population viability analysis. *Annual Review of Ecology and Systematics* 23:481–506.

Boyce, M. S., P. R. Vernier, S. E. Nielsen, and F. K. A. Schmiegelow. 2002. Evaluating resource selection functions. *Ecological Modelling* 157:281–300.

Boyle, B. 2002. Restoring credibility to government science. *Seattle Times,* February 27.

Brick, P. D., D. Snow, and S. Van De Wetering, eds. 2001. *Across the Great Divide: Explorations in collaborative conservation and the American West.* Washington, D.C.: Island Press.

Bricker, S. B., C. G. Clement, D. E. Pirhalla, S. P. Orlando, and D. R. G. Farrow. 1999. *National estuarine eutrophication assessment: Effects of nutrient enrichment in the nation's estuaries.* National Oceanic and Atmospheric Administration, National Ocean Service, National Center for Coastal Ocean Science. Silver Spring, Md.

Briscoe, A. D. 2001. Parallel evolution of red-green color vision in bees and butterflies. *American Zoologist* 41:1398.

Broecker, W. S. 1997. Thermohaline circulation, the Achilles heel of our climate system: Will man-made CO_2 upset the current balance? *Science* 278:1582–88.

Brook, B. W., M. A. Burgman, H. R. Akçakaya, J. J. O'Grady, and R. Frankham. 2002. Critiques of PVA ask the wrong questions: Throwing the heuristic baby out with the numerical bathwater. *Conservation Biology* 16:262–63.

Brook, B. W., J. J. O'Grady, A. P. Chapman, M. A. Burgman, H. R. Akçakaya, and R. Frankham. 2000. Predictive accuracy of population viability analysis in conservation biology. *Nature* 404:385–87.

Brookshire, D. S., M. McKee, and G. Watts. 1994. *Economic analysis of proposed critical habitat designation in the Colorado River basin for the razorback sucker, humpback chub, Colorado squawfish, and bonytail.* Final Report to the U.S. Fish and Wildlife Service. Department of Economics, University of New Mexico, Albuquerque.

Brookshire, D. S., M. McKee, and C. Schmidt. 1995. *Economic analysis of critical habitat designation in the Virgin River basin for the woundfin and Virgin River chub.* Final report to the U.S. Fish and Wildlife Service. Department of Economics, University of New Mexico, Albuquerque.

Brown Jr., G. M., and J. F. Shogren. 1998. The economics of the Endangered Species Act. *Journal of Economic Perspectives* 12:3–20.

Brownlow, C. A. 1996. Molecular taxonomy and the conservation of the red wolf and other endangered carnivores. *Conservation Biology* 10:390–96.

Buck, E. H., M. L. Corn, and P. Baldwin. 2001. *Endangered species: Difficult choices.* Congressional Research Service Report IB10072. Washington, D.C.: National Council for Science and the Environment.

Buechner, M., and R. M. Sauvajot. 1996. Conservation and zones of human activity: The spread of human disturbance across a protected landscape. Pp. 605–29 in *Biodiversity in managed landscapes: Theory and practice*, ed. R. C. Szaro and D. W. Johnston. New York: Oxford University Press.

Burgman, M. A. 2005. *Risks and decisions for conservation and environmental management.* Cambridge, U.K.: Cambridge University Press.

Burgman, M. A., D. R. Breininger, B. W. Duncan, and S. Ferson. 2001. Setting reliability bounds on habitat suitability indices. *Ecological Applications* 11:70–78.

Burgman, M. A., S. Ferson, and H. R. Akçakaya. 1993. *Risk assessment in conservation biology.* New York: Springer.

Burgman, M. A., and J. C. Fox. 2003. Bias in species range estimates from minimum convex polygons: Implications for conservation and options for improved planning. *Animal Conservation* 6:19–28.

Burkholder, J. M., E. J. Noga, C. H. Hobbs, and H. B. Glasgow Jr. 1992. New "phantom" dinoflagellate is the causative agent of major estuarine fish kills. *Nature* 358: 407–10.

Burney, D. A., H. F. James, L. P. Burney, S. L. Olson, W. Kikuchi, W. L. Wagner, M. Burney, et al. 2001. Fossil evidence for a diverse biota from Kaua'i and its transformation since human arrival. *Ecological Monographs* 71:615–41.

Burnham, K. P., and D. R. Anderson. 2002. *Model selection and multimodel inference: A practical information-theoretic approach.* 2d ed. New York: Springer.

Burnham, W., T. J. Cade, A. Lieberman, J. P. Jenny, and W. R. Heinrich. 2006. Hands-on restoration. Pp. 237–46 in *The Endangered Species Act at thirty: Renewing the conservation promise*, ed. D. D. Goble, J. M. Scott, and F. W. Davis. Washington, D.C.: Island Press.

Busack, C. A., and J. B. Shaklee, eds. 1995. *Genetic diversity units and major ancestral lineages of salmonid fishes in Washington.* Technical report RAD 95-02. Washington Department of Fish and Wildlife. Olympia.

Busby, P. J., T. C. Wainwright, G. J. Bryant, L. J. Lierheimer, R. S. Waples, F. W. Waknitz, and I. V. Lagomarsino. 1996. *Status review of West Coast steelhead from Washington, Idaho, Oregon, and California.* Technical memorandum NMFS-NWFSC-27. U.S. Department of Commerce, National Oceanic and Atmospheric Administration. Seattle.

Byers, J. A. 1997. *American pronghorn: Social adaptations and the ghosts of predators past.* Chicago: University of Chicago Press.

Cade, T. J., and W. Burnham, eds. 2003. *Return of the peregrine: A North American saga of tenacity and teamwork.* Boise, Idaho: Peregrine Fund.

Caffrey, J., M. Brown, W. B. Tyler, and M. Silberstein. 2002. *Changes in a California estuary: A profile of Elkhorn Slough.* Moss Landing, Calif.: Elkhorn Slough Foundation.

Calflora 2005. California wild plant database. http://www.calflora.org/.

California Department of Finance. Demographic Research Unit. 2002. *The data source handbook.* Sacramento. Also available online at http://www.dof.ca.gov/html/demograp/repndat.asp.

California Department of Fish and Game. 2002. *California wildlife habitat relationships*

(CWHR) system. Sacramento. Also available online at http://www.dfg.ca.gov/whdab/html/cwhr.html.

———. 2003. *Special animals list.* http://www.dfg.ca.gov/whdab/pdfs/SPanimals.pdf

———. 2005. *The status of rare, threatened, and endangered plants and animals of California 2000–2004.* Sacramento. Also available online at http://www.dfg.ca.gov/hcpb/species/t_e_spp/ann_te_rpt.shtml.

California Resources Agency. 1995. *Official Policy on Conservation Banks.* April 7. Sacramento. Also available online at http://ceres.ca.gov/wetlands/policies/mitbank.html.

California Rice Commission. 1997. Habitats in California. Chap. 2 in *Special status wildlife species use of rice cultivation lands in California's Central Valley,* prepared by Resource Management International. Sacramento. Also available online at http://www.calrice.org/a_special_status/index.htm.

Callicott, J. B. 1986. On the intrinsic value of non-human species. Pp. 138–72 in *The preservation of species: The value of biological diversity,* ed. B. G. Norton. Princeton, N.J.: Princeton University Press.

Cameron, J. 1929. *The Bureau of Biological Survey: Its history, activities, and organization.* Baltimore, Md.: Johns Hopkins University Press.

Carlson, C. 2003. Lawsuits planned to protect Florida panther. *Miami Herald,* April 24.

Carlton, J. T. 1993. Neoextinctions of marine invertebrates. *American Zoologist* 33:499–509.

Carpenter, G. A., S. Gopal, S. Macomber, S. Martens, C. E. Woodcock, and J. Franklin. 1999. A neural network method for efficient vegetation mapping. *Remote Sensing of Environment* 70:326–38.

Carpenter, S. R. 2002. Ecological futures: Building an ecology of the long now. *Ecology* 83:2069–83.

Carrigg, D. 2002. Balancing housing and growth pressures with limited resources: It's time for leadership. *Western City* 78:13–23.

Carroll, R., C. Augspurger, A. Dobson, J. Franklin, G. H. Orians, W. Reid, R. Tracy, D. S. Wilcove, and J. Wilson. 1996. Strengthening the use of science in achieving the goals of the Endangered Species Act: An assessment by the Ecological Society of America. *Ecological Applications* 6:1–11.

Carson, R., W. M. Hanemann, R. J. Kopp, J. A. Krosnick, R. C. Mitchell, S. Presser, P. A. Ruud, and V. K. Smith. 1994. *Prospective interim lost use value due to DDT and PCB contamination in the Southern California bight.* Report to the National Oceanic and Atmospheric Administration. Berkeley, Calif.

Carson v. Blazer. 1810. 2 Binn. 475. Pennsylvania Supreme Court.

Cart, J., and K. R. Weiss. 2004. Battle lines drawn on protection of species. *Los Angeles Times,* December 5.

Cart, T. W. 1972. "New Deal" for wildlife: A perspective on federal conservation policy, 1933–1940. *Pacific Northwest Quarterly* 63:113–20.

———. 1973. The Lacey Act: America's first nationwide wildlife statute. *Forest History* 17:4–13.

Caswell, H. 2001. *Matrix population models: Construction, analysis, and interpretation.* Rev. ed. Sunderland, Mass.: Sinauer Associates.

Cavalli-Sforza, L. L., and A. W. Edwards. 1967. Phylogenetic analysis: Models and estimation procedures. *Evolution* 21:550–70.

Cawley, R. M. 1993. *Federal land, western anger: The Sagebrush Rebellion and environmental politics.* Lawrence: University Press of Kansas.

Ceballos, G., and P. R. Ehrlich. 2002. Mammal population losses and the extinction crisis. *Science* 296:904–7.

Center for Biological Diversity v. Lohn. 2003. 296 F. Supp. 2d 1223. U.S. District Court for the Western District of Washington.

Center for Maximum Potential Building Systems. 2002. *Charting common ground for salmon and buildings.* Austin, Texas.

Channell, R., and M. V. Lomolino. 2000a. Dynamic biogeography and conservation of endangered species. *Nature* 403:84–86.

———. 2000b. Trajectories toward extinction: Spatial dynamics of the contraction of geographical ranges. *Journal of Biogeography* 27:169–79.

Chicago Metropolis 2020. 2003. *The metropolitan plan: Choices for the Chicago region.* http://www.metropolisplan.org/plan.pdf.

Chicago Wilderness. 1999. *Biodiversity recovery plan.* http://www.chicagowilderness .org/pubprod/brp/index.cfm.

———. 2001. *Atlas of biodiversity.* http://www.chicagowilderness.org/pubprod/atlas/ index.cfm.

Chichilnisky, G., and G. Heal. 1998. Economic returns from the biosphere. *Nature* 391:629–30.

CITES ("Convention on International Trade in Endangered Species of Wild Fauna and Flora"). 1973. *United States Treaties and Other International Agreements* 27, pt. 1087. March 3. Washington, D.C.

CITES Secretariat. 1996. Summary Record, CITES Animals Committee, 12th Meeting, Antigua, Guatemala, September 11–14 1995. Geneva. Also available online at http://www.cites.org/common/com/ac/12/12AC-SumRec.pdf.

City of Chicago. Department of the Environment. 2001. *Chicago's energy plan.* http://www.chpcentermw.org/pdfs/021024CEP-BronsonCuttica-BostonMA.pdf.

City of Seattle. Office of the Mayor. 2002. Mayor proposes quicker action on creek and shoreline restoration. http://www.cityofseattle.gov/mayor/issues/I-80.htm.

City of Seattle. Salmon Team. 2001. *Seattle's Urban Blueprint for Habitat Protection and Restoration.* http://www.seattle.gov/salmon/blueprintdoc.htm.

Clark, J. A., and E. Harvey. 2002. Assessing multi-species recovery plans under the Endangered Species Act. *Ecological Applications* 12:655–62.

Clark, J. A., J. M. Hoekstra, P. D. Boersma, and P. M. Kareiva. 2002. Improving U.S. Endangered Species Act recovery plans: Key findings and recommendations of the SCB recovery plan report. *Conservation Biology* 16:1510–19.

Clark, J. A., and R. M. May. 2002. Taxonomic bias in conservation research. *Science* 297:191–92.

Clark, J. R. 1999. Testimony of Jamie Rappaport Clark, Director, Fish and Wildlife Service, Department of the Interior, before the Senate Committee on Environment and Public Works, Subcommittee on Fisheries, Wildlife, and Drinking Water. May 27. http://epw.senate.gov/107th/cla_5-27.htm.

Clark, J. S., S. R. Carpenter, M. Barber, S. Collins, A. Dobson, J. A. Foley, D. M. Lodge, et al. 2001. Ecological forecasts: An emerging imperative. *Science* 293:657–60.

Clemen, R. T. 1996. *Making hard decisions: An introduction to decision analysis.* 2d ed. Pacific Grove, Calif.: Duxbury Press.

Code of Federal Regulations. 2004. 50:402.02. Interagency cooperation, Endangered Species Act of 1973 as amended.

Coggins, G. C. 1983. Grizzly bears don't stop at customs: A preface to transboundary problems in natural resources law. *University of Kansas Law Review* 32:1–16.

Coggins, G. C., and I. S. Russell. 1982. Beyond shooting snail darters in pork barrels: Endangered species and land use in America. *Georgetown Law Journal* 70:1433.

Cohen, A. N., and J. T. Carlton. 1998. Accelerating invasion rate in a highly invaded estuary. *Science* 279:555–58.

Cohen, H. 2000. Federal animal protection statutes. *Animal Law* 1:143–53.

Commissioners of Fisheries of the State of California. 1878. *Biennial report for the years 1876 and 1877*. Sacramento: California State Printing Office.

Committee on Rare and Endangered Wildlife Species. Bureau of Sport Fisheries and Wildlife. U.S. Department of the Interior. 1966. *Rare and endangered fish and wildlife of the United States*. (Also called "The Redbook.") Resource publication no. 34.

Confer, J. L., and K. Knapp. 1992. Golden-winged warbler (*Vermivora chrysoptera*). Pp. 369–83 in *Migratory nongame birds of management concern in the Northeast*, ed. K. J. Schneider and D. M. Pence. Newton Corner, Mass.: U.S. Fish and Wildlife Service.

Conner, R. N. 1988. Wildlife populations: Minimally viable or ecologically functional? *Wildlife Society Bulletin* 16:80–84.

Connor v. Burford. 1988. 848 F. 2d 1441. U.S. Court of Appeals for the 9th Judicial Circuit.

Convention on Nature Protection and Wild Life Preservation in the Western Hemisphere. December 10, 1940. 56 *U.S. Statutes at Large* 1534, Treaty Series no. 981, *United Nations Treaty Series* no. 193.

Convention with Great Britain for the Protection of Migratory Birds. August 16, 1916. 39 *U.S. Statutes at Large* 1702, Treaty Series No. 628.

Cooper, J. F. 1823. *The pioneers, or the sources of the Susquehanna*. From *The leatherstocking tales* 1:246–50. New York: Library of America, 1985.

Cooperman, M. S., and D. F. Markle. 2003. The Endangered Species Act and the National Research Council's interim judgment in Klamath Basin. *Fisheries* 28:10–19.

Corrado, A. 2000. *Campaign finance reform: Beyond the basics*. Washington, D.C.: The Century Foundation.

Costanza, R., R. d'Arge, R. de Groot, S. Farberk, M. Grasso, B. Hannon, K. Limburg, et al. 1997. The value of the world's ecosystem services and natural capital. *Nature* 387:253–60.

Coulson, T., G. M. Mace, E. Hudson, and H. Possingham. 2001. The use and abuse of population viability analysis. *Trends in Ecology and Evolution* 16:219–21.

County of San Mateo Planning Commission. 1982. *San Bruno Mountain Area Habitat Conservation Plan*. Redwood City, Calif.: County of San Mateo.

Cracraft, J. 1983. Species concepts and speciation analysis. Pp. 159–87 in *Current ornithology*, vol. 1, ed. R. F. Johnston. New York: Plenum.

Crandall, K. A., O. R. P. Bininda-Emonds, G. M. Mace, and R. K. Wayne. 2000. Considering evolutionary processes in conservation biology. *Trends in Ecology and Evolution* 15:290–95.

Crellin, G. 2002. *An assessment of Endangered Species Act on real property values*. Technical report for the National Association of Realtors. Washington, D.C.

Crocker, T., and J. Tschirhart. 1992. Ecosystems, externalities, and economics. *Environmental and Resource Economics* 2:551–67.

Cronon, W. 1983. *Changes in the land: Indians, colonists, and the ecology of New England*. New York: Hill and Wang.

———. 1995. Introduction: In search of nature. Pp. 23–56 in *Uncommon ground: Rethinking the human place in nature*, ed. W. Cronon. New York: W.W. Norton.

Crooks, K. R. 2002. Relative sensitivities of mammalian carnivores to habitat fragmentation. *Conservation Biology* 16:488–502.

Crouse, D. T., L. A. Mehrhoff, M. J. Parkin, D. R. Elam, and L. Y. Chen. 2002. Endangered species recovery and the SCB study: A U.S. Fish and Wildlife Service perspective. *Ecological Applications* 12:719–23.

Culver, M., W. E. Johnson, J. P. Slattery, and S. J. O'Brien. 2000. Genomic ancestry of the American puma (*Puma concolor*). *Journal of Heredity* 91:186–97.

Czech, B., and P. R. Krausman. 1997. Public opinion on species and endangered species conservation. *Endangered Species Update* 14:7–10.

———. 2001. *The Endangered Species Act: History, conservation biology, and public policy*. Baltimore, Md.: Johns Hopkins University Press.

Czech, H. A., and K. C. Parsons. 2002. Agricultural wetlands and waterbirds: A review. *Waterbirds* 25:56–65.

Daily, G. C. 1997. *Nature's services: Societal dependence on natural ecosystems*. Washington, D.C.: Island Press.

———. 1999. Developing a scientific basis for managing Earth's life support systems. *Conservation Ecology* 3:14.

———. 2001. Ecological forecasts. *Nature* 411:245.

———. 2003. Time to rethink conservation strategy. *Science* 300:1508–9.

Daily, G. C., S. Alexander, P. R. Ehrlich, L. Goulder, J. Lubchenco, P. A. Matson, H. A. Mooney, et al. 1997. Ecosystem services: Benefits supplied to human societies by natural ecosystems. *Issues in Ecology* 2:1–18.

Daily, G. C., G. Ceballos, J. Pacheco, G. Suzán, and A. Sánchez-Azofeifa. 2003. Countryside biogeography of Neotropical mammals: Conservation opportunities in agricultural landscapes of Costa Rica. *Conservation Biology* 17:1814–26.

Daily, G. C., and P. R. Ehrlich. 1996. Nocturnality and species survival. *Proceedings of the National Academy of Sciences of the United States of America* 93:11709–12.

Daily, G. C., P. R. Ehrlich, and G. A. Sánchez-Azofeifa. 2001. Countryside biogeography: Utilization of human-dominated habitats by the avifauna of southern Costa Rica. *Ecological Applications* 11:1–13.

Daily, G. C., and K. Ellison. 2002. *The new economy of nature: The quest to make conservation profitable*. Washington, D.C.: Island Press.

Dales, J. H. 1968. *Pollution, property, and prices*. Toronto: University of Toronto Press.

Dalton, R. 2002. Fur flies over lynx survey's suspect samples. *Nature* 415:107.

———. 2003. Ecologists seek to turn tide on Colorado River. *Nature* 423:793.

Daly, M. 2003. Two private firms to review status of owl, murrelet. *Seattle Times*, September 30.

Daniels, T. L. 1999. *When city and country collide: Managing growth in the metropolitan fringe*. Washington, D.C.: Island Press.

Darwin, C. 1859. *The origin of species by means of natural selection, or the preservation of favoured races in the struggle for life*. A facsimile of the first edition. Cambridge, Mass.: Harvard University Press.

Daubert v. Merrell Dow Pharmaceuticals. 1993. 509 U.S. 579. U.S. Supreme Court.

David Taussig and Associates. 2003. *Development impact fee schedule*. Report to Riverside County. Riverside, Calif.

Davis, F. W., D. D. Goble, J. M. Scott. 2006. Renewing the conservation commitment. Pp. 296–306 in *The Endangered Species Act at thirty: Renewing the conservation promise*, ed. D. D. Goble, J. M. Scott, and F. W. Davis. Washington, D.C.: Island Press.

Davis, F. W., D. M. Stoms, A. D. Hollander, K. A. Thomas, P. A. Stine, D. C. Odion, M. I. Borchert, et al. 1998. *The California Gap Analysis Project: Final Report*. University of California, Santa Barbara. http://www.biogeog.ucsb.edu/projects/gap/gap_rep.html.

Dawson, D., and J. Shogren. 2001. An update on priorities and expenditures under the Endangered Species Act. *Land Economics* 77:527–32.

De Alessi, M. 2003. *Saving endangered species privately: A case study of Earth Sanctuaries, Ltd.* San Francisco: Pacific Research Institute.

DeAngelis, D. L. 1992. *Dynamics of nutrient cycling and food webs*. London: Chapman and Hall.

Decker, J. F. 1979. *Prostitution: Regulation and control*. Littleton, Colo.: F. B. Rothman.

Defenders of Wildlife v. Babbitt. 1997. 958 F. Supp. 670. U.S. District Court for the District of Columbia.

Defenders of Wildlife v. Norton. 2001. 258 F. 3d 1136. U.S. Court of Appeals for the 9th Judicial Circuit.

———. 2002. 239 F. Supp. 2d 9. U.S. District Court for the District of Columbia.

De Groot, R. S. 1992. *Functions of nature: Evaluation of nature in environmental planning, management and decision making*. Groningan, Netherlands: Wolters-Noordhoff.

Dennis, B., P. L. Munholland, and J. M. Scott. 1991. Estimation of growth and extinction parameters for endangered species. *Ecological Monographs* 61:115–43.

Desimone, J., and M. C. Farrelly. 2001. Price and enforcement effects on cocaine and marijuana demand. *Economic Inquiry* 41:98–115.

Dewey, J. 1910. *The influence of Darwin on philosophy and other essays in contemporary thought*. New York: Henry Holt.

Diamond, J. M., J. Terborgh, R. F. Whitcomb, J. F. Lynch, P. A. Opler, C. S. Robbins, D. S. Simberloff, and L. G. Abele. 1976. Island biogeography and conservation: Strategy and limitations. *Science* 193:1027–32.

Díaz, S., and M. Cabido. 2001. Vive la différence: Plant functional diversity matters to ecosystem processes. *Trends in Ecology and Evolution* 16:646–55.

Dietz, T., and P. C. Stern. 2002. Exploring new tools for environmental protection. Pp. 3–15 in *New tools for environmental protection: Education, information, and voluntary measures*, ed. T. Dietz and P. C. Stern. Washington, D.C.: National Academies Press.

Dixon, L. 1995. The transaction costs generated by Superfund's liability approach. Pp. 171–85 in *Analyzing Superfund: Economics, science, and law*, ed. R. Revesz and R. Stewart. Washington, D.C.: Resources for the Future.

Dizon, A. E., C. Lockyer, W. F. Perrin, D. P. Demaster, and J. Sisson. 1992. Rethinking the stock concept: A phylogeographic approach. *Conservation Biology* 6:24–36.

Docker, M. F., and D. D. Heath. 2003. Genetic comparison between sympatric anadromous steelhead and freshwater resident rainbow trout in British Columbia, Canada. *Conservation Genetics* 4:227–31.

Donahue, D. 2005. The Endangered Species Act and its current set of incentive tools for species protection. Pp. 25–64 in *Species at risk: Using economic incentives to shelter endangered species on private lands*, ed. J. Shogren. Austin: University of Texas Press.

Donald, P. F., R. E. Green, and M. F. Heath. 2001. Agricultural intensification and the collapse of Europe's farmland bird populations. *Proceedings of the Royal Society B: Biological Sciences* 268:25–29.

Doremus, H. 1997. Listing decisions under the Endangered Species Act: Why better science isn't always better policy. *Washington University Law Quarterly* 75:1029–56.

————. 2006. Lessons learned. Pp. 195–207 in *The Endangered Species Act at thirty: Renewing the conservation promise*, ed. D. D. Goble, J. M. Scott, and F. W. Davis. Washington, D.C.: Island Press.

Dorsey, K. 1998. *The dawn of conservation diplomacy: U.S.-Canadian wildlife protection treaties in the progressive era.* Seattle: University of Washington Press.

Doughty, R. W. 1975. *Feather fashions and bird preservation: A study in nature protection.* Berkeley: University of California Press.

Dowling, T. E., W. L. Minckley, M. E. Douglas, P. C. Marsh, and B. D. Demarais. 1992. Response to Wayne, Nowak and Phillips and Henry: Use of molecular characters in conservation biology. *Conservation Biology* 6:600–3.

Drake, J. A., H. A. Mooney, F. di Castri, R. H. Groves, F. J. Kruger, M. Rejmánek, and M. Williamson, eds. 1989. *Biological invasions: A global perspective.* New York: John Wiley.

Dudley, J. P. 1999. Coevolutionary implications of an endemic Pleistocene megaherbivore fauna for insular floras of the California Channel Islands. *Conservation Biology* 13:209–10.

Dunlap, T. R. 1988. Sport hunting and conservation, 1880–1920. *Environmental Review* 12:51–60.

Earn, D. J., S. A. Levin, and P. Rohani. 2000. Coherence and conservation. *Science* 290:1360–64.

Ecological Society of America. 1926. *Naturalist's guide to the Americas*, ed. V. E. Shelford. Baltimore: Williams and Wilkins.

Edwards Jr., T. C., E. T. Deshler, D. Foster, and G. G. Moisen. 1996. Adequacy of wildlife habitat relation models for estimating spatial distributions of terrestrial vertebrates. *Conservation Biology* 10:263–70.

Ehrenfeld, D. 1988. Why put a value on biodiversity? Pp. 212–16 in *Biodiversity*, ed. E. O. Wilson. Washington, D.C.: National Academies Press.

Ehrlich, P. R. 1988. The loss of diversity: Causes and consequences. Pp. 21–27 in *Biodiversity*, ed. E. O. Wilson. Washington, D.C.: National Academies Press.

Ehrlich, P. R., and I. Hanski. 2004. *On the wings of checkerspots: A model system for population biology.* New York: Oxford University Press.

Ehrlich, P. R., and B. H. Walker. 1998. Rivets and redundancy. *BioScience* 48:387.

Elith, J. 2000. Quantitative methods for modeling species habitat: Comparative performance and an application to Australian plants. Pp. 39–58 in *Quantitative methods for conservation biology*, ed. S. Ferson and M. A. Burgman. New York: Springer-Verlag.

Elith. J., and M. A. Burgman. 2003. Habitat models for population viability analysis. Pp. 203–35 in *Population viability in plants*, ed. C. A. Brigham and M. W. Schwartz. Heidelberg, Denmark: Springer-Verlag.

Elith, J., M. A. Burgman, and H. M. Regan. 2002. Mapping epistemic uncertainties and vague concepts in predictions of species distributions. *Ecological Modelling* 157:313–29.

Ellner, S. P., and J. Fieberg. 2003: Using PVA for management despite uncertainty: Effects of habitat, hatcheries, and harvest on salmon. *Ecology* 84:1359–69.

Elphick, C. S., and L. W. Oring. 2003. Conservation implications of flooding rice fields on winter waterbird communities. *Agriculture, Ecosystems and Environment* 94:17–29.

Elton, C. S. 1958. *The ecology of invasions by animals and plants.* London: Chapman and Hall.

Endangered Species Technical Bulletin. 1980. Service withdraws proposals to list 1,876 Species. January 1.

Endangered Species Committee. 1985. Rules for applying for Endangered Species Act exemptions and for Endangered Species Act Committee consideration of such applications. *Federal Register* 50:8122–31.

Environmental Defense. 2003. *Red-cockaded woodpecker conservation bank: International Paper Company, Southlands Experimental Forest, Bainbridge, Georgia.* http://www.environmentaldefense.org/article.cfm?ContentID=2664.

Environmental Protection Information Center (EPIC) v. National Marine Fisheries Service (NMFS). 2004. C-02-5401-EDL, filed March 2 (U.S. District Court for the Northern District of California).

EPA (Environmental Protection Agency), USFWS (U.S. Fish and Wildlife Service), NMFS (National Marine Fisheries Service), and NOAA (National Oceanic and Atmospheric Administration). 2001. Memorandum of agreement between the Environmental Protection Agency, Fish and Wildlife Service, and National Marine Fisheries Service regarding enhanced coordination under the Clean Water Act and Endangered Species Act. *Federal Register* 66:11201–17.

Estrada, A., R. Coates-Estrada, and D. A. Meritt. 1997. Anthropogenic landscape changes and avian diversity at Los Tuxtlas, Mexico. *Biodiversity and Conservation* 6:19–43.

Fagan, W. F., R. S. Cantrell, and C. Cosner. 1999. How habitat edges change species interactions. *American Naturalist* 153:165–82.

Feldman, T. D. 1995. Local solutions to land use conflict under the Endangered Species Act: Habitat conservation planning in Riverside County. Ph.D. diss., University of California, Riverside.

Ferrier, S., G. Watson, J. Pearce, and M. Drielsma. 2002. Extended statistical approaches to modeling spatial pattern in biodiversity in northeast New South Wales. Species-level modeling. *Biodiversity and Conservation* 11:2275–307.

Fieberg, J., and S. P. Ellner. 2000. When is it meaningful to estimate an extinction probability? *Ecology* 81:2040–47.

Fields, P. A., J. B. Graham, R. H. Rosenblatt, and G. N. Somero. 1993. Effects of expected global climate change on marine faunas. *Trends in Ecology and Evolution* 8:361–67.

Filion, F. L., J. P. Foley, and A. J. Jacquemot. 1994. The economics of global ecotourism. Pp. 235–52 in *Protected area economics and policy: Linking conservation and sustainable development,* ed. M. Munasinghe and J. McNeely. Washington, D.C.: World Bank.

Finnoff, D., and J. Tschirhart. 2003a. Harvesting in an eight-species ecosystem. *Environmental Economics and Management* 45:589–611.

———. 2003b. Protecting an endangered species while harvesting its prey in a general equilibrium ecosystem model. *Land Economics* 79:160–80.

Fischman, R. L. 2003. *The national wildlife refuges: Coordinating a conservation system through law.* Washington, D.C.: Island Press.

Fisher, M. 2004. Governors unsure about how to fix Endangered Species Act. Dec. 4. *Riverside Press Enterprise.*

Fisher, R. N., A. V. Suarez, and T. J. Case. 2002. Spatial patterns in the abundance of the coastal horned lizard. *Conservation Biology* 16:205–15.

Flannery, T. F. 1995. *The future eaters: An ecological history of the Australasian lands and people.* New York: George Braziller.

———. 2001. *The eternal frontier: Ecological history of North America and its peoples.* New York: Atlantic Monthly Press.

Flores, D. 1991. Bison ecology and bison diplomacy: The southern plains from 1800–1850. *Journal of American History* 78:465–85.

Floyd, T. 2001. Complexity simplified (but who's paying attention?). *Ecology* 82:904–5.

Fluharty, D. 2000. Habitat protection, ecological issues, and implementation of the Sustainable Fisheries Act. *Ecological Applications* 10:325–37.

Foin, T. C., S. P. D. Riley, A. L. Pawley, D. R. Ayres, T. M. Carlsen, P. J. Hodum, and P. V. Switzer. 1998. Improving recovery planning for threatened and endangered species. *BioScience* 48:177–84.

Folke, C., C. S. Holling, and C. Perrings. 1996. Biological diversity, ecosystems and the human scale. *Ecological Applications* 6:1018–24.

Ford, M. J. 2004. Conservation units and preserving diversity. Pp. 338–57 in *Evolution illuminated: Salmon and their relatives,* ed. A. P. Hendry and S. C. Stearns. Oxford: Oxford University Press.

Fox, J., and A. Nino-Murcia. 2005. Status of species conservation banking in the United States. *Journal of Conservation Biology* 19 (4): 996–1007.

Fox, S. 1981. *The American conservation movement: John Muir and his legacy.* Madison: University of Wisconsin Press.

Fox, W. 1993. What does the recognition of intrinsic value entail? *Trumpeter* 10:101.

Fraser, D. J., and L. Bernatchez. 2001. Adaptive evolutionary conservation: Towards a unified concept for defining conservation units. *Molecular Ecology* 10:2741–52.

Freary v. Cooke. 1779. 14 Mass. 488. Massachusetts Supreme Judicial Court.

Fredrickson, R., and P. Hedrick. 2002. Body size in endangered Mexican wolves: Effects of inbreeding and cross-lineage matings. *Animal Conservation* 5:39–43.

Freeman III, A. M. 1993. *The measurement of environmental and resource values: Theory and methods.* Washington, D.C.: Resources for the Future.

Friedman, C. S., M. Thomson, C. Chun, P. L. Haaker, and R. P. Hedrick. 1997. Withering syndrome of the black abalone, *Haliotis cracherodii* (leach): Water temperature, food availability and parasites as possible causes. *Journal of Shellfish Research* 16:403–11.

Fritts, S. H., and L. N. Carbyn. 1995. Population viability, nature reserves, and the outlook for gray wolf conservation in North America. *Restoration Ecology* 3:26–38.

Fulton, W. B. 2000. *Guide to California planning.* 2d ed. Point Arena, Calif.: Solano Press.

Gabrielson, I. N. 1943. *Wildlife refuges.* New York: Macmillan.

GAO (General Accounting Office). 1992. *Endangered Species Act: Types and numbers of implementing actions.* GAO/RCED-92-131BR. Washington, D.C.: U.S. Government Printing Office. Also available online at http://archive.gao.gov/d32t10/146775.pdf.

———. 1995. *Endangered Species Act: Information on species protection on nonfederal lands.* Report to congressional requesters, GAO/RCED-95-16. Washington, D.C. Also available online at http://www.gao.gov/archive/1995/rc95016.pdf.

———. 2002. *Canada lynx survey: Unauthorized hair samples submitted for analysis.* Statement of Ronald Malfi, acting managing director, Office of Special Investigations. Testimony before the Committee on Resources, U.S. House of Representatives. GAO-02-496T. Washington, D.C. Also available online at http://resources committee.house.gov/archives/107cong/fullcomm/2002mar06/malfi.pdf.

————. 2003. *Endangered Species. Fish and Wildlife Service uses best available science to make listing decisions, but additional guidance needed for critical habitat designations.* GAO-03-803. Washington, D.C. Also available online at http://www.gao.gov/htext/d03803.html.

Gaston, K. J. 2000. Global patterns in biodiversity. *Nature* 405:220–27.

Geller, J. B. 1999. Decline of a native mussel masked by sibling species invasion. *Conservation Biology* 13:661–64.

Gende, S. M., R. T. Edwards, M. F. Willson, and M. S. Wipfli. 2002. Pacific salmon in aquatic and terrestrial ecosystems. *BioScience* 52:917–28.

Gerber, L. R., and L. T. Hatch. 2002. Are we recovering? An evaluation of recovery criteria under the U.S. Endangered Species Act. *Ecological Applications* 12:668–73.

Gerber, L. R., and G. R. VanBlaricom. 2001. Implications of three viability models for the conservation status of the western population of Steller sea lions (*Eumetopias jubatus*). *Biological Conservation* 102:261–69.

Gharrett, A. J., and W. W. Smoker. 1991. Two generations of hybrids between even- and odd-year pink salmon (*Oncorhynchus gorbuscha*): A test for outbreeding depression? *Canadian Journal of Fisheries and Aquatic Sciences* 48:1744–49.

Gifford Pinchot Task Force v. U.S. Fish and Wildlife Service. 2004. 378 F. 3d 1059. U.S. Court of Appeals for the 9th Judicial Circuit.

Gilbert, C. R., ed. 1992. *Rare and endangered biota of Florida.* Vol. 2. *Fishes.* Gainesville: University Press of Florida.

Gill, F. B. 1980. Historical aspects of hybridization between blue-winged and golden-winged warblers. *Auk* 97:1–18.

Gittleman, J. L., and M. E. Gompper. 2001. The risk of extinction: What you don't know will hurt you. *Science* 291:997–99.

Gladfelter, W. B. 1982. White band disease in *Acropora palmata*: Implications for the structure and growth of shallow reefs. *Bulletin of Marine Science* 32:639–43.

Glaeser, E., and J. Gyourko. 2002. *The impact of zoning on housing affordability.* Cambridge, Mass.: Harvard University Press.

Glomb, S. 1995. Protecting coastal ecosystems. *Endangered Species Bulletin* 20:4–7.

Goble, D. D. 1999. Salmon in the Columbia Basin: From abundance to extinction. Pp. 229–63 in *Northwest lands and peoples: Readings in environmental history,* ed. D. D. Goble and P. W. Hirt. Seattle: University of Washington Press.

Goble, D. D., and E. T. Freyfogle. 2002. *Wildlife law: Cases and materials.* New York: Foundation Press.

Goble, D. D., J. M. Scott, and F. W. Davis, eds. 2006. *The Endangered Species Act at thirty: Renewing the conservation promise.* Washington, D.C.: Island Press.

Goldburg, R. J., M. S. Elliott, and R. L. Naylor. 2001. *Marine aquaculture in the United States: Environmental impacts and policy options.* Arlington, Va.: Pew Oceans Commission.

Goodpaster, K. E. 1978. On being morally considerable. *Journal of Philosophy* 75:308–25.

Gordon Jr., R. E., J. K. Lacy, and J. R. Streeter. 1997. Conservation under the Endangered Species Act. *Environment International* 23:359–419.

Grant, P. R., and B. R. Grant. 1992. Hybridization of bird species. *Science* 256:193–97.

Greater London Authority. 2002. *Connecting with London's nature: The mayor's biodiversity strategy.* London.

Greenwald, D. N., K. F. Suckling, and M. Taylor. 2006. The listing record. Pp. 51–67 in *The Endangered Species Act at thirty: Renewing the conservation promise*, ed. D. D. Goble, J. M. Scott, and F. W. Davis. Washington, D.C.: Island Press.

Groot, C., and L. Margolis. 1991. *Pacific salmon life histories.* Vancouver: University of British Columbia Press.

Groves, C. R., L. S. Kutner, D. M. Stoms, M. P. Murray, J. M. Scott, M. Schafale, A. S. Weakley, and R. L. Pressey. 2000. Owning up to our responsibilities: Who owns lands important for biodiversity? Pp. 275–300 in *Precious heritage: The status of biodiversity in the United States*, ed. B. A. Stein, L. S. Kutner, and J. S. Adams. New York: Oxford University Press.

Gunderson, L., and C. Folke. 2003. Toward a "science of the long view." *Conservation Ecology* 7:15.

Gustafson, R. G., T. C. Wainwright, G. A. Winans, F. W. Waknitz, L. T. Parker, and R. S. Waples. 1997. Status review of sockeye salmon from Washington and Oregon. Technical memorandum NMFS-NWFSC-33. U.S. Department of Commerce, National Oceanic and Atmospheric Administration. Seattle.

Guterman, L. 2000. Have ecologists oversold biodiversity? Some scientists question experiments on how numerous species help ecosystems. *Chronicle of Higher Education* 47:A24–A26.

Haig, S. M., and J. D. Ballou. 1995. Genetic diversity among two avian species formerly endemic to Guam. *Auk* 112:445–55.

Haig, S. M., T. D. Mullins, and E. D. Forsman. 2004. Subspecific relationships and genetic structure in the spotted owl. *Conservation Genetics* 5:683–705.

Haig, S. M., T. D. Mullins, E. D. Forsman, P. Trail, and L. Wennerberg. 2004. Genetic identification of spotted owls, barred owls, and their hybrids: Legal implications of hybrid identity. *Conservation Biology* 18:1347–57.

Haila, Y. 2002. A conceptual genealogy of fragmentation research: From island biogeography to landscape ecology. *Ecological Applications* 12:321–34.

Halliday, T. R. 1980. The extinction of the passenger pigeon (*Ectopistes migratorius*) and its relevance to contemporary conservation. *Biological Conservation* 17:157–62.

Halpern, B. S. 2003. The impact of marine reserves: Do reserves work and does reserve size matter? *Ecological Applications* 13:S117–37.

Halpern, E., and J. Wilson. 2003. A sellout, or just practical? He's the biologist who pioneered use of land swaps to help builders develop acreage where endangered species live. Critics call him a traitor. *Los Angeles Times*, March 14.

Hanski, I. 1999. *Metapopulation ecology.* Oxford: Oxford University Press.

Hard, J. J., R. G. Kope, W. S. Grant, F. W. Waknitz, L. T. Parker, and R. S. Waples. 1996. Status review of pink salmon from Washington, Oregon, and California. Technical memorandum NMFS-NWFSC-25. U.S. Department of Commerce, National Oceanic and Atmospheric Administration. Seattle.

Hargrove, E. C. 2000. Toward teaching environmental ethics: Exploring problems in the language of evolving social values. *Canadian Journal of Environmental Education* 5:1–20.

Harris, F. A., and D. MacDonald. 2003. President's hook: Relevance in public policy. *Fisheries* 28:4–6.

Hart, J. F. 1996. Colonial land use law and its significance for modern takings doctrine. *Harvard Law Review* 109:1252–59.

———. 2004. Fish, dams, and James Madison: Eighteenth-century species protection and the original understanding of the takings clause. *Maryland Law Review* 63:287–319.

Hartley, E. N. 1957. *Ironworks on the Saugus.* Norman: University of Oklahoma Press.

Harvell, C. D., K. Kim, J. M. Burkholder, R. R. Colwell, P. R. Epstein, D. J. Grimes, E. E. Hofmann, et al. 1999. Emerging marine diseases: Climate links and anthropogenic factors. *Science* 285:1505–10.

Hays, S. P. 1957. *The response to industrialism: 1885–1914.* Chicago: University of Chicago Press.

———. 1959. *Conservation and the gospel of efficiency: The progressive conservation movement, 1890–1920.* Cambridge, Mass.: Harvard University Press.

Healey, M. C. 1991. Life history of chinook salmon (*Oncorhynchus tshawytscha*). Pp. 311–94 in *Pacific salmon life histories*, ed. C. Groot and L. Margolis. Vancouver: University of British Columbia Press.

Hein, D. 1995. Traditional education in natural resources. Pp. 75–88 in *A new century for natural resources management*, ed. R. L. Knight and S. F. Bates. Washington, D.C.: Island Press.

Heppell, S. S., and L. B. Crowder. 1998. Prognostic evaluation of enhancement programs using population models and life history analysis. *Bulletin of Marine Science* 62:495–507.

Heppell, S. S., L. B. Crowder, and D. T. Crouse. 1996. Models to evaluate headstarting as a management tool for long-lived turtles. *Ecological Applications* 6:556–65.

Heywood, V. H., ed. 1995. *Global biodiversity assessment.* Cambridge, U.K.: UNEP and Cambridge University Press.

Hilborn, R., T. P. Quinn, D. E. Schindler, and D. E. Rogers. 2003. Biocomplexity and fisheries sustainability. *Proceedings of the National Academy of Sciences of the United States of America* 100:6564–68.

Hirzel, A. H., V. Helfer, and F. Metral. 2001. Assessing habitat-suitability models with a virtual species. *Ecological Modelling* 145:111–21.

Hitt, N. P., C. A. Frissell, C. C. Muhlfeld, and F. W. Allendorf. 2003. Spread of hybridization between native westslope cutthroat trout (*Oncorhynchus clarki lewisi*) and nonnative rainbow trout (*Oncorhynchus mykiss*). *Canadian Journal of Fisheries and Aquatic Sciences* 60:1440–51.

Hobday, A. J., and M. J. Tegner. 2000. Status review of white abalone (*Haliotis sorenseni*) throughout its range in California and Mexico. Technical memorandum NOAA-TM-NMFS-SWR-035. U.S. Department of Commerce, National Oceanic and Atmospheric Administration. http://www.nmfs.noaa.gov/pr/readingrm/statrvws/whiteab.pdf.

Hoekstra, J. M., J. A. Clark, W. F. Fagan, and P. D. Boersma. 2002a. A comprehensive review of Endangered Species Act recovery plans. *Ecological Applications* 12:630–40.

Hoekstra, J. M., W. F. Fagan, and J. E. Bradley. 2002b. A critical role for critical habitat in the recovery planning process? Not yet. *Ecological Applications* 12:701–7.

Holmes, E. E. 2001. Estimating risks in declining populations with poor data. *Proceedings of the National Academy of Sciences of the United States of America* 98:5072–77.

Holmes, E. E., and W. F. Fagan. 2002. Validating population viability analyses for corrupted data sets. *Ecology* 83:2379–86.

Home Builders Association of Northern California v. U.S. Fish and Wildlife Service. 2003. 268 F. Supp. 2d 1197. U.S. District Court for the Eastern District of California.

Hood, L. C. 1998. *Frayed safety nets: Conservation planning under the Endangered Species Act.* Washington, D.C.: Defenders of Wildlife.

Hooper, D. U., M. Solan, A. Symstad, S. Díaz, M. O. Gessner, N. Buchmann, V. Degrange, et al. 2002. Species diversity, functional diversity, and ecosystem functioning. Pp. 195–208 in *Biodiversity and ecosystem functioning: Synthesis and perspectives,* ed. M. Loreau, S. Naeem, and P. Inchausti. Oxford: Oxford University Press.

Hornaday, W. T. 1931. *Thirty years war for wild life: Gains and losses in the thankless task.* New York: Charles Scribner's Sons.

Horner-Devine, M. C., G. C. Daily, P. R. Ehrlich, and C. L. Boggs. 2003. Countryside biogeography of tropical butterflies. Conservation Biology 17: 168-177.

Horwitz, M. J. 1977. *The transformation of American law, 1780–1860.* Cambridge, Mass.: Harvard University Press.

Hosmer, D. W., and S. Lemeshow. 2000. *Applied logistic regression.* 2d ed. New York: John Wiley.

Houck, O. A. 1993. The Endangered Species Act and its implementation by the U.S. Departments of Interior and Commerce. *University of Colorado Law Review* 64:277–370.

Hughes, J. B., G. C. Daily, and P. R. Ehrlich. 1997. Population diversity: Its extent and extinction. *Science* 278:689–92.

———. 2002. Conservation of tropical forest birds in countryside habitats. *Ecology Letters* 5:121–29.

Humphries, C. J., P. H. Williams, and R. I. Vane-Wright. 1995. Measuring biodiversity value for conservation. *Annual Review of Ecology and Systematics* 26:93–111.

Huntley, B. 1995. Plant species' response to climate change: Implications for the conservation of European birds. *Ibis* 1 (137): S127–38.

Huntsman, G. R. 1994. Endangered marine finfish: Neglected resources or beasts of fiction? *Fisheries* 19:8–15.

Hurst, J. W. 1956. *Law and the conditions of freedom in the nineteenth-century United States.* Madison: University of Wisconsin Press.

Hutchings, J. A. 2001. Conservation biology of marine fishes: Perceptions and caveats regarding assignment of extinction risk. *Canadian Journal of Fisheries and Aquatic Science* 58:108–21.

Hynning, C. J. 1939. *State conservation of resources.* Washington, D.C.: U.S. Government Printing Office.

Ihlanfeldt, K., and T. Shaughnessy. 2002. An empirical investigation of the effects of impact fees on housing and land markets. Paper presented at the Lincoln Institute of Land Policy, Cambridge, Mass., July 10–12. Product code CPO2A13..

Inciardi, J. A. 1986. *The war on drugs: Heroin, cocaine, crime, and public policy.* Palo Alto, Calif.: Mayfield.

Inhabitants of the Towns of Stoughton, Sharon, and Canton v. Baker. 1808. 4 Mass. 522. Massachusetts Supreme Judicial Court.

Innes, R., S. Polasky, and J. Tschirhart. 1998. Takings, compensation, and endangered species protection on private lands. *Journal of Economic Perspectives* 12:35–52.

Irvin, W. R. 1995. Statement of William Robert Irvin to the United States Senate Committee on Environmental and Public Works, Subcommittee on Drinking Water, Fisheries, and Wildlife. July 13.

Irwin, E. 2002. The effects of open space on residential property values. *Land Economics* 78 (4): 465–80.

Isenberg, A. 2000. *The destruction of the bison.* New York: Cambridge University Press.

IUCN (International Union for the Conservation of Nature). 1994. *IUCN Red list categories.* Gland, Switzerland: IUCN Council.

———. 2003. *Red list of threatened species.* http://www.redlist.org.

Jackson, J. B. C., M. X. Kirby, W. H. Berger, K. A. Bjorndal, L. W. Botsford, B. J. Bourque, R. H. Bradbury, et al. 2001. Historical overfishing and the recent collapse of coastal ecosystems. *Science* 293:629–37.

Jakobsson, K. M., and A. K. Dragun. 1996. *Contingent valuation and endangered species: Methodological issues and applications,* ed. W. E. Oates. Cheltenham, U.K.: Edward Elgar.

James, F. C. 1980. Miscegenation in the dusky seaside sparrow? *BioScience* 30:800–1.

Jasny, M., J. Reynolds, and A. Notthoff. 1997. *A leap of faith: Southern California's experiment in natural community conservation planning.* New York: Natural Resources Defense Council.

Jenkins, C. N., R. D. Powell, O. L. Bass Jr., and S. L. Pimm. 2003. Demonstrating the destruction of the habitat of the Cape Sable seaside sparrow (*Ammodramus maritimus mirabilis*). *Animal Conservation* 6:29–38.

Jenkins, M. 1992. Species extinction. Pp. 192–205 in *Global biodiversity,* ed. B. Groombridge. World Conservation Monitoring Centre. London: Chapman and Hall.

Jensen, D. B., M. Torn, and J. Harte. 1993. *In our own hands: A strategy for conserving California's biological diversity.* Berkeley: University of California Press.

Johnson, L. B. 1965. Natural beauty: Message from the president of the United States. *Congressional Record* 111:2087.

Johnson, O. W., W. S. Grant, R. G. Kope, K. Neely, F. W. Waknitz, and R. S. Waples. 1997. Status review of chum salmon from Washington, Oregon, and California. Technical memorandum NMFS-NWFSC-32. U.S. Department of Commerce, National Oceanic and Atmospheric Administration. Seattle.

Johnson, O. W., M. H. Ruckelshaus, W. S. Grant, F. W. Waknitz, A. M. Garrett, G. J. Bryant, K. Neely, and J. J. Hard. 1999. Status review of coastal cutthroat trout from Washington, Oregon, and California. Technical memorandum NMFS-NWFSC-37. U.S. Department of Commerce, National Oceanic and Atmospheric Administration. Seattle.

Jonas, A. E. G., and D. Wilson, eds. 1999. *The urban growth machine: Critical perspectives two decades later.* New York: State University of New York Press.

Jorgenson, D., and P. Wilcoxon. 1990. Environmental regulation and U.S. economic growth. *Rand Journal of Economics* 21:314–40.

Kant, I. 1785. *Foundations of the metaphysics of morals.* Trans. L. W. Beck, 1959. New York: Bobbs Merril.

Kappel, C. V. 2005. Losing pieces of the puzzle: Threats to marine, estuarine, and diadromous species. *Frontiers in Ecology and the Environment* 3:275–82.

Kareiva, P. M., S. Andelman, D. F. Doak, B. Elderd, M. Groom, J. Hoekstra, L. Hood, et al. 1998. *Using science in habitat conservation plans.* National Center for Ecological Analysis and Synthesis. http://www.aibs.org/books/resources/hcp-1999-01-14.pdf.

Kareiva,, P., T. H. Tear, S. Solie, M. L. Brown, L. Sotomayor, and C. Yuan-Farrell. 2006. Nongovernmental organizations. Pp. 176–92 in *The Endangered Species Act at thirty: Renewing the conservation promise,* ed. D. D. Goble, J. M. Scott, and F. W. Davis. Washington, D.C.: Island Press.

Karl, J. W., L. K. Svancara, P. J. Heglund, N. M. Wright, and J. M. Scott. 2002. Species commonness and the accuracy of habitat-relationship models. Pp. 573–80 in *Predict-*

ing species occurrences: Issues of accuracy and scale, ed. J. M. Scott, P. J. Heglund, M. L. Morrison, J. B. Haufler, M. B. Raphael, W. A. Wall, and F. B. Samson. Washington, D.C.: Island Press.

Keith, D. A., M. McCarthy, H. Regan, T. Regan, C. Bowles, C. Drill, C. Craig, et al. 2004. Protocols for listing threatened species can forecast extinction. *Ecology Letters* 7:1101–8.

Kennedy, T., S. Naeem, K. Howe, J. Knops, D. Tilman, and P. B. Reich. 2002. Biodiversity as a barrier to ecological invasion. *Nature* 417:636–38.

King County. Endangered Species Act Policy Coordination Office. 2002a. *Conserving salmon: King County accomplishments and action plan.* Seattle.

———. 2002b. Endangered Species Act Policy Coordination Office. *Overview of laws and policies for critical areas protection in King County.* Seattle.

Kleijn, D., F. Berendse, R. Smit, and N. Gilissen. 2001. Agri-environment schemes do not effectively protect biodiversity in Dutch agricultural landscapes. *Nature* 413:723–25.

Klute, D. S., M. J. Lovallo, and W. M. Tzilkowski. 2002. Autologistic regression modeling of American woodcock habitat use with spatially dependent data. Pp. 335–43 in *Predicting species occurrences: Issues of accuracy and scale*, ed. J. M. Scott, P. J. Heglund, M. L. Morrison, J. B. Haufler, M. B. Raphael, W. A. Wall, and F. B. Samson. Washington, D.C.: Island Press.

Knapp, S. 2003. Dynamic diversity. *Nature* 422:475.

Knowlton, N. 2001. The future of coral reefs. *Proceedings of the National Academy of Sciences of the United States of America* 98:5419–25.

Koslow, J. A., G. W. Boehlert, J. D. M. Gordon, R. L. Haedrich, P. Lorance, and N. Parin. 2000. Continental slope and deep-sea fisheries: Implications for a fragile ecosystem. *ICES Journal of Marine Science* 57:548–57.

Kostow, K. E., ed. 1995. *Biennial report on the status of wild fish in Oregon.* Portland: Oregon Department of Fish and Wildlife.

Kostyack, J. 1998. Surprise. *Environmental Forum* 15:19–28.

Kousky, C. 2004. Chicago skyscrapers go dark for migratory birds. *Terrain.org* online journal. Issue 15, fall/winter. http://www.terrain.org/articles/15/kousky.htm.

Krebs, J. R., J. D. Wilson, R. B. Bradbury, and G. M. Siriwardena. 1999. The second Silent Spring? *Nature* 400:611–12.

Kremen, C., N. M. Williams, and R. W. Thorp. 2002. Crop pollination from native bees at risk from agricultural intensification. *Proceedings of the National Academy of Sciences of the United States of America* 99:16812–16.

Kulik, G. 1985. Dams, fish, and farmers: Defense of public rights in eighteenth-century Rhode Island. Pp. 25–50 in *The countryside in the age of capitalist transformation*, ed. S. Hahn and J. Prude. Chapel Hill: University of North Carolina Press.

Kyle, D. G. 1998. *Spectacles of death in ancient Rome: Approaching the ancient world.* New York: Routledge.

Lafferty, K. D., R. O. Swenson, and C. C. Swift. 1996. Threatened fishes of the world: *Eucyclogobius newberryi Girard*, 1857 (Gobiidae). *Environmental Biology of Fishes* 46:254.

Landis, J. D., and M. Reilly. 2002. *How we will grow: Baseline projections of California's urban footprint through the year 2100.* Institute of Urban and Regional Development. Berkeley: University of California.

Landis, J. D., M. Smith-Heimer, M. Larice, M. Reilly, M. Corley, and O. Jerchow. 2000. *Raising the roof: California housing development and constraints, 1997–2020.*

Prepared by the University of California, Berkeley Institute of Urban and Regional Development, in collaboration with HCD. Sacramento: California Department of Housing and Community Development.

Langford, I. H., A. Kontogianni, M. S. Skourtos, S. Georgiou, and I. J. Bateman. 1998. Multivariate mixed models for open-ended contingent valuation data: Willingness to pay for conservation of monk seals. *Environmental and Resource Economics* 12:443–56.

Launer, A. E., and D. D. Murphy. 1994. Umbrella species and the conservation of habitat fragments: A case of a threatened butterfly and a vanishing grassland ecosystem. *Biological Conservation* 69:145–53.

Laurance, W. F., S. G. Laurance, L. V. Ferreira, J. M. Rankin-de Merona, C. Gascon, and T. E. Lovejoy. 1997. Biomass collapse in Amazonian forest fragments. *Science* 278:1117–18.

Lavorel, S., and E. Garnier. 2002. Predicting changes in community composition and ecosystem functioning from plant traits: Revisiting the Holy Grail. *Functional Ecology* 16:545–56.

Lawton, J. H., and V. K. Brown. 1993. Redundancy in ecosystems. Pp. 255–70 in *Biodiversity and ecosystem function*, ed. E. D. Schulze and H. A. Mooney. New York: Springer-Verlag.

Lawton, J. H., and R. H. May, eds. 1994. *Extinction rates*. Oxford: Oxford University Press.

Legal Information Institute. 2005. *Constitutions, statutes, and codes.* Ithaca, N.Y.: Legal Information Institute. Also available online at http://www.law.cornell.edu/statutes .html.

Lens, L., S. Van Dongen, K. Norris, M. Githiru, and E. Matthysen. 2002. Avian persistence in fragmented rainforest. *Science* 298:1236–38.

Leopold, A. 1930. Report to the American Game Conference on an American game policy. (Also called "American Game Policy of 1930.") *Transactions of the Seventeenth American Game Conference* 17:284.

———. 1933. *Game management.* New York: Charles Scribner's Sons.

———. 1953. *Round river: From the journals of Aldo Leopold,* ed. L. B. Leopold. New York: Oxford University Press.

———. 1991. Threatened species (1936). Pp. 230–34 in *The river of the mother of God and other essays,* ed. S. L. Flader and J. Baird Callicott. Madison: University of Wisconsin Press.

Levine, J. M. 2000. Species diversity and biological invasions: Relating local process to community pattern. *Science* 288:852–54.

Levine, J. M., and C. M. D'Antonio. 1999. Elton revisited: A review of evidence linking diversity and invasibility. *Oikos* 87:15–26.

Levine, J. M., T. Kennedy, and S. Naeem. 2002. Neighbourhood scale effects of species diversity on biological invasions and their relationship to community patterns. Pp. 114–24 in *Biodiversity and ecosystem functioning: Synthesis and perspectives,* ed. M. Loreau, S. Naeem, and P. Inchausti. Oxford: Oxford University Press.

Lewison, R. L., S. A. Freeman, and L. B. Crowder. 2004. Quantifying the effects of fisheries on threatened species: The impact of pelagic longlines on loggerhead and leatherback sea turtles. *Ecology Letters* 7:221–31.

Link, A. S., and R. L. McCormick. 1983. *Progressivism.* Arlington, Ill.: Harlan Davidson.

Lint, J., and J. Martin. 2005. Introduction. Pp. 1–9 in *Northwest forest plan—The first ten years (1994–2003): Status and trend of northern spotted owl populations and habitat* (draft), ed. J. Lint. Washington, D.C.: U.S. Department of Agriculture. Also available online at http://www.reo.gov/monitoring/10yr-report/northern-spotted-owl/documents/owl_text%20and%20tables.pdf.

Lockwood, J. L., G. J. Russell, J. L. Gittleman, C. C. Daehler, M. L. McKinney, and A. Purvis. 2002. A metric for analyzing taxonomic patterns of extinction risk. *Conservation Biology* 16:1137–42.

Lodge, D. M. 1993. Biological invasions: Lessons for ecology. *Trends in Ecology and Evolution* 8:133–37.

Lomolino, M. V. 2004. Introduction to conservation biogeography. Pp. 294–96 in *Frontiers of biogeography*, ed. M. V. Lomolino and L. R. Heaney. Sunderland, Mass.: Sinauer Associates.

Lomolino, M. V., and R. Channell. 1995. Splendid isolation: Patterns of range collapse in endangered mammals. *Journal of Mammalogy* 76:335–47.

———. 1998. Range collapse, re-introductions, and biogeographic guidelines for conservation. *Conservation Biology* 12:481–84.

Lomolino, M. V., R. Channell, D. R. Perault, and G. A. Smith. 2001. Downsizing nature: Anthropogenic dwarfing of species and ecosystems. Pp. 223–44 in *Biotic homogenization: The loss of diversity through invasion and extinction*, ed. M. McKinney and J. Lockwood. London: Plenum Press.

Loomis, J. B., and D. S. White. 1996. Economic benefits of rare and endangered species: Summary and meta-analysis. *Ecological Economics* 18:197–206.

Loreau, M., S. Naeem, and P. Inchausti, eds. 2002. *Biodiversity and ecosystem functioning: Synthesis and perspectives*. Oxford: Oxford University Press.

Loreau, M., S. Naeem, P. Inchausti, J. Bengtsson, J. P. Grime, A. Hector, D. U. Hooper, et al. 2001. Biodiversity and ecosystem functioning: Current knowledge and future challenges. *Science* 294:806–8.

Lubchenko, J. 1998. Entering the century of the environment: A new social contract for science. *Science* 279:491–97.

Luck, G. W., G. C. Daily, and P. R. Ehrlich. 2003. Population diversity and ecosystem services. *Trends in Ecology and Evolution* 18:331–36.

Luck, G. W., T. H. Ricketts, G. C. Daily, and M. Imhoff. 2004. Alleviating spatial conflict between people and biodiversity. *Proceedings of the National Academy of Sciences of the United States of America* 101:182–86.

Ludwig, D. 1999. Is it meaningful to estimate a probability of extinction? *Ecology* 80:298–310.

Lund, T. A. 1976. Early American wildlife law. *New York University Law Review* 51:703–30.

MacCall, A., and X. He. 2002. *Status review of the southern stock of bocaccio (Sebastes paucispinis)*. Santa Cruz, Calif.: Santa Cruz Laboratory, Southwest Fisheries Science Center, and National Marine Fisheries Service. Also available online at http://santacruz.nmfs.noaa.gov/files/pubs/00366.pdf.

Mack, R. N., D. Simberloff, W. M. Lonsdale, H. Evans, M. Clout, and F. A. Bazzaz. 2000. Biotic invasions: Causes, epidemiology, global consequences and control. *Issues in Ecology* 5:1–22.

Maestas, J. D., R. L. Knight, and W. C. Gilgert. 2002. Cows, condos, or neither: What's best for rangeland ecosystems? *Rangelands* 24:36–42.

———. 2003. Biodiversity across a rural land-use gradient. *Conservation Biology* 17 (5): 1425–34.

Manly, B. F. J., L. L. McDonald, D. L. Thomas, T. L. McDonald, and W. P. Erickson. 2002. *Resource selection by animals: Statistical design and analysis for field studies.* 2d ed. Dordrecht, Netherlands: Kluwer.

Mansfield, K. G., and E. D. Land. 2002. Cryptorchidism in Florida panthers: Prevalence, features, and influence of genetic restoration. *Journal of Wildlife Diseases* 38:693–98.

Manson, C. 1994. Natural communities conservation planning: California's new ecosystem approach to biodiversity. *Environmental Law* 24:603–15.

———. 2003. Testimony of Craig Manson, assistant secretary for fish and wildlife and parks, Department of the Interior, before the Subcommittee on Fisheries, Wildlife and Water of the Senate Committee on Environment and Public Works, regarding the designation of critical habitat under the Endangered Species Act. April 10. http://laws.fws.gov/TESTIMON/2003/2003april10.html.

———. 2004. Endangered and threatened wildlife and plants: Proposed designation of critical habitat for the Santa Barbara County District population segment of the California tiger salamander. *Federal Register* 69:3064.

Mapes, L. V. 2001. Lynx-fur furor focuses on science role. *Seattle Times*, December 30.

Marbled Murrelet v. Lujan. 1992. No. C91-522, filed April 17. U.S. District Court for the Western District of Washington.

Margules, C. R., and R. L. Pressey. 2000. Systematic conservation planning. *Nature* 405:243–53.

Martin, E. T. 1879. Among the pigeons. *Chicago Field* 10:385–86.

Martin, P. S. 1984. Prehistoric overkill. Pp. 354–403 in *Quaternary extinctions: A prehistoric revolution,* ed. P. S. Martin and R. G. Klein. Tucson: University of Arizona Press.

Matlock, R. B., D. Rogers, P. J. Edwards, and S. G. Martin. 2002. Avian communities in forest fragments and reforestation areas associated with banana plantations in Costa Rica. *Agriculture, Ecosystems, and Environment* 91:199–215.

May, R. M. 1974. *Stability and complexity in model ecosystems.* Princeton, N.J.: Princeton University Press.

May, R. M., J. H. Lawton, and N. E. Stork. 1995. Assessing extinction rates. Pp. 1–24 in *Extinction rates,* ed. J. H. Lawton and R. M. May. Oxford: Oxford University Press.

McCann, K. S. 2000. The diversity-stability debate. *Nature* 405:228–33.

McCann, K. S., A. Hastings, and G. R. Huxel. 1998. Weak trophic interactions and the balance of nature. *Nature* 395:794–97.

McCarthy, M. A., and L. S. Broome. 2000. A method for validating stochastic models of population viability: A case study of the mountain pygmy-possum (*Burramys parvus*). *Journal of Animal Ecology* 69:599–607.

McCarthy, M. A., D. Keith, J. Tietjen, M. A. Burgman, M. Maunder, L. Master, B. Brooks, et al. 2004. Comparing predictions of extinction risk using models and subjective judgement. *Acta Oecologica* 26:67–74.

McCarthy, M. A., H. P. Possingham, J. R. Day, and A. J. Tyre. 2001. Testing the accuracy of population viability analysis. *Conservation Biology* 15:1030–38.

McClanahan, T. R., and R. Arthur. 2001. The effect of marine reserves and habitat on populations of East African coral reef fishes. *Ecological Applications* 11:559–69.

McClanahan, T. R., and N. A. Muthiga. 1998. An ecological shift in a remote coral atoll of Belize over 25 years. *Environmental Conservation* 25:122–30.

McElhany, P., M. H. Ruckelshaus, M. J. Ford, T. Wainwright, and E. P. Bjorkstedt. 2000. *Viable salmonid populations and the recovery of evolutionarily significant units.* Technical memorandum NMFS-NWFSC-42. U.S. Department of Commerce, National Oceanic and Atmospheric Administration. Seattle.

McFarlin v. Essex Company. 1852. 64 Mass. 304 (10 Cush.). Massachusetts Supreme Judicial Court.

McGerr, M. 2003. *A fierce discontent: The rise and fall of the progressive movement in America, 1870–1920.* New York: Free Press.

McGuire, A. D., J. M. Melillo, L. A. Joyce, D. W. Kicklighter, A. L. Grace, B. Moore III, and C. J. Vorosmarty. 1992. Interactions between carbon and nitrogen dynamics in estimating net primary productivity for potential vegetation in North America. *Global Biogeochemical Cycles* 6:101–24.

McNeely, J. A., and S. J. Scherr. 2002. *Ecoagriculture: Strategies to feed the world and save wild biodiversity.* Washington, D.C.: Island Press.

McNulty, F. 1966. *The whooping crane: The bird that defies extinction.* New York: E. P. Dutton.

McPhail, J. D., and C. C. Lindsey. 1986. Zoogeography of the freshwater fishes of Cascadia (the Columbia system and rivers north to the Stikine). Pp. 615–37 in *The zoogeography of North American freshwater fishes,* ed. C. H. Hocutt and E. O. Wiley. New York: John Wiley.

Meine, C. D. 1988. *Aldo Leopold: His life and work.* Madison: University of Wisconsin Press.

———. 1995. The oldest task in human history. Pp. 7–36 in *A new century for natural resources management,* ed. R. L. Knight and S. F. Bates. Washington, D.C.: Island Press.

Meyer, S. 2001. Community politics and endangered species protection. Pp. 138–65 in *Protecting endangered species in the United States: Biological needs, political realities, economic choices,* ed. J. Shogren and J. Tschirhart. Cambridge, U.K.: Cambridge University Press.

Miami Herald. 2003. Florida panther fatalities rising on state's roadways. June 18.

Middle Rio Grande Conservancy District v. Babbitt. 2000. 206 F. Supp. 2d 1156. U.S. District Court for the District of New Mexico.

Mill, J. S. 1863. *Utilitarianism.* London: Longmans.

Millennium Ecosystem Assessment. 2003. *Ecosystems and human well-being: A framework for assessment.* Washington, D.C.: Island Press. Also available online at http://pubs.wri.org/pubs_description.cfm?PubID=3927.

———. 2005a. *Ecosystems and human well-being: Biodiversity synthesis.* Washington, D.C.: World Resources Institute.

———. 2005b. *Living beyond our means: Natural assets and human well-being.* Statement from the Board. Washington, D.C. Also available online at http://www.maweb .org/en/products.aspx.

Miller, G. 1996. Ecosystem management: Improving the Endangered Species Act. *Ecological Applications* 6:715–17.

Millett, K. 2004. Birds on a cool green roof. *Chicago Wilderness Magazine.* Summer. http://www.chicagowildernessmag.org/issues/summer2004/greenroof.html.

Mills, L. S. 2002. False samples are not the same as blind controls: Informal efforts to "test" a laboratory corrupt the data stream, where integrity is crucial. *Nature* 415:471.

Milstein, M. 2004. Scientists predict gloomy future for coastal marbled murrelets. *Portland Oregonian*, May 5.

Missouri v. Holland. 1920. 252 U.S. 416. U.S. Supreme Court.

Mladenoff, D. J., T. A. Sickley, and A. P. Wydeven. 1999. Predicting gray wolf landscape recolonization: Logistic regression models vs. new field data. *Ecological Applications* 9:37–44.

Montgomery, C., G. Brown Jr., and M. Darius. 1994. The marginal cost of species preservation: The northern spotted owl. *Environmental Economics and Management* 26:111–28.

Moritz, C. 1994. Defining "evolutionarily significant units" for conservation. *Trends in Ecology and Evolution* 9:373–75.

———. 2002. Strategies to protect biological diversity and the evolutionary processes that sustain it. *Systematic Biology* 51:238–54.

Morris III, W. J. 1997. *I've seen all the rooms: Female prostitution in Las Vegas.* Winston-Salem, N.C.: Wake Forest University.

Morris, W., D. F. Doak, M. Groom, P. M. Kareiva, J. Fieberg, L. Gerber, P. Murphy, and D. Thompson. 1999. *A practical handbook for population viability analysis.* Washington, D.C.: The Nature Conservancy.

Morrison, S. A., and D. T. Bolger. 2002. Lack of an urban edge effect on reproduction in a fragmentation-sensitive sparrow. *Ecological Applications* 12:398–11.

Morton, T. 1637. *New English Canaan.* Photo-reprint. Amsterdam.

Murphy, M. T. 2003. Avian population trends within the evolving agricultural landscape of the eastern and central United States. *Auk* 120:20–34.

Musick, J. A. 1999. Criteria to define extinction risk in marine fishes: The American Fisheries Society initiative. *Fisheries* 24:6–14.

Musick, J. A., M. M. Harbin, S. A. Berkeley, G. H. Burgess, A. M. Eklund, L. Findley, R. G. Gilmore, et al. 2000. Marine, estuarine, and diadromous fish stocks at risk of extinction in North America (exclusive of Pacific salmonids). *Fisheries* 25:6–30.

Myer, S. M. 2001. Community politics and endangered species protection. Pp. 138–65 in *Protecting endangered species in the United States: Biological needs, political realities, economic choices,* ed. J. Shogren and J. Tschirhart. Cambridge, U.K.: Cambridge University Press.

Myers, J. M., R. G. Kope, G. J. Bryant, D. Teel, L. J. Lierheimer, T. C. Wainwright, W. S. Grant, et al. 1998. *Status review of chinook salmon from Washington, Idaho, Oregon, and California.* Technical memorandum NMFS-NWFSC-35. U.S. Department of Commerce, National Oceanic and Atmospheric Administration. Seattle.

Myers, N., R. A. Mittermeier, C. G. Mittermeier, G. A. B. Da Fonseca, and J. Kent. 2000. Biodiversity hotspots for conservation priorities. *Nature* 403:853–58.

Myers, R. A., S. A. Levin, R. Lande, F. C. James, W. W. Murdoch, and R. T. Paine. 2004. Hatcheries and endangered salmon. *Science* 303:1980.

Myers, R. A., and B. Worm. 2003. Rapid worldwide depletion of predatory fish communities. *Nature* 423:280–83.

Naeem, S. 1998. Species redundancy and ecosystem reliability. *Conservation Biology* 12:39–45.

———. 2000. Reply to Wardle et al. *Bulletin of the Ecological Society of America* 81:241–46.

————. 2001. How changes in biodiversity may affect the provision of ecosystem services. Pp. 3–33 in *Managing human dominated ecosystems*, ed. V. Hollowel. St. Louis: Missouri Botanical Garden Press.

————. 2002a. Autotrophic-heterotrophic interactions and their impacts on biodiversity and ecosystem functioning. Pp. 96–114 in *The functional consequences of biodiversity: Empirical progress and theoretical extensions*, ed. A. Kinzig, S. W. Pacala, and D. Tilman. Princeton, N.J.: Princeton University Press.

————. 2002b. Ecosystem consequences of biodiversity loss: The evolution of a paradigm. *Ecology* 83:1537–52.

Naeem, S., D. Hahn, and G. Schuurman. 2000a. Producer-decomposer co-dependency influences biodiversity effects. *Nature* 403:762–64.

Naeem, S., J. M. H. Knops, D. Tilman, K. M. Howe, T. Kennedy, and S. Gale. 2000b. Plant diversity increases resistance to invasion in the absence of covarying extrinsic factors. *Oikos* 91:97–108.

Naeem, S., and S. Li. 1997. Biodiversity enhances ecosystem reliability. *Nature* 390:507–9.

Naeem, S., L. J. Thompson, S. P. Lawler, J. H. Lawton, and R. M. Woodfin. 1994. Declining biodiversity can alter the performance of ecosystems. *Nature* 368:734–37.

Naeem, S., and J. P. Wright. 2003. Disentangling biodiversity effects on ecosystem functioning: Deriving solutions to a seemingly insurmountable problem. *Ecology Letters* 6:567–79.

National Association of Home Builders v. Norton. 2003. 340 F. 3d 835. U.S. Court of Appeals for the 9th Judicial Circuit.

National Research Council. Committee on Scientific Issues in the Endangered Species Act. 1995. *Science and the Endangered Species Act.* Washington, D.C.: National Academies Press.

————. Committee on Protection and Management of Pacific Northwest Anadromous Salmonids. 1996a. *Upstream: Salmon and society in the Pacific Northwest.* Washington, D.C.: National Academies Press.

————. Commission on Engineering and Technical Systems. 1996b. *Stemming the tide: Controlling introductions of nonindigenous species by ships' ballast water.* Washington, D.C.: National Academies Press.

————. Committee on Grand Canyon Monitoring and Research. 1999a. *Downstream: Adaptive management of Glen Canyon Dam and the Colorado River ecosystem.* Washington, D.C.: National Academies Press.

————. Committee on Ecosystem Management for Sustainable Marine Fisheries. 1999b. *Sustaining marine fisheries.* Washington, D.C.: National Academies Press.

————. Committee on Missouri River Ecosystem Science. 2002a. *The Missouri River ecosystem: Exploring the prospects for recovery.* Washington, D.C.: National Academies Press.

————. 2002b. Committee on Endangered and Threatened Fishes in the Klamath River Basin. *Scientific evaluation of biological opinions on endangered and threatened fishes in the Klamath River Basin.* Interim report. Washington, D.C.: National Academy Press.

————. Committee on the Alaska Groundfish Fishery and Steller Sea Lions. 2003a. *The decline of the Steller sea lion in Alaskan waters: Untangling food webs and fishing nets.* Washington, D.C.: National Academies Press.

———. Committee on Oil in the Sea: Inputs, Fates, and Effects. 2003b. *Oil in the sea 3: Inputs, fates, and effects.* Washington, D.C.: National Academies Press.

———. 2004a. Committee on Endangered and Threatened Fishes in the Klamath River Basin. *Endangered and threatened fishes in the Klamath River Basin: Causes of decline and strategies for recovery.* Washington, D.C.: National Academies Press.

———. 2004b. Committee on Endangered and Threatened Species in the Platte River Basin. *Endangered and threatened species of the Platte River.* Washington, D.C.: National Academies Press.

———. 2004c. Committee on Water Resources Management, Instream Flows, and Salmon Survival in the Columbia River Basin. *Managing the Columbia River: Instream flows, water withdrawals, and salmon survival.* Washington, D.C.: National Academies Press.

———. Committee on Atlantic Salmon in Maine. 2004d. *Atlantic salmon in Maine.* Washington, D.C.: National Academies Press.

———. Committee on Assessing and Valuing the Services of Aquatic and Related Terrestrial Ecosystems. 2005. *Valuing ecosystem services: Toward better environmental decision-making.* Washington, D.C.: National Academies Press.

National Wildlife Federation v. NMFS. 2003. 254 F. Supp. 2d 1196. U.S. District Court for the District of Oregon.

NatureServe. 2003. Home page. http://www.natureserve.org.

Nee, S., and R. M. May. 1997. Extinction and the loss of evolutionary history. *Science* 278:692–94.

Nelson, G. J., and N. I. Platnick. 1981. *Systematics and biogeography: Cladistics and vicariance.* New York: Columbia University Press.

Nelson, W. E. 1975. *Americanization of the common law.* Cambridge, Mass.: Harvard University Press.

New Mexico Cattle Growers Association v. U.S. Fish and Wildlife Service. 2001. 248 F. 3d 1277. U.S. Court of Appeals for the 10th Judicial Circuit.

Nicholls, C. I., M. Parrella, and M. A. Altieri. 2001. The effects of a vegetational corridor on the abundance and dispersal of insect biodiversity within a northern California organic vineyard. *Landscape Ecology* 16:133–46.

Nielsen, J. L., ed. 1995. *Evolution and the aquatic ecosystem: Defining unique units in population conservation.* Bethesda, Md.: American Fisheries Society.

Nielsen, J. L., J. M. Scott, and J. L. Aycrigg. 2001. Letter to the editor. Endangered species and peripheral populations: Cause for conservation. *Endangered Species Update* 18:193–94.

NMFS (National Marine Fisheries Service). 1991. Notice of policy: Policy on applying the definition of species under the Endangered Species Act to Pacific salmon. *Federal Register* 56:58612–18.

———. 1992. Office of Protected Resources. *Recovery planning guidelines.* Silver Spring, Md.

———. 1994. Listing endangered and threatened species and designating critical habitat: Initiation of status reviews of pink salmon, chum salmon, sockeye salmon, chinook salmon, and sea-run cutthroat trout populations in Washington, Oregon, Idaho, and California. *Federal Register* 59:46808–10.

———. 1997. Threatened fish and wildlife: Change in listing status of Steller sea lions under the Endangered Species Act. *Federal Register* 62:24345–55.

———. National Oceanic and Atmospheric Administration. 1998. *Biological opinion: Water withdrawal for the Columbia River.* Washington, D.C.

———. 2000a. Reinitiation of consultation on the Federal Columbia Power System (FCRPS) including the Juvenile Fish Transportation Program and nineteen Bureau of Reclamation projects in the Columbia Basin. http://www.nwr.noaa.gov/1publcat/bo/2000/2000.html.

———. 2002a. Endangered and threatened wildlife and plants: 12-month finding for a petition to list the barndoor skate (*Dipturus laevis*) as threatened or endangered. *Federal Register* 67:61055–61.

———. 2002b. Endangered and threatened wildlife and plants: 12-month finding on a petition to list the Atlantic white marlin as threatened or endangered. *Federal Register* 67:57204–7.

———. 2002c. Endangered and threatened wildlife and plants: 12-month finding for a petition to list southern resident killer whales as threatened or endangered under the Endangered Species Act (ESA). *Federal Register* 67:44133–38.

———. 2002d. Office of Protected Resources. *Biennial report to Congress on the recovery program for threatened and endangered species.* Silver Spring, Md.

———. 2002e. Endangered and threatened wildlife and plants: 12-month finding on a petition to list bocaccio as threatened. *Federal Register* 67:69704–8.

———. 2003a. *Updated status of federally listed ESUs of West Coast salmon and steelhead.* July. West Coast Salmon Biological Review Team, Northwest Fisheries Science Center, Seattle, and Southwest Fisheries Science Center, Santa Cruz, Calif.

———. 2003b. Endangered and threatened species: Final endangered status for a distinct population segment of smalltooth sawfish (*Pristis pectinata*) in the United States. *Federal Register* 68:15674–80.

———. 2003c. Fisheries of the exclusive economic zone off Alaska: Steller sea lion protection measures for the groundfish fisheries off Alaska. *Federal Register* 68:204–36.

———. 2004a. Endangered and threatened species: Proposed policy on the consideration of hatchery-origin fish in Endangered Species Act listing determinations for Pacific salmon and steelhead. *Federal Register* 69:31354–59.

———. 2004b. Endangered and threatened species: Establishment of species of concern list, addition of species to species of concern list, description of factors for identifying species of concern, and revision of candidate species list under the Endangered Species Act. *Federal Register* 69:19975–79.

———. 2004c. Pink abalone (*Haliotis corrugata*): Species of concern profile. http://www.nmfs.noaa.gov/prot_res/species/concern/profiles/pink_abalone.pdf.

———. 2004d. Green abalone (*Haliotis fulgens*): Species of concern profile http://www.nmfs.noaa.gov/prot_res/species/concern/profiles/green_abalone.pdf.

———. 2005a. Policy on the consideration of hatchery-origin fish in Endangered Species Act listing determinations for Pacific salmon and steelhead. *Federal Register* 70:37204–16.

———. 2005b. Endangered and threatened wildlife and plants: Endangered status for southern resident killer whales; final rule. *Federal Register* 70:69903–12.

NOAA (National Oceanic and Atmospheric Administration. 2001. NOAA wins first prosecution using satellite-based vessel monitoring system. Press release 2001-R153. http://www.publicaffairs.noaa.gov/releases2001/dec01/noaa01r153.html.

Nordhaus, W. D., and J. Tobin. 1972. Is growth obsolete? Pp. 1–80 in *Economic research: Retrospect and Prospect, Economic Growth*. Vol. 5. National Bureau of Economic Research Fiftieth Anniversary Colloquium. New York: Columbia University Press.

Norris, D., N. Phelps, and D. J. Schubert. 2001. *Canned hunts: The newest American "sport."* Silver Spring, Md.: Fund For Animals.

Norse, E. A., C. B. Grimes, S. Ralston, R. Hilborn, J. C. Castilla, S. R. Palumbi, D. Fraser, and P. M. Kareiva. 2003. Marine reserves: The best option for our oceans? *Frontiers in Ecology and the Environment* 1:495–502.

Norton, B. G. 1987. *Why preserve natural variety? Studies in moral, political, and legal philosophy*. Princeton, N.J.: Princeton University Press.

———. 1991. *Toward unity among environmentalists*. New York: Oxford University Press.

———. 2005. *Sustainability: A philosophy of adaptive ecosystem management*. Chicago: University of Chicago Press.

Norton, B. G., and A. Steinemann. 2003. Environmental values and adaptive management. Pp. 514–48 in *Searching for sustainability: Interdisciplinary essays on the philosophy of conservation biology*, ed. B. G. Norton. New York: Cambridge University Press.

Nosil, P., B. J. Crespi, and C. P. Sandoval. 2002. Host-plant adaptation drives the parallel evolution of reproductive isolation. *Nature* 417:440–43.

Noss, R. F., M. A. O'Connell, and D. D. Murphy. 1997. *The science of conservation planning: Habitat conservation under the Endangered Species Act*. Washington, D.C.: Island Press.

Novak, W. J. 1996. *The people's welfare*. Chapel Hill: University of North Carolina Press.

Nowak, J. E., and R. E. Rotunda. 2000. *Constitutional law*. 6th ed. St. Paul, Minn.: West Group.

Nowak, R. M. 1992. The red wolf is not a hybrid. *Conservation Biology* 6:593–95.

O'Brien, S. J., and E. Mayr. 1991. Bureaucratic mischief: Recognizing endangered species and subspecies. *Science* 251:1187–88.

Office of Management and Budget (OMB). 2003. *Regulatory analysis*. Circular A-4. September 17. Washington, D.C.

Office of the President. 1981. Executive order 12291 of February 17. Federal regulation. *Federal Register* 46:13193–98.

Olson, D. M., E. Dinerstein, E. D. Wikramanayake, N. D. Burgess, G. V. N. Powell, E. C. Underwood, J. A. D'amico, et al. 2001. Terrestrial ecoregions of the world: A new map of life on earth. *Bioscience* 51:933–38.

Orfield, M. W. 1997. *Metropolitics: A regional agenda for community and stability*. Washington, D.C.: Brookings Institution Press.

Pain, D. J., D. Hill, and D. I. McCracken. 1997. Impact of agricultural intensification of pastoral systems on bird distributions in Britain 1970–1990. *Agriculture, Ecosystems and Environment* 64:19–32.

Paine, R. T. 2002. Trophic control of production in a rocky intertidal community. *Science* 296:736–39.

Palmer, M., and T. A. Maurer. 1997. Does diversity beget diversity: A case study of crops and weeds. *Journal of Vegetation Science* 8:235–40.

Palmer, T. S. 1899. A review of economic ornithology in the United States. *U.S. Department of Agriculture Yearbook* 259–92.

Palumbi, S. R. 2002. *Marine reserves: A tool for ecosystem management and conservation.* Arlington, Va.: Pew Oceans Commission.

Parmesan, C., and G. Yohe. 2003. A globally coherent fingerprint of climate change impacts across natural systems. *Nature* 421:37–42.

Pascual, M. A., and M. D. Adkison. 1994. The decline of the Steller sea lion in the northeast Pacific: Demography, harvest, or environment? *Ecological Applications* 4:393–403.

Patlis, J. 2001. Paying tribute to Joseph Heller with the Endangered Species Act: When critical habitat isn't. *Stanford Environmental Law Journal* 20:133.

Patterson, J. 1999. Growth management efforts and the takings clause: Planning for growth. *Western City* 75:8.

Paulsen, C. M., and R. A. Hinrichsen. 2002. Experimental management for Snake River spring/summer chinook (*Oncorhynchus tshawytscha*): Trade-offs between conservation and learning for a threatened species. *Canadian Journal of Fisheries and Aquatic Sciences* 59:717–25.

Pauly, D. 1995. Anecdotes and the shifting baseline syndrome of fisheries. *Trends in Ecology and Evolution* 10:430.

Pauly, D., V. Christensen, J. Dalsgaard, R. Froese, and F. Torres Jr. 1998. Fishing down marine food webs. *Science* 279:860–63.

Pavlik, B. M. 2003. Plants that protect ecosystems: A survey from California. *Biodiversity and Conservation* 12:717–29.

Peery, C. A., K. L. Kavanagh, and J. M. Scott. 2003. Pacific salmon: Setting ecologically defensible recovery goals. *BioScience* 53:622–23.

Perlman, D. L., and G. Adelson. 1997. *Biodiversity: Exploring values and priorities in conservation.* Malden, Mass.: Blackwell Science.

Perrings, C. 1995. Biodiversity conservation as insurance. Pp. 69–77 in *The economics and ecology of biodiversity decline: The forces driving global change,* ed. T. M. Swanson. Cambridge, U.K.: Cambridge University Press.

Peters, R. L., and T. E. Lovejoy, eds. 1994. *Global warming and biological diversity.* New Haven, Conn.: Yale University Press.

Peterson, G. D., G. S. Cumming, and S. R. Carpenter. 2003. Scenario planning: A tool for conservation in an uncertain world. *Conservation Biology* 17:358–66.

Pew Oceans Commission. 2003. *America's living oceans: Charting a course for sea change.* Arlington, Va..

Pfeifer, S. 2003. New plan to protect bird endangers the same projects: Latest proposal to protect the gnatcatcher could halt a toll road extension and the Rancho Mission Viejo home development. *Los Angeles Times,* April 25.

Pfisterer, A. B., and B. Schmid. 2002. Diversity-dependent production can decrease the stability of ecosystem functioning. *Nature* 416:84–86.

Phillips, J. C. 1934. *Migratory bird protection in North America.* Special publication no. 4, American Committee for International Wild Life Protection.

Pianin, E. 2003. Judge orders river level lowered; Endangered Species Act takes precedence, ruling says. *Washington Post,* August 7.

Pienkowski, M. W., ed. 1998. Forum papers: Biodiversity and high-nature-value farming systems. *Journal of Applied Ecology* 35:948–90.

Pinchot, G. 1947. *Breaking new ground.* New York: Harcourt Brace.

Pisani, D. J. 1996. Forests and conservation, 1865–1890. Pp. 124–40 in *Water, land,*

and law in the West: The limits of public policy, 1850–1920, ed. D. J. Pisani. Lawrence: University Press of Kansas.

Pitkin v. Olmstead. 1790. 1 Root's Reports 217. Hartford County Superior Court, Connecticut.

Pittock, A. B. 1999. Coral reefs and environmental change: Adaptation to what? *American Zoologist* 39:10–29.

Platt, R. H. 1996. *Land use and society: Geography, law, and public policy.* Washington, D.C.: Island Press.

Polasky, S., and H. Doremus. 1998. When the truth hurts: Endangered species policy on private land with imperfect information. *Environmental Economics and Management* 35:22–47.

Power, M. E., D. Tilman, J. A. Estes, B. A. Menge, W. J. Bond, L. S. Mills, G. C. Daily, J. C. Castilla, J. Lubchenco, and R. T. Paine. 1996. Challenges in the quest for keystones. *BioScience* 46:287–309.

Powles, H., M. J. Bradford, R. G. Bradford, W. G. Doubleday, S. Innes, and C. D. Levings. 2000. Assessing and protecting endangered marine species. *ICES Journal of Marine Sciences* 57:669–76.

Puget Sound Technical Recovery Team. 2002. Planning ranges and preliminary guidelines for the delisting and recovery of the Puget Sound Chinook salmon evolutionarily significant unit. April 30. http://www.nwfsc.noaa.gov/trt/trtpopesu.pdf.

Purvis, A., P. M. Agapow, J. L. Gittleman, and G. M. Mace. 2000a. Nonrandom extinction and the loss of evolutionary history. *Science* 288:328–30.

Purvis, A., J. L. Gittleman, G. Cowlishaw, and G. M. Mace. 2000b. Predicting extinction risk in declining species. *Proceedings of the Royal Society of London, Series B: Biological Sciences* 267:1947–52.

Pyare, S., and J. Berger. 2003. Beyond demography and delisting: Ecological recovery for Yellowstone's grizzly bears and wolves. *Biological Conservation* 113:63–73.

Quinn, T. C. 1993. A review of homing and straying of wild and hatchery-produced salmon. *Fisheries Research* 18:29–44.

Rabalais, N. N., and R. E. Turner. 2001. *Coastal hypoxia: Consequences for living resources and ecosystems.* Washington, D.C.: American Geophysical Union.

Raffaelli, D., W. H. Van der Putten, L. Persson, D. A. Wardle, O. L. Petchey, J. Koricheva, V. D. Heijden, J. Mikola, and T. Kennedy. 2002. Multi-trophic dynamics and ecosystem processes. Pp. 147–54 in *Biodiversity and ecosystem functioning: Syntheses and perspectives*, ed. M. Loreau, S. Naeem, and P. Inchausti. Oxford: Oxford University Press.

Ralls, K., S. R. Beissinger, and J. F. Cochrane. 2002. Guidelines for using population viability analysis in endangered species management. Pp. 521–50 in *Population viability analysis*, ed. S. R. Beissinger and D. R. McCullough. Chicago: University of Chicago Press.

Raubenheimer, E. J. 2000. Development of tusks and tusklessness in African elephant (*Loxodonta africana*). *Koedoe* 43:57–64.

Rausser, G., and A. Small. 2000. Valuing research leads: Bioprospecting and the conservation of genetic resources. *Journal of Political Economy* 108:173–206.

Raven, P. R., and E. O. Wilson. 1992. A fifty-year plan for biodiversity surveys. *Science* 258:1099–1100.

Rawls, John. 1971. *A theory of justice.* Oxford: Clarendon Press.

Reaves, D. W., R. A. Kramer, and T. Holmes. 1999. Does question format matter? Valuing an endangered species. *Environmental and Resource Economics.* 14:365–83.

Reed, J. M. 1996. Using statistical probability to increase confidence of inferring species extinction. *Conservation Biology* 10:1283–85.

Reed, J. M., L. S. Mills, J. B. Dunning Jr., E. S. Menges, K. S. McKelvey, R. Frye, S. Beissinger, M. C. Anstett, and P. Miller. 2002. Emerging issues in population viability analysis. *Conservation Biology* 16:7–19.

Regan, T. 1983. *The case for animal rights.* Berkeley: University of California Press.

Rejmánek, M. 2003. The rich get richer: Responses. *Frontiers in Ecology and the Environment* 1:122–23.

Rhymer, J. M., and D. Simberloff. 1996. Extinction by hybridization and introgression. *Annual Review of Ecological Systematics* 27:83–109.

Ricker, W. E. 1972. Hereditary and environmental factors affecting certain salmonid populations. Pp. 19–160 in *The stock concept in Pacific salmon,* ed. R. C. Simon and P. A. Larkin. H. R. Macmillan Lectures in Fisheries. Vancouver: University of British Columbia Press.

Ricketts, T. H., G. C. Daily, P. R. Ehrlich, and J. P. Fay. 2001. Countryside biogeography of moths in a fragmented landscape: Biodiversity in native and agricultural habitats. *Conservation Biology* 15:378–88.

Ricketts, T. H., E. Dinerstein, T. Boucher, T. M. Brooks, S. H. M. Butchart, M. Hoffman, J. F. Lamoreux, et al. 2005. Pinpointing and preventing imminent extinctions. *Proceedings of the National Academy of Science* 102:18497–501.

Rinkevich, S. E., and S. C. Leon. 2000. Stakeholders assist species recovery in the Southwest. *Endangered Species Bulletin* 25:28–29.

Riverside County Habitat Conservation Agency. 1996. *Habitat conservation plan for the Stephens' kangaroo rat in western Riverside County, California.*

Robbins, C. S., and E. T. Blom, eds. 1996. *Atlas of the breeding birds of Maryland and the District of Columbia.* Maryland Ornithological Society and Maryland Department of Natural Resources. Pittsburgh: University of Pittsburgh Press.

Roby, D. D., D. E. Lyons, D. P. Craig, K. Collis, and G. H. Visser. 2003. Quantifying the effect of predators on endangered species using a bioenergetics approach: Caspian terns and juvenile salmonids in the Columbia River estuary. *Canadian Journal of Zoology* 81:250–65.

Rohlf, D. J. 1989. *The Endangered Species Act: A guide to its protections and implementation.* Stanford: Stanford Environmental Law Society.

———. 2001. Jeopardy under the Endangered Species Act: Playing a game protected species can't win. *Washburn Law Journal* 41:114–58.

Rojas, M. 1992. The species problem and conservation: What are we protecting? *Conservation Biology* 6:170–78.

Rolston III, H. 1994. *Conserving natural value: Perspectives in biological diversity.* New York: Columbia University Press.

Roosevelt Campobello International Park Commission v. U.S. Environmental Protection Agency. 1982. 684 F. 2d 1041. U.S. Court of Appeals for the 1st Judicial Circuit.

Roosevelt, T. 1893. *The wilderness hunter.* New York: G. P. Putnam's Sons.

Root, T. L., J. T. Price, K. R. Hall, S. H. Schneider, C. Rosenzweig, and A. Pounds. 2003. "Fingerprints" of global warming on wild animals and plants. *Nature* 421:57–60.

Rosenberg, A. A. 2002. The precautionary approach from a manager's perspective. *Bulletin of Marine Science* 70:577–88.

Rosenzweig, M. L. 2003a. Reconciliation ecology and the future of species diversity. *Oryx* 37:194–205.

———. 2003b. *Win-win ecology: How the Earth's species can survive in the midst of human enterprise.* Oxford: Oxford University Press.

———. 2006. Beyond set-asides. Pp. 259–73 in *The Endangered Species Act at thirty: Renewing the conservation promise,* ed. D. D. Goble, J. M. Scott, and F. W. Davis. Washington, D.C.: Island Press.

Rothman, D. J., E. Rose, T. Awaya, B. Cohen, A. Daar, S. L. Dzemeshkevich, C. J. Lee, et al. 1997. The Bellagio Task Force Report on transplantation, bodily integrity, and the international traffic in organs. *Transplantation Proceedings* 29:2739–45.

Roy, J., B. Saugier, and H. A. Mooney, eds. 2001. *Terrestrial productivity.* San Diego: Academic Press.

Rubidge, E. 2003. Molecular analysis of hybridization between native westslope cutthroat trout (*Oncorhynchus clarki lewisi*) and introduced rainbow trout (*O. mykiss*) in southeastern British Columbia. Master's thesis, Department of Zoology, University of British Columbia.

Rubidge, E., P. Corbett, and E. B. Taylor. 2001. A molecular analysis of hybridization between native westslope cutthroat trout (*Oncorhynchus clarki lewisi*) and introduced rainbow trout (*O. mykiss*) in southeastern British Columbia. *Journal of Fish Biology* 59:42–54.

Rubin, J., G. Helfand, and J. Loomis. 1991. A benefit-cost analysis of the northern spotted owl. *Journal of Forestry* 89:25–30.

Ruckelshaus, M., P. McElhany, and M. J. Ford. 2002a. Recovering species of conservation concern: Are populations expendable? Pp. 305–29 in *The importance of species—perspectives on expendability and triage,* ed. Peter M. Kareiva and S. A. Levin. Princeton, N.J.: Princeton University Press.

Ruckelshaus, M. H., P. Levin, J. Johnson, and P. M. Kareiva. 2002b. The Pacific salmon wars: What science brings to the challenge of recovering species. *Annual Review of Ecology and Systematics* 33:665–706.

Ruckelshaus, M. H., P. McElhany, M. McClure, and S. Heppell. 2004. Chinook salmon in Puget Sound: Effects of spatially correlated catastrophes on persistence. Pp. 208–18 in *Species conservation and management: Case studies,* ed. R. Akçakaya, M. Burgman, O. Kindvall, C. C. Wood, P. Sjögren-Gulve, J. S. Hatfield, and M. A. McCarthy. New York: Oxford University Press.

Ruhl, J. B. 1999. How to kill endangered species, legally: The nuts and bolts of the Endangered Species Act "HCP" permits for real estate development. *Environmental Lawyer* 5:345–405.

Rundle, H. D., L. Nagel, J. W. Boughman, and D. Schluter. 2000. Natural selection and parallel speciation in sympatric sticklebacks. *Science* 287:306–8.

Russ, G. R., A. C. Alcala, and A. P. Maypa. 2003. Spillover from marine reserves: The case of *Naso vlamingii* at Apo Island, the Philippines. *Marine Ecology Progress Series* 264:15–20.

Russ, G. R., A. C. Alcala, and A. P. Maypa, H. P. Calumpong, and A. T. White. 2004. Marine reserve benefits local fisheries. *Ecological Applications* 14:597–606.

Ryder, O. A. 1986. Species conservation and systematics: The dilemma of subspecies. *Trends in Ecology and Evolution* 1:9–10.

Sacramento Bee. 2003a. South county adrift; supervisor's plan: To hell with the hawk. August 10.

————. 2003b. Not so critical; habitat designation has become distraction. August 22.

Sagoff, M. 1988. *The economy of the Earth: Philosophy, law, and the environment.* Cambridge, U.K.: Cambridge University Press.

————. 1997. Muddle or muddle through: Takings jurisprudence meets the Endangered Species Act. *William and Mary Law Review* 38:825–993.

Salzman, J., and J. B. Ruhl. 2001. Apples for oranges: The role of currencies in environmental trading markets. *Environmental Law Reporter* 31:11438–74.

SANDAG (San Diego Association of Governments). 2001. *Solving the San Diego Region's Housing Crisis.* Affordable Housing Policy Resource Report. San Diego.

Sanderson, E. W., M. Jaiteh, M. A. Levy, K. H. Redford, A. V. Wannebo, and G. Woolmer. 2002. The human footprint and the last of the wild. *Bioscience* 52:891–904.

Sarewitz, D. 2004. How science makes environmental controversies worse. *Environmental Science and Policy* 7:385–403.

Sarkar, S. 2005. *Biodiversity and environmental philosophy: An introduction.* New York: Cambridge University Press.

Savage-Rumbaugh, S., and R. Lewin. 1994. *Kanzi: The ape at the brink of the human mind.* New York: John Wiley.

Sawyer, R. 1986. *Slavery in the twentieth century.* London: Routledge and Kegan.

Schindler, D. E., S. R. Carpenter, J. J. Cole, J. F. Kitchell, and M. L. Pace. 1997. Influence of food web structure on carbon exchange between lakes and the atmosphere. *Science* 277:248–51.

Schlesinger, W. H. 1997. *Biogeochemistry: An analysis of global change.* 2d. ed. San Diego: Academic Press.

Schmidt, N. M., and P. M. Jensen. 2003. Changes in mammalian body length over 175 years adaptations to a fragmented landscape. *Conservation Ecology* 7 (2): 6. http://www.consecol.org/vol7/iss2/art6.

Schonfeld, A. 1985. International trade in wildlife: How effective is the Endangered Species Treaty? *California Western International Law Journal* 15:111–60.

Schorger, A. W. 1955. *The passenger pigeon: Its natural history and extinction.* Norman: University of Oklahoma Press.

Schulze, E. D., and H. A. Mooney, eds. 1993. *Biodiversity and ecosystem function.* New York: Springer-Verlag.

Schwartz, M. K., K. L. Pilgrim, K. S. McKelvey, E. L. Lindquist, J. J. Claar, S. Loch, and L. F. Ruggiero. 2004. Hybridization between Canada lynx and bobcats: Genetic results and management implications. *Conservation Genetics* 5:349–55.

Schwartz, M. W. 1999. Choosing the appropriate scale of reserves for conservation. *Annual Review of Ecology and Systematics* 30:83–108.

Schwartz, M. W., N. L. Jurjavcic, and J. M. O'Brien. 2002. Conservation's disenfranchised urban poor. *BioScience* 52:601–6.

Scott, J. M., F. W. Davis, B. Csuti, B. Butterfield, C. Groves, H. Anderson, S. Caicco, et al. 1993. GAP analysis: A geographical approach to protection of biological diversity. *Wildlife Monographs* 123:1–41.

Scott, J. M., F. W. Davis, G. McGhie, and C. Groves. 2001. Nature reserves: Do they capture the full range of America's biological diversity? *Ecological Applications* 11:9999–10004.

Scott, J. M., D. D. Goble, L. K. Svancara, and A. Pidgorna. 2006. By the numbers. Pp. 16–35 in *The Endangered Species Act at thirty: Renewing the conservation promise*, ed. D. D. Goble, J. M. Scott, and F. W. Davis. Washington, D.C.: Island Press.

Scott, J. M., P. J. Heglund, M. L. Morrison, J. B. Haufler, M. B. Raphael, W. A. Wall, and F. B. Samson. 2002. *Predicting species occurrences: Issues of accuracy and scale*. Washington, D.C.: Island Press.

Scott, T. A., R. Standiford, and N. Pratini. 1995. Private landowners are critical to saving California biodiversity. *California Agriculture* 49:50–57.

Scott, T. A., and J. E. Sullivan. 2000. The selection and design of multiple species preserves. *Environmental Management* 26:S37–53.

Seattle Times. 2002. Leery of grizzly tests, legislator demands review of all endangered-species studies. January 10.

Seattle Public Utilities. n.d.a *Salmon-friendly gardening*. http://www.seattle.gov/util/Services/Yard/Natural_Lawn_&_Garden_Care/Salmon_Friendly_Gardening/index.asp.

———. n.d. *The Street Edge Alternatives Project*. http://www.seattle.gov/util/About_SPU/Drainage_&_Sewer_System/Natural_Drainage_Systems/Street_Edge_Alternatives/index.asp.

Sechrest, W., T. M. Brooks, G. A. B. da Fonseca, W. R. Konstant, R. A. Mittermeier, A. Purvis, A. B. Rylands, and J. L. Gittleman. 2002. Hotspots and the conservation of evolutionary history. *Proceedings of the National Academy of Sciences of the United States of America* 99:2067–71.

Shaffer, M. L. 1981. Minimum population sizes for species conservation. *BioScience* 31:131–34.

Shaffer, M. L., J. M. Scott, and F. Casey. 2002. Noah's options: Initial cost estimates of a national system of habitat conservation areas in the United States. *BioScience* 52:439–43.

Shelden, K. E. W., D. P. DeMaster, D. J. Rugh, and A. M. Olson. 2001. Developing classification criteria under the U.S. Endangered Species Act: Bowhead whales as a case study. *Conservation Biology* 15:1300–7.

Shogren, J., R. Smith, and J. Tschirhart. 2005. The role of private information in designing conservation incentives for property owners. Pp. 217–32 in *Species at risk: Using economic incentives to shelter endangered species on private lands*, ed. J. Shogren. Austin: University of Texas Press.

Shogren, J., and M. Toman. 2000. Climate change policy. Pp. 125–68 in *Public policies for environmental protection*, 2d ed., ed. P. Portney and R. Stavins. Washington, D.C.: Resources for the Future.

Shogren, J., J. Tschirhart, A. Ando, T. Anderson, S. Beissinger, D. Brookshire, G. Brown, D. Coursey, S. Meyer, and S. Polasky. 1999. Why economics matters for endangered species protection. *Conservation Biology* 13:1257–67.

Shuford, W. D., G. W. Page, and J. E. Kjelmyr. 1998. Patterns and dynamics of shorebird use of California's Central Valley. *Condor* 100:227–44.

Sierra Club. 2003. *Politics and issues: Campaign finance reform, dirty money = forest destruction*. http://www.sierraclub.org/politics/clean_elections/logging.asp.

Sierra Club v. U.S. Fish and Wildlife Service. 2001. 245 F. 3d 434. U.S. Court of Appeals for the 5th Judicial Circuit.

Simberloff, D. S. 1988. The contribution of population and community biology to conservation science. *Annual Review of Ecology and Systematics* 19:473–511.

Simberloff, D. S., and L. G. Abele. 1976. Island biogeography theory and conservation practice. *Science* 191:285–86.

Simpson, G. G. 1966. Mammalian evolution on southern continents. *Neues Jahrbuch für Geologie und Paläontologie* 125:1–18.

Sinden, A. 2004. The economics of endangered species: Why less is more in the economic analysis of critical habitat designations. *Harvard Environmental Law Review* 28:129–214.

Snow, D. 1996. The pristine silence of leaving it all alone. Pp. 27–38 in *A wolf in the garden: The land rights movement and the new environmental debate*, ed. P. D. Brick and R. M. Cawley. Savage, Md.: Rowman and Littlefield.

Soulé, M. E. 1983. What do we really know about extinction? Pp. 111–24 in *Genetics and conservation: A reference for managing wild animal and plant populations*, ed. C. M. Shonewald-Cox, S. M. Chambers, B. MacBryde, and W. L. Thomas. London: Benjamin/Cummings.

———. 1991. Conservation: Tactics for a constant crisis. *Science* 253:744–50.

Soulé, M. E., A. C. Alberts, and D. T. Bolger. 1992. The effects of habitat fragmentation on chaparral plants and vertebrates. *Oikos* 63:39–47.

Soulé, M. E., J. A. Estes, J. Berger, and C. Martinez del Rio. 2003. Ecological effectiveness: Conservation goals for interactive species. *Conservation Biology* 17:1238–50.

Southern California Association of Governments (SCAG). 2001. *State of the region: Measuring progress in the 21st century.* http://www.scag.ca.gov/publications/sotr01/sortofc.html.

Southwest Center for Biological Diversity v. Babbitt. 2000. 215 F. 3d 58. U.S. Court of Appeals for the District of Columbia Judicial Circuit.

Spirit of the Sage Council v. Norton. 2003. 294 F. Supp. 2d 67. U.S. District Court for the District of Columbia.

Springer, A. M., J. A. Estes, G. B. van Vliet, T. M. Williams, D. F. Doak, E. M. Danner, K. A. Forney, and B. Pfister. 2003. Sequential megafaunal collapse in the North Pacific Ocean: An ongoing legacy of industrial whaling? *Proceedings of the National Academy of Sciences of the United States of America* 100:12223–28.

Spring Valley Water Works v. Schottler. 1884. 110 U.S. 347. U.S. Supreme Court.

Standiford, R. B., and T. Scott. 2001. Value of oak woodlands and open space on private property values in Southern California. Special issue. *Investigación Agraria: Sistemas Y Recursos Forestales (Towards The New Forestlands Commercial And Environmental Benefits Accounting: Theories And Applications,)* ed. P. Campos Palacin 1:137–52.

Stanford Environmental Law Society. 2001. *The Endangered Species Act.* Palo Alto, Calif.: Stanford University Press.

Steadman, D. W. 1995. Prehistoric extinctions of Pacific island birds: Biodiversity meets zooarchaeology. *Science* 267:1123–31.

Steadman, D. W., and P. S. Martin. 1984. Extinctions of birds in the late Pleistocene of North America. Pp. 466–77 in *Quaternary extinctions: A prehistoric revolution*, ed. P. S. Martin and R. J. Klein. Tucson: University of Arizona Press.

Stein, B. A., L. L. Master, and L. E. Morse. 2002. Taxonomic bias and vulnerable species. *Science* 297:1807.

Steinberg, T. 1991. *Nature incorporated.* Amherst: University of Massachusetts Press.

Stiffler, L., and R. McClure. 2003. Spawning coho and dying early in restored creeks: Polluted stormwater appears to be lethal. *Seattle Post-Intelligencer*, February 6.

Stohlgren, T. J., D. T. Barnett, and J. T. Kartesz. 2003. The rich get richer: Patterns of plant invasions in the United States. *Frontiers in Ecology and the Environment* 1:11–14.

Stohlgren, T. J., D. Binkley, G. W. Chong, M. A. Kalkhan, L. D. Schell, K. A. Bull, Y. Otsuki, G. Newman, M. Bashkin, and Y. Son. 1999. Exotic plant species invade hot spots of native plant diversity. *Ecological Monographs* 69:25–46.

Stokstad, E. 2002. Fur flies over charges of misconduct. *Science* 295:250–51.

Stone, C. 1987. *Earth and other ethics: The case for moral pluralism.* New York: Harper and Row.

Strassel, K. A. 2002. The missing lynx; the latest Clinton scandal has fur flying in Washington. *Wall Street Journal*, January 24.

Strickland, D. 2001. Residents rally to prevent sprawl. *Los Angeles Times*, May 21.

Stuart, C., and T. Stuart. 1996. *Africa's vanishing wildlife.* Washington, D.C.: Smithsonian Institution Press.

Suarez, A. V., D. T. Bolger, and T. J. Case. 1998. Effects of fragmentation and invasion on native ant communities in coastal Southern California. *Ecology* 79:2041–56.

Suckling, K., and M. Taylor. 2006. Critical habitat and recovery. Pp. 75–89 in *The Endangered Species Act at 30: Renewing the conservation promise*, ed. D. D. Goble, J. M. Scott, and F. W. Davis. Washington, D.C.: Island Press.

Sullivan, J. E., and T. A. Scott. 2000. The Western Riverside County Multiple Species Habitat Conservation Plan: A study in the evolution of HCPs. *Endangered Species Update* 17:28–34.

Sunding, D. 2005. The economics of environmental regulation of housing development. *Housing and Society* 32 (1): 23–38.

Sunding, D., and B. Arnold. 2003. *Environmental Regulation of Land Use Changes: Framework and Application to the Housing Industry.* University of California, Berkeley.

Swain, H. 2006. A reality check from Florida. Pp. 137–40 in *The Endangered Species Act at thirty: Renewing the conservation promise*, ed. D. D. Goble, J. M. Scott, and F. W. Davis. Washington, D.C.: Island Press.

Symposium. 1992. *The Monist* 75 (2): 119–276.

Takacs, D. 1996. *The idea of biodiversity: Philosophies of paradise.* Baltimore, Md.: Johns Hopkins University Press.

Tarlock, A. D. 2006. The dynamic urban landscape. Pp. 127–36 in *The Endangered Species Act at thirty: Renewing the conservation promise*, ed. D. D. Goble, J. M. Scott, and F. W. Davis. Washington, D.C.: Island Press.

Taylor, B. L. 1995. The reliability of using population viability analysis for risk classification of species. *Conservation Biology* 9:551–58.

Taylor, E. B. 1991. A review of local adaptation in Salmonidac, with particular reference to Pacific and Atlantic salmon. *Aquaculture* 98:185–207.

Taylor, E. B., C. J. Foote, and C. C. Wood. 1996. Molecular genetic evidence for parallel life-history evolution within a Pacific salmon (sockeye salmon and kokanee, *Oncorhynchus nerka*). *Evolution* 50:401–16.

Taylor, E. B., M. D. Stamford, and J. S. Baxter. 2003. Population subdivision in westslope cutthroat trout (*Oncorhynchus clarki lewisi*) at the northern periphery of its range: Evolutionary inferences and conservation implications. *Molecular Ecology* 12:2609–22.

Taylor, M. F. J., K. F. Suckling, and J. J. Rachlinski. 2005. The effectiveness of the Endangered Species Act: A quantitative analysis. *BioScience* 55:335–49.

Taylor, P. W. 1986. *Respect for nature: A theory of environmental ethics.* Princeton, N.J.: Princeton University Press.

Tear, T. H., J. M. Scott, P. H. Hayward, and B. Griffith. 1993. Status and prospects for success of the Endangered Species Act: A look at recovery plans. *Science* 262:976–77.

Teel, D. J., G. B. Milner, G. A. Winans, and W. S. Grant. 2000. Genetic population structure and origin of life history types in chinook salmon in British Columbia, Canada. *Transactions of the American Fisheries Society* 129:194–209.

Tennant, T., M. F. Allen, and F. Edwards. 2001. *Perspectives in conservation biology in Southern California: I. Current extinction rates and causes.* Tucson, Ariz.: Center for Conservation Biology. Also available online at http://repositories.cdlib.org/ccb/SCAextinctions.

Tennessee Valley Authority v. Hill. 1978. 437 U.S. 153. U.S. Supreme Court.

Terborgh, J., L. Lopez, P. Nuñez, M. Rao, G. Shahabuddin, G. Orihuela, M. Riveros, et al. 2001. Ecological meltdown in predator-free forest fragments. *Science* 294:1923–26.

Thompson, B. H. Jr. 2006. Managing the working landscape. Pp. 101–26 in *The Endangered Species Act at thirty: Renewing the conservation promise*, ed. D. D. Goble, J. M. Scott, and F. W. Davis. Washington, D.C.: Island Press.

Thompson, J. N., and B. M. Cunningham. 2002. Geographic structure and dynamics of coevolutionary selection. *Nature* 417:735–38.

Thompson, T. C. 1985. The life course and labor of the colonial farmer. *Historical New Hampshire* 40:135–47.

Thoreau, H. D. 1849. *A week on the Concord and Merrimack Rivers* 31. New York: Library of America, 1989.

Thorgaard, G. H. 1983. Chromosomal differences among rainbow trout populations. *Copeia* 1983:650–62.

Thornton, R. D. 1991. Searching for consensus and predictability: Habitat conservation planning under the Endangered Species Act of 1973. *Environmental Law* 21:604–55.

Thorsnes, P. 2002. The value of a suburban forest preserve: Estimates from sales of vacant residential building lots. *Land Economics* 78 (3): 426–41.

Tigas, L. A., D. H. van Vuren, and R. M. Sauvajot. 2002. Behavioral responses of bobcats and coyotes to habitat fragmentation and corridors in an urban environment. *Biological Conservation* 108:299–306.

Tilman, D. 1997. Community invasibility, recruitment limitation, and grassland biodiversity. *Ecology* 78:81–92.

Tilman, D., and J. A. Downing. 1994. Biodiversity and stability in grasslands. *Nature* 367:363–65.

Tilman, D., R. M. May, C. L. Lehman, and M. A. Nowak. 1994. Habitat destruction and the extinction debt. *Nature* 371:65–66.

Tilman, D., P. B. Reich, J. Knops, D. Wedin, T. Mielke, and C. L. Lehman. 2001a. Diversity and productivity in a long-term grassland experiment. *Science* 294:843–45.

Tilman, D., J. Fargione, B. Wolff, C. D'Antonio, A. Dobson, R. Howarth, D. Schindler, W. H. Schlesinger, D. Simberloff, and D. Swackhamer. 2001b. Forecasting agriculturally driven global environmental change. *Science* 292:281–84.

Tucker, G. M. 1997. Priorities for bird conservation in Europe: The importance of the farmed landscape. Pp. 79–116 in *Farming and birds in Europe: The common agricultural policy and its implications for bird conservation*, ed. D. J. Pain and M. W. Pienkowski. San Diego: Academic Press.

Turner, F. J. 1894. The significance of the frontier in American history. Pp. 119–227 in *Annual report of the American Historical Association for the year 1893.* Washington, D.C.: American Historical Association.

United Nations. 1996. *The International Bill of Human Rights.* Fact sheet no. 2 (rev. 1). Geneva.

United States v. McCullagh. 1915. 221 F. 288. U.S. District Court for the District of Kansas.

United States v. Shauver. 1914. 214 F. 154. U.S. District Court for the Eastern District of Arkansas. Appeal dismissed, 1919. 248 U.S. 594. U.S. Supreme Court.

U.S. Census Bureau. 2004. Home page. http://www.census.gov/.

———. 2005. *New privately owned housing units authorized valuation for regions, divisions, and states.* Table 2av, showing building permits by state. November. http://www.census.gov/const/C40/Table2/tb2v2004.txt.

U.S. Coast Guard. 2001. *Pollution incidents in and around U.S. waters: A spill/release compendium: 1968–2000.* http://www.uscg.mil/hq/g-m/nmc/response/stats/aa.htm.

U.S. Commission on Ocean Policy. 2004. *Preliminary report of the U.S. Commission on Ocean Policy: Governor's draft.* Washington, D.C. Also available online at http://oceancommission.gov/documents/prelimreport/welcome.html.

U.S. Congress. 1912. Senate. Report no. 675, 62d Cong., 2d sess.

———. 1972. House. Committee on Merchant Marine and Fisheries, Subcommittee on Fisheries and Wildlife Conservation. *Predatory mammals and endangered species: Hearings before the Subcommittee on Fisheries and Wildlife Conservation of the House Committee on Merchant Marine and Fisheries.* 92d Cong., 2d sess., 144.

———. 1982. House. Conference Report no. 835, 97th Cong., 2d sess. Reprinted in *United States Code Congressional and Administrative News*, 1982:2860.

U.S. Department of the Interior. 1967. Native fish and wildlife: Endangered species. *Federal Register* 32:4001.

———. 1977a. Whether hybrids are covered by the Endangered Species Act. Memorandum from Acting Assistant Solicitor, Fish and Wildlife, to Deputy Associate Director, Federal Assistance, U.S. Fish and Wildlife Service. May 18. Washington, D.C.

———. 1977b. Reconsideration of solicitor's opinion with regard to hybrids. Memorandum from Deputy Associate Director, Federal Assistance, U.S. Fish and Wildlife Service, to Solicitor's Office. July 22. Washington, D.C.

———. 1977c. Whether hybrids are covered by the Endangered Species Act. Memorandum from Acting Assistant Solicitor, Fish and Wildlife, to Deputy Associate Director, Federal Assistance, U.S. Fish and Wildlife Service. August 2. Washington, D.C.

———. 1983a. Status of hybrid offspring of two endangered species. Memorandum from Assistant Solicitor, Fish and Wildlife, to Regional Solicitor, Northeast Region. September 21. Washington, D.C.

———. 1990b. Memorandum from Assistant Solicitor, Fish and Wildlife, to Director, U.S. Fish and Wildlife Service. December 14. Washington, D.C.

U.S. Department of the Interior and U.S. Department of Commerce. 1997. *American Indian tribal rights, federal-tribal trust responsibilities, and the Endangered Species Act.* Secretarial order no. 3206. http://www.fws.gov/endangered/tribal/Esatribe.htm.

USFWS. 1978a. Endangered and threatened wildlife and plants: De-listing of the Mexican duck. *Federal Register* 43:32258–61.

———. 1979. Endangered and threatened wildlife and plants: Notice of withdrawal of five expired proposals for listing of 1,876 species, and intent to revise 1975 plant notice which includes most of these species. *Federal Register* 44:70796–97.

———. 1981a. Endangered and threatened wildlife and plants: Proposed redefinition of "harm." *Federal Register* 46:29490–92.

———. 1981b. Endangered and threatened wildlife and plants: Final redefinition of "harm." *Federal Register* 46:54748–50.

———. 1983a. Endangered and threatened species listing and recovery priority guidelines. *Federal Register* 48:43098–105.

———. 1983b. Endangered and threatened species listing and recovery priority guidelines: Correction. *Federal Register* 48:51985.

———. 1983c. Final rule to reclassify Arctic peregrine falcon from endangered to threatened; clarify the status of American peregrine falcon (*Falco americanus anatum*) in some parts of its range; and classify all free-flying peregrine falcons in the conterminous 48 United States under similarity of appearance provisions under section 4(e) of the Act. *Federal Register* 48:10520.

———. 1985. Endangered and threatened wildlife and plants: Interior population of the least tern determined to be endangered. *Federal Register* 50:21784–92.

———. 1986. Endangered and threatened wildlife and plants: Proposed threatened status for the Florida population of Audubon's crested caracara. *Federal Register* 51:22838–42.

———. 1987. Endangered and threatened wildlife and plants: Reclassification of the American alligator to threatened due to similarity of appearance throughout the remainder of its range. *Federal Register* 52:21059–64.

———. 1988. Determination of endangered status for Stephen's kangaroo rat. *Federal Register* 53:38465–69.

———. 1990a. Endangered and threatened wildlife and plants: Determination of threatened status for the Mojave population of the desert tortoise. *Federal Register* 55:12178–91.

———. 1990b. *Policy and guidelines for planning and coordinating recovery of endangered and threatened species.* Recovery and delisting of endangered species program. Washington, D.C. Also available online at http://www.fws.gov/endangered/recovery/90guide.pdf.

———. 1991a. Endangered and threatened wildlife and plants: Endangered status for the Lower Keys population of the rice rat (silver rice rat); final rule. *Federal Register* 56:19809–14.

———. 1991b. Endangered and threatened wildlife and plants: Threatened status under "similarity of appearance" provisions for *Felis concolor* in Florida. *Federal Register* 56:40265–67.

———. 1992. Endangered and threatened wildlife and plants: Threatened status for the Louisiana black bear and related rules. *Federal Register* 57:588–95.

———. 1993. Endangered and threatened wildlife and plants: Determination of threatened status for the coastal California gnatcatcher. *Federal Register* 58:16742–57.

———. 1996a. Endangered and threatened wildlife and plants: Notice of final decision on identification of candidates for listing as endangered or threatened. *Federal Register* 61:64481–85.

———. 1996b. Endangered and threatened wildlife and plants: Reclassification of *Erigeron maguirei* (Maguire daisy) from endangered to threatened. *Federal Register* 61:31054–58.

———. 1996c. Endangered and threatened wildlife and plants: Final listing priority guidance for fiscal year 1997. *Federal Register* 61:64475–81.

———. 1996d. Issuance of permit for incidental take of endangered species (Stephens kangaroo rat), *Federal Register* 61 (124): 33135.

———. 1997a. Endangered and threatened wildlife and plants: Determination of endangered status for the cactus ferruginous pygmy-owl in Arizona. *Federal Register* 62:10730–47.

———. 1997b. Endangered and threatened wildlife and plants: Final rule to list the northern population of the bog turtle as threatened and the southern population as threatened due to similarity of appearance. *Federal Register* 62:59605–23.

———. 1998. Endangered and threatened wildlife and plants: New 12-month finding for a petition to list the Florida black bear. *Federal Register* 63:67613–18.

———. 1999a. Endangered and threatened wildlife and plants: Determination of threatened status for the plant *Helianthus paradoxus* (Pecos sunflower). *Federal Register* 64:56581–90.

———. 1999b. Endangered and threatened wildlife and plants: Emergency rule to list the Sierra Nevada distinct population segment of California bighorn sheep as endangered. *Federal Register* 64:19300–9.

———. 1999d. Endangered and threatened wildlife and plants: Final rule to remove the plant *Echinocereus lloydii* (Lloyd's hedgehog cactus) from the federal list of endangered and threatened plants. *Federal Register* 64:33796–800.

———. 1999e. Endangered and threatened wildlife and plants: Notice of intent to clarify the role of habitat in endangered species conservation. *Federal Register* 64:31871–74.

———. 1999f. Final rule: Safe harbor agreements and candidate conservation agreements with assurances. *Federal Register* 64:32706–16.

———. 1999g. Final rule with correction: Safe harbor agreements and candidate conservation agreements with assurances. *Federal Register* 64:52676.

———. 1999h. *Status review for westslope cutthroat trout in the United States.* U.S. Fish and Wildlife Service, Regions 1 and 6: Portland, Ore., and Denver, Colo. Also available online at http://mountain-prairie.fws.gov/species/fish/wct/cutthroat1.pdf.

———. 1999i. *U.S. Fish and Wildlife Service approves International Paper's red-cockaded woodpecker habitat conservation plan.* USFWS press release, February 18. http://www.fws.gov/southeast/news/1999/r99-021.html.

———. 1999j. Endangered and threatened wildlife and plants: Final listing priority guidance for the fiscal year 2000. *Federal Register* 64:57114–19.

———. 2000. Endangered and threatened wildlife and plants: Designation of critical habitat for the tidewater goby. *Federal Register* 65:69693–717.

———. 2001. Final Rule: Response to public comments on amending general permitting regulations relating to habitat conservation plans, Safe harbor agreements and candidate conservation agreements with assurances. *Federal Register* 66:6483–87.

———. 2002a. Endangered and threatened wildlife and plants: Candidate status review for Rio Grande cutthroat trout. *Federal Register* 67:39936–47.

———. 2002b. Endangered and threatened wildlife and plants: Notice of intent to prepare a status review for the westslope cutthroat trout. *Federal Register* 67:56257–59.

USFWS. 2003a. Endangered and threatened wildlife and plants: Designation of critical habitat for the coastal California gnatcatcher (*Polioptila californica*) and determination of distinct vertebrate population segment for the California gnatcatcher (*Polioptila californica*). *Federal Register* 68:20227–312.

———. 2003b. Endangered and threatened wildlife and plants: Final rule to reclassify and remove the gray wolf from the list of endangered and threatened wildlife in portions of the conterminous United States; establishment of two special regulations for threatened gray wolves. *Federal Register* 68:15804–61.

———. 2003c. Endangered and threatened wildlife and plants: Listing of the central California distinct population segment of the California tiger salamander; reclassification of the Sonoma County and Santa Barbara County distinct populations from endangered to threatened; special rule. *Federal Register* 68:39892–93.

———. 2003f. Endangered and threatened wildlife and plants: Reconsidered finding for an amended petition to list the westslope cutthroat trout as threatened throughout its range. *Federal Register* 68:46989–7009.

———. 2003g. *Guidance for the establishment, use, and operation of conservation banks.* Washington, D.C.: U.S. Fish and Wildlife Service. Also available online at http://www.fws.gov/endangered/policies/conservation-banking.pdf.

———. 2003h. Safe harbor agreements and candidate conservation agreements with assurances; Revisions to the regulations. *Federal Register* 68:53320–27.

———. 2003i. Endangered and threatened wildlife and plants: Designation of critical habitat for the gulf sturgeon; final rule. *Federal Register* 68:13369–495.

———. 2003j. Draft handbook for candidate conservation agreements with assurances and enhancement of survival permit processing. *Federal Register* 68:37170–73. Also available online at http://www.fws.gov/endangered/candidates/ccaa_handbook_contents/handbooktext.pdf.

———. 2004a. Endangered and threatened wildlife and plants: 90-day finding for a petition to list the eastern subspecies of the greater sage-grouse as endangered. *Federal Register* 69:933–36.

———. 2005. Conservation plans and agreements. Database. http://ecos.fws.gov/conserv_plans/public.jsp.

USFWS (U.S. Fish and Wildlife Service) and NMFS (National Marine Fisheries Service). 1986. Interagency cooperation: Endangered Species Act of 1973, as amended; final rule. *Federal Register* 51:19926–63.

———. 1994a. Endangered and threatened wildlife and plants: Notice of interagency cooperative policy for peer review in Endangered Species Act activities. *Federal Register* 59:34270.

———. 1994b. Endangered and threatened wildlife and plants: Notice of interagency cooperative policy for the ecosystem approach to the Endangered Species Act. *Federal Register* 59:34274–77.

———. 1994c. Endangered and threatened wildlife and plants: Notice of interagency cooperative policy on information standards under the Endangered Species Act. *Federal Register* 59:34271.

———. 1994d. Endangered and threatened wildlife and plants: Notice of interagency cooperative policy for Endangered Species Act section 9 prohibitions. *Federal Register* 59:34272.

———. 1994e. Endangered and threatened wildlife and plants: Notice of interagency cooperative policy regarding the role of state agencies in Endangered Species Act activities. *Federal Register* 59:34274–75.

————. 1994f. Endangered and threatened wildlife and plants: Notice of interagency cooperative policy on recovery plan participation and implementation under the Endangered Species Act. *Federal Register* 59:34272–73.

————. 1996a. Notice of availability of final handbook for habitat conservation planning and incidental take permitting process. *Federal Register* 61:63854–57.

————. 1996b. Policy regarding the recognition of distinct vertebrate population segments under the Endangered Species Act. *Federal Register* 61:4722–25.

————. 1996c. Notice of policy for conserving species listed or proposed for listing under the Endangered Species Act while providing and enhancing recreational fishing opportunities. *Federal Register* 61:27978–82.

————. 1996d. *Endangered species petition management guidance.* U.S. Department of the Interior, Fish and Wildlife Service, Division of Endangered Species, Washington, D.C.; and U.S. Department of Commerce, National Oceanic and Atmospheric Administration, National Marine Fisheries Service, Endangered Species Division, Silver Spring, Md.

————. 1996e. Policy regarding the recognition of distinct population segments under the Endangered Species Act. *Federal Register* 61:4722–4725.

————. 1996f. Endangered and threatened wildlife and plants: Proposed policy and proposed rule on the treatment of intercrosses and intercross progeny (the issue of "hybridization"); request for public comment. *Federal Register* 61:4710–13.

————. 1997. *Making the ESA work better: Implementing the 10 point plan and beyond.* Washington, D.C.

————. 1998. Habitat conservation plan assurances ("No Surprises") rule. *Federal Register* 63:8859–73.

————. 1999a. Notice of availability of Final Endangered Species Consultation Handbook for procedures for conducting consultation and conference activities under section 7 of the Endangered Species Act. *Federal Register* 64:31285–87.

————. 1999b. Announcement of final safe harbor policy. *Federal Register* 64:32717–26.

————. 1999c. Announcement of final policy for candidate conservation agreements with assurances. *Federal Register* 64:32726–36.

————. 1999d. Endangered and threatened wildlife and plants: Final listing priority guidance for fiscal year 2000. *Federal Register* 64:57114–19.

————. 1999e. Notice of availability of Final Endangered Species Consultation Handbook for procedures for conducting consultation and conference activities under section 7 of the Endangered Species Act. *Federal Register* 64:31285.

————. 2000a. Notice of availability of a final addendum to the handbook for habitat conservation planning and incidental take permitting process. *Federal Register* 65:35242–47.

————. 2000b. Announcement of draft policy for evaluation of conservation efforts when making listing decisions. *Federal Register* 65:37102–8.

————. 2000c. Policy regarding controlled propagation of species listed under the Endangered Species Act. *Federal Register* 65:56916–22.

————. 2000d. Endangered and threatened species: Final endangered status for a distinct population segment of anadromous Atlantic salmon (*Salmo salar*) in the Gulf of Maine. *Federal Register* 65:69459–83.

————. 2003a. Policy for evaluation of conservation efforts when making listing decisions. *Federal Register* 68:15100–15.

————. 2003b. Policy for evaluation of conservation efforts when making listing decisions. *Federal Register* 68:15100.

USFWS (U.S. Fish and Wildlife Service), BLM (Bureau of Land Management), NPS (National Park Service), BIA (Bureau of Indian Affairs), USFS (U.S. Forest Service), and NOAA (National Oceanic and Atmospheric Administration). 2003. Joint counterpart Endangered Species Act section 7 consultation regulations. *Federal Register* 68:68254–65.

Utter, F. M., D. Chapman, and A. R. Marshall. 1995. Genetic population structure and history of chinook salmon of the upper Columbia River. Pp. 149–65 in *Evolution and the aquatic ecosystem: Defining unique units in population conservation,* ed. J. L. Nielsen. Symposium 17. Bethesda, Md.: American Fisheries Society.

VanBlaricom, G. R., and J. A. Estes. 1998. *The community ecology of sea otters.* New York: Springer-Verlag.

Van Manen, F. T., J. D. Clark, S. E. Schlarbaum, K. Johnson, and G. Taylor. 2002. A model to predict the occurrence of surviving butternut trees in the southern Blue Ridge Mountains. Pp. 491–97 in *Predicting species occurrences: Issues of accuracy and scale,* ed. J. M. Scott, P. J. Heglund, M. L. Morrison, J. B. Haufler, M. B. Raphael, W. A. Wall, and F. B. Samson. Washington, D.C.: Island Press.

Vargas, A. M., M. Lockhart, P. Marinar, and P. Gober. 1996. The reintroduction process: black-footed ferrets as a case study. Pp. 829–34 in *Proceedings: American Zoo and Aquarium Association Western Regional Conference.* May 15–19. Denver: American Zoo and Aquarium Association.

Varner, G. E. 1998. *In nature's interests? Interests, animal rights, and environmental ethics.* New York: Oxford University Press.

Vartanyan, S. L., V. E. Garutt, and A. V. Sher. 1993. Holocene dwarf mammoths from Wrangel Island in the Siberian Arctic. *Nature* 362:337–39.

Vitousek, P. M., J. Aber, R. W. Howarth, G. E. Likens, P. A. Matson, D. W. Schindler, W. H. Schlesinger, and G. D. Tilman. 1997a. Human alteration of the global nitrogen cycle: Causes and consequences. *Issues in Ecology* 1:1–16.

Vitousek, P. M., H. A. Mooney, J. Lubchenco, and J. M. Melillo. 1997b. Human domination of Earth's ecosystems. *Science* 277:494–99.

Vogler, A. P., and R. DeSalle. 1994. Diagnosing units of conservation management. *Conservation Biology* 8:354–63.

Volpe, J. P., E. B. Taylor, D. W. Rimmer, and B. W. Glickman. 2000. Evidence of natural reproduction of aquaculture-escaped Atlantic salmon in a coastal British Columbia river. *Conservation Biology* 14:899–903.

Vrijenhoek, R. C. 1996. Conservation genetics of North American desert fishes. Pp. 367–97 in *Conservation genetics: Case histories from nature,* ed. J. C. Avise and J. L. Hamrick. London: Chapman and Hall.

Wainwright, T. C., and R. G. Kope. 1999. Methods of extinction risk assessment developed for U.S. West Coast salmon. *ICES Journal of Marine Science* 56:444–48.

Walker, B. H. 1992. Biodiversity and ecological redundancy. *Conservation Biology* 6:18–23.

Wallace, A. R. 1876. *The geographical distribution of animals: With a study of the relations of living and extinct faunas as elucidating the past changes of the Earth's surface.* London: Macmillan.

————. 1901. *Darwinism: An exposition of the theory of natural selection, with some of its applications.* 3rd ed. London: Macmillan.

Wallington, T. J., R. J. Hobbs, and S. A. Moore. 2005. Implications of current ecological thinking for biodiversity conservation: A review of the salient issues. *Ecology and Society* 10 (1): 15, http://www.ecologyandsociety.org/vol10/iss1/art15.

Walsh, R. G., R. D. Bjonback, R. A. Aiken, and D. H. Rosenthal. 1990. Estimating the public benefits of protecting forest quality. *Journal of Environmental Management* 30:175–89.

Walters, M. J. 1992. *A shadow and a song: The struggle to save an endangered species.* White River, Vt.: Chelsea Green.

Waples, R. S. 1991. Pacific salmon (*Oncorhynchus* spp.) and the definition of "species" under the Endangered Species Act. *Marine Fisheries Review* 53:11–22.

———. 1995. Evolutionarily significant units and the conservation of biological diversity under the Endangered Species Act. Pp. 8–27 in *Evolution and the aquatic ecosystem: Defining unique units in population conservation,* ed. J. L. Nielsen. Symposium 17. Bethesda, Md.: American Fisheries Society.

Waples, R. S., R. G. Gustafson, L. A. Weitkamp, J. M. Myers, O. W. Johnson, P. J. Busby, J. J. Hard, et al. 2001. Characterizing diversity in salmon from the Pacific Northwest. *Journal of Fish Biology* Suppl. A 59:1–41.

Waples, R. S., D. J. Teel, J. M. Myers, and A. R. Marshall. 2004. Life-history divergence in chinook salmon: Historic contingency and parallel evolution. *Evolution* 58:386–403.

Wardle, D. A., M. A. Huston, J. P. Grime, F. Berendse, E. Garnier, W. K. Lauenroth, H. Setälä, and S. D. Wilson. 2000. Biodiversity and ecosystem function: An issue in ecology. *Bulletin of the Ecological Society of America* 81:235–39.

Warner, K., and M. Molotch. 1995. Power to build: How development persists despite local controls. *Urban Affairs Review* 30 (3): 378–406.

Watling, L., and E. A. Norse. 1998. Disturbance of the seabed by mobile fishing gear: A comparison to forest clearcutting. *Conservation Biology* 12:1180–97.

Wayne, R. K., and S. M. Jenks. 1991. Mitochondrial DNA analysis implying extensive hybridization of the endangered red wolf (*Canis rufus*). *Nature* 351:565–68.

Weitkamp, L. A., P. Busby, and K. Neely. 1997. Geographical variation in life histories of salmonids. Pp. 20–22 in *Estuarine and ocean survival of northeastern Pacific salmon: Proceedings of the workshop,* ed. R. L. Emmett and M. H. Schiewe. March 20–22. Newport, Ore.

Weitkamp, L. A., T. C. Wainwright, G. J. Bryant, G. B. Milner, D. J. Teel, R. G. Kope, and R. S. Waples. 1995. *Status review of coho salmon from Washington, Oregon, and California.* Technical memorandum NMFS-NWFSC-24. U.S. Department of Commerce, National Oceanic and Atmospheric Administration. Seattle.

Wellman, C. 1985. *A theory of rights.* Totowa, N.J.: Rowman and Allenheld.

Wetzel, R. G. 2001. *Limnology: Lake and river ecosystems.* 3rd ed. San Diego: Academic Press.

Whitbourne, R. 1620. *A discourse and discovery of New-found-land.* Photo-reprint. London: William Barret.

Whitehouse, A. M. 2002. Tusklessness in the elephant population of the Addo Elephant National Park, South Africa. *Journal of Zoology* 257:249–54.

Whittaker, R. H. 1960. Vegetation of the Siskiyou Mountains, Oregon and California. *Ecological Monographs* 30:279–338.

Wiens, J. A. 2002. Predicting species occurrences: Progress, problems, and prospects. Pp. 739–49 in *Predicting species occurrences: Issues of accuracy and scale,* ed. J. M. Scott,

P. J. Heglund, M. L. Morrison, J. B. Haufler, M. B. Raphael, W. A. Wall, and F. B. Samson. Washington, D.C.: Island Press.

Wilcove, D. S., and M. McMillan. 2006. The class of '67. Pp. 45–50 in *The Endangered Species Act at thirty: Renewing the conservation promise*, ed. D. D. Goble, J. M. Scott, and F. W. Davis. Washington, D.C.: Island Press.

Wilcove, D. S., D. Rothstein, J. Dubow, A. Phillips, and E. Losos. 1998. Quantifying threats to imperiled species in the United States: Assessing the relative importance of habitat destruction, alien species, pollution, overexploitation, and disease. *BioScience* 48:607–15.

———. 2000. Leading threats to biodiversity: What's imperiling U.S. species. Pp. 239–54 in *Precious heritage: The status of biodiversity in the United States*, ed. B. A. Stein, L. S. Kutner, and J. S. Adams. New York: Oxford University Press.

Wilkinson, C. F. 1992. Language, law and the eagle bird. Pp. 8–21 in *The eagle bird: Mapping a new west*. ed. C. F. Wilkinson. New York: Pantheon.

Willamette–Lower Columbia Technical Recovery Team. 2003. *Interim report on viability criteria for Willamette and Lower Columbia Basin Pacific salmonids*. March 18. http://www.nwfsc.noaa.gov/trt/viability_criteria.htm.

Williams, D. F., E. A. Cypher, P. A. Kelly, K. J. Miller, N. Norvelli, S. E. Phillips, C. D. Johnson, and G. W. Colliver. 1998. *Recovery plan for the upland species of the San Joaquin Valley, California*. U.S. Fish and Wildlife Service, Region 1, Portland, Ore. Also available online at http://esrpweb.csustan.edu/publications/pubhtml.php?doc= sjvrp&file=cover.html.

Williams, P. H., and C. J. Humphries. 1996. WORLDMAP and prioritisation for conservation: Integration of systematic data for conservation evaluation. Pp. 98–99 in *Biodiversity assessment: A guide to good practice*, ed. A. C. Jermy, D. Long, J. S. Sands, N. E. Stork, and S. Winser. Champaign, Ill.: Balogh Scientific Books.

Wilson, E. O., ed. 1988a. The current state of biological diversity. Pp. 3–18 in *Biodiversity*, ed. E. O. Wilson. Washington, D.C.: National Academies Press.

———. 1988b. *Biodiversity*. Washington, D.C.: National Academies Press.

Wilson, J. 2003a. Riverside County set to approve big land plan, a species trade-off. *Los Angeles Times*, June 17.

———. 2003b. U.S. officials cut protected habitat throughout state. *Los Angeles Times*, August 7.

Winans, G. A., P. B. Aebersold, and R. S. Waples. 1996. Allozyme variability of *Oncorhynchus nerka* in the Pacific Northwest, with special consideration to populations of Redfish Lake, Idaho. *Transactions of the American Fishery Society* 125:645–63.

Withler, F. C. 1982. Transplanting Pacific salmon. *Canadian Technical Report of Fisheries and Aquatic Science* 1079:1–27.

Wondolleck, J. M., and S. L. Yaffee. 2000. *Making collaboration work: Lessons from innovation in natural resource management*. Washington, D.C.: Island Press.

Wood, C. C. 1995. Life history variation and population structure in sockeye salmon. Pp. 195–216 in *Evolution and the aquatic ecosystem: Defining unique units in population conservation*, ed. J. L. Nielsen. Bethesda, Md.: American Fisheries Society.

Wood, P. M. 1997. Biodiversity as the source of biological resources: A new look at biodiversity values. *Environmental Values* 6:251–68.

———. 2000. *Biodiversity and democracy: Rethinking society and nature*. Vancouver: University of British Columbia Press.

Woods, M. 1997. Tiger economies. *Geographical Magazine* 69:38–42.

Woodwell, G. M. 2002. On purpose in science, conservation, and government: The functional integrity of the earth is at issue not biodiversity. *Ambio* 31:432–36.

Worster, D. 1977. *Nature's economy: A history of ecological ideas.* New York: Cambridge University Press.

Wyoming Farm Bureau Federation v. Babbitt. 2000. 199 F. 3d 1224. U.S. Court of Appeals for the 10th Judicial Circuit.

Xu, Z., and D. N. Bengston. 1997. Trends in national forest values among forestry professionals, environmentalists, and the news media, 1982–1993. *Society and Natural Resources* 10:43–59.

Yaffee, S. L. 1982. *Prohibitive policy: Implementing the federal Endangered Species Act.* Cambridge, Mass.: MIT Press.

———. 2006. Collaborative decision making. Pp. 208–20 in *The Endangered Species Act at thirty: Renewing the conservation promise,* ed. D. D. Goble, J. M. Scott, and F. W. Davis. Washington, D.C.: Island Press.

Zaniewski, A. E., A. Lehmann, and J. M. Overton. 2002. Predicting species spatial distributions using presence-only data: A case study of native New Zealand ferns. *Ecological Modelling* 157:261–80.

Zink, R. M., G. F. Barrowclough, J. L. Atwood, and R. C. Blackwell-Rago. 2000. Genetics, taxonomy, and conservation of the threatened California gnatcatcher. *Conservation Biology* 14:1394–405.

Index

Italicized page numbers refer to boxes, figures, and tables.

Abalone, 249–50, 253
Abundance, myth of, 6–7, 9
Adaptive management, 5, 52, 95, 121, 154
Additive indexes, 54–57
Administrative Procedure Act (1946), 99
Adverse modification standards, 21; and
    conservation banking, 230; and criti-
    cal habitat designations, 113–17; and
    private landowner concerns, 121; sci-
    ence underlying, 104, 117–20,
    119–20
Aesthetic value, 1, 15, 37, 39, 94, 109
Agricultural landscapes: in California,
    260–72; and cost-benefit analyses,
    186; and countryside, 180, 256–74;
    and CWHR database analysis,
    263–72; and land use planning, 215;
    research to inform policy, 272–74
Agrochemicals, 273
Akaike's Information Criterion, 170
Alameda whipsnake *(Masticophis lateralis
    euryxanthus)*, 113, 234
Alaskan sockeye salmon *(Oncorhynchus
    nerka)*, 74, 143
Alliance for Zero Extinctions, 68
Alonso-Muth-Mills framework, 192
Alsea Valley Alliance v. Evans, 108
American alligator *(Alligator mississippien-
    sis)*, 134, 157
American black bear *(Ursus americanus)*,
    157–58

American Fisheries Society (AFS), 244–46
American Game Policy (1930), 12
Animal rights, 42–44
Anthropocentrism, 36–37, 51
Anthropogenic impacts. *See* Human im-
    pacts
Aquaculture, 247
Aransas National Wildlife Refuge (Tex.),
    14
*Arizona Cattle Growers Association v.
    USFWS*, 229
Arnold, Keith, 238
Artificial propagation, 105, 107–8, *110*
Atlantic salmon *(Salmo salar)*, 247
Atlas of Biodiversity (Chicago Wilderness),
    285
At-risk species conservation, 4, 6–23, 180;
    and environmental movement,
    14–22; and market dominance, 7–9;
    and myth of abundance, 6–7, 9; and
    scientific management, 9–14

Babbitt, Bruce, 21–22
Bald eagle *(Haliaeetus leucocephalus)*, 1, 3,
    11, 134, 185, 188
Baselines, 33, 82, 118, 182, 255
Bay checkerspot butterfly *(Euphydryas
    editha bayensis)*, 94, 240, 242
BedZED (Beddington Zero-Energy Devel-
    opment), 279
Benefits. *See* Cost-benefit analyses
Bengston, David, 47
"Best available science" mandate, 60,
    97–100, 300n4; and critical habitat

designations, 114, 165; and hybrids, 161; and jeopardy/adverse modification standards, 117; and listing processes, 20, 108; and value-neutrality, 95
"BioBlitz" (Central Park), 276
Bioclimatic ranges, 271
Biodiversity (Wilson), 127
Biodiversity Act (South Africa), 150
Biodiversity protection, 4–5, 49–58; and biological definitions, 53–57; and conservation biogeography, 66–67; and ecosystem functioning, 82–83; and natural processes, 73–74; in public policy discourse, 50–53, 57–58; social goals and policy objectives in, 51–53; and urban landscapes management, 275–87
Biodiversity Strategy (London, Eng.), 281
Biogeochemical functions, 72, 76; and ecosystem functioning, 81–82, 84
Biological definitions of biodiversity, 53–57
Biological diversity, continuum of, 144–49
Biological invasions. See Invasive species
Biotechnology, 183
Black-capped vireo (Vireo atricapilla), 188
Black-footed ferret (Mustela nigripes), 43, 67
Blazer, Carson v., 7
Blue-winged warblers (Vermivora pinus), 156
Bog turtle (Clemmys muhlenbergii), 157
Bonytail chub (Gila elegans), 187
Bronzed cowbird (Molothrus aeneus), 266
Brown pelicans (Pelecanus occidentalis), 29
Brown tree snake (Boiga irregularis), 155
Brussard, Peter, 54
Buffalo (Bison bison), 7–9
Bull trout (Salvelinus confluentus), 254
Burford, Connor v., 100
Burger, Warren, 37, 40
Burying beetle (Nicrophorus americanus), 80
Bush (George H. W.) administration, 21
Bush (George W.) administration, 22, 300n4
Bycatch, 244, 246, 254–55
Byers, John, 63–64

Cactus ferruginous pygmy-owl (Glaucidium brasilianum cactorum), 108, 134

CALFLORA database, 261
California condor (Gymnogyps californianus), 1, 67
California Department of Fish and Game (CDFG), 232, 234, 236
California Environmental Quality Act (CEQA), 207
California gnatcatcher. See Coastal California gnatcatcher
California red-legged frog (Rana aurora draytonii), 105, 234
California Resources Agency, 209, 212, 232
California tiger salamander (Ambystoma californiense), 105–6
California Wildlife Habitat Relationships database. See CWHR
Calumet Open Space Reserve (Chicago, Ill.), 286
Canada lynx (Lynx canadensis), 157–58
Captive breeding, 107–8, 155
Carbon dioxide (CO2), 72, 82
Carson v. Blazer, 7
Caspian terns (Sterna caspia), 123
CCAs (Candidate conservation agreements), 22, 33–35
Center for Biological Diversity v. Lohn, 108
Center for Natural Lands Management, 236
Center for the New American Dream (Tacoma Park, Md.), 281
Central Park (New York City), 276
Chicago Metropolis 2020, 286
Chicago Wilderness, 284–86
Churchill, Winston, 217
CITES, 17, 26–28, 47, 158–60, 159, 160
Cities. See Urban landscapes
CitySpaces (Chicago, Ill.), 285
Clean Water Act (1972), 218
Climate change, 4, 72, 111, 187, 239–40, 250, 252
Clinton administration, 21
Coastal California gnatcatcher (Polioptila californica californica), 106–7, 196–204, 198–201, 203, 210, 234
Colonial laws, 1, 6–7
Colorado pikeminnow (Ptychocheilus lucius), 187–88
Committee on Rare and Endangered Wildlife Species, 15–16, 25
Connor v. Burford, 100

Conservation banking, 228–43; case study, 237–38; current status of, 237; ecological success of, 239–42; economic success of, 238–39; mechanics of, 233–37; potential benefits of, 229–31; regulatory provisions of, 232–33; timelines, 35

Conservation biogeography, 61–69, 257–59

Conservation credits, 48, 234–39; ratios, 237, 240–41

Conservation easements, 235, 237–39

Consultations, 19–21; and critical habitat designations, 117; and recovery plans, 122; science underlying, *110*, 117–20, *119–20*; timelines, 28–29

Contingent evaluation surveys, 184–86

Controlled propagation policy, 34, 154–55

Convention on Biological Diversity, 77

Convention on Nature Protection and Wild Life Preservation in the Western Hemisphere (1940), 10, 27

Convention with Great Britain for the Protection of Migratory Birds (1916), 10

Cooke, Freary v., 7

Cooper, James Fenimore, 22

Cornerstones Conservation Bank (San Diego, Calif.), 235

Cost-benefit analyses, 116–17, 179, 181–89, 274

Countryside, 256–74; biogeography of, 257–59; in California, 260–72; and CWHR database analysis, 263–72, *264, 265, 266, 267, 268, 269; and private landowner concerns, 259–60; research to inform policy,* 272–74

Courts. *See* Lawsuits

Crestridge Conservation Bank (San Diego, Calif.), 235

Critical habitat designations, 18, 19–21, 164–74; and "best available science" mandate, 98–101; and cost-benefit analyses, 187; and development interests, 191; and housing industry, 196–204, *198–201, 203*; and marine biodiversity, 249, 251, 254; multilevel framework for, 165–68, *167, 169*; science underlying, 104, *110*, 113–17; timelines, 27, 34–35; using logistic regression, 168, 170–71; using population viability, 171–74, *173*

CWHR (California Wildlife Habitat Relationships) database, 263–72; correlation of reproduction, cover, and feeding values, 269–70, *269*; habitat value by species, 267–69, *268*; potential biases of, 270–72; species habitat associations, 266–67, *266, 267*; species richness by habitat, 263–66, *264, 265*

Daley, Richard M., 285

Darling, J. N. ("Ding"), 12

Darwin, Charles, 50–51, 76

Data Quality Act (2000), 100, 102

Daubert v. Merrell Dow Pharmaceuticals, 102

Decision making: and "best available science" mandate, 103; and cost-benefit analyses, 182; and science underlying ESA, 105, 109, 121, 123, 125–26; and urban landscapes management, 276

Defenders of Wildlife, 43

Defenders of Wildlife v. Babbitt, 99

Defenders of Wildlife v. Norton, 111

Delisted species: and continuum of biological diversity, 147–48; and ecosystem services, 95; and hybrids, 156, 161; and natural processes, 77; science underlying, 122; timelines, 29–30, 32

Democracy of value objectification, 44–47

Deontological value, 36, 39–41, 46

Depauperate systems, 74, 77

Desert tortoise *(Gopherus agassizii)*, 157, 188

Development interests, 3, 179–80; and "best available science" mandate, 100–101, 103; and conservation banking, 228–43; and cost-benefit analyses, 186; and countryside, 257, 261; and critical habitat designations, 115; and incidental take permits, 20–21; and land use planning, 190–96, *194 (see also* Land use planning); and mitigation banking, 48, 218–27, *221, 222, 223*; and urban landscapes management, 277–78. *See also* Housing industry

Dewey, John, 50–51, 57

Difference definitions of biodiversity, 53–56, 58

Dignity, 39–40, 42–43, 45

Disease, 247, 249–50

Disentangled bank, 76–78

DPSs (distinct population segments), 127–49; and continuum of biological diversity, 147–48; and marine biodiversity, 245–46; nonsalmonid, 134; in Pacific salmon, 129, 133, *133*, 136, *136*, 138, 143, 145–46; science underlying, 105, 106–7, 108, *110*, 111; timelines, 33. *See also* ESUs

Duck Stamp Act (1934), 11, 13

Dusky seaside sparrow *(Ammodramus maritimus nigrescens)*, 30, 106, 155

Dwyer, William, 31

Earth Summit (Johannesburg 2002), 72

Earth Summit (Rio de Janeiro 1992), 72, 77

Eastern timber wolf *(Canis lupus lycaon)*, 107, 170–71

East Plum Creek Conservation Bank, 235

Ecological diversity, 129–35, *130, 131,* 141

Ecological exchangeability, 141–43

Ecological fungibility, 241–42

Ecological processes, 70–71, 73, 75–79

Ecological Society of America, 68, 101

Ecological value, 80–81. *See also* Ecosystem services

Economic impact analyses, 190–205; and conservation banking, 238–39; cost-benefit analyses, 181–89; and critical habitat designations, 114–17; and development interests, 100, 190–96, *194*; and housing industry, 190, 196–204, *198–201, 203*; and land use planning, 211–13, 215–16; and sustainable development, 77

Economic justification: and biodiversity protection, 51, 55; and Reagan administration, 19–20, 98; timelines, 27, 29; and value, 37–40, 43, 45, 46–48

Ecosystem functions, 81–96; and biodiversity, 82–83; and listed species, 83–91, *85, 86, 87, 88, 89, 90, 91*; preservation of, 91–96, *94*

Ecosystem protection, 5, 32, 148, 253–55

Ecosystem services, 4; and biodiversity definition, 55; and cost-benefit analyses, 77, 182; and countryside, 256–57, 259; and extinctions, 38–39; preservation of, 80–96, *94*; and value, 41

Ecotourism, 184

Eelgrass limpet *(Lottia alveus alveus)*, 250

Efficiency question, 181–82

Ehrenfeld, David, 38–39

Elkhorn coral *(Acopora palmata)*, 250

Elton, Charles, 73

Empirical models, 165–68, *167*

Endangered species, 109; and cost-benefit analyses, 184–85, 187–88; and development interests, 191; and ESUs in Pacific salmon, 133; and land use planning, 206; and marine biodiversity, 247–48, 251–54; and private landowner concerns, 180; similarity-of-appearance, 157. *See also* Listed species; *names of species*

Endangered Species Act (ESA 1973), 15, 17–18; amendments and revisions to, 18–22, 24, 27–30, 98; authorization for, 29, 31; and "best available science" mandate, 98; broader vision of, 290; timelines, 24–35

Endangered Species Committee, 19, 28, 47–48

Endangered Species Conservation Act (ESCA 1969), 16–17, 24, 26, 97

Endangered Species Preservation Act (ESPA 1966), 16, 24–26, 97

Endowment funds, 236–39

Energy and Water Development Appropriations Act (1979), 28

Environmental Defense, 238

Environmental Protection Information Center v. NMFS, 111

Erwin, Terry, 54–55

ESUs (evolutionarily significant units): alternative definitions for, 134–44, *136, 139, 145*; and continuum of biological diversity, 144–49; in Pacific salmon, 127, 129–34, *130, 131, 132, 133*, 135–44, *136, 139, 145*; science underlying, 106, 108–9, *110*, 122; timelines, 31

European Union, 258

Evolutionary legacy, 129, 139

Evolutionary processes: and conservation biogeography, 62–63, 68–69; and continuum of biological diversity, 148–49; and hybridization, 150; as natural processes, 70–71, 75–79

Exemptions, 18–20, 27–30, 47–48

Existence value, 43–44

Expert models, 165–68, *167*

Extinction debts, 63

Extinction risk, 3; and artificial propagation, 107–8; and conservation banking, 233–34, 240–41; and countryside, 262; and critical habitat designations, 115; and ecosystem services, 80, *94*, 95; and lawsuits, 108, 111–12; and listing processes, 109–13, *110*; and marine biodiversity, 245, 255; and natural processes, 74–78; in Progressive Era, 13–14; timelines, 30

Extinctions, 6–9; and conservation banking, 240; and conservation biogeography, 61–68; and cost-benefit analyses, 183; and countryside, 260; and critical habitat designations, 172; human impact on, 72, 74, 150; and hybridization, 155–56; and marine biodiversity, 247

Fading Trails: The Story of Endangered American Wildlife, 14–15

Falk, Donald, 54

Farming. *See* Agricultural landscapes

Federal Aid to Wildlife Restoration Act (1937), 13

Federal government: and "best available science" mandate, 97–103; and critical habitat designations, 117; and environmental movement, 14–17; and hybrids, 155–58; in Progressive Era, 10–13; timelines for actions of, 24; and value objectification, 44–48

Federal Register, 157

Field, Stephen J., 8

Fishery management, 252–53

Fishing, 184, 246–47, 251–53

Flannery, Timothy, 64

Florida panther *(Felis concolor coryi)*, 106, 153, 157

Florida scrub jay *(Aphelocoma coerulescens)*, 188

Flow modification, 248

Footprint analyses, 280–82

Forestry, 12, 257

Freary v. Cooke, 7

Game management, 11–12, 22

Game Management (Leopold), 12

GAP Analysis Program mapping, 68, 166, 263

Gene conservation groups, 147

General Accounting Office (GAO), 108, 117, 188

General Equilibrium Ecosystem Model, 184

Genetic diversity: and cost-benefit analyses, 183; and critical habitat designations, 115; and ESUs in Pacific salmon, 129–35, *132*, 138, 140–41; and hybrids, 156, 161; and natural processes, 76

Genetic exchangeability, 141–43

Geographic distributions, 4, 61–69; and conservation banking, 235–36; and critical habitat designations, 99; and ecosystem functioning, 83; in Pacific salmon, 129–33, *130, 131*

GEUs (geminate evolutionary units), 139–41

Gifford Pinchot Task Force v. USFWS, 114

Gingrich, Newt, 21

GIS (geographic information system), 165–66, 170, 212

Golden-cheeked warbler *(Dendroica chrysoparia)*, 237–38

Golden-winged warbler *(Vermivora chrysoptera)*, 156

Gray wolf *(Canis lupus)*, 32, 34, 134, 170–71, 188

Great auk *(Alca impennis)*, 6–7

Greater London Authority, 276

Green accounting, 187

Green-building policies, 282, 285

Green loggerhead sea turtle *(Chelonia mydas)*, 250

Green procurement policies, 281

Green rooftops, 278, 285

Green sea turtle *(Chelonia mydas)*, 188

"Green-slime perspective," 70–71

Green streets, 278

Greenwich Millennium Village (London, Eng.), 279

Grizzly bear *(Ursus arctos horribilis)*, 3, 14, 123, 134, 184

Growth Management Act (Wash.), 283
Gulf sturgeon *(Acipenser oxyrinchus desotoi)*, 34, 115

"Habitat banking" (Hawaii), 232–33
Habitat conservation plans. *See* HCPs
Habitat loss, 4, 16; and conservation banking, 241–42; and countryside, 260–63; and marine biodiversity, 244, 247; and urban landscapes management, 275
Habitat modification, 72–73, 76
Habitat protection: and "best available science" mandate, 101; and colonial laws, 6; and ecosystem services, 93–94; and environmental movement, 16; and market dominance, 7–8; and natural processes, 76–78; in Progressive Era, 11–13; and "similarity of appearance" clause, 157; timelines, 25, 34–35
Habitat suitability models, 116
Habitat value by species, 267–70, *268, 269*
Handbook for Habitat Conservation Planning and Incidental Take Permitting Process, 34
Hart, John, 7
Hayes, David, 214
HCPs (Habitat conservation plans): and conservation banking, 229–33; and conservation biogeography, 67; and countryside, 260–61; and incidental take permits, 20–21; and land use planning, 207, 208–16, *211*; and private landowner concerns, 22; science underlying, *110*; timelines, 29, 31–33; and value, 48
Hedonic modeling, 215
Hickory Pass Ranch Conservation Bank, 237–38
Holland, Missouri v., 10
Home Builders Association of Northern California v. USFWS, 99, 113
Housing industry: and cost-benefit analyses, 187; and countryside, 261; and economic impact analyses, 190, 196–204, *198–201, 203*, 300n1(Ch.15); and land use planning, 207–8, *208*. *See also* Development interests

HSIs (habitat suitability indices), 165–66
Human-dominated landscapes, 3, 5, 111, 179, 256–58, 272, 288–90
Human Footprint, 68
Human impacts, 71–73; and conservation banking, 240; and conservation biogeography, 63; and hybrids, 150, 156, 161; and marine biodiversity, 244, 246–48, 251, 255
Humpback chub *(Gila cypha)*, 187
Hunting, 11, 13, 238, 259
Hybrids, 150–63; and CITES, 158–60, *159, 160*; controlled propagation policy, 154–55; history of, 150–55, *151, 152*; hybrid policy, 151–53; intercross policy, 153–54; and listing processes, 105, 107, *110*, 156–58, 160–62; Migratory Bird Treaty Act (1918), 158; natural hybrid origin, 156; "similarity of appearance" clause, 156–58; timelines, *151*

Ideology, 51–52
Inca dove *(Columbina inca)*, 266
Incentives: and cost-benefit analyses, 181–83; and land use planning, 215–16; timelines, 33. *See also* "No surprises" policy; CCAs; HCPs; SHAs
Incidental take permits, 20–21; and "best available science" mandate, 98, 300n3; and conservation banking, 229–31; and jeopardy/adverse modification standards, 118; and land use planning, 212–14; and recovery plans, 122; timelines, 29
Industrialization, 6, 7–9, 279
"The Influence of Darwinism on Philosophy" (Dewey), 50
Instrumental value, 36–39, 47
Intercross policy, 153–54
Interior least tern *(Sterna antillarum athalassos)*, 105
International Biogeography Society, 68
International commerce, 16–18, 26, 28, 30, 158–60, *159, 160*
International Convention Advisory Commission, 28
International Paper HCP, 48, 219–21, 225
International Union for the Conservation of Nature and Natural Resources. *See* IUCN

Interstate commerce, 10, 16, 18, 26, 28
Intrinsic value, 36–37; and biodiversity
  protection, 51–52; to listed species,
  39–41, 43; metric for quantifying,
  45–48, 46
Invasive species, 72–74, 76, 83, 244, 249,
  252, 254, 262
Inventory definitions of biodiversity,
  53–56, 58
Irvine Ranch Company (Calif.), 209,
  212
IUCN: habitat classification system,
  83–84, 86; Redbook, 16, 25, 74, 93,
  94, 172, 244–45
Ivory-billed woodpecker *(Campephilus
  principalis)*, 14

Jaguar *(Panthera onca)*, 80, 93
Janzen, Daniel, 54
Jasper Ridge Biological Preserve, 240
Jeopardy standards, 19–21; and "best available science" mandate, 98; and cost-
  benefit analyses, 181; and critical
  habitat designations, 113–15, 117;
  and natural processes, 79; and private
  landowner concerns, 121; science underlying, 104, 117–20, 119–20;
  timelines, 26, 28–29; and value, 40,
  47
Johnson, Lyndon, 15
Johnson's seagrass *(Halophila johnsonii)*,
  33, 249
Johnston, David, 237–38
Johnston, Jacquelyn, 237
Journal of Wildlife Management, 12

Kant, Immanuel, 39, 41–45, 50
Kelp bass *(Paralabrax clathratus)*, 185
Kemp's ridley sea turtle *(Lepidochelys kem-
  pii)*, 116, 246, 250
Key deer *(Odocoileus virginianus clavium)*,
  25
Key silverside *(Menidia conchorum)*, 247
Keystone species, 38–39, 74, 109
Killer whale *(Orcinus orca)*, 108, 134
Kirtland's warbler *(Dendroica kirtlandii)*,
  27

Lacey Act (1900), 10, 28
Land and Water Conservation Fund Act
  (1963), 16, 24–25

Land use planning, 179, 206–17; and
  colonial laws, 7; and development interests, 190–96, 194; and HCPs, 207,
  208–9; and MSHCPs, 209–16, 211;
  need for new management options,
  207–8, 208; in Progressive Era, 11;
  timelines, 33; and urban landscapes
  management, 276–77; and wildland-
  urban interface, 206–7
Language, 50–53, 57–58
Last of the Wild, 68
Lawsuits: and "best available science" mandate, 99–102; and critical habitat designations, 99, 115–16; and extinction
  risk, 108, 111–12; and listing processes, 93, 108. *See also names of
  cases*
Leadbeater's possum *(Gymnobelideus leadbeateri)*, 185
Least Bell's vireo *(Vireo bellii pusillus)*, 210,
  239
Leatherback sea turtle *(Dermochelys coriacea)*, 246–47
LEED (Leadership in Energy and Environmental Design), 282
Legislature. *See* Federal government
Leopold, Aldo, 12–14, 149
"Lights Out Chicago," 286
Linnaean shortfall, 67
Listed species, 16–18; and conservation
  banking, 228–42; and countryside,
  259–60; and CWHR database,
  260–63, 271–72; and ecosystem
  functioning, 83–91, 85, 86, 87, 88,
  89, 90, 91; and HCPs, 209; listable
  units, 105–9; and marine plants, 33,
  249; and mitigation banking,
  220–27, 222, 223; timelines, 25; and
  urban landscapes management, 277;
  and value, 39–41, 45. *See also* Endangered species; *names of species*
Listing processes: amendments and revisions to, 18–21; and "best available
  science" mandate, 97–103; and conservation biogeography, 67; and critical habitat designations, 114, 117;
  and ecosystem services, 93, 95; and
  hybrids, 105, 107, 110, 156–58,
  160–62; and marine biodiversity,
  244–45; science underlying, 105–13,
  110; timelines, 25–29, 35

Lloyd's hedgehog cactus *(Echinocereus lloydii)*, 156
Loggerhead sea turtle *(Caretta caretta)*, 188, 246
Logistic regression, 168, 170–71
Lohn, Center for Biological Diversity v., 108
Lovejoy, Thomas, 57
Lucas v. South Carolina Coastal Council, 212
Lujan, Marbled Murrelet v., 111
Lumbering. *See* Timber harvesting

Magnuson Fisheries Conservation and Management Act (1976), 15
Management units (MUs), 137, 146
Mangrove rivulus *(Rivulus marmoratus)*, 247
Manson, Craig, 114
Marbled murrelet *(Brachyramphus marmoratus marmoratus)*, 188
Marbled Murrelet v. Lujan, 111
Marine biodiversity, 180, 244–55; conservation strategies, 251–54; threats to, 246–50
Marine Mammal Protection Act (MMPA 1972), 15
Marine plants, 33, 249
Marine reserves, 251–53
Market: and conservation banking, 236; and cost-benefit analyses, 181, 183; and land use planning, 207; triumph of, 6; and value, 39–40, 42–45, 47, 51
Market dominance, 7–9
Market price, 39–40
Martin, Paul, 64
McCullagh, United States v., 10
McFarlin v. Essex Company, 8
Mediterranean monk seal *(Monachus monachus)*, 185
Merrell Dow Pharmaceuticals, Daubert v., 102
Mexican duck *(Anas platyrhynchos diazi)*, 161
Mexican wolves *(Canis lupus baileyi)*, 65
Micronesian kingfisher *(Halcyon cinnamomina cinnamomina)*, 155
Middle Rio Grande Conservancy District v. Babbitt, 99, 113
Migratory Bird Conservation Act (1929), 11

Migratory Bird Hunting Stamp Act (1934), 11, 13
Migratory bird protection, 10–11, 13, 262, 276, 280, 286
Migratory Bird Treaty Act (1918), 10, 158
Millennium Ecosystem Assessment, 228
Minimally viable population, 75, 78, 171
Mississippi gopher frog *(Rana capito sevosa)*, 105
Missouri v. Holland, 10
Mitigation banking, 48, 218–20, *221*; with species, 220–27, *222, 223. See also* Conservation banking
Monetary metric, 37–40, 43, 45, 46–48
Monocultures, 77, 259
Morton, Thomas, 6
Mountain yellow-legged frog *(Rana muscosa)*, 210
MSHCPs (multispecies conservation plans), 5, 95, 123, 209–16, *211*, 260
MtDNA (mitochondrial DNA), 135–38, 146
Multispecies conservation plans, 5, 95, 123, 209–16, *211*

NASA Earth Observing System Terrestrial Ecosystem Model, 84
National Academy of Sciences, 30
National Association of Home Builders, 108, 192, 196
National Environmental Policy Act (NEPA 1970), 15
National Forest Management Act, 31
National Marine Fisheries Service (NMFS), 18; and critical habitat designations, 113–17; and ESUs in Pacific salmon, 129, 134, 140, 146–48; and hybrids, 153–54, 157; and jeopardy/adverse modification standards, 117–20, *119–20*; and listing processes, 105–9, 111–12, 245; and marine biodiversity, 253; and private landowner concerns, 121; and recovery plans, 121–22; timelines, 31–33; and urban landscapes management, 283
National Oceanic and Atmospheric Association (NOAA), 184
National Research Council (NRC), 101, 105, 108, 117, *119–20*, 182

Native species, 63–67, 72, 259, 261–62, 280

Natural processes, 70–79; and biodiversity loss, 73–74; as ecological and evolutionary processes, 70–71; and habitat protection, 76–78; human impact on, 71–73; and species preservation, 75–76

Nature: as entangled bank, 76–77; preservation of, 70–79; as resource, 8

The Nature Conservancy (TNC), 43

Nature reserves, 4, 11–15, 25, 256–57, 261

NatureServe, 84

NCCPs (Natural Community Conservation Plans), 209, 212, 232, 260

NeighborSpaces (Chicago, Ill.), 285

New Deal, 11–12

New Mexico Cattle Growers Association v. USFWS, 114, 116

Nickels, Greg, 284

Nitrogen: deposition of, 72, 248, 258; fixation of, 76, 81; mobilization of, 82, 84, 87–90, *89, 92*

Nixon, Richard M., 26, 288

Nonlisted hybrids, 162

Northern spotted owl *(Strix occidentalis caurina)*, 31, 158, 185, 187–88, 212

Northwest Salmon Recovery Planning, 149

"No surprises" policy, 22, 121, 210, 214; timelines, 31, 33, 35

NPP (Net primary production), 81–82, 84, 86–90, *86, 87, 88, 92*

Office of Management and Budget (OMB), 98, 100, 117

Olive ridley sea turtle *(Lepidochelys olivacea)*, 246, 250

Olmstead, Pitkin v., 7

OpenLands Project (Chicago, Ill.), 280

Open space, 3, 204, 215, 278

Opportunity costs, 186–88

Origin of Species (Darwin), 50, 76

Overexploitation, 244, 246–47, 251–52, 255

Pacific salmon *(Oncorhynchus* spp.), 60, 106, 127–49; background on, 128; and "best available science" mandate, 101; biology of, 128–29; ESUs in, 129–34, *130, 131, 132, 133*; ESUs in (alternative definitions), 134–44, *136, 139, 145*; ESUs in (and continuum of biological diversity), 144–49; and marine biodiversity, 245, 247, 254; role of science in management of, 108–9, 111, *119–20*, 122, 123; timelines, 31; and urban landscapes management, 282–84

Pacific yew *(Taxus brevifolia)*, 183

Parallel evolution, 143–44, *145*

Passenger pigeon *(Ectopistes migratorius)*, 7–8, 22

Pecos sunflower *(Helianthus paradoxus)*, 156

Peer review, 32, 100, 102, 108, *119*

Pelican Island National Wildlife Refuge (Fla.), 11

Penalty metric, 46–48, 46

Peregrine falcon *(Falco peregrinus)*, 155, 157, 185, 188

Pesticides, 30, 279–80

Pew Oceans Commission, 246

Phylogenetic analyses, 64, 68; and biodiversity loss, 74; phylogenetic species concept (PSC), 138–39, *139*, 146; and species preservation, 75

Phylogeographic analyses, 64, 68, 134–37

Pinchot, Gifford, 9, 12, 15

Pitkin v. Olmstead, 7

Plant species, 27, 30, 33, 229, 249, 260–61. *See also names of plant species*

Pleasanton Ridge Conservation Bank (Livermore, Calif.), 234

Pollution, 244, 248–49, 251–52, 255, 280

Population matrix models, 116

Population viability analyses. *See* PVAs

Prairie Stone Facility (Sears Roebuck), 280

Predators, 63–65, 74, 221, 246, 253

Prehistoric ranges, 63–68

Private landowners: and cost-benefit analyses, 181–82; and countryside, 259–60; and critical habitat designations, 3; and incidental take permits, 3, 20–21; and land use planning, 206–7; science underlying limitations on, 120–21; timelines, 29, 33; and value, 48. *See also* Development interests

Progressive Era, 9–14, 22

Pronghorn antelopes, 63–65

Property rights, 9, 78–79, 211–12
Pseudoabsences, 166
Public hearings, 19, 27, 30
Public opinion surveys, 184–86
Public policy discourse, 50–53, 57–58
Public support: and critical habitat designations, 115–16; and extinction risk, 111–12; and listing processes, 108; and symbolic species, 3
PVAs (population viability analyses), 109, 111, 122, 171–74, *173*

Rainbow trout *(Oncorhynchus mykiss)*, 107, 128, 143–44, 146–47, 157, 161–62
Rain gardens, 278–79
Raven, Peter, 67
Razorback sucker *(Xyrauchen texanus)*, 187–88
Reagan administration, 19–20, 98
Recovery planning, 18; and "best available science" mandate, 98, 101; and conservation banking, 236; and conservation biogeography, 62, 67–68; and cost-benefit analyses, 187–88; and critical habitat designations, 114, 117, 172, *173*; and ecosystem services, 94–95; and jeopardy/adverse modification standards, *119*; for Pacific salmon, 149; science underlying, 104, *110*, 121–23; timelines, 27, 30–32, 34
Recreation: and cost-benefit analyses, 181, 183–84, 186–87; and ecosystem services, 94; timelines, 33; and urban landscapes management, 276; and value, 38–39
Redbook (IUCN), 16, 25, 74, 93, *94*, 172, 244–45
Red-cockaded woodpecker *(Picoides borealis)*, 38–39, 48, 188, 219, 221–22
Red wolf *(Canis rufus)*, 107, 153
Refuge systems, 4, 11–15, 25, 256–57, 261
Reproductive isolation, 128–33, 135
Ringed turtle dove *(Streptopelia risoria)*, 266
Rio Grande silvery minnow *(Hybognathus amarus)*, 113
Rockfish bocaccio *(Sebastes paucispinis)*, 245, 250, 252
Rolston, Holmes, 37

Roosevelt, Franklin D., 12
Roosevelt, Theodore, 9, 11
Roosevelt Campobello International Park Commission v. EPA, 100
Rosy periwinkle *(Catharanthus roseus)*, 183
Ruhl, J. B., 21
Run-off, 248–49

Safe harbor agreements. *See* SHAs
Sagoff, Mark, 44, 46
San Bruno elfin butterfly *(Callophrys mossii bayensis)*, 29
San Bruno Mountain (Calif.) HCP, 29, 209
SANDAG (San Diego Association of Governments), 197
San Joaquin kit fox *(Vulpes macrotis mutica)*, 239
San Timoteo Canyon state park, 215
Sarkar, Sahotra, 56
SCAG (Southern California Association of Governments), 197
Scenario planning, 111, 122–23
Schottler, Spring Valley Water Works v., 8
Science, 104–26, *110*; advancing role of, 104–5, 112–13, 116–17, 120, 121, 123–26, *124*; "best available science" mandate, 97–103; and critical habitat designations, 104, 113–17; and jeopardy/adverse modification standards, 104, 117–20, *119–20*; and listing processes, 105–13; and private landowner concerns, 120–21; and recovery plans, 104, 121–23
Scientific management, 6, 9–14, 22
Scrimshaw, 27–28, 30
Seagrass *(Zostera marina)*, 250
Sea-run cutthroat trout *(Oncorhynchus clarki)*, 31
Seattle (Wash.) biodiversity conservation, 282–84
Seattle Creek Restoration Initiative, 284
Seattle's Urban Blueprint for Habitat Protection and Restoration, 283
Sea turtles, 30, 246, 250
Sedimentation, 248–49
Service areas, 235–36
Set-asides, 5, 179, 261–63, 277
Shadow price, 39–40
SHAs (Safe harbor agreements), 22, 32–35, 218–19, 222, *223*, 226

Shauver, United States v., 10
Shoreline Master Plan (Seattle, Wash.), 284
Sierra Club v. USFWS, 34, 114
Simberloff, Daniel, 68
"Similarity of appearance" clause, 156–58
Simpson, George Gaylord, 61, 63
Smalltooth sawfish *(Pristis pectinata)*, 246
Snail darter *(Percina tanasi)*, 18, 27, 40
Social goals/values, 51–53, 181–82, 184
Society for Conservation Biology, 68
Soulé, Michael, 62
"Sound science" model, 102
Southern sea otter *(Enhydra lutris nereis)*, 38
Southwest Center for Biological Diversity v. Babbitt, 100
Spatial scale, 61–69
Species habitat associations, 266–67, *266, 267*
Species habitat models, 270–71
Species richness by habitat, 263–66, *264, 265*
Spirit of the Sage Council v. Norton, 35
Spring Valley Water Works v. Schottler, 8
Staghorn coral *(Acropora cervicornis)*, 250
State governments, 9–11, 13, 75, 112; timelines, 25, 26, 28, 30, 32
Statistical models: and critical habitat designations, 165–68, *167, 169*; and ecosystem services, 84–93, *85, 86, 87, 88, 89, 90, 91, 92*
Steadman, David, 64
Steelhead *(Oncorhynchus mykiss)*, 31, 106, *119–20*, 128, 143–44, 146–47, 247
Stellar sea-lion *(Eumetopias jubatus)*, 101, 111, 251–53
Stephens' kangaroo rat *(Dipodomys stephensi)*, 207, 213
Stewardship, urban, 276–77
Stone, Christopher, 52
Street Edge Alternatives (Seattle, Wash.), 278–79
Striped shiner *(Luxilus chrysocephalus)*, 185
Subspecies, 105–7, 111, 271–72
Superfund, 188
Sweet Home, Babbitt v., 32, 212
Symbolic species, 1, 11, 18

Takacs, David, 53–54, 57
Take regulations: and colonial laws, 6; and conservation banking, 241; and cost-benefit analyses, 181; and hybrids, 157–58; and private landowner concerns, 3, 120–21; in Progressive Era, 9–13; timelines, 26. *See also* incidental take permits
Tellico Dam, 18, 27–28, 40–41
Temporal scale, 61–69
Tennessee Valley Authority v. Hill, 17, 18–19, 23, 27, 37, 40–41, 47, 100
Theory of value, 51–52
Thoreau, Henry David, 22
Threatened species: and cost-benefit analyses, 184–85; and countryside, 258, 260; and critical habitat designations, 172; and ecosystem functioning, 84, 95–96; and environmental movement, 16–18; and ESUs in Pacific salmon, 133; and hybrids, 156–57, 161; and listing processes, 109; and marine biodiversity, 244–50, 252, 254; and natural processes, 76–79; and private landowner concerns, 180; timelines, 26–27, 35. *See also* Listed species
"Threatened Species" (Leopold), 14
Tidewater goby (Eucyclogobius newberryi), 247, 249, 253–54
Tilman, David, 63
Timber harvesting, 31, 38–39, 186–87
Tokogenetic lineages, 138
Topminnow *(Poeciliopsis monacha)*, 155
Totoaba *(Cynoscion macdonaldi)*, 248
Travel-cost method, 38–39
Trophic structure, 81–82, 84, 87–91, *89, 90, 91*
Tsonga, Paul, 69
Turner, Frederick Jackson, 8–9

Union of Concerned Scientists, 300n4
"Urban Conservation Treaty for Migratory Birds" (USFWS), 286
Urban landscapes, 275–87; biodiversity conservation in Seattle, 282–84; and biodiversity management, 279–80; in California, 260–72; Chicago Wilderness, 284–86; conservation agenda for, 286–87; and cost-benefit analyses, 188; and countryside, 180, 256–74; and CWHR database analysis, 263–72; and development interests, 277–78; ecological retrofitting of,

Urban landscapes (*continued*)
278–79; and habitat-friendly design, 279; reducing biodiversity-destructive footprint of, 280–82; research to inform policy, 272–74; and stewardship, 276–77; and sustainable development, 282; and wildland-urban interface, 206–7. *See also* Development interests; Housing industry
U.S. Biological Survey, 14
U.S. Bureau of Land Management (BLM), 15
U.S. Bureau of Reclamation, *119*
U.S. Commission on Ocean Policy, 246
U.S. Constitution, 44–45, 206, 212
U.S. Department of the Interior, 13, 15, 18, 25, 98, 117, 151
U.S. Environmental Protection Agency, 30, 100
U.S. Fish and Wildlife Service (USFWS): and conservation banking, 229–39; and critical habitat designations, 99, 113–17, 249; and DPSs, 129, 134, 147–48; and housing industry, 202; and hybrids, 151–57, 161; and jeopardy/adverse modification standards, 18, 117–18, *119*, 120; and listed species, 84; and listing processes, 19, 105–9, 111–12; and marine biodiversity, 249, 253; and mitigation banking, 48, 219–20; and multispecies HCPs, 209; and "No surprises" policy, 22, 121, 210, 214; and private landowner concerns, 121; in Progressive Era, 13–14; and recovery plans, 95, 121–22; timelines, 25, 28, 30, 32–35; and urban landscapes management, 280, 285–86
U.S. Green Building Council, 282
U.S. Ocean Commission, 253
Utah prairie dog *(Cynomys parvidens)*, 16
Utilitarian welfare calculus, 41–44

Value-neutrality, 80, 93, 95, 98
Value objectification, 44–45
Values, 36–48; and biodiversity protection, 41, 49–53; and ecosystem services, 80–81, 93; instrumental value, 36–39, 47; interaction of penalty and monetary metrics, 46–48; intrinsic

value, 36–37, 39–41, 43, 45–46, *46*; and redundant species, 83; utilitarian welfare calculus, 41–44; value objectification, 44–45
Vertebrate Population Policy, 32–33
Vessel monitoring systems, 253
Virgin River chub *(Gila seminuda)*, 187

Wallace, Alfred Russel, 66
Wallacean shortfall, 59, 66–67, 69
Warranted but precluded findings, 20, 29, 103
Watt, James, 19–20, 28
Weeks-McLean Migratory Bird Act (1913), 10
Western Riverside County Multi-Species HCP, 213–15
Western trout *(Oncorhynchus spp.)*, 157
Westslope cutthroat trout *(Oncorhynchus clarki lewisi)*, 107, 161–62
Whitbourne, Richard, 6
White croaker *(Genyonemus lineatus)*, 185
White River spinedace *(Lepidomeda albivallis)*, 188
Whittaker, R. H., 53, 55
Whooping crane *(Grus americana)*, 14, 188
Wilderness, 15–16
Wilderness Act (1964), 14–15
Wild Free-Roaming Horses and Burros Act (1971), 15
Wildlands Inc., 221
Wildland-urban interface, 206–7
Wildlife management, 6–7, 9–14, 206–7
Wildlife Society, 12
Wilson, E. O., 54, 67, 127
Wilson, Pete, 209
Wood, Paul, 54–56
Wooly mammoths, 65–66
Working landscapes, 179–80, 256–57
World Conservation Union. *See* IUCN
WorldMap, 68
Woundfin *(Plagopterus argentissimus)*, 187
Wyoming Farm Bureau Federation v. Babbitt, 34

Yellowstone National Park, 32, 34

Zoos, 16, 76